# THE FINAL BABYLON

## America and the Coming of Antichrist

*"And the woman... is that great city, which reigneth over the kings of the earth"*
*Revelation 17:18*

Douglas W. Krieger
Dene McGriff
S. Douglas Woodward

# THE FINAL BABYLON

## *AMERICA AND THE COMING OF ANTICHRIST*


**Douglas W. Krieger**
**Dene McGriff**
**S. Douglas Woodward**



**FAITH HAPPENS**
OKLAHOMA CITY

# *THE FINAL BABYLON:*

## *AMERICA AND THE COMING OF ANTICHRIST*

*FAITH HAPPENS*
*OKLAHOMA CITY*
*PRINTED IN THE UNITED STATES OF AMERICA*

*WWW.FAITH-HAPPENS.COM*



ISBN-13: 978-1490947068

ISBN-10: 149094706X

ALL IMAGES FROM WIKIPEDIA COMMONS, PUBLIC DOMAIN UNLESS OTHERWISE NOTED

COVER DESIGN BY WOODWARD

ALL SCRIPTURE TAKEN FROM THE KING JAMES VERSION OF THE BIBLE UNLESS OTHERWISE NOTED

# Table of Contents

***Tables of Figures*** ..... ***ix***

***Dedication*** ..... ***xi***

***FOREWORD: The City Sliding Down the Hill*** ..... ***xiii***

***Chapter 1: The Contrarian Prophetic Scenario*** ..... ***3***

Rome Has Not Revived ..... 3

Just How Much is America Declining? ..... 7

Is America Sanctioned by God? ..... 10

Will the Antichrist be Muslim? ..... 14

So Is America Omitted in Bible Prophecy? ..... 17

Conclusion ..... 23

***Chapter 2: Who Is Babylon?*** ..... ***25***

Mystery Babylon ..... 25

Hunting for Catholic Apostasy ..... 28

The Mother of Fortifications and Her Leopard Child ..... 33

Historical Babylon and the Islamic Scenario ..... 43

A Not So Literal Interpretation of Babylon ..... 52

Conclusion – The Economic and Political Babylon ..... 57

***Chapter 3: Why a New Look at Babylon is NOT So New*** ..... ***61***

America as Babylon Not A New Insight ..... 61

Does Nationalism Cause Blindness? ..... 63

Revered Eschatology Scholars Speak Out ..... 64

The Clash of the Titans ..... 65

The Daughter of Babylon ..... 70

Why We Are Critical of American Evangelicals ..... 72

The Sell-out of the American Press ..... 74

Is the Rapture Why America Falls? ..... 76

A Balanced Gospel ..... 77

The Role of America Today....79
Conclusion....83

***Chapter 4: Is America a Christian Nation?....85***

The Myth of America's Christian Beginnings....85
The Pretext for Patriotism Among Christians....87
Were our Founding Fathers Christians?....88
Jefferson and "Nature's God"....92
The Founding Fathers – The Neo-Pagans....94
The Rosicrucians: A Rose by Any Other Name....104
Masonic Deception....108
Barton's "Christian-Speak" = Apostasy....109
"GAOTU" – "Great Architect Of the Universe"....111
Illuminati Symbolism....112
America: The New Atlantis....116
Conclusion....117

***Chapter 5: Why America IS the Final Babylon....121***

The Most Compelling Arguments....121
One: America's Historical Religious Aspirations Reflect Babylonian Religion....122
Two: America's National Symbols Reflect Egyptian Paganism....123
Three: America's Inclusion of Nazi Socialism Corrupted Our Government....127
Four: America's Financial Dominance Unlikely to be Usurped before the Lord Returns....129
Five: America's Military Dominates the World – We Remain the One and Only Superpower....135
Will America Relinquish the Geopolitical Reins?....140
Our Failure to Make America Accountable....145

**Chapter 6: The Colossus of Commercial Babylon......................149**

What Does the Dollar Sign Symbolize?.............................. 149

More than a Mere City?.................................................. 150

The Rise of America's Commercial Empire......................... 153

Don't Count America Out ................................................ 160

Getting Deeper and Deeper in Debt ................................... 163

Sure We're in Bad Shape, but Compared to Whom? .......... 166

Where is the Global Economy Going?................................ 170

How to End America's Dominance? Sack the Dollar!........ 174

The Remarkable Rebound of America.............................. 175

Isn't Hyperinflation a Real Threat?.................................... 177

Conclusion........................................................................ 181

**Chapter 7: The First World Empire .............................................185**

The Many Methods of Empire Building ............................. 185

A Short History of Canaan (Tyre and Sidon, aka the Phoenicians) ............................................................ 188

The Sidonians.................................................................... 193

Phoenicia, the Merchants of Tarshish, and the Celts ........... 196

God's Disdain for Corrupt Commerce ............................... 203

Other Witnesses against Modern Tyre and Tarshish............. 206

Conclusion: The Final Condemnation of Tyre, Tarshish, and Babylon ............................................................... 208

**Chapter 8: Prophecy and the Powers of Seven..........................215**

Seventy (70) and the Perfection of Judgment...................... 215

Seventy Years of Gentile Judgment ................................... 217

Why Tyre and Babylon Are Prophetically Identical ........... 221

The Annihilation of Ahab and Worshippers of BAAL ......... 225

The Lesson from Another Ahab: Get Out Quick! .............. 229

The Prophetic Principle of Postponement........................... 231

Daniel's Prophecy of the 70 Weeks ....................................234
Why Did the Seventy Years of Captivity Happen? ..............239
The Anti-Hero of Daniel – the Antichrist ..........................240
Conclusion: Tying it All Together .....................................243

***Chapter 9: When Antichrist Reveals Himself in America, Will We Recognize Him? ..........249***

Political Professions of Faith ...........................................249
Orchestrating the Madding Crowd .....................................254
The Division of Labor in the Third Reich ...........................260
Hating in the Name of Christ and Country ..........................264
Impulse for a New Christian Ecumenism? ...........................266
Betraying the Meaning of the Kingdom of God ....................269
Justification by the Providence of God ...............................273

***Chapter 10: The Judgment of Babylon ..........277***

The Stage is Set ..............................................................277
The First Woe ..................................................................282
The Second Woe ...............................................................289
The Third Woe ..................................................................296
Summing Up .....................................................................303

***AFTERWORD: Democratic Globalism and the Fate of America ..........307***

The World's Commercial Empire .........................................307
America's True Golden Rule ..............................................308
Commerce as Empire .........................................................312
Who Are the True Agents of Change? ..................................315
Conclusion .......................................................................321

***Appendix: The Burden of Babylon ..........327***

***Selected Bibliography ..........334***

***About the Authors ..........338***

# Tables of Figures

Figure 1 - The *Euro*, Europe's Common Currency ..... 5
Figure 2 - The European Union ..... 7
Figure 3 – Jefferson, The Cause for Democracy's End ..... 11
Figure 4 - The City of London Financial District ..... 12
Figure 5 - *The End of America* ..... 15
Figure 6 - The Colossus of Nebuchadnezzar's Dream ..... 19
Figure 7 - A Vision of Babylon ..... 25
Figure 8 - The Whore of Babylon ..... 29
Figure 9 - Cybele: The Goddess of Fortifications ..... 36
Figure 10 - Nimrod Inspects the Tower of Babel ..... 40
Figure 11 - Babylon in 2005, a cultural center funded by the U.N. to engender Iraqi Pride (a 180-degree composite photo) ..... 44
Figure 12 - Wall Street ..... 58
Figure 13 - What Did the Founding Father's Intend? ..... 85
Figure 14 - Benjamin Franklin ..... 95
Figure 15 - Lillback's *Sacred Fire* ..... 98
Figure 16 - The Jefferson Bible ..... 100
Figure 17 - James Madison ..... 103
Figure 18 - The Reverse Side of the Great Seal ..... 105
Figure 19 - Billington's *Fire in the Minds of Men* ..... 112
Figure 20 - The Layout of the Pentagram in Washington DC ..... 113
Figure 21 - A Satanic Pentagram ..... 115
Figure 22 – Lord Francis Bacon on Newfoundland Postage Stamp 116
Figure 23 - The Original Layout of Washington DC ..... 124
Figure 24 - The U.S. Military Spend compared to the Rest of the World ..... 135
Figure 25 - The 10 Kingdoms of the Club of Rome and the U.N. ..... 139
Figure 26 - The Logo for President Obamas Visit, March 20-23, 2013 ..... 144
Figure 27 - The *Plus Ultra* and the Spanish REAL of 1768 ..... 150
Figure 28 - Gross National Product (GNP) by Rank Comparing Actual Data from 2005 with 2050 Forecasted Data ..... 152
Figure 29 - Debt as a Percent of GDP: USA, Japan, & Germany ..... 161

Figure 30 - The Velocity of Money as a Measure of Inflation............178
Figure 31 - A 9' Giant with Full Copper Armor, discovered in 1925 in Walkerton, Indiana (1 of 8 co-located skeletons) ..............................186
Figure 32 - Phoenicia and its Key Cities.................................................188
Figure 33 - Mt. Hermon, Near Caesarea Philippi ..................................194
Figure 34 - The Kensington Runestone in Alexandria, MN, discovered there in 1897 (dating circa: 1100 AD)...............................199
Figure 35 - Tyre's Commercial Empire ....................................................200
Figure 36 - A Gold Coin from Carthage with a World Map?................201
Figure 37 - *Palestra* ruins (athlete training center) in Ancient Tyre..........................................................................................218
Figure 38–The stele of BAAL, the god of Tyre holding a Thunderbolt (found in Ugarit)................................................................................222
Figure 39 - Jehu Bowing Before the Assyrian King, Shalmanessar III, 827 B.C. from the Black Obelisk of Shalmanessar.................................224
Figure 40 - The view from Mount Megiddo, looking northeast across the Jezreel Valley in Israel (Mount Tabor arises on the horizon)...227
Figure 41 - Recapping the Seventies in Judgment...................................247
Figure 42 – Luther's cover to the 1543 edition, *The Jews and Their Lies*..................................................................................................251
Figure 43 - "*Gott Mit Uns*" - God With Us ..................................................253
Figure 44 - *Reichskirche* Flag, circa 1936, Nazi Germany ......................254
Figure 45 - The Cross and the Swastika...................................................257
Figure 46 - The Pope's Nuncio, Archbishop Orsenigo with Hitler and Joachim von Ribbentrop ......................................................269
Figure 47 - Ahab, Jezebel, and Elijah.........................................................286
Figure 48 - The Valley of Jehoshaphat......................................................297

# Dedication

The three co-authors' lives have been touched by a number of wonderful saints that have gone on to be with our Lord. We dedicate this book to three saints whom we hold in highest esteem in our hearts. If there be merit in this book, it owes much to the grace and wisdom we received from these great disciples of Jesus Christ.

**Corrie ten Boom** (1892 – 1983) – In the face of Nazi terror, Corrie and her Dutch family stood together with God's ancient people in godly resistance to tyranny. She risked all, because "a faith worth dying for is a faith worth living for." Because of her acts and unwavering commitment to the gospel of Jesus Christ, she endured hardship as a good soldier of Jesus Christ – without compromise. Full of the Savior's love, Corrie "tramped" all over the world to declare His divine love, even to those who once persecuted her and her loved ones.

**J.R. Church** (1938 – 2011) – For decades J.R. declared the supernatural essence of the Scripture, and, more than any other eschatological teacher of his generation, unlocked breathtaking secrets of the Bible. He spoke with more people about the signs of the time and testified to the Hope of Glory than any other person we know. Many can attest to his lifelong commitment of earnest study in God's Word and the palpable joy which emanated from his person when privileged to have him share a new prophetic insight recently attained, testifying to the imminent return of our Savior.

**David Flynn** (1963 – 2012) – David was a unique Christian apologist, tailor-made for our times. Besides his self-effacing character and tranquility of spirit, he never ceased to astound with insight into the supernatural character of the Bible, with truths that did much to authenticate the inspiration of God's Word. By studying his works, we continue to be blessed. More than any other author/researcher of our day, David "broke the code" in the interconnections between science and the Scripture, between classic mythology and biblical truth. His research left us in awe of the "Wonderful Numbers of Sacred Canon." His was a special gift we sorely miss.

## *FOREWORD:*
# The City Sliding Down the Hill

By Cris Putnam

I AM HONORED TO INTRODUCE *THE FINAL BABYLON* BY THREE DISTINGUISHED AUTHORS WHOM I RESPECT. NO DOUBT I WAS ASKED TO PREFACE THIS WORK BECAUSE OF MY OWN RECENT ventures into the genre of speculative eschatology, co-authoring with Thomas Horn: *Petrus Romanus the Final Pope is Here* and *Exo-Vaticana*. The former volume is referenced in *The Final Babylon*. Please note that without a careful reading, one could construe a conflict. However, I perceive no disagreement between the scenario presented here and my own. Like the false prophet, Babylon in the Bible is the symbol or *type* of any religious system that opposes God. Likewise, the Antichrist and his "base of operations" – "Mystery Babylon" of Revelation 17-18 is also a commercial center of political power that imposes its will on the world. While it is hard to conceive a better match for the economic/political constituent than the case argued by Krieger, McGriff, and Woodward, the spiritual component is also entirely consistent with my own ideas about idolatrous Romanism. Indeed, if the Tribulation and return of Christ are truly upon us, then the thesis presented in *The Final Babylon* is not only compelling, *it is necessary*. Nevertheless, I anticipate that many will demur.

Naysayers may counter: "Surely America has been the 'City upon a Hill' used by God to evangelize the world?" Indeed, this once *was* the case; but today in particular the northeast U.S. is one of the largest unchurched regions in the world. The irony is that the "City upon a Hill" reference as applied to America began with a sermon called "A Model of Christian Charity" and was written in 1630 by the Puritan leader John Winthrop as his community of followers sailed to New England. In sharp relief, it is not an overstatement to lament today that we likely would require missionaries *from* Africa to evangelize New England. While those Puritan values were formative in the founding of our great nation, hundreds of years later we are reaching the extremity of a sharp decline. Founding Father John Adams wrote, "Our Constitution was made only for a moral and religious people. It is wholly inadequate to the government of any other."[1] James Madison echoed these words with this statement: "We have staked the whole future of American civilization, not upon the power of government, far from it. We have staked the future of all of our political institutions upon the capacity of mankind of self-government; upon the capacity of each and all of us to govern ourselves, to control ourselves, to sustain ourselves *according to the Ten Commandments of God.*" [Emphasis added]

Accepting this at face value, we should not be surprised that under the Bush administration the Patriot Act effectively gutted the Constitutional freedoms once enjoyed by our citizens. No matter what we once were, as a rule we are no longer a moral and religious people. Our leadership is all too often lacking in ethical, let alone biblical motivation when making decisions behind closed doors on behalf of the country. We are all the worse for this lapse.

Growing up in the Bible belt during the late 1960s and early 1970s, I recall a lingering remnant of traditional American values. Although I really did not become a Christian until adulthood, there was a sense of common decency and respect generally absent in our American culture today. The radical existentialism of the 1960s led to postmodernism and the deconstruction of traditional morals upon which our country was based. Not surprisingly, this has led to a moral decline few would have thought possible a few decades ago. It has prompted strident

---

[1] John Adams, "Message from John Adams to the Officers of the First Brigade of the Third Division of the Militia of Massachusetts," Belief Net, accessed May 1, 2013
http://www.beliefnet.com/resourcelib/docs/115/Message_from_John_Adams_to_the_Officers_of_the_First_Brigade_1.html.

and largely counterproductive political responses from mostly well-intended evangelical believers. For instance, social scientist Robert Hunter recently observed, "Speaking as a Christian myself, contemporary Christian understandings of power and politics are a very large part of what has made contemporary Christianity in America appalling, irrelevant, and ineffective – part and parcel of the worst elements of our late-modern culture today, rather than a healthy alternative to it."[2] He was possibly speaking of the loudest voices in the movement we know as *The Moral Majority*, which while well-intended actually did more harm than good by *coupling Christianity to a specific political agenda* rendering evangelicalism into a non-ingratiating caricature of itself.

But it is not just our political inclinations that are no longer aligned with biblical mandates. American Christians have largely been seduced by "the world"; that is, its ideals and methodology. The President of Southeastern Baptist Theological Seminary, Daniel Akin has written, "The church of the Lord Jesus has been seduced by a skilled seductress: the American dream."[3] Interestingly, one of the worst offenders, televangelist Jim Bakker, (infamous for his PTL Club theme park, gold plated bathroom fixtures and air conditioned dog house) had a radical epiphany in prison. Afterward, he suggested that Revelation's prostitute, the "whore of Babylon", "is materialism."[4] Despite the lessons learned by its worst offenders over the past two decades, the consumer mentality of our culture infects the believing church to an even greater extent today.

Since the lesson of Revelation 17–18 has stood as perennial warning for all Christendom throughout the ages (as does all of

---

[2] James Davison Hunter, *To Change the World: The Irony, Tragedy, and Possibility of Christianity in the Late Modern World* (Oxford University Press: 2010), p. 95.

[3] "*Radical* by David Platt Editorial Reviews" Amazon, accessed May 1, 2013, http://www.amazon.com/Radical-Taking-Faith-American-Dream/dp/B00A16O7A2.

[4] "The Re-education of Jim Bakker," *Christianity Today* (Dec. 7, 1998), p. 62.

Scripture in providing relevant instruction) inasmuch as Christian leaders have often been led astray by the grandeur of the world system, it certainly applies no less to North American evangelicals at this precarious moment. The text before you speaks not only to the idolatrous influence of an end time commercial empire (18:11); but also to the arrogance of its people's imagined *invincibility* (18:7–8). As the sole remaining super power, when one searches for the political entity or "system" upon which the Antichrist will build his empire, the U.S. is a hard candidate to beat.

Cultural critic Neil Postman argues that Western society is now a "technopoly," a culture that worships technology. He attributes this to rampant scientism and a constant progression of new improved technology fueling an ostensibly better and better quality of life. Postman argues that in a technopoly "people are conceived of not as children of God or even as citizens but as consumers - that is to say, as markets."[5] Whereas Christian ministries surely do not intend such a *worldly* approach to bringing about the Kingdom of God, their methods, however inadvertently, sneak it in nevertheless. We see this overtly when Ministry "success" is measured by growing market percentages and comparative statistics. One would be hard pressed to deny that American Christianity has developed the "business model mentality" where quantified success trumps the organic intimacy of the *ecclesia***.** Instead of building and expanding vibrant personal relationships, growing congregations are viewed as "our slice of the *burgeoning markets." A prominent case in point:* Rick Warren's unholy union with marketing guru and management consultant Peter Drucker. This manner of commercialism creates a corrosive naturalistic ethos in the Church of Jesus Christ that undermines our commitment to a biblical perspective on evangelism and discipleship. Hunter writes that powerful commercial interests em-

---

5 Neil Postman, *Technopoly: The Surrender of Culture to Technology*. Kindle Edition (Random House, Inc.). Kindle Locations 610-612.

bedded in our ecclesiastical institutions makes, "resistance to [such] effects nearly impossible."[6] In other words, most of American evangelicalism has been assimilated into the technopoly. The Babylon of Revelation 17-18 portrays this technopoly well; furthermore, given its inability to serve as censor to its own unethical motives ("only money matters"), as the colossus of international trade, it dominates as the principal exporter of immorality.

To be more conclusive in this indictment, pornography is a huge business in the United States with total sales estimated to be $12.62 to 13.33 billion per year. Then there is the horrendous matter of abortion. Since Roe vs. Wade in 1973, (as of this writing), there have been over 56 million American children sacrificed on the altar of easy sex and convenience.[7] Even worse, the Protestant mainline denominations – Episcopal,[8] Evangelical Lutheran Church of America (ELCA),[9] and Presbyterian Church in the United States of America (PCUSA)[10] – are knowingly leading people to hell. Not satisfied with merely condoning homosexuality as an acceptable alternative sexual practice and lifestyle, they are ordaining homosexual *clergy to preside over their congregations*. Ignoring the clear warnings in Scripture, they thumb their noses at God, denying His clear teaching against homosexuality, inverting His created order. And what's worse, the so-called *Emergent Church* embraces by the droves, the "spirit of the age" – enthusiastically announcing

---

[6] Hunter, *To Change the World*, p. 209.

[7] "Abortion Counter" accessed May 1, 2013 http://www.numberofabortions.com/

[8] Mireya Navarro, "Openly Gay Priest Ordained in Jersey," *The New York Times*, December, 17, 1989.

[9] ELCA News Service, "ELCA Assembly Opens Ministry to Partnered Gay and Lesbian Lutherans," *ELCA.org*, August 21, 2009, http://www.elca.org/Who-We-Are/Our-Three-Expressions/Churchwide-Organization/Communication-Services/News/Releases.aspx?a=4253.

[10] Eric Marrapodi, "First Openly Gay Pastor Ordained in the PCUSA Speaks," *CNN.com*, October 10, 2011, http://religion.blogs.cnn.com/2011/10/10/first-openly-gay-pastor-ordained-in-the-pcusa-speaks/.

*same sex marriage* as something God leads us now to "affirm and accept."[11]

Jesus connected such debauched choices to the time of His return saying, "Likewise also as it was in the days of Lot; they did eat, they drank, they bought, they sold, they planted, they builded" (Luke 17:28). Jesus' allusion to Lot living in Sodom inescapably implies the widespread acceptance of sexual immorality in the last days. It should go without saying (but I find it necessary to be explicit lest I fail to make my point clear), Jesus' analogy elucidates that the state of the world in the last days will reflect Sodom and Gomorrah, which the reader will recall was literally "blown away" in judgment by God for its rampant sexual immorality. Consequently, should we really be so astonished that Muslim peoples, who value modesty, think of the U.S. as the "great Satan" when the most popular TV show on the planet is *Baywatch*? As the major exporter of immorality, America will certainly drink the cup of fornication and the cup of wrath (Rev. 14:8–10; 16:19; 17:4; 18:6). Biblical scholar Craig Keener observed:

> Whereas Rome was the Babylon of John's day, however, it was only one of several actors in Babylon's role. Subsequent history reminds us that just as the false prophetess of Thyatira was a new Jezebel, the false prophet of Pergamum a new Balaam, the evil emperor a new Nero, and Rome a new Babylon, so the empires of history continue to return in successive incarnations that repeat the same basic lies. That the Babylon of John's day has fallen, however, like most Babylons since and all that have preceded it, gives us courage that *the final Babylon, too, will perish before the glory of God's invading kingdom.*[12] [Emphasis added]

---

[11]Nicola Menzie. "Rob Bell on Gay Marriage Support: God Pulling Us Ahead to Affirm Gay Brothers, Sisters," Christian Post (March 22, 2013) accessed May 2, 2013 http://www.christianpost.com/news/rob-bell-on-gay-marriage-support-god-pulling-us-ahead-to-affirm-gay-brothers-sisters-92395/

[12]Craig S. Keener, *The NIV Application Commentary: Revelation* (Grand Rapids, MI: Zondervan Publishing House, 2000), p. 434.

So is America the final Babylon? If you believe that the return of Jesus Christ is within the next decade or so then this conclusion seems inevitable. But don't take my word for it. You have in your hands the work of three immensely qualified authors who have laid out a systematic well-reasoned argument to that end. But one major caveat is in order: in reading this book you will likely come under conviction that your patriotism, however well-meaning and based as it is no doubt upon the finest ideals that America possessed in its early history, may now be no better than idolatry. For America's governing philosophy no longer consists of such noble principles. It has been defaced by an anti-biblical utopianism on the one hand which diminishes personal liberty and an atheistic materialism on the other which consumes the soul of its people. Should we challenge the justice of God or His righteousness in calling our nation to account for its impact upon our world? Ultimately the reader must decide whether the epithet *Babylon the Great*, aka *Mystery Babylon*, is indeed, as these authors assert, an invective proclaimed by the angel of Revelation 18:1-3 against the United States of America:

> [1] *After these things I saw another angel coming down from heaven, having great authority, and the earth was illuminated with his glory.*
>
> [2] *And he cried mightily with a loud voice, saying, "Babylon the great is fallen, is fallen, and has become a dwelling place of demons, a prison for every foul spirit, and a cage for every unclean and hated bird!*
>
> [3] *For all the nations have drunk of the wine of the wrath of her fornication, the kings of the earth have committed fornication with her, and the merchants of the earth have become rich through the abundance of her luxury."*

***Cris Putnam***
*North Carolina, June 2013*

***The Final Babylon***

## *Chapter 1:*
# The Contrarian Prophetic Scenario

## Rome Has Not Revived

TO CONTRADICT A MENTOR IS A PAINFUL ACT. WHEN YOU CHOOSE TO DO SO IN THE CAUSE OF TRUTH, IT'S BEST TO FIRST ACKNOWLEDGE HOW MUCH YOU RESPECT AND REVERE THE ONE that taught you so much.

In this book, not only do we contradict one of our most valued mentors, we challenge three of them. We take no pleasure in calling a particular aspect of their teaching into question. However, in doing so we know we are not without the company and support of other researchers and authors.

While we're hesitant to reckon our mentors mistaken regarding a major aspect of their prophetic teaching, as Luther said at his inquest, (to paraphrase) "Unless Scripture and reason persuade me otherwise, here I stand: I can do no other."[1] With that note of deference, we present a *contrarian* prophetic scenario.

The "standard scenario" of Bible prophecy reflects the thinking of popular writers (and mentors) Hal Lindsey, Tim LaHaye, and the late Grant Jeffrey. In particular, their important prophetic interpretation for the end times was built on a crucial but controversial view that even they were reluctant to advance for obvious reasons. That fundamental premise: *America must decline as a world power and a united Europe must come forward to dominate geopolitics.* Then the Antichrist will appear in these last days and head the alliance of ten "kings" composed of na-

---

[1] The full quotation is reputed as follows: "Unless I am convinced by the testimony of the Scriptures or by clear reason (for I do not trust either in the pope or in councils alone, since it is well known that they have often erred and contradicted themselves), I am bound by the Scriptures I have quoted and my conscience is captive to the Word of God. I cannot and will not recant anything, since it is neither safe nor right to go against conscience. May God help me. Amen." Martin Luther's speech at the Diet of Worms may or may not have included the famous line I cite—"Here I stand. I can do no other. God help me. Amen."

tion-states historically belonging to the Roman Empire. There are many facets of the prophecies pertaining to the last days, but the issue of the Antichrist and the "league of nations" supporting his ascendancy remains pivotal.

The "Lindsey/LaHaye/Jeffrey" argument builds on a particular passage, Daniel 9:24-27. We quote it here for the reader's convenience:

> 24 *"Seventy weeks have been decreed for your people and your holy city, to finish the transgression, to make an end of sin, to make atonement for iniquity, to bring in everlasting righteousness, to seal up vision and prophecy and to anoint the most holy place.*
>
> 25 *So you are to know and discern that from the issuing of a decree to restore and rebuild Jerusalem until Messiah the Prince there will be seven weeks and sixty-two weeks; it will be built again, with plaza and moat, even in times of distress.*
>
> 26 *Then after the sixty-two weeks the Messiah* ***will be cut off*** *and have nothing, and* ***the people of the prince who is to come will destroy the city and the sanctuary****. And its end will come with a flood; even to the end there will be war; desolations are determined.*
>
> 27 *And* ***he will make a firm covenant with the many for one week,*** *but in the middle of the week he will put a stop to sacrifice and grain offering; and on the wing of abominations will come one who makes desolate, even until a complete destruction, one that is decreed, is poured out on the one who makes desolate."*

In verse 26, Messiah the Prince is "cut off" (put to death). Thereafter, the "greatly beloved" prophet predicts the *prince of the people to come will destroy the city and the sanctuary.* Scholars uniformly believe this references the destruction of Jerusalem and Herod's Temple by Titus and the Roman army in 70 A.D.

The "***prince*** *of this people to come*" references the Antichrist (although this appellation isn't used literally in the Books of Daniel or Revelation). Nonetheless, this same evil figure which dominates Daniel's visions (Daniel's anti-hero) is also known as the king of "fierce countenance" (Daniel 8:23)[2] and the "Little Horn" (Daniel 7:8 and 8:9). [3]

Thus, the *standard scenario* proclaims the countries through which the Antichrist obtains power – his powerbase – comprise a revived Roman Empire. After all, it was the "the people to come" — the Romans – that destroyed the city and sanctuary. At issue, however, is what is implied by the identifier "the people to come." Are we talking Romans? Do we literally mean Italians or Europeans? Or could this mean a people who are their descendants? The standard scenario has held that "the people of the prince" means Europeans and specifically, a confederation of European peoples. During the past 50 years, the aforementioned writers sold over 75 million books promoting the standard prophetic scenario. Especially during the last two decades (save the last five years), it appeared that a *United States of Europe* was inevitable. The pieces of the puzzle of the standard scenario seemed to be falling perfectly into place.

**Figure 1 - The *Euro*, Europe's Common Currency**

Since the European Common Market came about as a result of The Treaty of Rome (1957) and its goal was the unification of European nations, many authors such as Lindsey, LaHaye (and a

---

[2] *"And in the latter time of their kingdom, when the transgressors are come to the full, a king of fierce countenance, and understanding dark sentences, shall stand up."* (Daniel 8:23)

[3] We could go further as the personage we know as *Antichrist* has over 30 names in the Old Testament. One of the most auspicious: "the Assyrian" – mentioned by the prophets Isaiah and Micah, seems to infer a connection to the ancient ruler of Babylon, *Nimrod.*

host of others), drew the conclusion that the Roman Empire was about to be revived and its headquarters would be in Rome.[4] Further developments since continued to increase the unity of Europe including the formation of a European Parliament and a common currency – the *Euro*. But the headquarters of the European Community continue in Brussels, Belgium, and there are no plans to move it to Rome.

Still, it was anticipated this union would accomplish financial, diplomatic, and eventually military dominance as the United States correspondingly diminished in all these categories.[5] Moreover, while this unification transpired, America seemed to be doing its best to spend itself into oblivion even as its citizens grew more tolerant toward sexual immorality and many other new lows established in the name of social responsibility.

However, in the past five years, the puzzle pieces have disassembled and the European Union appears to be falling apart. Nevertheless, the standard apocalyptic scenario continues on, with the majority still assuming European unity will advance and the "powerbase" of the Daniel's evil prince will be in Rome or another megalopolis in Europe. Thus, we believe it is time to challenge the standard scenario. We believe the core assump-

---

[4] It was first heralded with the emergence of the European Common Market (Treaty of Paris—1952), and then later, the European Union through a series of three additional treaties.

[5] In regards to efforts to achieve world socialism by the wealthy elite, the inability for Europe to become the dominant player in the "Gentile world" is not their only disappointment. The United Nations has also failed to deliver a unified world government. The UN leans heavily upon the United States for fiscal and military resources, without which it would prove even more irrelevant than it already has. Perennially the UN is at center stage of middle-eastern issues, specifically the "Palestinian question". However, it has a dismal record enforcing its will upon Israel, the Palestinians, or other members of the Arab community. Most recently, it demonstrated its weakness in failing to right the course of several "rogue" nations, most notably Iran (in restricting nuclear armaments) and Syria (in stopping the murder of its citizens). If the UN is to be the locus for the power and authority of the Antichrist (a particular scenario that LaHaye advanced in his "Left Behind" series), a dramatic turn of events is surely demanded.

tions were misunderstood. We have written this book to be a catalyst to rethink how events are likely to play out and who the player is that comprises the powerbase of Antichrist.

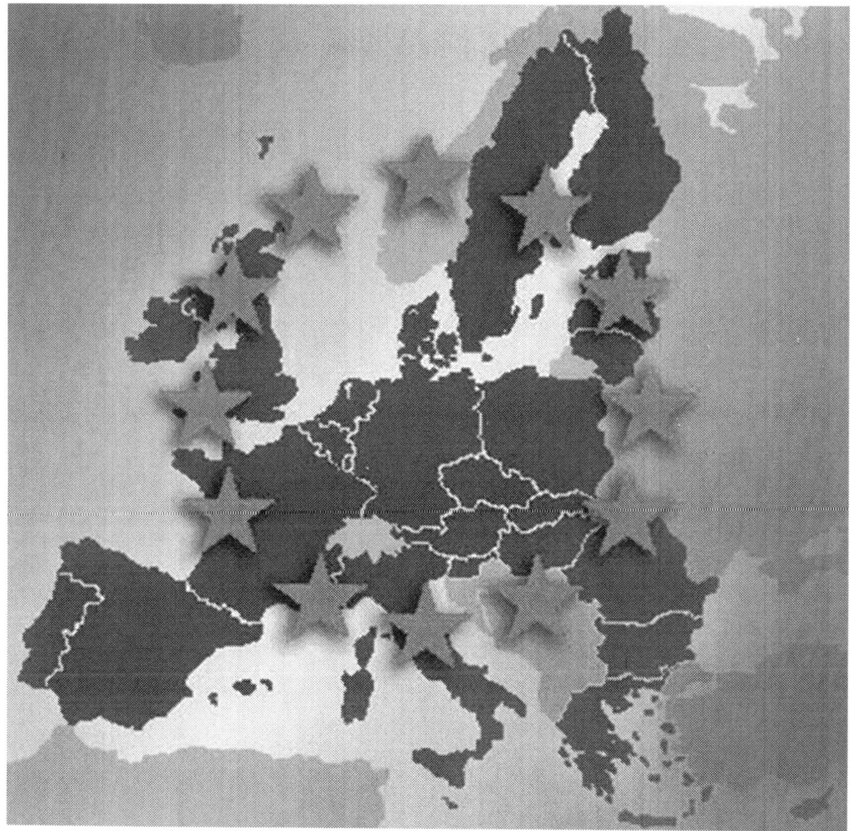

**Figure 2 - The European Union**

## Just How Much is America Declining?

Grant Jeffrey, in his last book before joining our Lord in heaven, *One Nation under Attack*, was explicit in predicting the absence of America in Bible prophecy. In a number of statements from a section of his final work, Jeffrey makes his position plain:

> The United States is not mentioned specifically in biblical prophecy. It does not appear by name or by geographical reference in the detailed descriptions of events that will occur

> during the last-days generation. Christ will return... but the one nation in the West that has benefitted from God's blessing is absent from the prophetic accounts of the critical last-day's events.
>
> There is a strange silence regarding the political and military presence and strategic influence of the United States leading up to the two major prophesied wars [the "Gog/Magog War" and the "Battle of Armageddon"]... Since every nation on earth will be involved at the Battle of Armageddon, it is certain that America will be present in some fashion, but the lack of a specific mention of America as a key player indicates that the United States will no longer be a leading power in the world. [6]

Given that the United States invests more in its military defense than the next ten top nations combined, the authors of this book ask, "How can this possibly be true?" America dominates the world with more military force than any previous empire, including ancient Rome or the British Empire at the height of its supremacy. What can explain the lack of any prophetic reference to the American Empire? What combination of forces will be capable of draining America's power in only a few short years?

Jeffrey suggests America can be transformed into mediocrity (like the British in the previous generation) in less than a decade as a result of political liberalism. *The socialist agenda will be our undoing*. As the late Margaret Thatcher, Prime Minister of England once said, "Socialism works until it runs out of other people's money to spend." On that point, we do *not* disagree.

Jeffrey voices a strong faith in America's divine favor and innate goodness. "No longer will there be a freedom-defending global superpower that works for human rights and fights against the military aggression of other nations. There will no longer be a world power that is committed to advancing free enterprise and the prosperity that comes as a result of free-market capitalism." Jeffrey's unshakeable confidence in America's mor-

---

[6] Jeffrey, Grant, *One Nation Under Attack: How Big-Government Liberals are Destroying the America You Love*, Waterbrook Press, Colorado Springs, 2012, pp. 4-5.

al uprightness permeates his lament: "At a time in history when the political influence, economic power, and military force of the United States could be called into service to oppose this unprecedented spread of evil in the world, America will be sliding into obscurity. The fall of the American Empire is already at an advanced stage. In fact, the end of America's story will come in your lifetime." [7] While we agree that the timing of the U.S.A.'s concluding chapter is imminent, *America's final "Act" (to mix a metaphor) features a plot twist most in the audience don't anticipate.*

Because America may falter at this momentous point in history (just before the seven-year period known as the "Tribulation" begins), the forces of evil cannot be held in check. Jeffrey predicts, "The Antichrist soon will rise to power and enslave the nations of the *revived Roman Empire.* Initially, he will rule the member nations of *the European Union (EU)* as well as a number of Mediterranean nations. Once the Antichrist has consolidated his power over this confederation, he will gain control of the entire world."[8] [Emphasis added] However, to cinch this geopolitical transition, America must decline – dramatically.

Jeffrey cites a number of current developments signaling America's collapse.

- The work of foreign financiers working in conjunction with U.S. officials to manipulate our currency ensuring its soon failure;
- The rise of a totalitarian regime in America – an imperial presidency achieving a new level of control with Barack Obama.
- A deliberate strategy to undermine free-market capitalism because a military approach to take over America would be doomed to failure.

Jeffrey recognizes that the progressive decline of America is more than political partisan programs. "The agenda has been steadily advanced regardless of whether the presidential ad-

---

[7] Ibid., p. 7.
[8] Ibid.

ministration was Republican or Democratic." [9] And factors outside the direct control of "the elite," especially the so-called Arab Spring, have played no small part in creating massive geopolitical turmoil leading to unforeseen changes.

However, the current international political state of affairs remains substantially the same as it has since World War II. So far, the ascendancy of Europe has not materialized – America still dominates. During 2011 and 2012, the failure of numerous European economies (the southern nations of Italy, Greece, Spain, and Portugal) has downgraded the prospects for the 27 nation confederacy. The cracks in the wall have widened with the more stable northern nations (notably France and Germany) balking at EU demands to come to the aid of their weaker colleagues. EU currency has weakened upon prospects that the union will fail. Consequently, it now stands wholly uncertain whether Europe will achieve – at least in the short-term – the dominion depicted in the classic *literal* interpretation of the Book of Daniel.

Some have gone so far as to argue that America must be completely destroyed before Europe can fulfill its prophetic destiny. However, claiming that this austere fate awaits us seems to be "reaching." What we contend happens to America toward the latter half of the Tribulation period (a divine appointment in which *utter destruction occurs at the hands of America's enemies*), others argue happens before the Tribulation begins – enabling Europe to take center stage. If so, the destruction of America is imminent indeed.

## Is America Sanctioned by God?

While we have quoted Grant Jeffrey, similar quotes could be selected from Hal Lindsey or Tim LaHaye. And like Jeffrey, Lindsey, LaHaye, and most evangelicals assume that America has been a bulwark for liberty and morality in the world.

---

[9] Ibid., p. 13.

**Figure 3 – Jefferson, The Cause for Democracy's End**

It is for this reason that critics of evangelicals complain *we are conservative theologically because we are conservative politically.* In other words, conservatism is an implicit mode of thinking no matter what issue is under debate. Regardless of that more complicated argument, nonetheless it has been frequently observed how theological conservatives are quick to *defend old-fashioned American values*, assuming that our actions in the world today result from those sacrosanct motives.

However, we question whether the mission of America is truly to be "the last and best hope of freedom" in a world full of oppressive dictators and power-hungry regimes. Rather, we suspect that rationalization is what we tell ourselves to justify safeguarding national corporate interests, especially when the liberation of the oppressed had no apparent connection to our actions. In effect, have we heard this self-serving justification so many times that a negative assessment of our national behavior lies beyond consideration? Likewise, does America deserve such high standing in the minds of evangelical ministers? Or do we fail to speak prophetically to our society, calling into question the actions of our institutions? *There are our ideals and then there are our actions.* How well do our actions achieve our ideals?

**Figure 4 - The City of London Financial District**

There is little question that Capitalism is the world's most effective form of economic structure to facilitate widespread wealth. America's strength politically owes much to a capitalist approach building business and creating opportunity. However, there is also little question that left to their own devices, corporations and those who lead them seek monopolistic advantage to generate better returns on investment, enriching themselves and their shareholders (as they are commissioned to do), acting out of self-interest (just as the founder of capitalism Adam Smith argued they should). Why fight against greed if "greed is good?"[10]

But are all parties truly well-served in the process?

Unfortunately, there are far too many examples adduced by Capitalism's critics that wealthy "owners of capital" make life miserable for laborers. To be more specific, by merely fulfilling their "mission statement," and by most accounts, corporations and their executives often conduct business in ways detrimental to their employees, their communities, and their homeland. The

---

[10] As the fictional character Gordon Gekko famously asserted in the 1987 Oliver Stone film, *Wall Street*. Gekko was played by Michael Douglas who won an Academy Award for Best Actor in this role.

bigger they are the more likely they are to exploit their opportunity in the marketplace. Goodness knows, the powerful don't willingly give up their competitive advantages. As one of the executives at Microsoft used to say: "We just want our fair share of the market... and for us that is at least 95%."

The lesson learned: no *perfect* economic system exists. There is no utopia. As Jesus said, "The poor you have with you always" (Matthew 26:11, paraphrased). Furthermore, as if the words of Jesus were intended as an excuse, there seems to be little incentive for any capitalist enterprise to "play fair" if it can cheat and get away with it. That's why business ethics are essential to the maintenance of a just society – and why perfectly just societies will always be out of reach.

The American government intends to facilitate commerce while providing a series of checks and balances to monitor the formations of "trusts" and anticompetitive conspiracies among businesses as well as take on the responsibility to manage monopolies (like power, water, and waste entities) on behalf of the citizenry. Unfortunately, this necessary activity of government often fails in its mission due to its own bureaucracy and sometimes inept personnel. It also fails because politicians require getting re-elected; and getting re-elected takes money which corporations are only too happy to supply – in exchange for certain "considerations." Far too often, politicians are "in the tank" out of the debt they owe to the corporations who help get them elected. Hence, accountability to the electorate from the rank and file politician often falls short. Thus, regardless of whether we can strike the right balance between the private and public sectors, the point remains: it's ill-advised to assume God ordains any single economic theory or sanctions only one political model.

In a fallen world, with sinful men and women running the system, we are much more likely to encounter institutions at odds with the law of God, and what is more, struggle to uncover examples where love for neighbor is practiced by those in charge. America, at times, has been a beacon of light. But over the past 60 years, this beacon has grown increasingly dim. Does this mean that America is set up for a fall? These authors believe "not in the short-term." In fact, we argue that this powerful self-interest is a strong reason for why America's place at the top will persist well into the last days before Jesus Christ returns.[11]

## Will the Antichrist be Muslim?

In the past several years, there have been a number of prophecy scholars who have considered the possibility that the Antichrist will be a Muslim. Logically, it is assumed that his power base will be Islam and its various *kingdoms* allied as enemies of Israel. In the past few years, Chuck Missler made the point that the Roman Empire was not just composed of the western nations of Europe but also an "eastern leg" – nations we know as *Mesopotamia* (a region whose name means "between two rivers," i.e., the Tigris and the Euphrates), inferring that a "revived Roman Empire" might suggest the nations of Islam will fulfill the prophecy of Daniel. Additionally, since the semi-successful U.S. involvement in Iraq (helping to rebuild that nation after deposing Saddam Hussein), the physical restoration of Babylon (only to a limited extent thus far) has become more than a mere possibility. Connecting this historical fact with biblical exegesis, Missler argues that the prophecies of Jeremiah 50 and 51 referring to the destruction of "the daughter of Babylon" (likewise seen in Isaiah 47 and elsewhere) have never been literally fulfilled. These prophecies call for the devastation of the *daughter of Babylon* so completely it can never be restored. His interpretation assumes that ancient Babylon in Iraq and the *daughter of Babylon* (Jeremiah and Isaiah's prophecy) refer to one and the same city. As we have already made plain, we do not share that perspective.

---

[11] For those familiar with biblical eschatology, we are specifically arguing that America continues to operate deep into the Great Tribulation (the final three and one-half years of Daniel's 70th Week); indeed, it appears that the United States isn't destroyed until the onslaught of the Day of the Lord.

Still, Chuck Missler doesn't stand alone. There are others who echo the view that Islam is at the center of the alliance of nations spawning Antichrist. Mark Hitchcock, a popular prophecy author and well-respected spokesperson for eschatology amongst evangelicals, has seconded Missler's motion. He believes the physical, historical Babylon will soon be rebuilt and become one of the major "capitols" for the Antichrist.

**Figure 5 - *The End of America***

Then there is author John Price. In his fine book, *The End of America* (2009), he supports the related notions that Islam is the religion of Antichrist, the Antichrist will be Muslim, and the City of Babylon, Iraq, will be rebuilt. He believes that Islam will attack America – specifically, terrorists will destroy many of our major cities through detonating suitcase nukes smuggled into our country. Price argues several American cities are destined for obliteration; their destruction constitutes the fulfillment of the Old Testament prophecies. Upon concluding his thesis, he calls Jews and Christians to heed the advice of Jeremiah 51:6: *"Flee out of the midst of Babylon, and deliver every man his soul: be not cut off in her iniquity; for this is the time of the LORD'S vengeance; he will render unto her a recompense."* Price goes so far to identify lands far away from America that will be safe havens from war and unlikely to be subjected to Islamic control.

Finally, the irrepressible Jack Van Impe warns of Christianity and Islam being merged into an amalgam ("Chrislam"). Not too long ago, Van Impe charged megachurch pastor and best-selling evangelical author Rick Warren of *promoting* Chrislam. This led to a split between Van Impe and TBN (Trinity Broadcasting Network) who refused to air Van Impe's episode in which he made the controversial allegation.[12] Despite this, Van Impe continues to warn viewers of a pending merger of these religions. For Van Impe, true Christianity and its devoted followers will become a target of persecution, imprisonment and martyrdom.

*Of course, given enough time (not just years, but decades or even centuries), any number of scenarios are certainly possible.* The issue is made more acute, however, if we speculate that the return of Jesus Christ is possible (if not probable) within the next 20 years. Once we establish a time limit in order to evaluate a "most likely" scenario (and those who study prophecy are likely to conduct such evaluations), one or two scenarios are judged worthy of consideration, while others (such as those summarized above) seem nigh unto impossible. For instance, we might ask, "Could Babylon become one of the world's most dominant cities within a single decade? Who would be willing to provide the financing to accomplish this herculean task?"

On the other hand, we could continue speculating about the traditional scenario and ask, "Could Europe become a dominant military presence within the next ten years? Given its struggles to support its mostly socialist economies, where will it come up with the revenues to build an invincible military? If money matters (and it universally does), the prospects for a radical shift in wealth, political influence, and military capability – away from the United States to Europe – seems remote.

Likewise, while the monetary capacity of Arab states to the average American seems virtually infinite, the chances an alliance of Islamic states could collectively become the primary military power of the end times also seems, well, astronomically small. So far, Arab states (including Iran) haven't exactly domi-

---

[12] See http://blog.beliefnet.com/news/2011/10/what-is-chrislam-and-does-anybody-really-preach-it.php.

nated Israel – let alone Europe, America, or Asia. Given most prophetic scenarios envisage the destruction of nations surrounding Israel as a fulfillment of Psalm 83 and Isaiah 17 – not to mention the Gog and Magog passages of Ezekiel 37 and 38 – supposing that Antichrist appears bound to ride an Arabian "beast" seems inherently self-contradictory.

## So Is America Omitted in Bible Prophecy?

To entertain such stupefying suppositions as outlined above, it appears the only way any of these circumstances could materialize would be with the realization of a magnificently difficult pre-condition. That pre-condition would be *the demise of the United States*. Mind you, in this context we are not talking a decisive weakening, but a total dismantling. We argue this dramatic change in the geo-political situation could only be imagined with sudden and catastrophic events that stretch the credibility of thc person proposing them.

Consequently, we must ask what the pivotal questions are for these authors: "Could America be eliminated as the dominant financial player in the world? Could the Anglo-American alliance that connects Wall Strcct bankers with "City of London" financiers cease to control the world's economies? What would happen to the world financial system in the wake of such a financial Armageddon? Would there really be any survivors? Wouldn't every nation's economy be dramatically affected and driven to its knees?" We raise these questions for we are mindful that, as they say, when America sneezes the rest of the world catches pneumonia.

When we turn to the issue of military dominance, we feel compelled to ask key questions like, "How could America's military be disabled and made ineffectual? Short of a hidden set of alien technologies, the stuff of "alien conquest movies," who could make war with the United States?[13] True, our cities might

---

[13] Joseph Farrell in his books, has raised the possibility that a "breakaway civilization" exists (building on the original idea by UFO expert and research-

be vulnerable to attack from any number of threats. It is suggested they are susceptible (1) to suitcase bombs from Islamic terrorists (Price), (2) an Iranian electromagnetic pulse (EMP) device exploded high above U.S. territory (Missler et al), or even (3) a surprise missile attack launched from Soviet, Chinese, or North Korean submarines lurking off our coastline (Note: we know these would-be enemies quietly cruise daily in nearby international waters). But it's hard to imagine any scenario (absent the direct judgment of God) that would wipe out strategic U.S. military assets consisting of 11 carrier groups and 80 plus submarines spread throughout the world, half of which project strategic nuclear weapons and all of which are nuclear powered.

There are strong reasons why most Bible preachers argue judgment lies on America's doorstep (or has already entered our front door). In fact, a consensus exists amongst prophecy pundits that the moral laxity of our nation deserves the judgment of God. Immorality, abortion, the advocacy of homosexuality as a "normal" lifestyle – all of these attributes of American culture today constitute a repudiation of God's Law. Going further, authors like John McTernan (*As America Has Done to Israel*) and David Brennan (*The Israel Omen*) point out the fantastic timing "coincidence" between destructive natural calamities and American efforts to push Israel in "giving up land for peace" as a means to settle the "Palestinian Issue." Whether we are talking about 2005 Hurricane Katrina or the 1994 Northridge Earthquake in Los Angeles, these authors demonstrate God (through His provi-

---

er, Richard Dolan). The supposition goes this way: Powerful Nazi technologies lived on after World War II and continued to be financed by intelligence agencies (mostly the CIA) after wars' end. Massive stockpiles of gold, stored in the Philippines by the Japanese, have provided the hard capital necessary to finance weapons development "off the books." This has resulted in advanced military capabilities that are waiting in the wings and could be deployed. These technologies likely include anti-gravity aircraft, laser-powered weapons, zero-point energy weapons, and even super soldiers and teleportation. These weapons would neutralize conventional weapons, nullifying American arms. "Resistance would be futile." See Farrell's latest book, *Covert Wars and Breakaway Civilizations,* Adventures Unlimited Press, (2012)

dential rule over nature) may have judged America already for its failure to support Israel's security and right to its ancient land.

**Figure 6 - The Colossus of Nebuchadnezzar's Dream**

Author Jonathan Cahn in his recent best-selling book, *The Harbinger,* has also asserted America may be under God's judgment for all the reasons above. He discusses Isaiah 9:10-11 describing God's judgment on Israel in the eighth century BC and proposes this is a pattern that seems to be playing out in America today. What happened to the United States in the 911 tragedy might signify a similar "harbinger" (a warning) that speaks of an even greater calamity heading our way should our nation not repent and dramatically change its present course.

As stated above, the traditional scenario relies upon America not just taken down a rung or two, but being pulled off the ladder entirely. There are two principal reasons. One is due to a logical argument applied to biblical interpretation; the second rests upon speculation about the events surrounding the rapture of the Church.

The first justification for maintaining America isn't identified "anywhere in end time's prophecy" is the argument from silence (*argumentum a silentio*). It is claimed that because America is not mentioned specifically by name through the great prophets of the Bible, America must not play a part in the final days before Jesus Christ returns.

The argument that America isn't directly disclosed in the Bible is hard to refute. It seems rather obvious that America would not be mentioned by name. If it were, it would be a most stunning confirmation of the supernatural character of Scripture. Certainly, the reader recognizes that other great empires such as Egypt and Greece were mentioned by name. But then, those nations and peoples existed employing those names at the time the Bible was written. Certainly Rome was not identified by name in the Old Testament, but it was obviously referenced too many times to mention in the New. Why? The New Testament was contemporary to the Roman era. Therefore, among theologians who assume biblical inspiration, few disagree that Rome was symbolized by the "two legs" of the great metallic colossus dreamed by Nebuchadnezzar and interpreted by Daniel (See Daniel 2).

Likewise, the Roman Empire appears unmistakably represented within the Book of Revelation. John the Revelator connects it implicitly to Daniel's writing (compare Daniel 7:1-7 with Revelation 13:1-4). Indeed, the Bible is a time-connected book recording true history and predicting upcoming events in space-time – although its predictions about the future make liberal use of simile and metaphor. Daniel used imagery and symbol when predicting the coming of Greece (and later Rome) before the angels (or "archons") of these lands came on the scene (see Daniel 10:20). In this pertinent respect, America would be no different. If America were revealed in the Bible, it would only be declared through imagery and symbol. And given America dominates the world in ways that no other empire ever has before in history, supposing America *to be overlooked by the prophecies of the Bible implies the Bible's prophets possessed meager intuition.* Therefore, the argument from silence isn't really that compelling. Indeed, when the reader thinks about it carefully, it seems somewhat baffling that for so long it has been a prominent aspect of the dispute regarding whether America is absent during the "end times."

Likewise, for a variety of reasons we also challenge the second rationale justifying America's absence in biblical predictions. This subsequent rationale has to do with the physical consequences of the rapture. The rhetorical question is often asked, "What will happen to the world when millions (or hundreds of millions) of believers are suddenly "translated" from mortal bodies to immortal bodies to meet Christ in the air?" Typically, proponents of the "America-goes-missing-in-action" argument base their conclusions on the notion many of its people – tens of millions – vanish into thin air because of the *rapture.* The familiar scenario: all at once thousands upon thousands disappear at critical moments leaving jets to fall from the sky and cars to careen out of control. As the bumper sticker said in the 1970s, "Warning: In Case of Rapture, Car will be Unmanned."

Please take note: we are not challenging the idea of a pre-tribulation Rapture. For not unlike the evangelical community, the three authors of this book do not agree on its timing. Woodward continues to maintain that the Rapture happens well before the physical return of Jesus Christ in great glory ("*Looking for that blessed hope, and the glorious appearing of the great God and our Savior Jesus Christ*" - Titus 2:13) while McGriff and Krieger maintain a "pre-wrath" view – and a rapture very late in the Tribulation period. Regardless, the authors agree *the rapture does not constitute the primary cause for America's potential diminished place in the world.* We have other reasons to challenge that facet of the traditional scenario. Nevertheless, we still feel it necessary to speak to the "rapture rationale."

First, to argue that America is especially harmed by the snatching away of believers in this most magnificent supernatural event, infers that America has a far greater percentage of believers as citizens than do other nations in "the West" or the rest of the world. That may or may not be true (only God knows for sure!) But even if it is true, it seems unlikely America would be impacted far more than other nations that fly airplanes, sail ships, or sport millions of vehicles active at any given moment. At the root of our objection is a sense of *parochial arrogance that citizens of the United States are predominantly Christian.* That may have been true at one time. But those that are truly blessed with the saving knowledge of Jesus Christ are likely far fewer than "the statistics" convey. Indeed, despite the fact that most surveys indicate a majority of American's see themselves as "Christian" the state of our society suggests otherwise. As Jesus proclaimed in Matthew 7:21-23, *"Not every one that saith unto me, Lord, Lord, shall enter into the kingdom of heaven; but he that doeth the will of my Father which is in heaven. Many will say to me in that day, Lord, Lord, have we not prophesied in thy name? And in thy name have cast out devils? And in thy name done many wonderful works? And then will I profess unto them, I never knew you: depart from me, ye that work iniquity."* In short, the fruits of our country aren't what they used to be. Much of our produce, spiritually speaking, has gone rotten.

Secondly, trying to understand how the Rapture will "go down" (or we go up!) is not a matter that our finite human minds can conjecture with any accuracy (compared to what will really occur). If we believe in the providence of God, we believe He is able to foresee the activities of every person on earth simultaneously – indeed, He does so every day. That fact is impossible for the human mind to "take in." But just because we can't "figure out how He does it" doesn't make it less true. If the rapture happens in a moment, in the twinkling of an eye (not a blinking but a twinkling—not a split-second, but a nano-second), it is conceivable that the physical characteristics may not involve the utter chaos generally imagined. God is able to engineer anything – even the fact that airplanes won't fall out of the sky and cars won't pile up on the interstate. Having said that, it is also possible that the rapture of the church will happen, as our friend David Lowe suggests, amidst worldwide cataclysms – the opening of Revelation's sixth seal and the great earthquake that causes every mountain and island to move from its place (Revelation 6:14).[14] If so, chaos will reign.

Should this happen (to be more specific, should the resurrection of the quick and the dead be a physical cause for this worldwide catastrophe as Lowe speculates) those "left behind" will be calling for the rocks to cover them from the wrath of the Lord of Heaven (Isaiah 2:10,19; Revelation 6:17). The rapture will hardly be the first thing on their minds or the explanation they pose to explain the sudden destruction that has come upon them (I Thessalonians 5:3). Logically, after coming out of the caves (or bomb shelters as the case may be), those missing, even if it is vast sum (and we think it is) will be easily explained away by survivors *as a direct consequence of the immense catastrophe.*

## Conclusion

"Because America isn't mentioned in the Bible" by name, that is, does not constitute a sufficient reason for biblical schol-

---

[14] The idea that any mechanism could cause every island and mountain to move from its place is now conceivable. As part of the 2012 "scare", Charles Hapgood's theory of a crustal shift resulting from a magnetic pole shift was brought once again to the foreground.

Charles Hapgood is now perhaps the best remembered early proponent. In his books *The Earth's Shifting Crust* (1958) (which includes a foreword by Albert Einstein that was written before the theory of plate tectonics was developed)[11] and *Path of the Pole* (1970). Hapgood, building on Adhemar's much earlier model, speculated that the ice mass at one or both poles over-accumulates and destabilizes the Earth's rotational balance, causing slippage of all or much of Earth's outer crust around the Earth's core, which retains its axial orientation.

Based on his own research, Hapgood argued that each shift took approximately 5,000 years, followed by 20,000- to 30,000-year periods with no polar movements. Also, in his calculations, the area of movement never covered more than 40 degrees. Hapgood's examples of recent locations for the North Pole include Hudson Bay (60°N, 73°W), the Atlantic Ocean between Iceland and Norway(72°N, 10°E) and Yukon (63°N, 135°W).

However, in his subsequent work *The Path of the Pole*, Hapgood conceded Einstein's point that the weight of the polar ice would be insufficient to bring about a polar shift. Instead, Hapgood argued that the forces that caused the shifts in the crust must be located below the surface.

ars to dismiss the United States as a possible fulfillment of the final Babylon. In this important regard, scholars such as the late J.R. Church, the venerable Noah Hutchings, Reverend R.A. Coombs, and a host of other authors like Tom Horn, John Price, Patrick Heron, Stewart Best, Allen Bonck, Rob Skiba – and these authors – challenge the Lindsey/ Jeffrey/ LaHaye view. Along with these "other" authors, we argue the Bible *does* prophesy specifically about America. Our nation is disclosed in the many attributes associated with the notorious entity called *the daughter of Babylon* in Jeremiah, Zechariah, and Isaiah as well as "Mystery Babylon" in the Book of Revelation.

Whether the Antichrist turns out to be an American, a Muslim from the Middle East, or a European King, is the overt topic which we will address. However, in this project, our focus covers the arising of the "powerbase" of Antichrist as well. Succinctly, *we assert that America plays a central role in Antichrist's appearance.* Moreover, we argue America continues dominating geopolitically well into the Great Tribulation and through its residual military (surviving what appears to be a vast destruction on the continent), will be instrumental in the events culminating in very last of the last days.

In short, we contend America is *THE FINAL BABYLON.*

## *Chapter 2:*
# Who Is Babylon?

## Mystery Babylon

IDENTIFYING "MYSTERY BABYLON" REMAINS ONE OF THE GREATEST OF PUZZLES AMONG MANY RIDDLES IN THE BOOK OF REVELATION. IN TIMES PAST, THIS MYSTERIOUS ENTITY *BABYLON* WAS identified with numerous different peoples, nations, and institutions. The reformers, Martin Luther and John Calvin regarded it to be the Roman Catholic Church. In fact, most evangelical leaders in times past (for instance John Wesley in the eighteenth century) made the same proclamation, sometimes at the risk of their livelihood if not lives. We know this anti-Catholic viewpoint as the *historicist* perspective. Furthermore, most of today's evangelical prophecy authors and teachers see the Pope as either the *Antichrist* or even more typically, the *False Prophet* of Revelation 13:11-14 who causes the whole world to worship the Beast.

**Figure 7 - A Vision of Babylon**

Doubtless the Roman Catholic Church was singled out because of the fervent hostility between Protestants and Catholics for almost 500 years. The debate turns on more than one issue.

First of all, Catholics and Protestants each accuse the other of heresy based upon the matter of authority. Catholics insist that the Pope is infallible and must be obeyed without question. Protestants assert only the Bible is authoritative. However, this fundamental topic only scratches the surface. Other disputes are legion: the nature of the sacraments; the substance of how one obtains salvation; the place of the priesthood in mediating the grace of God; the role of women; birth control; but especially the separation of church and state.

Despite the historical vitriol between these two Christian paths, today it is only the most orthodox followers within each tradition that continue to strongly object to the other. To a great extent, this disdain has dramatically diminished in America since John Kennedy became the first Catholic president in 1961. Since then, most Protestants have relaxed their doctrinal disputes against their Catholic antagonists. In fact, by 1993, the World Council of Churches hosted the Catholic Church in an ecumenical effort to combine forces to convert the world to a Christianized point of view. Needless to say, doctrinal differences were no longer emphasized. Only a loose notion of what it means to be Christian was mandatory for uniting.

Not so with many died-in-the-wool evangelicals (among whom we number ourselves). As orthodox believers in the Protestant tradition we generally remain suspicious of the Catholic hierarchy and many aspects of Catholic theology. Nowhere is this more pronounced than *in the issue of eschatology*. The matter of the so-called *historicist interpretation* of the Bible's prophetic passages still stimulates heated debate.[1]

In 2012, researchers and authors Tom Horn and Cris Putnam wrote an extensive and updated exposé of the Historicist point of view in their best-selling book *Petrus Romanus* (subtitled *The Final Pope is Here*). Horn and Putnam asserted that the next

[1] Catholic eschatology can best be described as *Post-Millennial*, meaning that the Church (the Catholic Church that is) will eventually sanctify all the earth and usher in the Kingdom of God.

pope elected (who is now elected, Francis I, George Mario Cardinal Bergoglio) will be pope contemporary to the return of Jesus Christ. The final pope is named *Petrus Romanus*, Peter the Roman. However, whether the new pope has *Pietro* hidden somewhere in his name (a matter of controversy already) will not be settled in the near term. Francis I now is the 112th pope. There are 111 others identified in an extra biblical prophecy purportedly owing to an Irish monk, St. Malachy of the twelfth century. His *prophecy of the popes*, published in 1595, allegedly named all 112 popes (from the beginning of the papal legacy to the end of time – at least as we know it) each with a terse poetic illusion generally no more than two to four lines. Horn and Putnam maintain, along with some Catholics and many Evangelicals, this pope will be the so-called False Prophet (of Revelation 13:6), a beast with two horns that speaks like a lamb but is a *dragon in sheep's clothing* (to mishandle the metaphor).

Calling the Pope a false prophet is bound to make enemies whether or not the name calling winds up being accurate. Scandals are plaguing the Roman Church once again and the odds-on supposition is that these events are hardly coincidental. Additionally, it is noteworthy that Horn and Putnam predicted the resignation of the former Pope Benedict XVI about one year ago (in 2011). They suggested the resignation would likely occur in 2012. In effect, they missed the predicted timeframe by only a few months. Not bad in the high-powered world of churchly politics.

Could Pope Francis I be *Petrus Romanus*? If this Pope has the name Peter listed somewhere in his background, chances are the St. Malachy prophecy continues to bat 1.000. However, it should be realized that whatever his full name, the Catholics regard all Popes standing in "the shoes of the fisherman" (the Apostle Peter), and he, like all popes, makes his abode within Rome (in Vatican City of course). Therefore, don't be surprised if Francis I has no trace of Peter anywhere in his name. The reason for his Malachy moniker, *Peter the Roman*, may take some searching out before it comes to light. And given that Francis I was formerly of the Jesuit Order, conservative Protestants are certainly on edge already (regardless of the Malachy prophecy) given Francis' recent coronation. (Note: Jesuit priests have long been seen as the defenders of the most aggressive form of Catholicism going back all the way to the "counter-reformation" of the sixteenth century when the order was approved in 1542, having been founded a few years prior by Ignatius Loyola).[2]

## Hunting for Catholic Apostasy

About two decades ago, conservative author Dave Hunt wrote a momentous study, *A Woman Rides the Beast* (1994) provided an exhaustive analysis of the anti-Catholic position. It remains a solid source of information about the historical conflict between Catholics and Protestants. Hunt's book provides exhaustive detail in its 500-plus pages chronicling the apostasy and abuses of Catholicism down through the ages. His tone is at best direct (at worst scathing), in detailing all the ways the Roman Catholic Church constitutes the whore of Revelation, the "woman who rides the beast" until the ten kings who reign with the Beast ultimately turn against her, eat her flesh, and burn her with fire. *"And the ten horns which thou sawest upon the beast, these shall hate the whore, and shall make her desolate and naked, and shall eat her flesh, and burn her with fire"* Revelation 17:16).[3]

---

[2] "The order is...well-versed in controversies, being the target of many itself, both in and out of the Catholic Church. Its detractors claim that its members are part of various conspiracies and secret organizations, while conservative Catholics chastise them for their modern views, especially on such issues as abortion, priestly celibacy, homosexuality, and liberation theology." See *http://www.wisegeek.org/what-is-the-jesuit-order.htm.*

[3] C.I. Scofield in his commentary on Revelation 18:2 summarizes his view of ecclesiastical and political Babylon and the fate of the harlot:

> "Babylon, "confusion," is repeatedly used by the prophets in a symbolic sense (*See Scofield* "Isaiah 13:2"), note 2. Two "Babylons" are to be distinguished in the Revelation: ecclesiastical Babylon, which is apostate Christendom, headed up under the Papacy; and political Babylon, which is the Beast's confederated empire, the last form of Gentile world-dominion. Ecclesiastical Babylon is "the great whore" Revelation 17:1

Hunt emphasizes that Babylon comprises a combination of spiritual and political power, a world system that unites politics and religion in a dominating and oppression manner. Hunt says:

> A paramount feature common to all was the unity between throne and altar, between prince and priest. "Separation of church and state" was as yet unheard of; in fact, the

**Figure 8 - The Whore of Babylon**

> opposite was true. The pagan priests-astrologers, magicians, sorcerers, soothsayers – were the emperor's close advisers and often the hidden influence controlling the empire. Thus a

---

and is destroyed by political Babylon Revelation 17:15-18 that the beast may be the alone object of worship; 2 Thessalonians 2:3; 2 Thessalonians 2:4; Revelation 13:15. The power of political Babylon is destroyed by the return of the Lord in glory... The notion of a literal Babylon to be rebuilt on the site of ancient Babylon is in conflict with Isaiah 13:19-22. But the language of Revelation 18:10; Revelation 18:16; Revelation 18:18 seems beyond question to identify "Babylon," the "city" of luxury and traffic, with "Babylon" the ecclesiastical centre, viz. Rome. The very kings who hate ecclesiastical Babylon deplore the destruction of commercial Babylon."

> principle characteristic of this woman [the whore], who is both a city and a spiritual entity, will be her adulterous relationships with secular governments.[4]

In other words, instead of holding human government accountable to the Law of God, the harlot religion conspires with the political "powers that be" to enrich itself at the expense of liberty and human dignity. Should it conflict with political authority, doctrine will be compromised.

For Hunt, the infamous Tower of Babel represents a religious enterprise, a stark symbol illustrating a means by which human beings seek godly power and overrule Yahweh's reign. Human efforts seek to join heaven and earth – to deny the place of God and to exalt the position of humanity. Once the sphere of God is dismissed – only human opinion sets the rules. No longer are political and civil union authorities judged by the decrees of God. With monotheism denied, humanity discards God's law out of hand.

However, this cosmological sword cuts both ways. Sacred institutions which seek political hegemony prostitute themselves. The "mystery" of Babylon conveys this scurrilous union:

> The city [of Babylon] was a political/civil union of earth's inhabitants at that time. The tower was clearly a religious enterprise, the means of reaching heaven. *Babel thus represents the unity of state and church, involving the entire world in the attempt to elevate man to God's level.* That this would be accomplished through a tower built by human genius and energy obviously represents man's religion of self-effort. Inasmuch as the entire world was united in this effort, we have the first example of world government and world religion joined as one. As man began in this unity, so he must end in it as well; such is the clear message on the woman's forehead [emphasis ours].[5]

---

[4] Dave Hunt. *A Woman Rides the Beast: The Roman Catholic Church and the Last Days* (Kindle Locations 469-472). Kindle Edition.

[5] Ibid., Kindle Locations 477-481.

When religion reinforces the State's position by demanding its members heed without question the mandate of human government, it ceases to function as the Lord of Heaven and Earth intended. From the eleventh-century Magna Carta forward, [6] Hunt asserts "Whatever her true motives, history bears full witness to the fact that whenever she has been able to do so, the Roman Catholic Church has suppressed and openly condemned such basic human rights as freedom of the press, speech, religion, and even conscience."[7] Then Hunt becomes more explicit:

> The antipathy of Roman Catholicism to basic human freedoms later created unholy alliances with the totalitarian governments of Hitler and Mussolini, who were praised by the pope and other Church leaders as men chosen by God. Catholics were forbidden to oppose Mussolini and were urged to support him. The Church virtually put the Fascist dictator in office (as it would Hitler a few years later). In exchange, Mussolini (in thc 1929 Concordat with the Vatican) made Roman Catholicism once again the official state religion, and any criticism of it was made a penal offense. The Church was granted other favors, including a vast sum in cash and bonds. [8]

Hunt also provides several citations from the Pulitzer-Prize winning historian Peter Viereck in his 1940 book *Meta-Politics: The Roots of the Nazi Mind* (that pre-dated the entrance of America into World War II) with this incisive analysis of what the Nazi government of Adolf Hitler would mean to the people of Germany after the war ended, and what their final words would be (Viereck was only too right in his ominous prediction):

---

[6] "The 1215 charter required King John of England to proclaim certain liberties and accept that his will was not arbitrary—for example by explicitly accepting that no "freeman" (in the sense of non-serf) could be punished except through the law of the land, a right that still exists. Magna Carta was the first document forced onto a King of England by a group of his subjects, the feudal barons, in an attempt to limit his powers by law and protect their privileges." See http://en.wikipedia.org/wiki/Magna_Carta.

[7] Ibid., Kindle Locations 509-510.

[8] Ibid., Kindle Locations 526-529.

> "Someday the same Germans (who voted for Hitler), now cheering Hitler's strut into Paris will say... 'We did not know what went on...' And when that day of know-nothing comes, there will be laughter in hell."[9]

A prescient observation if ever there was one.

A most incriminating example of the Church bowing to the State came with a "joint pastoral letter [from all the German bishops that] was read from the pulpits... January 3, 1937 [stating that] "the German bishops consider it their duty to support the head of the German Reich by all those means which the Church has at its disposal.... We must mobilize all the spiritual and moral forces of the Church in order to strengthen confidence in the Führer."[10] The fact that Hitler was a member in good standing of the Catholic Church was purely a political decision. As many authors have shown conclusively, Hitler believed in spiritualism, ancestor worship, the Theosophy of Blavatsky[11], and the myths of ancient Germany including Thule and Hyperborea.[12]

But the larger point is this: the government of the German Workers Party – National Socialism, the Nazis – was driven by spiritual motivations of the "hidden" (occult) kind and reinforced by the "public" Church in an effort to safeguard its wealth and

---

[9] Ibid., Kindle Locations 549.

[10] Ibid., Kindle Locations 568-571.

[11] Helena Petrovna Blavatsky, a Russian woman, along with Henry Steel Olcott, an American formerly serving in the Union Army, founded the Theosophical Society in the 1880s in America. Theosophy was the forebear to the New Age Movement and highly influential amongst the leadership of the Nazis.

[12] "Along with Thule, Hyperborea was one of several *terrae incognitae* to the Greeks and Romans, where Pliny, Pindar and Herodotus, as well as Virgil and Cicero, reported that people lived to the age of one thousand and enjoyed lives of complete happiness. Hecataeus of Abdera collated all the stories about the Hyperboreans current in the fourth century BC and published a lengthy treatise on them, lost to us, but noted by Diodorus Siculus (ii.47.1–2). Also, the sun was supposed to rise and set only once a year in Hyperborea; which would place it above or upon the Arctic Circle, or, more generally, in the arctic polar regions." See http://en.wikipedia.org/wiki/Hyperborea.

societal status. *The merger (or marriage) of the political and the spiritual is the defining characteristic of Babylon.* The two are inseparably bonded. This attribute will be incarnated once again (and in its fullest form) with THE FINAL BABYLON. The two beasts, one spiritual and one commercial/political, will act as one managing world affairs in the name of "what's best" for humankind.

Despite the purported beneficent aspirations, the lasting lesson remains: the Church of Jesus Christ must never compromise its position on the insufficiency of human government. The doctrine of "depravity" extends to human institutions as well as individuals. No one infallible exists; and no institution can, of its own accord, promise heaven on earth to its citizens. The *fall* of humankind must be constantly memorialized. Moreover, the sinfulness of human beings extends into all its institutions, no matter how worthy their ideals or how meritorious their causes. Good government takes the doctrine of depravity seriously and establishes checks and balances to mitigate against the excesses of sinful human beings. A "Babylonian government" asserts human reason and humanitarian values will establish utopia. The Bible says, "No!" Humanity's sin precludes "heaven on earth." That is why the Tower of Babel, among other things, symbolizes humanity's effort to bring "heaven down to earth" and why God sought to "spread humanity out." Unity achieved by a single human government would institutionalize evil – and "nothing would be impossible for them" – even the greatest evils.

In summary, the most essential element of Babylon is a form of *totalitarianism combining religious doctrine with political control, the religion providing justification for a dominating political authority.*

## The Mother of Fortifications and Her Leopard Child

Another resource often referenced in this evangelical condemnation of Catholicism is the classic book by Alexander Hislop, *The Two Babylons* (1858 – subtitled *The Papal Worship*

*Proved to Be the Worship of Nimrod and His Wife).* Hislop's "*two Babylons*" refer to the common religious perspective of ancient Chaldea, its capital city Babylon, and its alleged counterpart over the past 1,500 years, the Roman Catholic Church. However, our references in this section to Hislop's study *are not provided for that purpose* – although identifying Babylon with Catholicism was Hislop's primary intent. Instead, the connection we chart below relates to the founder of Babylon, *Nimrod*, aka *The Assyrian*, and his mother who Hislop contends comprise the realities behind the Catholic worship of Mary and her beloved baby. Moreover, for Hislop, *Nimrod and his mother are icons conveying the essential sin of Babylon as asserted above.*[13]

Hislop did an exhaustive study of the many mythological characters of Babylon, Egypt, Greece, and Rome in order to demonstrate that, among other practices, the worship of the Madonna and child was not so much adoration of Jesus Christ and his mother Mary, but instead stemmed from the worship of *Nimrod* and his mother *Shamiram* (in Greek, Semiramis). Nimrod and Semiramis (the more familiar version of her name) lived about 200 to 400 years after the Flood of Noah.

The study of these two figures looms large *since Nimrod embodies the Bible's first foreshadowing or archetype of the Antichrist.* In other words, we will spend some time on the subject of Nimrod here because *he provides a portrait of the Antichrist!*

According to Hislop, the mythological history of Orion, Osiris, and Apollo all are closely linked to Nimrod who was "a mighty hunter *before* the Lord." To quote Genesis 10:9 in its entirety, *"He was a mighty hunter before the LORD: wherefore it is said, 'Even as Nimrod the mighty hunter before the LORD'."* This phrase certainly begs the question of whether the ancient

---

[13] Hislop's work is subject to considerable criticism. But it is not clear that these criticisms are themselves without prejudice. The notion that Nimrod represents an iconic image of the nature of Babylonian religion seems probable even given the very limited references in the Bible. The question of whether Nimrod and Semiramis are truly the impetus behind the worship of the Madonna and Child can be distinguished and is a separate issue.

writer assumed his reader was familiar with a well-known proverb in the ancient world. So we must inquire rhetorically, "What is the writer of Genesis inferring with this proverb?" No doubt the adage is lost on modern hearers because today, if someone is called a Nimrod, it is akin to saying they are obviously stupid – since Nimrod thought he could build a tower tall enough to reach heaven! ("What a fool!") Nonetheless, if ever a name was "lost in translation" the meaning of Nimrod's name surely is it.

No doubt Genesis 10:9 has been subjected to numerous "strained" interpretations. However, from our study it should be translated, "a defiant and fearless hunter who the world revered *instead* of the Lord." A more accurate paraphrase would be "a ruthless hero, renown for hunting and other acts of courage and skill that encouraged the ancient world to regard him as supreme to the God of heaven." Transliterating this *into even more plainly stated blasphemous modern vernacular*, we could offer these words, "Just as the familiar saying goes: 'Nimrod is more awesome than God'."[14]

According to tradition and mythology both oral and written, there was no beast that Nimrod could not defeat. Indeed, Nimrod was considered the greatest hunter of the ancient world. In fact, he may have been the first to stalk prey from the back of a horse using a bow and arrow. Additionally, it is supposed that Nimrod was the first hunter who trained a leopard to stalk prey beside him. In fact, wearing leopard skins (a tradition of ancient kings), implicitly referenced Nimrod who *hunted* leopards and hunted *with* leopards.[15] Even the first portion of his name, *Nimr*, means *leopard*.

---

[14] It is noteworthy that the constellation *Orion* is also known as "the hunter."

[15] J.R. Church once detailed a different legend for why Nimrod wore leopard skins. The skins were the ones God made for Adam, the first King of the Earth, to cover Adam for his sins upon the Fall. The skins were passed down through Noah, Ham, Cush, to Nimrod. The leopard skins were the ensign, the emblem, of the Kingship of the world.

When we find that Osiris, the grand god of Egypt, under different forms, was thus arrayed in a leopard's skin or spotted dress, and that the leopard-skin dress was so indispensable a part of the sacred robes of his high priest, we may be sure that there was a deep meaning in such a costume. And what could that meaning be, but just to identify Osiris with the Babylonian god, who was celebrated as the "Leopard-tamer," and who was worshipped even as he was, as *Ninus* [whom the Greeks considered the queen who founded Nineveh in ancient Assyria], the CHILD in his mother's arms?[16] ...When Nimrod, as "the Leopard-tamer," began to be clothed in the leopard skin, as the trophy of his skill, his spotted dress and appearance must have impressed the imaginations of those who saw him; and he came to be called not only the "Subduer of the Spotted One" (for such is the precise meaning of Nimr – the name of the leopard), but to be called "The spotted one" himself.[17]

**Figure 9 - Cybele: The Goddess of Fortifications**

Additionally, Nimrod was also renowned for his building prowess. It is he, not Solomon, that the most adept Freemasons cite as the first "stonemason" and discoverer of primal secrets.

This was the way in which Osiris, "the son, the husband of his mother," was often exhibited, and what we learn of this god, equally as in the case of Khonso, shows that in his original he was none other than Nimrod. It is admitted that the secret system of Free Masonry was

[16] Ibid., Kindle Locations 744-747.
[17] Ibid., Kindle Locations 758-760.

originally founded on the Mysteries of the Egyptian Isis, the goddess-mother, or wife of Osiris. But what could have led to the union of a Masonic body with these Mysteries, had they not had particular reference to architecture, and had the god who was worshipped in them not been celebrated for his success *in perfecting the arts of fortification and building?* Now, if such were the case, considering the relation in which, as we have already seen, Egypt stood to Babylon, who would naturally be looked up to as their great patron of the Masonic art? The strong presumption is that Nimrod must have been the man. He was the first that gained fame in this way. As the child of the Babylonian goddess-mother, he was worshipped, as we have seen, in the character of *Ala mahozim,* "The god of fortifications" [see endnote for technical elaboration][18] Osiris, in like manner, the child of the Egyp-

---

[18] We cite below a fascinating note from BibleBelievers.org (http://www.biblebelievers.org.au/2bab040.htm). The essence of the note is that Hislop's analysis is not only correct, but it also identifies the true character the Romans worshipped as Mars to be in fact Nimrod, the first god of war, the god of forces, the god of fortifications. Is this not a fitting picture of Antichrist?

> The name *"Ala-Mahozim"* is never, as far as I know, found in any ancient uninspired author, and in the Scripture itself it is found only in a prophecy. Considering that the design of prophecy is always to leave a certain obscurity before the event, though giving enough of light for the practical guidance of the upright, it is not to be wondered at that an unusual word should be employed to describe the divinity in question. But, though this precise name be not found, we have a synonym that can be traced home to Nimrod. In SANCHUNIATHON, pp. 24, 25, *"Astarte, travelling about the habitable world,"* is said to have found *"a star falling through the air, which she took up and consecrated in the holy island Tyre."* Now what is this story of the falling star but just another version of the fall of Mulciber from heaven (see ante, p. 233), or of Nimrod from his high estate? For as we have already seen, Macrobius shows (Saturn., lib. i. cap. 21, p. 70) that the story of Adonis—the lamented one—so favourite a theme in Phoenicia, originally came from Assyria. The name of the great god in the holy island of Tyre, as is well known, was Melkart (KITTO'S Illus. Comment., vol. ii. p. 300), but this name, as brought from Tyre to Carthage, and from thence to Malta (which was colonised from Carthage), where it is found on a monument at this day, casts no little light on the subject. The name Melkart is thought by some to have been derived from Melek-eretz, or *"king of the earth"* (WILKINSON, vol. v. p. 18); but the way in which it is sculptured in Malta shows that it was really Melek-kart, *"king of the walled city."* (See WILKINSON'S Errata prefixed to vol. v.) Kir, the same as the Welsh Caer, found in Caer-narvon, etc., signifies *"an encompassing wall,"* or a *"city com-*

tian Madonna, was equally celebrated as "the strong chief of the buildings." This strong chief of the buildings was originally worshipped in Egypt with every physical characteristic of Nimrod.[19]

---

*pletely walled round;"* and Kart was the feminine form of the same word, as may be seen in the different forms of the name of Carthage, which is sometimes Car-chedon, and sometimes Cart-hada or Cart-hago. In the Book of Proverbs we find a slight variety of the feminine form of Kart, which seems evidently used in the sense of a bulwark or a fortification. Thus (Prov. x. 15) we read: *"A rich man's wealth is his strong city"* (Karit), that is, his strong bulwark or defense. Melk-kart, then, *"king of the walled city,"* conveys the very same idea as Ala-Mahozim. In GRUTER's Inscriptions, as quoted by Bryant, we find a title also given to Mars, the Roman war-god, exactly coincident in meaning with that of Melkart. We have elsewhere seen abundant reason to conclude that the original of Mars was Nimrod (p. 44. Note). The title to which I refer confirms this conclusion, and is contained in the following Roman inscription on an ancient temple in Spain:

> *"Malace Hispanie*
> *MARTI CIRADINO*
> *Templum communi voto*
> *Erectum."*

(See BRYANT, vol. ii. p. 454.) This title shows that the temple was dedicated to *"Mars Kir-aden,"* the lord of *"The Kir,"* or *"walled city."* The Roman C, as is well known, is hard, like K; and Adon, *"Lord,"* is also Aden. Now, with this clue to guide us, we can unravel at once what has hitherto greatly puzzled mythologists in regard to the name of Mars Quirinus as distinguished from Mars Gradivus. The K in Kir is what in Hebrew or Chaldee is called Koph, a different letter from Kape, and is frequently pronounced as a Q. Quir-inus, therefore, signifies *"belonging to the walled city,"* and refers to the security which was given to cities by encompassing walls. Gradivus, on the other hand, comes from *"Grah," "conflict,"* and *"divus," "god"*--a different form of Deus, which has been already shown to be a Chaldee term; and therefore signifies *"God of battle."* Both these titles exactly answer to the two characters of Nimrod as the great city builder and the great warrior, and that both these distinctive characters were set forth by the two names referred to, we have distinct evidence in FUSS's Antiquities, chap. vi. p. 348. *"The Romans,"* says he, *"worshipped two idols of the kind [that is, gods under the name of Mars], the one called Quirinus, the guardian of the city and its peace; the other called Gradivus, greedy of war and slaughter, whose temple stood beyond the city's boundaries."* 2bab040.htm

[19] Hislop, Alexander (2010-04-21). *The Two Babylons,* Kindle Edition (Kindle Locations 702-711).

Because of his indomitable capabilities, Nimrod came to be seen by the ancient world as a "god-man". Tom Horn speculates that Nimrod was more than just "larger than life." He was in fact a *Nephilim*—a demigod—a hybrid between man and angel (Genesis 6:4). It is interesting that, like angels, "the mighty ones" of which Nimrod became known as one, were depicted with wings!

> Let it only be borne in mind that "the birds"—that is, the "winged ones" – symbolized "the Lords of the mighty ones," and then the meaning is clear, viz., that men first "began to be mighty on the earth;" and then, that the "Lords" or Leaders of "these mighty ones" were deified. The knowledge of the mystic sense of this symbol accounts also for the origin of the story of Perseus, the son of Jupiter, miraculously borne of *Danae*, who did such wondrous things, and who passed from country to country on wings divinely bestowed on him... and of Icarus, the son of Daedalus, who, flying on wax-cemented wings over the Icarian Sea, had his wings melted off through his too near approach to the sun, and so gave his name to the sea where he was supposed to have fallen. The fables all referred to those who trod, or were supposed to have trodden, in the steps of Nimrod, the first "Lord of the mighty ones," *and who in that character was symbolized as equipped with wings [*emphasis ours*].*[20]

Regardless of whether Nimrod was truly a superman (a mixture of "divine" and human DNA akin to Hitler's envisioned Übermensch, based on the "over-man" as devised by Nietzsche), he was a *genuine legend in his own time* in more ways than one. And it is most intriguing that he was given "wings" in tribute.

Hislop provides extensive commentary that surpasses *stunning* in its implication. He suggests that the spires on the crown of kings refer to "mini towers" of Babylon which Nimrod founded, the towers built into the walls of Babylon, and the fortresses implied by them. Most readers know already that the walls of Babylon were so high and wide that the city was considered impregnable. As Nimrod was the founder of Babylon he was known as the "god of fortresses." If so, it provides a fascinating insight

---

[20] Ibid., Kindle Locations 650-658.

into the true meaning of Daniel 11:36-39, suggesting that the personage (the king) usually associated with the Antichrist might in fact refer to Nimrod and disclose an important trait of the future evil leader himself (that is, reinforce the significance of Babylon as the symbol of his kingdom):

**Figure 10 - Nimrod Inspects the Tower of Babel**

> 36 *And the king shall do according to his will; and he shall exalt himself, and magnify himself above every god, and shall speak marvelous things against the God of gods, and shall prosper till the indignation be accomplished: for that that is determined shall be done.* [Like Nimrod, he was be regarded as preeminent to the LORD]
>
> 37 *Neither shall he regard the God of his fathers* [suggesting he is Jewish but does not regard Jehovah as God], *nor the desire of women* [a controversial matter for interpretation], *nor regard any god: for he shall magnify himself above all* [just as Nimrod did].
>
> 38 *But in his* ***estate*** [his place of ruling, his pedestal as in a court] ***shall he honor the God of forces****: and a god whom*

*his fathers knew not* [as above] *shall he honor with gold, and silver, and with precious stones, and pleasant* things [no expense is spared on his priorities].

39 *Thus shall he do in the most strong holds* [literally, a well-fortified place] *with a strange god, whom he shall acknowledge and increase with glory: and he shall cause them* [perhaps the ten kings] *to rule over many, and shall divide the land for gain* [which we believe refers to Israel]. [Emphasis ours]

Hislop indicates that historians stumble on the "god of forces or fortifications" (to whom this god refers) while they easily identify the *goddess* of forces (Cybele, the Roman version of Semiramis). Hislop expounds this matter as follows:

In Daniel 11.38, we read of a god called *Ala Mahozine* -- i.e., the "god of fortifications." [See footnote referenced earlier.] Who this god of fortifications could be, commentators have found themselves at a loss to determine. In the records of antiquity the existence of any god of fortifications has been commonly overlooked; and it must be confessed that no such god stands forth there with any prominence to the ordinary reader. But of the existence of a goddess of fortifications, everyone knows that there is the amplest evidence. That goddess is *Cybele,* who is universally represented with a mural or turreted crown, or with a fortification, on her head. Why was Rhea or Cybele [so] represented? Ovid asks the question and answers it himself; and the answer is this: The reason he says, why the statue of Cybele wore a crown of towers was, "because she first erected them in cities." The first city in the world after the flood (from whence the commencement of the world itself was often dated) that had towers and encompassing walls, was Babylon; and *Ovid himself tells us that it was Semiramis, the first queen of that city, who was believed to have "surrounded Babylon with a wall of brick.*" Semiramis, then, the first deified queen of that city and tower whose top was intended to reach to heaven, must have been the prototype of the goddess who "first made towers in cities."[21] [Emphasis ours]

---

[21] Ibid., Kindle Locations 529-538.

Fortresses and crowns with spires (towers) seem to reinforce that the essence of this evil king (and his renowned mother), was to *trust in power, in fortifications, in military might* rather than in the god of ancient Israel. Remarkably (according to Hislop), the *spires of kingly crowns are in fact a reference to Nimrod and the Tower of Babel.* The original Nimrod may have been the first to adorn a *kingly crown meant to recall the spires or towers of Babylon.* The final Nimrod is destined to rule with ten kings. His crowning achievement (no pun intended) will be immense fortifications. The first Nimrod and his mother built the initial Walls of Babylon (that by the time of Nebuchadnezzar) would grow to over a hundred feet tall and be so wide that four chariots could ride abreast about the circuit surrounding the city. The final Nimrod will spare no expense in building the most extravagant military power the world has ever seen. If the future Nimrod is, as we assert, an American leader soon to reveal himself, *this prophecy stands ready to be immediately fulfilled.*

Another conservative biblical authority, perhaps the most famous of all dispensational scholars, C.I. Scofield comments:

> Summary: In the sense of the present world-system, the ethically bad sense of the word *[Kosmos]* refers to the "order," "arrangement," under which Satan has organized the world of unbelieving mankind upon his cosmic principle of force, greed, selfishness, ambition, and pleasure... *This world-system is imposing and powerful with armies and fleets;* is often outwardly religious, scientific, cultured, and elegant; but, seething with national and commercial rivalries and ambitions, is upheld in any real crisis *only by armed force,* and is dominated by Satanic principles.[22] [Emphasis added]

But why is this "god of fortifications" (if we have interpreted the essence of Daniel's passage correctly) so foreign to the God of the Hebrews? Because military might was not the "god" in which ancient Israel believed. Instead, Israel trusted in Jehovah to deliver them from their enemies. They were taught that a human

---

[22] *Scofield Bible,* Commentary on Revelation 13:8.

military institution could ensnare just as much as protect. When it came time to defeat Sennacherib's army of 185,000 men, the angel of God acted alone in the dark of night. As the passage sardonically states, *"When they arose early in morning, they were all dead bodies"* (2 Kings 19:35). Sennacherib's miserable defeat resulted, in part, from mocking King Hezekiah who trusted in the Lord alone; God would deliver Jerusalem from yet "another Assyrian." Hezekiah's amazing faith in the Lord was thoroughly vindicated.

For those keeping score, the final tally was this: Yahweh: 185,000. Sennacherib: 0.

Merely from reading the English translation, many commentators suggest that the "god of forces" (of Daniel 11:38) is a reference to a pantheistic belief espoused by the Antichrist. Thus, this god consists not of a transcendent being but rather a life-force like "the Force" in Star Wars who exists "immanent" in the creation. Nevertheless, the alternative concept proposed here (based upon Hislop's study) not only provides a more intriguing interpretation, it likely conveys a historically correct meaning.

The application for America today: Do the people of God trust in toting guns for self-protection and an invincible military to ensure our place in the world? Or do the people of God trust in the Lord for our safe-keeping? This is not to say that Americans shouldn't have the right to bear arms. Nor should we intentionally disparage America for having a strong military. But it reminds us who our real protector is – *The Lord of Heaven,* not the god of fortifications – lest we honor *Nimrod.* **The real meaning of "a Nimrod" is a world leader who trusts in strong defenses, military might, and powerful weapons.** This is the most essential truth behind the King of Babylon – *the archetype of Antichrist.*

## Historical Babylon and the Islamic Scenario

While a literal translation is generally preferred by orthodox interpreters of the Bible, in some cases a "literalist translation" may not disclose the true meaning behind the words of Scripture.

This may be especially so when we consider the meaning of Babylon of the Book of Revelation. In fact, when we come to the significance of MYSTERY BABYLON we are inclined to challenge a literalist interpretation for a variety of reasons, some exegetical, some practical.

For if we take the name *Babylon* to mean literally the historical city in Iraq, we must conclude the ancient city of Babylon will be physically restored. Since Antichrist comes on the scene in dramatic fanfare and reigns for a very short time (perhaps no more than three and one-half years), it appears that the rebuilding of Babylon would need to be well underway before Antichrist is revealed. It almost goes without saying: should Babylon be the subject of a massive rebuilding project, it will be no surprise if a leader surfaces soon thereafter to take the helm. Reckoning him Antichrist would almost be anti-climactic.

Dave Hunt dispensed with the notion that a literal Babylon was meant by the writer of Revelation with this concise assertion:

> Saddam [Hussein] has proudly imprinted his name on every brick being used in the reconstruction of ancient Babylon. As much hated as feared by his own people, one day Saddam will be deposed, as eventually happens to all tyrants [Hunt was proven correct in this prediction published in 1994!] It would not be surprising if the Iraqis, in order to erase the last vestige of Saddam's loathsome memory, thereafter bulldozed the proud structures he has erected at the site of ancient Babylon. Whether that happens or not, there is no way that this city, rebuilt after lying in ruins for more than 2000 years, could be mistaken for the Babylon which is the major subject of Revelation chapters 17 and 18.[23]

**Figure 11 - Babylon in 2005, a cultural center funded by the U.N. to engender Iraqi Pride (a 180-degree composite photo)**

[23] Hunt, op. cit., Kindle Locations 463-467.

Nonetheless, as we have pointed out previously, there is no shortage of prophecy scholars who proclaim such a literalist view. Mark Hitchcock, Joel Rosenberg, and John Price contend that Babylon, about 55 miles from Baghdad, will grow to magnificent proportions becoming the seat of power for Antichrist. Obviously, this anticipation of a Babylon building project provides support for their position that Antichrist is a Muslim and the final deception (the "Great Lie") the whole world accepts is *Islam.*

Another outspoken author (possibly a pseudonym for a Muslim not wishing to be exposed) is Joel Richardson, a favorite of Glenn Beck and writer for Joseph Farah's World Net Daily. Richardson is outspoken in his rancor toward Islam and his conviction that the Mahdi and the Antichrist are one and the same.[24]

And yet, there are a number of colossal problems asserting that Antichrist will be Muslim. Indeed, this proposition almost turns the traditional scenario of prophetic interpretation upside down. Moreover, *there are both practical and biblical factors that argue strongly against this view.*

First, the practical considerations: if we believe we live *in the very last of the last days* (which most students of Bible prophecy do), the questions of time and money becomes an important consideration. How could a global power muster the political resolve and put their money where they mouth is, a herculean effort costing countless dollars (or Euros!) necessary to transform Babylon (which is barely a tourist attraction at this moment in 2013) into a highly functional city to rival the other great cities of the world? A literalist interpretation insists upon this eventuality. And yet, the realities of such a building project boggle the mind. How long

---

[24] **"Richardson Posits That Muslim Mahdi Will Be The Antichrist."** In his book *The Islamic Antichrist* [WND Books, 2009], Richardson "makes the case that the biblical Antichrist is one and the same as the Quran's Muslim Mahdi." [*WorldNetDaily,* 8/3/09]. He also claims that Islam is "the primary vehicle that will be used by Satan to fulfill the prophecies of the Bible about the future political/religious/military system of the Antichrist." From *The Islamic Antichrist.* See http://mediamatters.org/research/2011 /02/17/who-is-joel-richardson-becks-end-times-prophet/176590.

would it take to assemble a consensus to accomplish this objective? How would the monies be amassed to make it happen? How long would the project take? Would any political regime last long enough to realize this goal? How could it be justified?

Secondly, the Bible plainly argues strongly against this scenario. Several authors, most notably Bill Salus in his book *Israelistine* (2008) and most recently, in his book entitled *Psalm 83* (2013), provide a compelling argument that the Arab nations immediately surrounding Israel will be destroyed in a devastating war. Their demise (or at least the striking down of their military force) happens when they conspire to destroy the Jews "to wipe out the name of Israel." The destruction of Damascus (prophesied in Isaiah 17) appears linked to this sequence of events. Israel emerges from this confrontation with a dominating presence, so much so that it no longer senses itself threatened by its neighbors.

Citing Psalm 83 (inspired by Salus' popular work), we offer a probable identification of the various tribes and tribal leaders identified there (our interpretation of the various tribes is based upon our research, not necessarily always reflecting Salus' considered opinion):

> [1] *Keep not thou silence, O God: hold not thy peace, and be not still, O God.*
>
> [2] *For, lo,* ***thine enemies make a tumult****: and they* ***that hate thee*** *have lifted up the head.*
>
> [3] *They have taken crafty counsel against thy people, and consulted against thy hidden ones.*
>
> [4] *They have said,* ***Come, and let us cut them off from being a nation; that the name of Israel may be no more in remembrance.***
>
> [5] ***For they have consulted together with one consent: they are confederate against thee:***
>
> [6] *The tabernacles of Edom* [ancient Assyria, principally Syria and Iraq today], *and the* Ishmaelites [generally considered the forebear of Arabs]; *of Moab* [Jordon], *and the Hagarenes* [probably Egypt, but certainly Syria];

7 *Gebal, and Ammon, and Amalek* [peoples in northern Israel and Lebanon]; *the Philistines [Gaza] with the inhabitants of Tyre* [Lebanon];

8 *Assur* [Iraq] *also is joined with them: they have holpen* [helped] *the children of Lot. Selah.*

9 *Do unto them as unto the Midianites* [south and east of Israel]; *as to Sisera, as to Jabin* [south of Israel, perhaps the Sinai], *at the brook of Kison* [northern Israel, near Haifa]:

10 *Which perished at Endor* [associated with the Philistines]: *they became as dung for the earth.*

11 *Make their nobles like Oreb, and like Zeeb: yea, all their princes as Zebah, and as Zalmunna:* [all of whom were Midianite generals slain by Gideon east of the Jordan River aka the East Bank]

12 *Who said, Let us take to ourselves the houses of God in possession.*

13 *O my God, make them like a wheel; as the stubble before the wind.*

14 *As the fire burneth a wood, and as the flame setteth the mountains on fire;*

15 *So persecute them with thy tempest, and make them afraid with thy storm.*

16 *Fill their faces with shame; that they may seek thy name, O LORD.*

17 *Let them be confounded and troubled forever; yea, let them be put to shame, and perish:*

18 ***That men may know that thou, whose name alone is JEHOVAH, art the most high over all the earth.*** (Psalm 83:1-18, emphasis added)

The Psalmist takes pains to list the ancient adjacent enemies of Israel who geographically encircle the land. He points out they are destined to act with one accord, as a confederation, to destroy *the name of Israel* (not Judah and not Palestine) once and for all! The Psalmist reckons them *enemies of Jehovah* and concludes by this expression that all these men should realize the true God is named *Jehovah* (by implication not *Allah*); and He is Lord over ALL the earth (including the nations now dominated by Islam), not just the Lord of Israel. The assumption is this Psalm does not reflect any previous war or uprising such as the 1967 (Six-day) war, the 1973 Yom Kippur War, or the Intifadas (of which there have been many over the past twenty-plus years).

It appears that a future, massive, but singular war as depicted in Psalm 83 sets the stage for a subsequent infamous war – a battle seen by Orthodox Jews to immediately precede the coming of Messiah – and evangelical prophecy scholars as setting the stage for the emergence and revealing of Antichrist.

Virtually all researchers believe that the so-called Gog and Magog War described in the book of Ezekiel (from which it derives its name) also involves key nations who espouse Islam; notably, Libya (i.e., ancient North Africa according to Herodotus), Ethiopia (i.e., today's Northern Sudan), Iran, and probably Turkey. As Salus points out, it isn't likely that the nations identified in Psalm 83 are merely overlooked in the war depicted in Ezekiel. Their absence in Ezekiel's account implicitly demonstrates their elimination by the conflagration predicted by the Psalmist. If correct, whenever the war of Ezekiel transpires, logically the war of Psalm 83 must have already happened first. The destruction of the armies from the surrounding nations establishes Israel as a nation of "unwalled villages" – a people dwelling securely. Ezekiel chapters 38 and 39 explicitly describe this state of affairs.

Unlike the war described in Psalm 83, students of prophecy know the Ezekiel passage well and its predicted future war. For readers not so familiar, allow me to quote the passage at length.

From Ezekiel chapter 38, beginning with verse 2:

> 2 *Son of man, set thy face against Gog, the land of Magog, the chief prince of Meshech and Tubal, and prophesy against him,*
>
> 3 *And say, Thus saith the Lord GOD; Behold, I am against thee, O Gog, the chief prince of Meshech and Tubal:*
>
> 4 *And I will turn thee back, and put hooks into thy jaws, and I will bring thee forth, and all thine army, horses and horsemen, all of them clothed with all sorts of armour, even a great company with bucklers and shields, all of them handling swords:*

5 ***Persia, Ethiopia, and Libya*** *with them; all of them with shield and helmet:*

6 ***Gomer, and all his bands; the house of Togarmah*** *of the north quarters* [most scholars suggest this is a reference to Turkish peoples while some continue to insist it includes peoples within Russia], *and all his bands: and many people with thee.*

7 *Be thou prepared, and prepare for thyself, thou, and all thy company that are assembled unto thee, and be thou a guard unto them.*

8 *After many days thou shalt be visited: in the latter years thou shalt come into the land that is brought back from the sword, and is gathered out of many people, against the mountains of Israel, which have been always waste: but it is brought forth out of the nations, and they shall dwell safely all of them.*

9 *Thou shalt ascend and come like a storm, thou shalt be like a cloud to cover the land, thou, and all thy bands, and many people with thee.*

10 *Thus saith the Lord GOD; It shall also come to pass, that at the same time shall things come into thy mind, and thou shalt think an evil thought:*

11 *And thou shalt say, I will go up to the land* ***of unwalled villages;*** *I will go to them that are at rest, that dwell safely, all of them dwelling without walls, and having neither bars nor gates,*

12 ***To take a spoil, and to take a prey*** [a different motive than the war of Psalm 83 which is to destroy the name Israel once and for all]; *to turn thine hand upon the desolate places that are now inhabited, and upon the people that are gathered out of the nations, which have gotten cattle and goods, that dwell in the midst of the land* [which happened throughout the twentieth century but especially since 1948 when Israel officially became a nation].

13 *Sheba, and Dedan* [a reference to Arabia], *and the merchants of Tarshish* [Tarshish, a city on the coast of Spain, hence a likely reference to Europe and probably America; we study this in depth later in this book], *with all the young lions thereof, shall say unto thee, Art thou come to take a spoil? hast thou gathered thy company to take a prey? to carry away silver and gold, to take away cattle and goods, to take a great spoil?*

> 14 *Therefore, son of man, prophesy and say unto Gog, Thus saith the Lord GOD; In that day when my people of Israel dwelleth safely, shalt thou not know it?*
>
> 15 *And thou shalt come from thy place out of the north parts, thou, and many people with thee, all of them riding upon horses, a great company, and a mighty army:*
>
> 16 *And* ***thou shalt come up against my people of Israel****, as a cloud to cover the land; it shall be in the latter days, and I will bring thee against my land, that the heathen may know me, when I shall be sanctified in thee, O Gog, before their eyes.*
>
> 17 *Thus saith the Lord GOD; Art thou he of whom I have spoken in old time by my servants the prophets of Israel, which prophesied in those days many years that I would bring thee against them?*
>
> 18 *And it shall come to pass at the same time when Gog shall come against the land of Israel, saith the Lord GOD, that my fury shall come up in my face.*
>
> 19 *For in my jealousy and in the fire of my wrath have I spoken, Surely in that day there shall be a great shaking in the land of Israel;*
>
> 20 *So that the fishes of the sea, and the fowls of the heaven, and the beasts of the field, and all creeping things that creep upon the earth, and all the men that are upon the face of the earth, shall shake at my presence, and the mountains shall be thrown down, and the steep places shall fall, and every wall shall fall to the ground.*
>
> 21 *And* ***I will call for a sword against him throughout all my mountains,*** *saith the Lord GOD: every man's sword shall be against his brother.*
>
> 22 *And I will plead against him with* ***pestilence and with blood; and I will rain upon him, and upon his bands, and upon the many people that are with him, an overflowing rain, and great hailstones, fire, and brimstone.***
>
> 23 *Thus will I magnify myself, and sanctify myself; and I will be known in the eyes of many nations, and they shall know that I am the LORD* [emphasis added].

And, continuing with the passage in Ezekiel 39:

> [1] *Therefore, thou son of man, prophesy against Gog, and say, Thus saith the Lord GOD; Behold, I am against thee, O Gog, the chief prince of Meshech and Tubal:*
>
> [2] *And I will turn thee back, and leave but the sixth part of thee* [five-sixths are destroyed], and *will cause thee to come up from the north parts, and will bring thee upon the mountains of Israel:*
>
> [3] *And I will smite thy bow out of thy left hand, and will cause thine arrows to fall out of thy right hand.*
>
> [4] ***Thou shalt fall upon the mountains of Israel****, thou, and all thy bands, and the people that is with thee: I will give thee unto the ravenous birds of every sort, and to the beasts of the field to be devoured.*
>
> [5] *Thou shalt fall upon the open field: for I have spoken it, saith the Lord GOD.*
>
> [6] *And I will send a fire on Magog, and among them that dwell carelessly in the isles* [the scope of God's judgment extends beyond Israel]: *and they shall know that I am the LORD.*
>
> [7] *So will I make my holy name known in the midst of my people Israel; and I will not let them pollute my holy name any more* [this action is a total "game-changer"]: *and the heathen shall know that I am the LORD, the Holy One in Israel* [emphasis ours].

The prophet testifies that the LORD will make an example of these armies, demonstrated by destroying five-sixths of the listed armies (39:2); He alone is the LORD, the Holy One in Israel.

A scholarly consensus over the past four decades asserts this war happens (1) before Daniel's seventieth week (most often equated with the Great Tribulation of the last days), or (2) early in this seven-year long period, but (3) not later than half-way through Daniel's seventieth week (or 3.5 years). By the end of the Gog-Magog war, Islam – for all intents and purposes – will exist only in select outposts around the world (one thinks of Indonesia), but *no longer in the Middle East.* Furthermore, many writer-researchers believe Antichrist reveals himself on the heels of this particular war. Consequently, it is probable Antichrist *has a major role to play in defeating the Islamic armies.*

Therefore, to say the least, it would seem illogical and especially unbiblical to contend Antichrist is a Muslim. *Defeating Islam* appears to be how the Antichrist asserts his power and authority around the world. *Far from being Muslim, Antichrist becomes a dominating world leader by eliminating Islam as a viable political and religious force to be reckoned with.* At this juncture, it would be apropos to recall the words of Jesus: *"And if a house be divided against itself, that house cannot stand"* (Mark 3:25).

To sum up: we believe that "denial is more than just a river in Egypt" – but we do not believe that Antichrist will be Muslim. And by the same token, THE FINAL BABYLON will not be a magnificently restored city in modern Iraq which becomes the future base of operations for the Antichrist.

## A Not So Literal Interpretation of Babylon

On the other hand, once we accept that *Babylon* is a metaphor for a politico-religious system opposed to God, we summarily dismiss the idea of a rebuilt Babylon in Iraq. Subsequently, if the physical Babylon is rejected, then the identity of Babylon must be deciphered by considering various symbols in the immediate context of Revelations' 22 chapters and by reference to prophecies in the Old Testament – passages that John the Revelator assumes the reader will understand (no doubt John perceives his audience to be believing Jews and highly dedicated gentile Christians during the first century). However, in reading his writing 1900 years after the fact, his extensive use of biblical metaphors and images (familiar to his first-century audience), increases our difficulty in deciphering – we do not find it easy to identify *prima facie* evidence disclosing the identity of Babylon.

To establish its identity, one of our first assignments is to distinguish the attributes of Babylon in Revelation 17 with those of Babylon in Revelation chapter 18. The Babylon of Revelation 17 presents an entity, a "whore" (itself an obvious metaphor) who is predominantly a spiritual institution or more precisely a spiritual system of beliefs that stands opposed to the God of the Bible, His Kingdom, and His plan to reshape and restore the world.

In Chapter 17 of Revelation, we read details surrounding Babylon's spiritual apostasy (our commentary is in [brackets]):

> 1 *And there came one of the seven angels which had the seven vials, and talked with me, saying unto me, Come hither; I will shew unto thee the judgment of the great whore that sitteth upon many waters* [which is defined below as many nations and peoples]:
>
> 2 *With whom the kings of the earth have committed fornication* [a phrase used throughout the Bible representing earthly powers opposed to Jehovah], *and the inhabitants of the earth have been made drunk with the wine of her fornication* [the people of earth are insensitive to the nature of Babylon].
>
> 3 *So he carried me away in the spirit* [a state that suggests it wasn't a physical transport] *into the wilderness: and I saw a woman sit upon a scarlet coloured beast, full of names of blasphemy, having seven heads and ten horns* [defined in Daniel and Revelation as co-regents with the "Beast system" of prior history and in this future time].
>
> 4 *And the woman was arrayed in purple and scarlet colour, and decked with gold and precious stones and pearls, having a golden cup in her hand* [referencing Jeremiah 51:7][25] *full of abominations and filthiness of her fornication:*
>
> 5 *And upon her forehead was a name written, MYSTERY, BABYLON THE GREAT, THE MOTHER OF HARLOTS AND ABOMINATIONS OF THE EARTH.*
>
> ***6 And I saw the woman drunken with the blood of the saints, and with the blood of the martyrs of Jesus*** [this appears to identify Babylon as a religious entity with associations with the true church of Jesus Christ]: *and when I saw her, I wondered with great admiration.*
>
> 7 *And the angel said unto me, Wherefore didst thou marvel? I will tell thee the mystery of the woman, and of the beast that carrieth her, which hath the seven heads and ten horns.*

---

[25] Jeremiah 51:7, *"Babylon hath been a golden cup in the LORD'S hand, that made all the earth drunken: the nations have drunken of her wine; therefore the nations are mad."*

8 *The beast that thou sawest was, and is not; and shall ascend out of the bottomless pit* [Abaddon/Apollyon—Rev 9:11), *and go into perdition: and they that dwell on the earth shall wonder, whose names were not written in the book of life from the foundation of the world, when they behold the beast that was, and is not, and yet is.*

9 *And here is the mind which hath wisdom. The seven heads are seven mountains, on which the woman sitteth* [while this identifies Rome, many other cities including Jerusalem claim to be built on seven hills].

10 *And there are seven kings: five are fallen, and one is, and the other is not yet come; and when he cometh, he must continue a short space* [a hotly contested list of former empires, concluding with Rome or the offspring of Rome, just as Jeremiah calls it a "daughter" of Babylon].

11 *And the beast that was, and is not, even he is the eighth, and is of the seven, and goeth into perdition* [the beast while the leader of an eighth empire is an empire that is of the same ilk as the seventh—with identical characteristics].

12 *And the ten horns which thou sawest are ten kings, which have received no kingdom as yet; but receive power as kings one hour with the beast* [a very short time in biblical terms, perhaps related to 3.5 years or the full term of Daniel's seventieth week—seven years].

13 *These have one mind, and shall give their power and strength unto the beast.*

14 *These shall make war with the Lamb, and the Lamb shall overcome them: for he is Lord of lords, and King of kings: and they that are with him are called, and chosen, and faithful.*

15 *And he saith unto me, The waters which thou sawest, where the whore sitteth, are peoples, and multitudes, and nations, and tongues* [suggesting that the waters are either (1) not real waters at all but a metaphor of an international collection of peoples or (2) a place, perhaps on the waters, that is recognized as an international seat of power – one thinks of the United Nations and New York].

16 *And the ten horns which thou sawest upon the beast, these shall hate the whore, and shall make her desolate and naked, and shall eat her flesh, and burn her with fire* [while the whore is carried by the beast, eventually the beast bucks her off

and the kings and beast destroy her. Woe unto the woman who thought she could ride the beast!]

[17] *For God hath put in their hearts to fulfill his will, and to agree, and give their kingdom unto the beast, until the words of God shall be fulfilled.*

[18] *And* ***the woman which thou sawest is that great city, which reigneth over the kings of the earth*** [and that "city" may be a metropolis or it may hearken to Nimrod, to his mother the queen of fortifications, and to the totalitarian world system that the mother and child represent in ages past and in a time yet to come].

Throughout this passage, there is interplay between the political power structure (the Beast and his ten kings) and the spiritual system (worldwide in scope) sitting on "many waters" equated with peoples, multitudes, nations, and tongues. The Beast was, and is not, but will be again (verse 11). Likewise, there are seven kings, five of which have already come and gone, one king which dominates at the time that the Book of Revelation was written, and another which will come. John declares the eighth synonymous with the seventh being *distinguished and identified as the Beast* since he goes into perdition (thrown into the lake of fire with the False Prophet, Revelation 19:20). This Beast will "carry" the whore but eventually betrays her, eating her flesh. The ten horns are ten kings (verse 12) distinguished as a separate list from the seven kings that most scholars equate with empires – five of which have already come and gone before the time of John the Revelator.[26]

However, before we assume the harlot to be a reference exclusively to the Roman Catholic Church, we best recall that Israel

[26] Most scholars identify these empires as Egypt, Assyria, Babylon, Media-Persia, Greece, five which are past; and Rome "which is" at the time of Revelation's writing, (the sixth) and the future kingdom (the seventh) with the beast the eighth, but he is really of the seven. Scholars dispute the exact empires. But the most important point is that all of these empires represent kingdoms opposed to the Kingdom of God and of His Christ. This is most especially true of the final empire, headed by the Beast, *which unites religious harlotry with political hegemony.*

was also graphically described as a spiritual harlot by several of its prophets. The characterization of such apostasy (depicted as harlotry) reaches its zenith in the Book of Hosea.

In Chapter 4 of Hosea, we read the words of this prophet who was directed by the Lord to take a prostitute for a wife, to demonstrate both the jealously of the Lord and His mercy to His unfaithful bride:

> 11 *Whoredom and wine and new wine take away the heart.*
>
> 12 *My people ask counsel at their stocks, and their staff declareth unto them: for the spirit of whoredoms hath caused them to err, and they have gone a whoring from under their God.*
>
> 13 *They sacrifice upon the tops of the mountains, and burn incense upon the hills, under oaks and poplars and elms, because the shadow thereof is good: therefore your daughters shall commit whoredom, and your spouses shall commit adultery.*
>
> 14 *I will not punish your daughters when they commit whoredom, nor your spouses when they commit adultery: for themselves are separated with whores, and they sacrifice with harlots: therefore the people that doth not understand shall fall.*
>
> 15 *Though thou, Israel, play the harlot, yet let not Judah offend; and come not ye unto Gilgal, neither go ye up to Bethaven, nor swear, The LORD liveth.*
>
> 16 *For Israel slideth back as a backsliding heifer:*

The frequent image of God betrothing Israel as a bride, and in the New Testament of the bride betrothed to Christ, *spotless* (the goal explicitly stated by the Apostle Paul) is familiar to most orthodox Jews and Christians. Note that Revelation 17:6 emphasizes how the whore is made drunk with the blood of the saints and the martyrs of Jesus (perhaps a reference to both Old and New Testaments believers?) This suggests both Judaism and Christianity, so-called, have played the harlot. Both religions calling Jehovah *God* have often combined religious sentiments with political ambitions; and by so doing, they have each at distinct times and in myriad ways *symbolically become* Babylon.

As alluded to above, the seven mountains upon which the empire of the Beast sits are usually identified as Rome, a city on seven hills. But others have suggested Jerusalem too is a city set on seven hills. *In fact, not only Jerusalem, but Mecca, Moscow, and almost* ***seventy other cities of the world*** *romantically claim to be a city set on seven hills.*[27] And since it is called the city where the Lord was crucified (an identifier not easily confused), Jerusalem symbolically comprises *Sodom and Egypt*, cities symbolically portrayed by John as enemies of the Kingdom of God. Thus, both Rome and Jerusalem are clearly identified as spiritual "Babylon" and as the correct interpretation of Babylon in Revelation 17. There is biblical precedent, indeed, precedent within the Book of Revelation itself, to understand Babylon NOT to be the literal Babylon in Iraq. Likewise, if being a city on seven hills is meant to identify Rome as the "literal" Babylon (which by definition, it isn't), that "plain" identity is challenged by the fact so many cities (seventy in all) claim to be cities set on seven hills. Perhaps it is more logical as well as biblical; to realize a city set on seven hills refers to the *metropolis* as a symbol of human habitation in rebellion against God.

Consequently, we feel justified in arguing Babylon to be any human institution that sets itself up against the God of the Bible, but especially those uniting spiritual with political authority, *to create a dominant totalitarian regime*, be it Jewish or Gentile.

Please realize: When it comes to judging apostasy, God is no respecter of persons or peoples. He is a jealous God who demands loyalty and fidelity. On the other hand, He showers endless blessings on those that are the object of His love.

## Conclusion – The Economic and Political Babylon

In contrast, the Babylon of Revelation chapter 18 is described as an economic colossus. Dominating global finance, it stands as the center of world commerce until it collapses from God's inescapable judgment. With the obliteration of Babylon, all the mer-

---

[27] See http://en.wikipedia.org/wiki/List_of_cities_claimed_to_be_built_on_seven_hills.

chants of the world weep and mourn. In a single hour its total devastation wipes out the wealth of the world's richest brokers and dealers. Discovering its identity, unlike its spiritual counterpart, does not require a doctorate in biblical exegesis and a second degree in ancient history. *One only has to take into account who is the "king of the hill" at this present moment in world affairs.*

And yet, to thoroughly consider the implications of the unexpected culprit and to compellingly prove its guilt requires no less from us than a carefully argued book to solidify the case. So it is we set about the task of writing one.

**Figure 12 - Wall Street**

From Revelation 18, we highlight the most essential verses as prologue:

> 10 *Standing afar off for the fear of her torment, saying, Alas, alas that great city Babylon, that mighty city! For in one hour is thy judgment come.*
>
> 11 *And the merchants of the earth shall weep and mourn over her; for no man buyeth their merchandise any more...* [clearly this Babylon is a commercial center of world commerce]
>
> 16 *And saying, Alas, alas that great city, that was clothed in fine linen, and purple, and scarlet, and decked with gold, and*

*precious stones, and pearls!* [The greatest wealth is contained therein!]

[17] *For in one hour so great riches is come to nought* [nothing]. *And every shipmaster, and all the company in ships, and sailors, and as many as trade by sea, stood afar off,*

[18] *And cried when they saw the smoke of her burning, saying, "What city is like unto this great city!"* [The image conveys this Babylon is a great seaport, unlike the land-locked Babylon of Iraq]

[19] *And they cast dust on their heads, and cried, weeping and wailing, saying, Alas, alas that great city, wherein were made rich all that had ships in the sea by reason of her costliness! For in one hour is she made desolate* [a sudden destruction that is echoed in chapters Jeremiah 50, 51 to be discussed later].

[20] *Rejoice over her, thou heaven, and ye holy apostles and prophets; for God hath avenged you on her* [not only is Babylon a spiritual whore, but a political harlot as well that has also been the source of persecution, intimidation, imprisonment, and murder of the righteous in many forms].

[21] *And a mighty angel took up a stone like a great millstone, and cast it into the sea, saying, Thus with violence shall that great city Babylon be thrown down, and shall be found no more at all* [a total destruction that suggests an annihilation of "biblical proportions!"]

[24] *And in her was found the blood of prophets, and of saints, and of all that were slain upon the earth* [whether Jewish, Christian, or of no religious commitment whatsoever, this Babylon is guilty of the killing of untold millions] *(Rev. 10, 11, 16-21, 24).*

Of whom is the author of Revelation speaking? While the Babylon of Revelation 17 is regarded as a spiritual harlot, Babylon the Great, this city of Great Power comprises the world's singular financial leviathan. In today's world, there is only one such city which qualifies, and only one such country comprising an unequaled amassing of wealth, economic control, and political hegemony. If this final Babylon of the last days consists of the combined forces of spirit and mammon, of religion and political power, its identification requires only a minute amount of analytical skill. Indeed, it is only the United States of America that musters the money and the might to be THE FINAL BABYLON of Revelation 18 (and as we shall study later) the *Daughter of Babylon* prophesied in Jeremiah 50-51, Isaiah 13, 47, and Zechariah 2.

As Pogo said, "We have met the enemy and he is us."[28]

---

28 See http://www.igopogo.com/final_authority.htm. Some doubt that Pogo said this!

*Chapter 3:*

# Why a New Look at Babylon is NOT So New

## America as Babylon Not A New Insight

OVER THE PAST FEW DECADES, SOME PROTESTANTS HAVE DARED SUPPOSE AMERICA TO BE THE "SEAT OF ANTICHRIST" – PERHAPS EVEN SPECULATING THAT ANTICHRIST MASQUERADES AS the then-current President of the United States. This stance, wedded with enough partisan vitriol to invigorate it from time to time, has occasionally replaced the much older judgment championed by Bible-believing Christians that the Catholic Church was *Mystery Babylon* and the Pope its Antichrist. Such intolerance with Rome has been easily justified because its religious rituals closely resemble those of ancient Babylon (see the earlier recap of Alexander Hislop's classic, *The Two Babylons* for details.). Indeed, the vitality of these charges has been customary since the time of Luther and Calvin, whether laid at the feet of the Roman "religious system" or the institution itself. As noted earlier, this notion represents the Protestant interpretive school we know as "historicism."[1]

However, despite how startled many readers may be at first blush, the idea "America is the Babylon of the last days" really isn't that new.

Here are a few examples:

- It was propounded in 1859 by Frances Rolleston in *Notes on the Apocalypse, as Explained by the Hebrew Scriptures: The Place in Prophecy of America and Australia Being Pointed Out.*[2]

---

[1] "All Historicists believe that the Papacy is that Anti-Christ, the Man of Sin of II Thessalonians 2, and a Beast of Revelation 13" (http://www. historicism.net/).
[2] Rolleston's book was recently republished in 2011. See http://www.amazon. com /Notes-Apocalypse-Explained-Hebrew-Scriptures/dp/1173735348

- Seventh-day Adventist Church expositor Uriah Smith in 1884 authored a text entitled *The United States in the Light of Prophecy; or, An Exposition of Rev. 13:11-17.*[3] Smith was insistent that America was the Second Beast of Revelation 13:11-17.
- More recently, 1998, R. A. Coombes, in *America, the Babylon: America's Destiny Foretold in Biblical Prophecy* presented thirty-three identifying markers which he claimed identified America as the Babylon of the End Times, the seat of Antichrist. He tallies sixty-six reasons why New York City is the bastion symbolically identified as Babylon the Great.

So perhaps it's acceptable for an immigrant pastor like the late S. Franklin Logsdon (*to wit a Canadian*), to express a contrary view of America in the 1960s:

> It is unthinkable that God who knows the end from the beginning would pinpoint such small nations as Libya, Egypt, Ethiopia and Syria in the prophetic declaration and completely overlook the wealthiest and most powerful nation on the earth. Too long have we evaded the question. Too long have we summarily grouped our country with the so-called revived Roman Empire. Too long have we persisted in terming the U. S. A. in prophecy as one of the 'lion's cubs,' thus giving her but an inferential mention in the shadow of a diminishing Britain. [4]

We might dismiss an Alex Jones or a Jesse Ventura who frets over the establishment of FEMA camps and incites angst amongst their respective viewers (perhaps) for provocation purposes. But how can we remain calm when we hear the view expressed by Noah Hutchings or the late J.R. Church that Logsdon was onto something.[5] Are these patriotic Americans disparaging the "red, white and blue?" Viewing the USA with suspicion as we

---

[3] See http://www.conservapedia.com/Antichrist.

[4] S. Franklin Logsdon – Sr. Pastor Moody Memorial Church, Chicago – c. 1967

[5] Noah Hutchings republished Logsdon's book and wrote a Part II to support his thesis in *The U.S. in Bible Prophecy* (2000). J.R. Church in *Guardians of the Grail* also cited Logsdon extensively in his book and posed the possibility that America could fulfill the role of the final Babylon.

do is sure to annoy the patriotic spirit of more than a few conservative readers.

A "Babylonian-like American empire" today hardly resembles the Papal influence lingering in Europe which was finally dealt a death-blow by French revolutionaries 220 years ago. Likewise, it is a far cry from the so-called *Pax Britannia* – not to mention light years beyond the state of affairs after "The Great War" marked by Woodrow Wilson's designs to "make the world safe for democracy." To be sure, Adolf Hitler lost no time demonstrating how hazardous the world remained after Wilson's League of Nations was formed. Concluding a "total victory" over the Axis enemies, nevertheless, America continued on in mortal conflict (and sometimes *combat* through various surrogates) conducting the so-called "Cold-war." But massive spending to fund an arms race with which its enemies could not keep pace, America won the contest and in the process built the most overwhelming military force and lop-sided advantage the world has ever known. Indeed, within a few decades, America's geopolitical antagonists cowered at the new leviathan. No sooner had Reagan's words been spoken, "Mr. Gorbachev: tear down this wall!" America found itself alone as the world's only remaining super power. Instead of realizing Khrushchev's threat to America ("We will bury you"), the Russian bear was tranquilized into a protracted hibernation from which it is only now shaking off the cobwebs.

## Does Nationalism Cause Blindness?

Failure to apprehend the meaning of Daniel's colossus as built upon the banks of the Tigris; and unaware or unwilling to recognize that Western Civilization marches inexorably toward "Gentile" global hegemony – politically, militarily, commercially, and even culturally – we who are proponents of Bible prophecy often mire ourselves in extraneous eschatological debates. Our most popular end-times scenarios mute the amplitude of our prophetic voice because of our unwillingness to discern the real source of political, financial, and spiritual despotism today. In our exuberance to proclaim our patriotism as well as our traditional evangelical perspective on "the last days," we relegate ourselves to the periphery in the war for the soul of civilization – and tragically – at the most critical moment in the battle.

Some spokespersons for prophetic topics unwittingly diminish Biblical relevance and infuse believers within the Western world with false hopes – that America's absence from prophetic writ suggests either an implosion by some manner of cataclysm (be it natural or man-made); or an ineffectual witness from the unintended consequences of the secret pre-tribulational rapture. Could it be that our eschatology itself is to blame for the church in America becoming the lukewarm Laodicean Church of Revelation, Chapter 3? In the anticipation of joining the resurrected and the raptured, are believers today ill-prepared to give a vibrant witness on behalf of the Testimony of Jesus? Has the belief in the "blessed hope of the Church" dampened the energizing Spirit of Prophecy – a Spirit which would have us as Christ's Bride, testify against the seat of Antichrist, aka Babylon the Great? Some critics of the Pre-tribulational rapture position often pose this criticism.

Moody Memorial's Sr. Pastor, Logsdon, countered and critiqued American evangelicals who asserted that "the USA is given only *inferential mention* in the context of the great prophetical panoply prior to the Day of the Lord." He inferred America's patriotic voices of prophecy reinforced this "benign critique" by misjudging our national motives. Perhaps naively, advocates for what we now call American *exceptionalism* (the world's "last and best hope for freedom") suppose her illuminating torch of liberty is lifted high to protect personal freedoms throughout our land and selflessly promote democracy throughout the whole earth. By *ipso facto* adopting nationalism as a secondary religion, many grievous sins in our land have been overlooked or marginalized.

## Revered Eschatology Scholars Speak Out

In 2000, Dr. Noah Hutchings, pastor of the Southwest Radio Bible Church, reprinted the treatise by S. Franklin Logsdon entitled, *Is the U.S.A. in Prophecy?* As alluded to earlier, Logsdon had written his brief book in 1968 declaring that America was the Babylon of Revelation 18. When he wrote these words, it was a risky proposition. The Cold War was at its height. The Soviet Union and the United States were locked into various wars through numerous surrogates (most famously, Vietnam). To say the least, given the tension of the time, Logsdon's declaration wasn't much welcomed in the heartland of America.

Thirty years later, Hutchings found his argument compelling and Hearthstone Publishing in Oklahoma City encouraged him to write a book on the subject drawing upon Logsdon's original work then out of copyright. He was somewhat reluctant to take the same position as Logsdon since he was and remains an unashamed patriot unwilling to convey even a single spec of disloyalty to the America he loves. And yet despite his misgivings, the insights of Logsdon coupled with his own, drew Hutchings fully into the effort.

Adding to his obvious consternation were the statements of radicals and liberals in the 1970s such as Eldridge Cleaver of the Black Panthers who declared, "Our job is to destroy Babylon." Chiming in, Harvard Law School graduate and attorney William Stringfellow shouted "Hallelujah" when describing the decline and fall of the American Empire he proclaimed in the 1970s. According to the *Chicago Sun-Times*, October 31, 1970, Stringfellow asserted the United States is the modern equivalent of Babylon, the "most rich and powerful of all nations which underwent a process of violent disintegration." Could it be the one thing upon which liberals and conservatives agree, is that the United States of America comprises THE FINAL BABYLON depicted in the Bible? How ironic that such could be the case!

## The Clash of the Titans

Hutchings cites Lord Byron who said, "Civilization goes like this: First freedom, and then glory, and then wealth, and then vice, and then corruption, and then barbarism, and then collapse." Where do we think the United States resides in Bryon's life-cycle of civilizations?

Dr. Hutchings speaks of the two great sovereign states which "will have especially incurred the indignation of the Lord. The one is 'the king of the north' or Russia (Ezekiel. 38:22). But prior to this nation's demise, another of even greater prominence stands slated for the consuming vengeance of the Lord. This nation is spiritually called 'Babylon'." [6]

Hutchings continues:

> Historical Babylon is to eventuate in two imposing branches, viz., religious Babylon, the ultimate of organized religion and prophetical, political Babylon, a powerful but God-forsaking end-time nation.
>
> God will put it into the hearts of Antichrist's ten kingdoms to utterly eliminate the "woman" or the false church which is religious Babylon (Rev. 17:16-17). He will also take counsel against prophetical, political Babylon and will cause a great nation to destroy her.
>
> Before this judgment falls, God will call for His people (those saved in the early part of Daniel's seventieth week) to flee this doomed nation and emigrate to Zion or Israel (Jer. 50:28)

Hutchings lists the characteristics of this Babylon drawing from Jeremiah 50, 51, Isaiah 47, and Revelation 17-19:

1. She is the offspring of a kingdom which will deteriorate from a position of world leadership.
2. She at one time was a cup of gold in the Lord's hand—a monetary instrument in the promotion of God's work.
3. She has a cosmopolitan population—a "mingled people."
4. She is the latest or youngest of nations, said to be "the hindermost."
5. She is an exceedingly wealthy country—"abundant in treasures."
6. She is the most powerful nation and termed "the hammer of the whole earth."

---

[6] Hutchings, Dr. Noah, *The U.S. in Prophecy*, Oklahoma City, Hearthstone Publishing, 2000, pp. 105-6.

7. Her scientific achievements excel all other nations.
8. She speaks with an influential voice in the world community.
9. She has established unprecedented national defenses.
10. She involves herself in global affairs.
11. She is singularly and lavishly generous in foreign aid.
12. She has the highest standard of living, even of an epicurean character.
13. She becomes a spiritual renegade, lapsing into idolatry and covetousness.
14. Through unrestrained permissiveness, a moral decadence ensues to the proportions of blatant turpitude.
15. She develops pride and haughtiness through egotistical bias and claims to "sit a queen," untouched by defeat and untouchable.
16. The "unsinkable titanic" of nations is slowly, subtly, and surely stripped of her gold.[7]

Wanting to remain slightly uncommitted to what is for him a most painful thesis (that America fulfills the prophecy since it unmistakably possesses these attributes), Hutchings surmises:

> Some end-time nation will answer to these descriptions. That nation, having been mightily blessed of God, will incur His indignation because of her godlessness. And when the hour of divine judgment arrives, an alliance of greater nations from the prophetical "north," possessing devastating, vulnerable weapons in formidable quantities, will strike unexpectedly, suddenly, and decisively.
>
> As the "woman" (the false church) shall be utterly eliminated, even so, the end-time nation, spiritually called Babylon, shall irreparably perish from the earth. Her beauty and pride shall no more restrain the hand of divine judgment than the impressiveness of Lucifer, the son of the morning, could prevent his fall and ultimate doom when he turned from God and through pride exalted himself.

---

[7] Ibid., pp. 106-7.

The late J.R. Church addressed the same issues in his book, *Guardians of the Grail* (1989). He began by expressing the same regret and disclaimer: "Being a patriotic citizen, I would much rather write about the good of our country than the bad. My heart still leaps when I see the flag and hear the national anthem."[8] But Church felt compelled to observe the facts set forth in the Scriptures:

> The beast upon which the woman sits may be identified as the ten-nation confederation of the revived Roman Empire. But MYSTERY BABYLON uses those ten nations as a vehicle upon which to rise to power. She appears to provide the direction and provide the motivation for those ten nations.
>
> BABYLON THE GREAT, then, may not be a part of the European group of nations. It may represent a nation who is in control of those nations. The United States today certainly fills that role.[9]

Church, like Hutchings, finds Logsdon's examination of the United States convincing. First, in reference to Jeremiah 50:12, "*Your mother shall be sore confounded...*" Logsdon noted that ancient Babylon was founded by Nimrod 1,600 years before the Christian era. It was destroyed in 683 BC and then rebuilt by Nebuchadnezzar about 100 years later. In regards to the United States, Britain was surely confounded by the Revolution and despite being the most powerful nation in the world, lost the colonies in America in what amounted to "guerilla warfare."

Secondly, Jeremiah 51:7 asserts, *"Babylon hath been a golden cup in the Lord's hand, that made all the earth drunken: the nations have drunken of her wine; therefore the nations are mad."* The nation which had once been mightily used by God and blessed by Him became so debauched that the nations (according to Logsdon) have been made drunken with her wine.

---

[8] J.R. Church, *Guardians of the Grail,* Oklahoma City: Prophecy Publications, 1989, p. 237

[9] Ibid., p. 239.

Thirdly, in Jeremiah 50:37, we read, *"A sword is upon their horses, and upon their chariots, and upon all the mingled people that are in the midst of her..."* Given that our country is known as the "melting pot of the world" the passage in Jeremiah reflects the cosmopolitan character we possess. Next, Jeremiah 51:13 contends, *"O thou that dwellest upon many waters, abundant in treasures, thine end is come, and the measure of thy covetousness."* Church points out...

> Dr. Logsdon suggested that the description could hardly fit the empire of ancient Babylon. The city was situated on the banks of the Euphrates River with its southern most point touching the Persian Gulf. The description in Jeremiah 51:13 seems to be indicative of the United States with the Atlantic Ocean along our eastern coast, the Pacific Ocean along our western coast, and the Gulf of Mexico to our south. *"O thou that dwellest upon many waters..."*

Church cites Jeremiah 50:23: *"How is the hammer of the whole earth cut asunder and broken!"* Rather than seeing the hammer as a violent vitriolic image, Church pointed out that the meaning of the verb in Hebrew instead conveys "create, shape, overpower, or overwhelm by force or influence." Thus, Logsdon's suggestion made sense to Church. God looked down through the corridors of time and saw our nation welding dominating, overpowering influence upon the nations of the whole world. The United States constitutes the *hammer of the entire earth* today.

Another verse from Jeremiah 51:53 helps make the case. *"Though Babylon should mount up to heaven, and though she should fortify the height of her strength..."* transcends the tower that helped make Babylon famous. Our country celebrates the fact that we were the first to land men on the moon and return them safely. America has mounted up to the heavens and our military strength is unassailable because of our dominant air power. The United States has ruled the skies for the past 70 years.

## The Daughter of Babylon

The authors we've just discussed have loved their country. But they noticed that the historical Babylon did not fulfill the prophecies of Jeremiah 50, 51, Isaiah 13, 47, and Zechariah 2. Additionally, the title, *Daughter of Babylon*, caught their attention. They noted the prophets spoke against this empire with great vindictiveness. From the description of this Babylon, they read how it would be utterly destroyed. The Babylon that had captured Judah and hauled off its inhabitants to the land of the Chaldeans was not destroyed as Isaiah and Jeremiah depict. Almost without struggle, it was conquered as the Medes and Persians slipped in under the city walls by damning the Euphrates River, then entering into the "impregnable" city when the water lowered. Additionally, they were well aware that the physical and historical city of Babylon continued on for hundreds of years with its identity intact.

However, Jeremiah could hardly be more adamant about the destruction of Babylon. This land would be devastated by enemies "from the north" (Medo-Persia advanced upon Babylon from the East). He also indicated a number of times that multiple enemies would come upon Babylon.

> 9 *For, lo, I will raise and cause to come up against Babylon an assembly of great nations from the north country: and they shall set themselves in array against her; from thence she shall be taken: their arrows shall be as of a mighty expert man; none shall return in vain.*
>
> 10 *And Chaldea* [the land, not just a single city] *shall be a spoil: all that spoil her shall be satisfied, saith the* LORD.

To put it simply: the Babylon of these biblical passages couldn't be the Babylon of ancient times. There are too many incongruities. Unless you subscribe to the view that Babylon in Iraq will be rebuilt to massive proportions (a theme we dealt with earlier), the Babylon of the Jeremiah 50, 51, and Isaiah 47, the *Daughter of Babylon,* must be a metaphor for a future empire. Of course, we believe that empire is the United States of America.

What is particularly worrisome concerns the utter destruction of this Babylon:

> [39] *Therefore the wild beasts of the desert with the wild beasts of the islands shall dwell there, and the owls shall dwell therein: and it shall be no more inhabited for ever; neither shall it be dwelt in from generation to generation.*
>
> [40] *As God overthrew Sodom and Gomorrah and the neighbour cities thereof, saith the LORD; so shall no man abide there, neither shall any son of man dwell therein.*
>
> [41] *Behold, a people shall come from the north, and a great nation, and many kings shall be raised up from the coasts of the earth.*

According to this scripture, the destruction of Babylon shall be complete, and in a manner akin to the destruction of Sodom and Gomorrah which was destroyed by "fire and brimstone." Could this reference suggest a nuclear holocaust will befall America?

From to this passage, we see that its destruction will be led by a king from the north ("hailing from the north" is mentioned in five different verses from Jeremiah 50, 51), with many kings raised up from the "coasts" of the earth (an expression of lands far away from Israel). As mentioned earlier, Dr. Hutchings speculated that the two titans of the end days are Russia and America. Likewise, author Allen Bonck (another senior writer and teacher) identifies Russia also as the captain of Babylon's enemies in his fine but brief book, *America the Daughter of Babylon*. He suggests the enemies of America consist of both Russia and Iran, citing Jeremiah 51:27-28:

> [27] *Set ye up a standard in the land, blow the trumpet among the nations, prepare the nations against her, call together against her the kingdoms of Ararat, Minni, and Ashchenaz; appoint a captain against her; cause the horses to come up as the rough caterpillers.*
>
> [28] *Prepare against her the nations with the kings of the Medes, the captains thereof, and all the rulers thereof, and all the land of his dominion.*

Bonck comments:

> The biblical nation of Ararat existed in the area of north-eastern Turkey and southern Russia. It lies in the region of the Caucus Mountains, between the Black and Caspian seas. The town of Ararat still exists today near Lake Sevan, in the [former] Soviet Union. The nation of Minni, is located in the modern nation of Iran, between lake Ermia, and Iran's modern capital of Tehran. The nation of Ashchenaz, like Ararat, is located in modern Russia, between the Black and Caspian seas, although Ashchenaz was further north. The Medes were located in north-western Iran [and are also associated with the Kurds who live in northern Iraq and southern Turkey].[10]

In a later chapter, we will discuss other reasons why traditional evangelical interpretative methods allow for the Daughter of Babylon to be a nation other than the Babylon of Nebuchadnezzar and Belshazzar. However, at this juncture our point is this: there are many venerable authors/researchers/scholars, which are great students of the Bible, but press the argument that America is the Babylon spoken of by the great Hebrew prophets. America is the principal power standing opposed to the Lord in the end of days. They do not agree with the traditional scenario; instead they amass stout biblical rationale to contend *America is the Daughter of Babylon.*

## Why We Are Critical of American Evangelicals

Therefore, after studying scores of books published on the subject of America's role in the last days – whether written by well-meaning futurists, historical interpreters, or those who would dismiss her engagement as purely symbolic, we conclude that the theology of the end-times (based upon Old Testament prophets such as Daniel, Zechariah, Isaiah, Ezekiel, and New Testament authors including select portions of the synoptic gospels, Paul's letters to his churches, Peter, Jude, and John the Revelator), demands contemporary interpretation revise the

---

[10] Allen Bonck, *America the Daughter of Babylon*, New York: iUniverse, 1989, 2008, p. 60.

view which has dominated our day. It must reconsider the meaning of the great Pre-millenarian insights of J.N. Darby and others from his era. We affirm the Word of God is living and will speak again to our generation with unmistakable clarity.

It was for this purpose that our co-author, Krieger some years ago joined the dedicated but non-harmonious chorus of domestic prophets and decided to pen two on-line texts. *Antichrist – Reflections on the Desolator* and *The Rise or Fall of American Empire?* Likewise, co-author McGriff for some time has written extensively on the financial corruption of the American economic system while *co-author* Woodward has made plain the depth of America's mostly-concealed institutional and governmental depravity post-World War II. In *Power Quest Book One* and *Two*, Woodward recited myriad seldom known facts: American scientists, eugenicists, industrialists, militarists and ideologues teamed with Nazi émigrés in abundance upon American soil (at the invitation of our Government no less!) in a remorseless effort to "protect" our republic from Communism and in the wake altered our country's values with their fiendish prescriptions to build a new world freed from the threat of the Marxist dialectic. The undesirable aftereffects of this bad medicine plague us still. *Although invisible to all but a discerning few, pilgrim Winthrop's "City set on a hill" now resembles Dante's Inferno on a mountaintop.* As Billy Graham's wife Ruth once said, "If God doesn't judge America, He'll have to apologize to Sodom and Gomorrah!"

No wonder such evangelical luminaries like the late David Wilkerson saw Babylon's sudden destruction fulfilled in America! That idyllic picture of our nation which we'd like to affirm has assuredly been blurred. Our country is now a faint image... a shadowy silhouette of her former self. Nevertheless, most red-blooded Americans remain convinced (despite increasing evidence to the contrary) that our global humanitarian vision persists even today. Most profess this *consensus rosy-colored reality* prevails – revitalized with an oft-repeated appeal of "God bless America" anytime an unforeseen adversary threatens our American dream.

## The Sell-out of the American Press

What is even more discouraging: the not-so-independent press fails to play their constructive role as a conscience for civil or political morality. With few exceptions, journalists are now oblivious to our nation's deficiencies. The occasional voice crying in the wilderness (we have in mind foreign policy critics like Chalmers Johnson or Noam Chomsky) has no public platform for expression except the seldom watched documentary available in the "backroom" of video store or a hard-to-find download on the Internet. The "Mike Wallaces" of *Sixty Minutes*, if they are to be found at all, are scarce when they should be vocal and visible in the public square.

Notwithstanding, the complicit press and our ascendant intelligence operatives, teaming up in an unspoken but obvious alliance to mislead, continues to churn out the most outlandish geopolitical hogwash. Our latest dose of "farsighted" analysis (we speak sarcastically of course) was foisted on the American public with the publication of a 140-page report released in December, 2012, by the National Intelligence Council (surely a misnomer), citing "trends" wherein America and the world are facing "a critical juncture in human history, which could lead to widely contrasting futures." This successful quest for prosaic ambiguity was offered by Chairman Christopher Kojm. The most highly touted "game-changers" – sites Kojm – are led by our "crisis-prone" global economy (this disingenuous metaphor is sure to offend even the most cautious theorist of conspiratorial activity!) "Black swans," like the collapse of the Euro or the juggernaut that is China's economy, threaten America's place in the world. And yet, the meandering report drones on, warning of global warming, an 8.3 billion world population by 2030, and a host of other gloomy prospects which "could" diminish the sphere's only super power.

*Good grief, Scotty: even the Government now sounds like date-setting millenarians which, upon reflection, could compel our good brother Hal Lindsey to wince from incredulity!*

But wait: there's the final conclusion and summary committed to our trust by *Bloomberg News* reporter Nicole Gaouette. She cautions the U.S. role in this new world order grows hard to predict since the degree to which domination continues over the international system will vary widely. After waiting for the gasps to quiet, she quotes from the Report: "Despite that, the United States most likely will remain 'first among equals' in 2030 (?)..."[11]

Did you catch that? "First among equals?" The question mark is ours because the 800 lb. Gorilla sits upon a bench beside measly chimps Gaouette terms "equals." Despite that dubious observation, she regards the Gorilla "first" among them! Such an oxymoronic statement could only be brought to you by the aforesaid co-opted press via a so-called "intelligence gathering" establishment playing rope-a-dope in a vain and surreptitious effort to dismiss the continuance of US leadership. "Lead from behind?" – *please!* If our leadership doesn't endure, we must immediately inquire, "Whose behind would be left?"

After diminishing American superiority in Nobel Prizes, Olympic Medals, educational prowess, and (to say the least, our incomparable military might), her analysis crescendos with this über-cautious, and perhaps worse, disingenuous deprecation: *Our economic clout has run amuck.* Well, pray tell – how is it that our President can, first, operate our third installment of quantitative easing, aka "QE3" (Bernanke's effort to stimulate the economy to the tune of $40B per month); secondly, attract three buyers of our Treasury Bills for every one we offer; and thirdly, pay next to nothing in interest to the world's most finicky "investors" hedging their assets? The conclusion is as plain as the picture of any particular dead president on a dollar bill: despite protests to the contrary (and scare tactics by both politicians and prophets alike) the one remaining currency of unques-

---

[11] Nicole Gaouette, *Bloomberg News, "Report sees world transformed... Forecast predicts falling U.S. power, spreading wealth, scarcer resources,"* http://www.bloomberg.com/news/2012-12-10/u-s-intelligence-agencies-see-a-different-world-in-2030.html.

tioned value on the planet is American. While it may be shrinking in stature, its resiliency easily outdoes the rest! But beyond the issue of financial prowess, America has no intention of rolling up its bed and stealing away into the night. The U.S.A. may no longer be that "City on the hill" but it is clear to even the most amateur observer that we fully intend to remain king of the hill.

## Is the Rapture Why America Falls?

Just the thought of evangelical prophetic brethren contradicting "American exceptionalism" because the rapture of the American church (amongst a few others outside our borders) will reduce our stranglehold on the global economy, military dominance, and world affairs generally, makes one think our most zealous Bible-believing prophets have forgotten who sits so comfortably at the controls. Perhaps it's because our most popular evangelical authors assume we've done far better in evangelizing America than we normally acknowledge? However one interprets the timing of the rapture of the Church (be it pre-trib, mid-trib, pre-wrath, post-trib – the authors in fact don't agree on this point) we nonetheless raise several interrogatives: Just how many airplanes do you suppose will remain in the sky unmanned? How many nuclear reactors will be left unattended? How many Wall Street markets will go askew for want of brokers and market-makers? What will be the number of cars careening out of control? How many "Jack and Jills" will go up the hill paired only to come down single? *Far fewer than the popular evangelical view espouses!*

That is why we differ with those who assume the *rapture* is the root cause for the resignation of America from its role of undisputed leadership in the world. Furthermore, as if our well-meaning sarcasm isn't pressing our luck with the reader already, we venture that those who believe the wingless lift-off of millions of Americans to fly the friendly skies will promptly lead to our undoing, such adherents lack a good grasp on the reality of our situation here in these United States.

To suppose it a factual statement worthy of affirmation, that many tens of millions of our fellow citizens will be saved from the wrath to come (because they have individually and sincerely received Jesus Christ as their personal savior), is itself a supposition worthy of indictment. We would suppose *just the opposite!* The unsaved are legion. The way we read biblical prophecy, America is not destined only to diminish... to go away quietly into that good night... but *to be utterly destroyed* (in fulfillment of the prophecies of Jeremiah, Isaiah, and John the Revelator) because far too many of its fiscal, military, and political leaders show little hint of Christian sentiments, let alone advocate the salvation it alone would supply society. Of course, it's never easy to properly position Christian convictions in the political realm.

## A Balanced Gospel

In January, 1934, Ludwig Mueller, Reich Bishop, issued the "Muzzling Order" designed to silence political statements from the pulpit in Germany. He proclaimed that the churches abstain from any manner of political commentary. The church service is for "the proclamation of the pure gospel, and for this alone."

Some Christians would find this injunction acceptable; after all, didn't Jesus say to *"Render therefore unto Caesar those things that are Caesar's and unto God those things that are God's"?* (Matthew 22:21). Perhaps when it comes to the political situation, we should keep our mouth shut. On the other hand, since the 1970s, evangelicals formed the "Christian right" and engaged actively in politics. Jerry Falwell (1933-2007) pastor of the Thomas Road Baptist Church in Lynchburg, Virginia, became the head of the Moral Majority, a movement for evangelicals which had a dramatic impact on several presidential elections.

But the fatal flaw, from our perspective, was restricting the Gospel of Christ to "moral issues" only – anti-abortion, anti-gay rights, and pro-family. [12] The Moral Majority appeared to be little

---

[12] According to Jim Marrs, "Following the attacks of September 11, 2001, Falwell, on Pat Robertson's *700 Club* TV show, said pagans, abortionists, femi-

more than the religious wing of the Republican Party. Christianity and conservatism were inextricably linked. This has led left-leaning Christian authors such as Chris Hedges, a graduate of Harvard Divinity School, to respond with an angry diatribe against the Christian "hard-right" which he paints as "American fascists" who war against America and seek to, in the words of the *Los Angeles Times*, "turn the United States into a Christian nation."

No doubt our readers will do a double-take on that summation of Hedges' thesis, assuming all Christians should be about the business of "*returning* the U.S. to the status of a 'Christian nation'" once more. Of course, we argue instead that enlightened Evangelicals must beware of presuming patriotism and spirituality go hand-in-hand. Christ stands apart from our country and government – judging how society conducts itself. We stand accountable before Him.

However, unlike the implications of Hedges' rhetoric, the separation of Church and State protects and secures *religious* rights – *not as arbiter or guarantor protecting secularism as the law of the land.* But that doesn't mean that proclaiming Christianity places a gag order on all political expression in the name of Christ. Evangelicals must take a stand against any and all governmental policies or programs that compromise the gospel of Jesus Christ. This is especially so when secular globalists suppose that America must be about the business of building a singular government absent of Kingdom principles.

And, unfortunately, we see this matter the one place where America unquestionably leads the way.

---

nists, gays, lesbians, the ACLU, and everyone else trying to secularize America "helped this happen." Marrs, *The Rise of the Fourth Reich*, pp. 293-4. However well-intentioned Falwell's explanation for connecting God's judgment on America with Bin Laden's terrorist team, the statement convicts the innocent and excuses the perpetrators. It is true that what evil seeks to achieve, God in fact redeems and uses for His purposes. God did use Al-Qaida for judgment. But how the prophet of God presents this message must be done with sensitivity to the victims and with condemnation to those responsible.

## The Role of America Today

Globalist Jim Garrison, President of The State of the World Forum and author of *America as Empire*, believes the mission of America is to lead (if not force) the world to a single government. He proclaims unequivocally, "No one can argue credibly that America today is not an empire. Militarily, economically, and culturally, the United States wields a hegemonic influence unparalleled in world history." The not-so-popular-with-Fox-News hypocrite champion of the not-so-meek, the mega-rich George Soros, offers this analysis: "The United States is the only country in the world that is in a position to initiate a change in the world order, to replace the Washington consensus with a global open society. To do so, we must abandon the unthinking pursuit of narrow self-interest and give some thought to the future of humanity." [13]

Jim Naisbitt, introducing Garrison's book, summarizes Garrison's position as a restatement of the global aspirations of Woodrow Wilson, President Franklin D. Roosevelt, and Harry S. Truman. Of that we cannot quibble. All argue globalism must be incorporated into our governmental institutions since the world already acts as a single global consumer – that is, it already implements *one financial system.* Naisbitt exclaims (much to our incredulity): "Leadership reminiscent of Wilson and Roosevelt is now needed again." He goes on to explain the "enforcer" role America must play to facilitate the transition:

> If (America) attains this level of greatness... then America could *be the final empire,* [is Naisbitt the Caiaphas of our day unwittingly prophesying our doom?] for what the next generation of global institutions could bequeath to the world is a democratic and integrated global system in which empire will no longer have a place. Garrison thus wants America to see itself as a transitional empire, one that uses its power to build

[13] Quoted by Garrison, p. 193.

> mechanisms that will institutionalize America as partner rather than as empire[14] [emphasis ours].

Toward the conclusion of his book, Garrison criticizes *fundamentalism* of all kinds (Jewish, Islam, and Christian in the chapter "America at the Choice Point"). He charges that all share an equally harmful apocalyptic worldview which counters the *optimism* of globalism (as if this were the first time Judaism, Christianity, and perhaps even Islam have challenged godless utopianism!) Thus, globalists and 'prophets' are at loggerheads.

He writes a synopsis of Christian eschatology which clearly demonstrates a thorough knowledge of the standard "apocalyptic scenario" made popular by Hal Lindsey and Tim LaHaye. And he sees their expressions of apocalyptic fervor detrimental to the future of humankind:

> The political ideology fostered by this apocalyptic theology combines a radical pessimism about human nature and current events with an equally radical optimism about God's plan for the elect. Quite literally, the worse the world situation becomes, the more expectant these believers become because they believe they are getting closer to Jesus's coming again and taking them to heaven. They have little regard for the environment because they believe the environment will be destroyed anyway. They have little sympathy for the poor and the dispossessed because they believe that economic dislocation and civil unrest are indicators of human depravity and a signal that the end is nigh. They have little support for the protection of civil liberties because they believe that strong action must be taken against the infidels and potential terrorists.[15]

Of course, if we do not present a "balanced gospel;" Garrison's criticism, although exaggerated and unsympathetic, is on point.

Moreover, keeping the Gospel "balanced" is quintessential to keeping it relevant. Neither the "left" nor the 'right' have all the answers and often miss the point. The Lordship of Christ ex-

---

[14]Garrison, Jim, *America as Empire: Global Leader or Rogue Power?* San Francisco, Berrett-Koehler Publishers, Inc., 2004, p. ix.
[15] Ibid., p. 159.

tends to all aspects of our lives – moral, social, economic, political, and everything in between. To *rightly present the gospel* means to model the coming Kingdom of God in the way we live our lives in the "here and now" (in Latin, the *hic et nunc* – "here at this place, now in this present moment"). This is the eschatological mission of Christians. Our lives are to serve as a reminder that the judgment of God is coming. Our distinctiveness is to be not only salt that preserves – but strong medicine that stings when applied. *American exceptionalism* may be no more than bravado and ballyhoo. *Christian exceptionalism* is equivalent to modeling the Kingdom of God *hic et nunc. That is the big distinction – and one generally lost on all utopians.*

This was assuredly the position of Dietrich Bonhoeffer (1906-1945) who was martyred – hanged by the Reich with piano wire – for his part in attempting to assassinate Hitler. Bonhoeffer preached against "cheap grace," a gospel which sanctioned splitting the realm of human life into more than one sphere, creating a dominion in our society where Christ could not be Lord. That is what the "Muzzling Order" did. It restricted religion into one "kingdom" and human government into another.

Erwin W. Lutzer, evangelical pastor of the Moody Church in Chicago, summarized what Christians should learn from the history of Hitler's German church: "We will discover that the Nazi era shouts its lessons to the church of America. It warns us, challenges us, and forecasts what might happen in the days ahead. Whether we heed its warnings, accept its challenges, and recognize its subtle deceptions is up to us." [16] Lutzer believes the end times are upon us. He preaches to prepare his congregation *now* for hard times ahead – even though he remains a pre-tribulational preacher who sees the rapture of the Church preceding the coming of Antichrist.[17]

---

[16] Lutzer, Hitler's Cross, op. cit., p. 130.

[17] Lutzer also states "Here in America the phrase "separation of church and state" is given a sinister twist by civil libertarians. To them, it means that religious people should not be allowed to practice their religion in the realm

Note: we will examine Hitler's impact on the Church in a later chapter as it discloses the tactics we can expect from Antichrist at some point in the years ahead.

At this point, we must declare Garrison and the globalists are deeply mistaken seeing in those who believe in the imminent return of Christ, culprits who are heaven-bent doomsayers wishing only for the worse to happen that we might speed up the redemptive process. If we heed the words of Jesus Christ and his proclamation that the Kingdom of God is at hand, we are motivated by an optimism which transcends the utopian vision. We seek a truly redeemed world – one which glistens and shimmers from the glory of Christ, unrestrained by the sin of humankind and its destructive works. In the picturesque words of Paul from the Letter to the Hebrews, we are like our father in faith, Abraham, seeking a city that is from God. *"For here have we **no continuing city*** (*meno* in the Greek, a place to sojourn or reside continually, and polis, our native town where we are "at home"), *but we seek one to come."* (Hebrews 13:14). We lack optimism when it comes to the globalist agenda – our faith lies elsewhere. The pessimism Garrisons criticizes, rests on 6,000 years of human history which teaches plainly and convincingly that when power is fully centralized, totalitarianism becomes inevitable.

There is an expression, "When the elephants dance, the grass suffers." In political affairs the analogue is, "When the elite rule absolutely, the poor suffer unconditionally." Garrison, like Wilson, Roosevelt, and almost all U.S. Presidents, wants the rich to rule.

Indeed, *utopian dreams are dreamlike only when they remain dreams.* When such lofty programs are implemented – always by totalitarian means – the weak are oppressed and human rights are eclipsed despite the euphoria emanating from idealistic platitudes and speeches. *That is the lesson of world*

---

that belongs to the state. Religion, we are told, should be practiced privately; the state must be "cleansed" from every vestige of religious influence. By insisting that the state be "free for all religions," organizations such as the ACLU in effect make it free for none." Lutzer, op. cit., p. 19.

*dictators from Nimrod's time to present day.* The fact that globalists believe a single government and a single leader would manage the affairs of humankind effectively – guided only by reason and not by the admonitions of the Bible – clearly infers that of all supposedly learned men and women, *utopians are the poorest students of history.* The French Revolution, starring Madame Guillotine, provides a most vivid visual aid arguing their supposedly considered opinion demands revision if not absolute reversal.

## Conclusion

In summation (and the timing of the rapture notwithstanding), the real fault in America lies within its "citadel of corruption" whose cup, once golden that served the Lord, grows morally disgusting and from whence earthly merchants wax rich through her wares. "*Come out of her My people, that you be not partakers of her sins and her plagues!*" (Rev. 18:4)

We must be mindful: Israel was delivered from Egypt by the Almighty's miraculous intervention. We dare say that John's impassioned plea for God's people to depart Babylon and the snare of her world-wide abominations may only be realized *through the rapture of the Saints* rather than a well-timed voluntary exodus. For like the majority of reticent Hebrews who refused to return to Jerusalem from Babylon with Zerubbabel, we predict the vast majority won't leave their familiar confines since they reject the reality we assert: Americans reside smack dab at the center of that "city" deserving God's greatest antipathy: *Babylon the Great!*

It is with grave compunction we, along with many other noteworthy voices in Evangelicalism over the past fifty years, assert the U.S.A. fulfills the dire prophecies of the Hebrew prophets. It is THE FINAL BABYLON.

*Chapter 4:*

# Is America a Christian Nation?

## The Myth of America's Christian Beginnings

MOST CONSERVATIVE AMERICANS BELIEVE THAT AMERICAN WAS FOUNDED "A CHRISTIAN NATION." WE ALSO BELIEVE THAT OUR NATIONAL MOTTO, "IN GOD WE TRUST" WAS part of the Constitution (it wasn't[1]), and that when Thomas Jef-

**Figure 13 - What Did the Founding Father's Intend?**

ferson wrote in our Declaration of Independence that "the Creator endowed us with certain unalienable rights" he meant the Hebrew God, Jehovah or the Christian God incarnate, Jesus Christ. Jefferson meant neither. But since conservatives believe this, they naturally chafe when hearing our current President, Barack Obama make plain the fact that America wasn't intended to be a nation only for Christians. They ask, "Don't we sing, 'God Bless America?' When President Obama sings it, does he think

---

[1] Adopted in 1956, it was an alternative to the unofficial motto of *E Pluribus Unum.*

God will bless us? If so, which God is he asking for a blessing?" President Barack Obama has stated that we Americans "do not consider ourselves a Christian nation, or a Muslim nation, but rather, a nation of citizens who are, uh, bound by a set of values."

John Eidsmoe, in the April, 2009 edition of the *New American* notes that:

> Obama has made similar statements in the past. In June 2007, he told CBS, "Whatever we once were, we are no longer a Christian nation — at least, not just. We are also a Jewish nation, a Muslim nation, a Buddhist nation, and a Hindu nation, and a nation of nonbelievers." Note the progression. In 2007, he said we are no longer 'just' a Christian nation. Now, in 2009, he says we "do not consider ourselves a Christian nation" at all.[2]

Of course, in making these statements, it is a legitimate issue to wonder exactly what President Obama's point is: To the extent he is underscoring that America is proud of its religious freedom, tolerance for the intolerant, and that our right to choose our religion – that religious freedom is as American as apple pie – even the most conservative of conservative Christians will likely say "Amen." For we celebrate the separation of Church and State. We do not want any one "Church" such as practiced by our mother country ("The Church of England"); neither do we want our "supreme leader" to mandate our manner of worship, or even that we should worship at all (especially since many choose to kneel at the altar of professional sports on Sunday mornings). It matters not whether our government is elected democratically.[3] We don't wish religious choice to be taken from us. Such a combination of political and priestly power almost certainly guarantees tyranny. Moreover, personal religious freedom is one of the liberties Americans hold dear.

---

[2] John Eidsmoe, "Obama, Not a Christian Nation" *New American*, April, 2009.

[3] King Henry VIII was the first English monarch who felt it was his responsibility to be the head of both the government and the Church. His obligation came about, as most readers know, because he wanted a divorce and the Pope refused to grant him one. So Henry divorced England from the Roman Church!

Of course, when an American citizen chooses to be Muslim, Hindu, or "none of the above" – it doesn't take much imagination to understand why in making that choice, believers in religions outside of the Judeo-Christian realm feel more comfortable with an America not dedicated (and never was so dedicated) to the proposition "we are a *Christian nation.*" Our nation is pluralist and inclusive. We want it that way, despite any zeal we may feel for our personal religious faith and whether or not we regard our faith to be the exclusive pathway to truly know God.

## The Pretext for Patriotism Among Christians

Nevertheless, a plethora of organizations in the USA are committed to the proposition that the fundamentals of American democracy are established on Christian mores. The notion that our republic was founded upon the secular reasoning of deists (and more worrying– pagans no matter how enlightened) seems alien to say the least.

This common presupposition assuredly explains the avalanche of "America's Shining Light for the Gentiles." Even just the tip of the iceberg as to those who proclaim America's Christian heritage is impressive: *WallBuilders, American Christian History Institute, Christian Discoveries, The Claremont Institute, The Declaration Foundation, America's Christian Heritage Week, National Alliance Against Christian Discrimination, Christian Legal Society, American Vision, National Lawyers Association, The Foundation for American Christian Education, The Gilder Lehrman Institute of American History, Peter Marshall Ministries, The Providence Forum, The Providence Foundation...* in fact, over 100 organizations are listed on the *WallBuilders* web site alone, acclaiming America's Founding Fathers to be rooted in biblical platitudes if not theistic doctrine.

With that much smoke there's got to be some fire... at least religious zeal that is. And indeed there is. However, and in spite of hope that the Founding Fathers held fast to "Christian assumptions" – the preponderance of their political philosophy hearkens not to the Bible but to Greece and Rome – i.e., the "Greco-Roman" worldview. Consider this fact: The Nation's Capital is not laden with Christian symbols but with pagan ones. We should ask but we generally don't, "What in the world is the goddess Minerva doing atop our nation's capital dome (or for that matter) the god Mars guarding the entry to our sacred citadel?" We are so used to seeing them standing there it never occurred to us that we should ask who invited them to be our sacred symbols.

## Were our Founding Fathers Christians?

No doubt many readers will be surprised to learn most of the progenitors of America were NOT Christians; nor were they even *theists.* While they believed in a deistic God who created the universe and who stood for moral principles, they did not consider Him particularly "personal" – which is the quality a theist fervently believes God possesses.

> Most historians define the "founding fathers" to mean a larger group, including not only the Signers and the Framers (of the U.S. Constitution) but also all those who, whether as politicians or jurists or statesmen or soldiers or diplomats or ordinary citizens, took part in winning American independence and creating the United States of America.[4] The eminent American historian Richard B. Morris, in his 1973 book *Seven Who Shaped Our Destiny: The Founding Fathers as Revolutionaries,* identified the following seven figures as the key founding fathers: Benjamin Franklin, George Washington, John Adams, Thomas Jefferson, John Jay, James Madison, and Alexander Hamilton.[5] [We will look at them in detail later.]
>
> Warren G. Harding, then a Republican Senator from Ohio, coined the phrase *Founding Fathers* in his keynote address to the 1916 Republican National Convention. He used it several times thereafter, most prominently in his 1921 inaugural address as President of the United States.[6]

---

4 en.wikipedia.org/wiki/Founding_Fathers_of_the_United_States#cite_note-1.
5 en.wikipedia.org/wiki/Founding_Fathers_of_the_United_States#cite_note-2.
6 en.wikipedia.org/wiki/Founding_Fathers_of_the_United_States#cite_note-3.

We would hasten to include such agnostics (at least regarding the "immortality of the soul") as the curmudgeon himself, Thomas Paine, whose *Common Sense* was but one of his contrarian publications to "Kingly and Priestly rule." No one person fanned the flames of the American Revolution more than Thomas Paine, and there was none his equal among the Founding Fathers in deploring Christianity.

> Paine greatly influenced the French Revolution. He wrote the *Rights of Man* (1791), a guide to Enlightenment ideas. Despite not speaking French, he was elected to the French National Convention in 1792. The Girondists regarded him as an ally, so, the Montagnards, especially Robespierre, regarded him as an enemy. In December of 1793, he was arrested and imprisoned in Paris, then released in 1794. He became notorious because of *The Age of Reason* (1793–94), his book advocating deism, promoting reason and freethinking, and arguing against institutionalized religion and Christian doctrines. He also wrote the pamphlet *Agrarian Justice* (1795), discussing the origins of property, and introduced the concept of a guaranteed minimum income [a first step toward socialism!].[7]

Deism – which afflicted a number of our Founding Fathers – ultimately led to anti-Trinitarian propositions on the nature of the Divine. The origins of creation are simply a manifestation of one's religious and philosophical belief systems whereby a supreme being, deigned to create the universe, can be determined by human reasoning and observation of the natural world alone. Hence, there is no need for faith, and particularly the Judeo-Christian type of faith – bits, parts and pieces may be used as a moral compass of sorts from these sources, but that's as far as one's faith need venture!

For the Deist, the creation is on "auto-pilot" – God is hardly a participant in the affairs of man. But if He is, it's a unilateral proposition – He does what He chooses to do in spite of any infractions on our parts to the contrary. Why intervene through miracles and revelations? That isn't the "natural order of

---

[7] See en.wikipedia.org/wiki/Thomas_Paine.

things." For Paine and his deist friends, all *supernatural* revelation (supposedly contained within sacred texts) results from the pre-enlightenment mind that didn't know any better. The "Great Architect of the Universe" (GAOTU)[8] has an undisclosed set of rules to run the universe and we poor, puny misanthropes may seek to determine that plan, but it remains beyond us to ever know the mind of the Almighty, let alone "change His mind" through prayer and supplication. If we would worship God truly, we should realize we do this for *our own benefit* – nothing more than a mere reminder we *are* indeed but poor, puny misanthropes. God doesn't require our worship; and frankly, could care less about getting it.

So says the Deist with a smug look of self-satisfaction.

To go one step further to make our point a bit more plain: Unbelievers suppose that the "God who reveals Himself" in history, in His Word, and through Jesus Christ, is simply the figment of our superstitious undereducated imaginations – with the less intellectually endowed having more *figments* than most (Moses, Jesus, Buddha, Mohammed and other "enlightened souls" apparently had a lot of figments). Most of those who embraced Deism wound up trumpeting the Age of Enlightenment. Most were nominal Christians who couldn't stomach a triune God, Jesus' divinity, miracles or inspired biblical texts. Especially disconcerting, was the notion of the *God of revelation and authority* – thus, "sacred canon" was but an illusion stemming from man's efforts to control elements of society. These sophisticated deists weren't atheists per se – but esteemed their own human reason, though finite, as the best that could be achieved given the limits of our construction. One and only one God was "out there somewhere, in some form" beyond our comprehension – and if one thinks about it long enough, it is only *reasonable* to conclude that *God alone* explains the universe. But that's

[8] A common and approved way of referring to God in Freemasonry.

all there is to it. Unitarianism and *universalism* (in its quasi-Christian expression) derive from Deism.[9]

It might be put pithily as follows: "If I only had a brain... Wait, I do have a brain and I better start using it!" Thus was born the aphorism *using our common sense*, along with its big brother, the supremacy of reason, aka the *Age of Enlightenment.*

So it is that we contend the birth of these United States had far more to do with instituting the values promulgated by the Age of Enlightenment than to inculcate Judeo-Christian tenants through the government of the people, by the people, and for the people. The Hebrew God wasn't really the guarantor of the nation. For most of the Founding Fathers, he was purposefully occluded from its origination. Our grandiose cause was man-made, not the result of answered prayer. God was but a distant observer. If man knew what was best for him, he would follow the rules that God had made plain in "natural law"[10] but not venture that Deity communicated in a clear-cut way, such as *special revelation.* That would require God "speak" in such a way that violates the chasm between the Holy God and the less-than-holy human being. *"For My thoughts are not your thoughts, nor are your ways My ways"* says the LORD. (Isaiah 55:8) While the Hebrew God wasn't inferring the chasm between God and man was unbridgeable (the Bible teaches it remains God's dream to live with humankind "face-to-face" thus restoring paradise lost), Gnosticism – an ancient cousin to Deism – was quick to conclude it was an expanse too wide to bridge.

Now this, in the course of human history, leads us to some interesting conclusions, the least of which disassociates humanity's collaborate efforts with the divine plan (i.e., infinitesimal man – though he exercises reason, is nonetheless excluded from

---

[9] Although some "Christian Universalists" would strongly argue against such an analysis – for Christian *universalism* was around long before Englishmen put foot on North American shores.

[10] Natural law according to Dictionary.com is a "principle or body of laws considered as derived from nature, right reason, or religion and as ethically binding in human society." It is not specifically connected to any one religion.

knowing the Divine plan – other than what he can reason to be its essential message and guidance). Again, our arrogant aspiration to discern the divine intent stands inconsistent with rightly knowing what God represents (and not truly "knowing Him"); and more importantly, realizing that we are to keep within the sphere of what God made us to be – knowing our limits that is – as we can discern them through reason.

## Jefferson and "Nature's God"

*Nature's God* (if there is such a being) is the god of Deism. Thanks to Thomas Jefferson, this "god" is the one embedded within the United States Constitution– not the God of revelation and authority, and certainly not the God of the Bible; for nature's god has literally nothing to do with either Moses or Jesus, and certainly nothing to do with Paul the Apostle to the Gentiles. These enlightened souls of sacred writ were at best only keen observers of Him Who dwells, from the vantage point as deists, in inaccessible ambiguity.

We dare say the "Founders" may have been, at best, impressed with the "moral authority" of the Bible's overall message as they felt the Bible was a record of the best morality that humanity had devised in its millennia of wanderings and wonderings. They may have taken, again at best, the Bible's so-called moral persuasions as general norms of governing civilization; however, the Christian religion was not responsible for emancipating humanity. That accolade was reserved for the *enlightenment* that gave birth to these United States. Viewing from their point in history at the end of the eighteenth century, the horrific history of Europe's priestly and "divinely appointed" monarchical rule is testimony enough of what Christianity begets. Consequently, they regarded Judeo-Christian revelation an impediment to the creation of a mutually beneficial covenant amongst all humanity. Only human reason can lead to a righteous society.

To assert the biblical covenants were key components to the American experiment, as it was often called – be the covenants in question Noahic, Abrahamic, Mosaic, Davidic, or the New

Covenant Jesus instituted – is rather a theistic reconstruction of secular history. This lack of a Christian consensus amongst the Founders is born out from a study published in 2003 by Frank Lambert[11] which examined the religious affiliations and beliefs of the Founders. The 1787 delegates to the Constitutional Convention had various affiliations and some *had none at all.* Lambert provides this recap: Most were Protestants except for three Roman Catholics: C. Carroll, D. Carroll, and Fitzsimons. Among the Protestant delegates to the Constitutional Convention, 28 were Church of England (Episcopalian post-Revolutionary War), eight were Presbyterians, seven were Congregationalists, two were Lutherans, two were Dutch Reformed, and two were Methodists, the total number being 49 (apparently Baptists were too brilliant to be found amongst the founders!)

Some of the most prominent Founding Fathers such as Thomas Jefferson and Benjamin Franklin were anti-clerical altogether – being vocal in their opposition to organized religion.[12] However, other notable founders, such as Patrick Henry, were strong proponents of the Christian faith.[13] Several of the Founding Fathers considered themselves to be deists or held beliefs very similar to that of deists. Deism was "the least common denominator" among those who were "men of faith." The phrase *"Nature's God"* was inserted into our Constitution by Thomas Jefferson, a deist whose intention was to lay the foundation of a "civil religion" based upon toleration and respect for all religious faiths. "So Jefferson helped create a society in which different religions could coexist peacefully because of the emphasis on morality over specific belief."[14] Put another way:

---

[11] Frank Lambert, *Founding Fathers and the Place of Religion in America*, (Princeton, NJ, Princeton University Press), 2003.

[12] See en.wikipedia.org/wiki/Founding_Fathers_of_the_United_States#cite_note-13.

[13] Perhaps this explains why he was willing to die if he couldn't have liberty!

[14] Paul Johnson, *The Almost-Chosen People, American History*, R. J. Maddox, ed., vol.I, 10th ed., Guilford, Conn: Dushkin Publishing Group, 1989, p. 37.

The American Deists of the Republican period abhorred both atheism and religious fanaticism. The *Age of Reason* (Paine) was written to dispute atheism and the evil trends Paine saw in France and Europe. To summarize, traditional Deism emphasized reason over revelation and that God/Allah is non-controlling. Human rights are based on Natural Law but morality, to Jefferson, [was based] on God/Allah... Paine wrote: "Religion has two principal enemies, fanaticism and infidelity, or that which is called atheism. The first requires to be combated by reason and morality, the other by natural philosophy." [15]

## The Founding Fathers – The Neo-Pagans

Let us delve into Richard B. Morris' *Seven Who Shaped Our Destiny: The Founding Fathers as Revolutionaries* – for these prominent plutocrats did more to shape our foundations than all the rest combined; although, we must add emphasis to the mercurial figure of one "father" in particular, *Thomas Paine*, whose distinction in the writing of *Common Sense*, was proclaimed by John Adams: "Without the pen of Paine, the sword of Washington would have been wielded in vain."

### Thomas Paine

Yes, the man who "stirred the American colonies to independence" and "history is to ascribe the American Revolution to Thomas Paine" (literally engraved upon his tombstone) had this to say about biblical revelation: "When I see throughout the greater part of this book (the Bible) scarcely anything but a history of the grossest vices and a collection of the most paltry and contemptible tales, I cannot dishonor my Creator by calling it by His name." Or, how about this testimony which vividly places Paine's real feelings in perspective:

"What is it the Bible teaches us? — Rapine, cruelty, and murder. What is it the Testament teaches us? — To believe that the Almighty committed debauchery with a woman engaged to be

[15] See "Who is Nature's God?" www.sullivan-county.com/news/deist1999/jeff_bible.htm .

married, and the belief of this debauchery is called faith. It is the fable of Jesus Christ, as told in the New Testament, and the wild and visionary doctrine raised thereon, against which I content. The story, taking it as it is told, is blasphemously obscene." [16]

Paine was the son of a Quaker. Nigh unto 175 years had passed since the Pilgrims landed on Plymouth Rock, a time when the Puritans held sway. Hence, we see how thoroughly Paine's comments demonstrate a wholly pagan opinion had won the day.

### Benjamin Franklin

Now, we open the mixed bag of one *Benjamin Franklin.* From his speech at the Constitutional Convention, we hear Franklin on a good day:

**Figure 14 - Benjamin Franklin**

"God governs in the affairs of man. And if a sparrow cannot fall to the ground without his notice, is it probable that an empire can rise without His aid? We have been assured in the Sacred Writings that except the Lord build the house, they labor in vain that build it. I firmly believe this. I also believe that, without His concurring aid, we shall succeed in this political building no better than the builders of Babel . . . In the beginning of the contest with Britain, when we were sensible of danger; we had daily prayers in this room for Divine protection. Our prayers, Sir, were heard, and they were graciously answered... do we imagine we no longer need His assistance?"[17]

---

[16] *The Bloody Christian Faith,* Thomas Paine and the *Age of Reason.*

[17] Constitutional Convention, Thursday June 28, 1787.

Of course, he could also be a bit indifferent to prayer. In regards to Franklin's request for prayer at the Constitutional Convention, he noted on his handwritten copy of the speech that, "the Convention, except three or four persons, thought prayers unnecessary."[18]

But what of Ben's nefarious pursuits, in spite of signing all the original documents of our beginning (the *Declaration of Independence,* the *Treaty of Paris*, and the *U.S. Constitution*), he was intimately involved in Freemasonry, let alone in three secret societies in America, France and England. Franklin was master of the *Nine Sisters Lodge,* from which sprang the French Revolution – in England he "joined a rakish political group founded by Sir Francis Dashwood called 'Monks of Medmenham Abbey' also known as the 'Hellfire Club.'"

Franklin's vision of America's beginnings was undergirded by Dashwood, a Member of Parliament and intimate friend of Franklin. The Hellfire Club took part in "forms of satanic worship" as well as "the occult, orgies and parties with prostitutes" – all of which were the "norm" – a most bizarre and ungodly "foundation" indeed!

Ever the scientist, Franklin appears to have, according to the *Sunday Times* article dated February 11, 1998, worked on a coterie of cadavers (at least four adults and six children) at a home under renovation.

The article states: "Initial estimates are that the bones are about two hundred years old and were buried at the time Franklin was living in the house, which was his home from 1757 to 1762 and from 1764 to 1775... Most of the bones show signs of having been dissected, sawn or cut... One skull has been drilled with several holes." The article goes on to state that experiments were performed on these bodies by Dr. William Hewson, who apparently worked alongside the founders of British surgery –

---

[18] For he also famously quipped that lighthouses were more useful than churches (i.e. when shipwrecked "instead of placing a chapel upon the rocks which caused his demise, it had been better to establish a lighthouse thereon").

the good doctor being one of Ben's buddies. Investigators are not sure these bodies were "anatomical specimens that Dr. Hewson disposed of." If the reader were to visit the home today, however, you would be assured that the bones amount to nothing more sinister than "the remains of William Hewson's anatomy school!" We surely hope so.

However, the article also states that the bones were "deeply buried, probably to hide them because grave robbing was illegal" – and suggests that more could and most probably are buried beneath Ben's home... but there's more to this macabre tale. Mixed in with the human remains were those of "animal" remains. These bones, according to the article, were charred or blackened, apparently by fire. Researchers are a bit dubious regarding these discoveries having any "medical" value and suggest that the remains of animals have something to do with *the Hellfire Club.* The "Club" consorted with Satanists wherein "ritual killings of both humans and animals" were rumored.

So were Franklin and his Hellfire friends only working with Hewson to provide the doctor with fresh bodies? Or was something much more hellish going on there? Christian J. Pinto in his Introduction to Tom Horn's *Apollyon Rising 2012* ventures the unspeakable. Indeed, Pinto's analysis certainly disturbs:

> If the humans were medical cadavers, why were they disposed of like so much trash beneath the house? Why not give them some kind of proper burial? If grave robbers could sneak into a graveyard to steal a body, they could also sneak in to put one back. Furthermore, why were the human remains mingled with those of animals? It is worth noting that Dr. Hewson developed an infection from working on one of his cadavers and died from it.

Regarding Franklin's views of Christianity and the Lord Jesus Christ – he answered an Ezra Stiles, then president of Yale University, with a retort that is expressive of folks like Paine and Jefferson; to wit: "I think the system of Morals and his (Jesus') Religion, as he left them to us, the best the world ever saw or is likely to see; but I apprehend it has received various corrupt changes, and I have, with most of the present Dissenters in England, some 'Doubts as to his divinity.'" Further, he suggests that there were "corrupt changes" in the Gospel records – altogether typical of the Founding Fathers, i.e., they complimented the "morality of Christ" but rejected His authority.

### George Washington

Moving to *George Washington,* we certainly hope for better things; however, we may be disappointed. For it isn't easy to get a clear reading on Washington's belief about God or Jesus Christ. We find it necessary to rely upon George's Episcopalian Bishop, James White, who provided naught but vague assertions as to Washington's faith:

**Figure 15 - Lillback's *Sacred Fire***

"I do not believe that any degree of recollection will bring to my mind any fact which would prove General Washington to have been a believer in the Christian revelation further than as may be hoped from his constant attendance upon Christian worship, in connection with the general reserve of his character."

Assisting the good bishop was the Rev. James Abercrombie who apparently ministered to Washington for years. When asked by a Dr. Bird Wilson regarding Washington's faith, Abercrombie replied:

"Sir, Washington was a Deist."

Upon Washington's farewell address as president, certain members of the Christian clergy tried to "obtain a confession of faith, or a clear denial, from Washington" – Thomas Jefferson commented on this in his journal, by saying:

> "Feb 1.—Dr. Rush tells me that he had it from Asa Green (chaplain to the Congress during Washington's presidency) that when the clergy addressed General Washington on his departure from the Government, it was observed in their consultation that he had never on any occasion said a word to the public which showed a belief in the Christian religion and they thought they should so pen their address as to force him at length to declare publicly whether he was a Christian or not. They did so. However, he observed, the old fox was too cunning for them. He answered every article in their address particularly except that, which he passed over without notice....I know that Governor Morris, who pretended to be in his secrets and believed himself to be so, has often told me that General Washington believed no more in the system (Christianity) than he did."

Pinto destroys the edifice erected to Washington's Christianity by authors Jerry A. Lillback and Jerry Newcombe, in their book, *George Washington's Sacred Fire*, in which they seek to unalterably prove Washington to be an ardent Christian.

After a thousand pages of "proof texts" – about the only quote Lillback and Newcombe could deduce from Washington was: "the Religion of Jesus Christ." After which, they set about to destroy their entire hypothesis by quoting Marquis de Lafayette, also a Freemason like Washington, as saying that Washington said: "Being no bigot myself to any mode of worship, I am disposed to indulge the professors of Christianity in the church, that road to Heaven, which to them shall seem the most direct, plainest, easiest, and least liable to exception." There is no need to worry that the camel can't pass through the needle's eye.

Yes, the "road to Heaven" is perhaps one of many pathways to glory? Frankly, Washington used wholly Masonic phraseology. Washington "viewed himself as an outsider to biblical Christianity" and simply *indulged Christians* by his church attendance. Perhaps Washington viewed himself as being a man of

"Christian character" – but this did not confirm his faith in Christ as the Son of God any more than Gandhi's admiration for Jesus made him a Christian instead of a Hindu. To be sure, Washington was a man of esteemed character, deserving of accolades, and worthy to be upheld as a great example of courage and honor. But that does not number him among the elect.

### Thomas Jefferson

How anyone amongst the patriotic pastors can conclude any semblance of Christianity to Tom Jefferson is beyond the pale of human history and reason! Pinto's remarks sentence Jefferson to the abyss, along with the entitlement of ANTICHRIST.

If there ever were a man utterly ruined and spoiled by vain philosophy, it was surely Thomas Jefferson. Along with Thomas Paine, he was America's greatest deceiver and antichrist—if you judge him according to the Scriptures. Jefferson, perhaps more than any other, typifies the last-days 'scoffers, walking after their own lusts' warned about in the Bible (2 Peter 3:3, KJV). Jefferson said this about the book of Revelation in a letter to General Alexander Smyth dated January 17, 1825:

**Figure 16 - The Jefferson Bible**

> "It is between fifty and sixty years since I read it (the book of Revelation) and I then considered it as merely the ravings of a maniac, no more worthy nor capable of explanation than the incoherences of our own nightly dreams."

In that same letter Jefferson made it clear to General Smyth that he had not repented of his tirade regarding the Apocalypse. It is silly to assume that because Jefferson thought Jesus was a fine teacher of morality Jefferson's horrific and damning statements made against Christendom and its biblical figures can be overlooked.

Here's what Jefferson said in a letter to William Short dated October 31, 1819:

> The greatest of all the Reformers of the depraved religion of his own country, was Jesus of Nazareth. Abstracting what is really His from the rubbish in which it is buried, easily distinguished by its luster from the dross of his biographers, and as separable from that as the diamond from the dunghill.

This outburst justified the writing of the infamous *Jefferson Bible* (titled: *The Life and Morals of Jesus of Nazareth*). Likewise, in a letter to John Adams dated January 24, 1814, Jefferson wrote:

> Where did we get the Ten Commandments? The book indeed gives them to us verbatim, but where did it get them? For itself tells us they were written by the finger of God on tables of stone, which were destroyed by Moses.... But the whole history of these books is so defective and doubtful, that it seems vain to attempt minute inquiry into it.... We have a right to entertain much doubt what parts of them are genuine... In the New Testament there is internal evidence that parts of it have proceeded from an extraordinary man; and that other parts are of the fabric of very inferior minds. It is as easy to separate those parts, as to pick out diamonds from dunghills.

Some of the "dunghills" alluded to in the Jefferson Bible included: the virgin birth, the miracles of Christ, the resurrection of Christ and His ascension into heaven – and, of course, that nightmarish text written by John on the supposed Isle of Patmos, the Revelation, which is completely omitted from the Jefferson "Bible." In another letter written to Short on April 13, 1820, Jefferson wrote concerning Jesus Christ:

"Among the sayings and discourses imputed to Him by His biographers, I find many passages of fine imagination, correct morality, and of the most lovely benevolence; and others, again, of so much ignorance, so much absurdity, so much untruth, charlatanism and imposture.... I separate, therefore, the gold from the dross... and leave the latter to the stupidity of some, and roguery of others of His disciples. Of this band of dupes and imposters, Paul was the... first corruptor of the doctrines of Jesus."

### John Adams

As America's third president and in retirement the close friend of Tom Jefferson, John Adams, along with Jefferson and Franklin, diligently worked as a committee to superintend the "masonic" design of the Great Seal of the United States.

Adam's was a Unitarian – his views on Christianity mirrored those of Paine, Jefferson and Franklin. Adams was an "enemy of the Cross of Christ" and boldly declared his animosity: "I almost shudder at the thought of alluding to the most fatal example of the abuses of grief which the history of mankind has preserved — the Cross. Consider what calamities that engine of grief has produced!" (From A letter written to Thomas Jefferson, dated September 3, 1816)

### James Madison

Madison's commitment to the strict separation between the State and Religion is definite, harboring as he did, egregious contempt for the clergy and their religious meddling in the affairs of State. If you were to ask of him whether the Founding Fathers sought to establish a "Christian State" he would be outraged and ask you if you had lost your marbles! "That diabolical, hell-conceived principle of persecution rages among some; and to their eternal infamy, the clergy can furnish their quota of impasse for such business..." [James Madison, letter to William Bradford, Jr., January 1774] Furthermore, he offered this pronouncement: "Ecclesiastical establishments tend to great ignorance and corruption, all of which facilitate the execution of mischievous projects." [James Madison, letter to William Bradford, Jr., January 1774] More lengthy judgments by Madison on the value of religion to government are provided below:

"What influence, in fact, have ecclesiastical establishments had on society? In some instances they have been seen to erect a spiritual tyranny on the ruins of the civil authority; on many instances they have been seen upholding the thrones of political tyranny; in no instance have they been the guardians of the liberties of the people. Rulers who wish to subvert the public liberty may have found an established clergy convenient auxiliaries. *A just government, instituted to secure and perpetuate it, needs them not.*" [Pres. James Madison, *A Memorial and Remonstrance,* addressed to the General Assembly of the Commonwealth of Virginia, 1785]

**Figure 17 - James Madison**

"Experience witnesseth that ecclesiastical establishments, instead of maintaining the purity and efficacy of religion, have had a contrary operation. During almost fifteen centuries has the legal establishment of Christianity been on trial. What has been its fruits? *More or less, in all places, pride and indolence in the clergy; ignorance and servility in the laity; in both, superstition, bigotry and persecution.*" [James Madison, *A Memorial and Remonstrance,* addressed to the General Assembly of the Commonwealth of Virginia, 1785]

"The experience of the United States is a happy disproof of the error so long rooted in the unenlightened minds of well-meaning Christians, as well as in the corrupt hearts of persecuting usurpers, that without a legal incorporation of religious and civil polity, neither could be supported. A mutual independence is found most friendly to practical Religion, to social harmony, and to political prosperity." [James Madison, Letter to F.L. Schaeffer, Dec 3, 1821]

Finally, it has been concluded that the Episcopalian Madison, like Washington, was simply a Deist in disguise – so it is said of him:

> A deist could go to church in the morning, rail against organized religion in the afternoon, and pen a speech in the evening praising the salutary effects of faith. Considered to have been a deist, James Madison, late in life, wrote, "Belief in a God All Powerful wise and good is so essential to the moral order of the World and to the happiness of man, that arguments which enforce it cannot be drawn from too many sources." [19]

### Alexander Hamilton and John Jay

There is some small consolation with two other Founding Fathers. When Alexander Hamilton was shot and killed in a duel with Aaron Burr on July 12, 1804, he was thought to have uttered in his dying breath: "I have a tender reliance on the mercy of the Almighty, through the merits of the Lord Jesus Christ. I am a sinner. I look to Him for mercy; pray for me."

Then there is John Jay – given the fact that our first Chief Justice of the Supreme Court, appointed by President George Washington, was truly an ardent follower of Christ – we are duly obliged to note his dedication to the Savior.

Both gentlemen, however, could hardly be considered vociferous advocates to the concept of a State dedicated to Christianity – although they favored men of Christian persuasion at the helm of government.

## The Rosicrucians: A Rose by Any Other Name

In January 2007, Speaker of the House Nancy Pelosi in the opening of the 110th Congress celebrated the passage of House Resolution 33 in recognizing "the thousands of Freemasons in every State of the Nation...Whereas the Founding Fathers of this great Nation and signers of the Constitution, *most of whom were Freemasons* (our emphasis), provided a well-rounded basis for

---

[19] James Breig, *Deism, One Nation Under A Clockwork God?*

developing themselves and others into valuable citizens of the United States."

David Barton in his book, *The Question of Freemasonry and the Founding Fathers,* wrongly asserts that the Founding Fathers' form of Freemasonry was "Christian" in its essence. Barton contends that Freemasonry was later corrupted by Albert Mackey and Albert Pike. His evidence for this supposed corruption is sketchy at best. Barton's view is not shared with scholars who work in this area and these authors who have read the Masonic texts of Pike and Hall. But even if one dismisses scholars championed by today's Freemasons, we must delve into the historic roots of Freemasonry to determine whether the "tree of masonry" can bear Christian fruit. Was Masonry meant to lend support to the gospel of Jesus Christ?

In Chris Pinto's *Secret Mysteries of America's Beginnings*, he traces American Masonry back to England during the time of Sir Francis Bacon (1561-1626). Sir Francis is considered by most to be the first grand master of modern Masonry. The doctrinal nexus of Freemasonry is the embrace of the world's religions alongside Christianity – this is the "inner core" juxtaposed to the "outer doctrine" of this secret society; furthermore, *Rosicrucianism*, the forerunner of Masonry, must likewise be misunderstood (in so far as its connection with that of Freemasonry) if Masonic ideals are seen to be Christian.

**Figure 18 - The Reverse Side of the Great Seal**

Bacon's confidant was a Dr. John Dee, who was the court astrologer for Queen Elizabeth I. Dr. Dee's sorcery was well known in the court wherein he would "summon demonic spirits to obtain secret knowledge." Dr. Dee was the "chief Rosicrucian" in England. The quest within Rosicrucianism has always been to know the secrets of science (i.e., knowledge) – hence, inquiring demonic powers (or "knowledge from a knowing one") regarding such knowledge is/was commonplace. Dee and Bacon were not "essentially Christian."

Sir Francis Bacon apparently made contact with one of these demonic spirits, including the goddess Pallas Athena – his "inspirer." *Dr. Dee bequeathed England's Rosicrucian Society to Bacon who in turn enclosed it within the system of Freemasonry.* Is there, therefore, any puzzle why Sir Francis Bacon became the father of the modern "scientific method?" Or, is it any wonder why the likes of Ben Franklin and Tom Jefferson were so enthralled by this "method" and religiously followed its pursuits? Not surprisingly, Rosicrucians are proud to claim Franklin and Jefferson as their own.[20] Once touted, unless repudiated, the taint contaminates and convicts.

---

[20] The **Rose Cross** originated as a Christian symbol in the first century, and was later adopted as the primary emblem of the Rosicrucians, an esoteric secret society that originated during the Renaissance. The rose symbolized the redemptive power of the blood of Christ; the symbol as a whole illustrated the triumph of spirit over matter. A deeper, hidden significance of the symbol is the union of the rose of Mary with the Cross of Christ, the union of the divine feminine with the divine masculine. According to author David Flynn, the rose was also a symbol of secrets, reminding Freemasons not to divulge the secrets which they were privileged to learn.

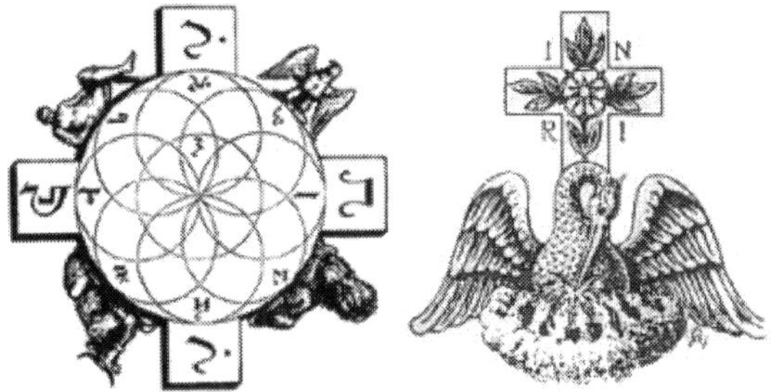


According to Rosicrucian philosophers, the whole Rosicrucian philosophy could be found in the symbol. The rose cross was adopted as a Hermetic occult symbol during the Middle ages, and was later popularized by the Nineteenth century magical order the Golden Dawn. The esoteric meaning of the cross is

The connection between Freemasonry, Rosicrucianism and Gnosticism is likewise irrefutable:

> "Rosicrucians and Freemasons such as George Washington, Benjamin Franklin, Thomas Jefferson, John Adams and Charles Thomson inspired the Constitution of the United States. Thomson, the designer of the Great Seal of the USA, was a member of Franklin's American Philosophical Society, the equivalent of the English 'Invisible College'. The Seal is inspired by the alchemical tradition, inherited from the allegory of the ancient Egyptian *Therapeutate.* The eagle, the olive branch, the arrows and the pentagrams are all occult symbols of the opposite: good and evil, male and female, war and peace, darkness and light. On the reverse (as also on the dollar bills) is the truncated pyramid, indicating the loss of the Old Wisdom, severed, and forced underground by the Church. The rays of ever-hopeful light, incorporating the 'all-seeing-eye', were used as a symbol during the French revolution. Before creating the Republic the USA wanted to create a monarchy. Charles III Stuart was contacted but he refused and the Republic was born.[21]
>
> "The Rosicrucian movement's origins are to be found in the intellectual desire to investigate the inheritance of ancient philosophy and to carry on the quest for the true origin of the human condition. Rosicrucianism, as it is known today, announced its rebirth with the publication of the two 'manifestos' in 1614 and 1615 in Germany. Their author, Christian Rosecreuz, is described as the founder of the ancient order of the Rose Cross. This revival of the Rosy Cross was an attempt to illustrate the more esoteric components of Gnosticism. During this revival Gnosticism found new expression in the promotion of a religious interpretation of alchemy supported by the study of numbers, a science that dates from the construction of the

quite similar to the original; the cross symbolizes the material plane, and the cycle of death and rebirth. The rose represents the unfolding nature of spiritual growth. When the equal armed cross is employed, it has a secret significance: the word lux, or light, can be found hidden in its arms. See webcache. googleusercontent.com/search?q=cache:X1crRjzjXqgJ:www.morrischia.com/ david/portfolio/boozy/research/rosicrucians.html+Rosicrucians+claim+Franklin +and+Jefferson+as+their+own&cd=3&hl=en&ct=clnk&gl=us.

[21] http://www.morrischia.com/david/portfolio/boozy/research/republic.html

> Temple, and the use of Geometry to define the quantity of perfection.
>
> "The manifestos, and the age of enlightenment they promoted, arrived in a Europe ready for profound changes. The Enlightenment in seventeenth and eighteenth centuries France owes its origin in large part to hermetic thought at the core of which we find Gnosticism and its belief in the religious philosophy of tolerance and natural harmony. This revival of Pythagoreanism and Platonism can be seen as an extension of the ancient practice of preserving wisdom through the use of geometry considered as sacred."[22]

Pinto rightly conjectures:

> "Like the Gnostics, the Rosicrucians craved knowledge; it was this desire that led them to worship Lucifer. The secret orders regard Lucifer as the 'angel of light' who, in the form of a serpent, bid mankind to partake of the 'Tree of Knowledge of Good and Evil' so that their eyes would be open and they could become as gods. This is the inner doctrine of Rosicrucianism, Freemasonry, and all the secret orders—and always has been. In the nineteenth century, when Masons like Pike and Mackey (along with leading occultists such as Eliphas Levi and Madame H. P. Blavatsky) described this doctrine in their writings, they were only admitting in print what had been secretly known for centuries. The difference was that with the revolutionary movement, freedom of religion allowed them to publish such things without fear of persecution."

## Masonic Deception

Manly P. Hall has been called "Masonry's greatest philosopher" in America's leading Masonic publication. Hall claims in his text, *The Secret Destiny of America*, deception and pretense are the tools of Masons to camouflage their intentions. The Christian faith broke up paganism's secret societies – driving many of them into obscurity. However, most simply redressed

---

[22] webcache.googleusercontent.com/search?q=cache:X1crRjzjXqgJ:www.morrischia.com/david/portfolio/boozy/research/rosicrucians.html+Rosicrucians+claim+Franklin+and+Jefferson+as+their+own&cd=3&hl=en&ct=clnk&gl=us

themselves in the garb of Christian phraseology, but kept the "secrets" within their core beliefs. Those initiated into the evolving secret societies were "bound to secrecy."

Hall contends that these secret societies have been operational in the Americas for centuries, and that our Founding Fathers of the American Revolution were intimately engaged in these secret societies. But before you brand Hall a conspiracy theorist, consider this relevant fact: How many pagan monuments to the Pantheon of the gods in Washington D.C. were erected by Christians? Or, were those involved in such overtly pagan monuments pretending to be Christians, but inwardly (let alone outwardly) they held to a secret and hidden agenda, just as their "greatest philosopher" tells us?

## Barton's "Christian-Speak" = Apostasy

David Barton's text, *Freemasonry and the Founding Fathers*, disturbingly defends the use of pagan symbols with the following contention (again, quoting from Christian J. Pinto in the preface to Thomas Horn's text, *Apollyon Rising 2012: The Lost symbol Found and the Final Mystery of the Great Seal Revealed)*:

> Americans in recent generations have not been trained in classical literature – a training that was routine in the Founding Era. Therefore, present-day Americans are not inclined to consider structures from the ancient empires (such as the pyramids), or to be familiar with their heroes (such as Cato, Cicero, and Aeneus), or even with their writers (such as Homer, Virgil, Herodotus, and especially Plutarch).
>
> If you take the time to look up the works of Homer, Virgil, etc., you will find that these ancient writers/philosophers were writing about the gods and goddesses of the ancient world. All of these gods are called *devils* in the Bible (I Corinthians 10:20). The same deception is used to describe the statue of Liberty, where reference is made to "Liberty's classical origins." The placard on Liberty Island goes on to say that the statue was based on the Roman goddess *Libertas*. Were the statue judged from a biblical viewpoint, it would tell of Liberty's *demonic* origins. The clever use of the word 'classic' is simply evidence of

> satanic duplicity. David Barton's incredible delusion seems to be that if Satan and his demons are put in a book designated as 'classical literature,' then they are somehow sanitized and no longer offensive to God. But in the Bible, God says, *"Thus shall ye say unto them, The gods that have not made the heavens and the earth, even they shall perish from the earth, and from under these heavens"* (Jeremiah 10:11).

Pinto has a worthy point for Americans to consider: *"Why would any Bible-believing Christian want to build statues and monuments to exalt spiritual powers that God has condemned to destruction?"* How quaint of the Founding Fathers to couch their symbolism within the context of "classical literature" wherein demons somehow derive an air of respectability, acceptance – a sort of a "learning tool"? Or is the adoration implicit in these statutes (to reluctantly reference the title of a Britney Spears' song) "not-so-innocent" after all?

God bless the Dutchman, *Erasmus*, the Catholic reformer (and certainly NOT an atheistic humanist as some ignorantly assume), who surmised their true ontological status: "Under the cloak of reviving ancient literature, paganism tries to rear its head, as there are those among Christians who acknowledge Christ only in name but inwardly breathe heathenism."[23]

As mentioned earlier, author David Barton, is President of the patriotic organization: *WallBuilders*. It seems harsh; nonetheless it remains true that tying Masonic symbolism and pagan statues to America's founding is not justified for Christians sensitive to the spiritual cosmology behind the Bible and the cosmic struggle that continues to rage. If Michael is the angel of Israel, who pray tell might be the angel of America? Could it be Apollyon (Apollo) as Tom Horn speculates is the spirit of Antichrist?

We must be careful to detect which "God is blessing America" lest we be singing to the top of our lungs a National Anthem based upon our evidence that its foundations are steeped in the

---

[23] See http://www.wayoflife.org/database/erasmus.html for a reasonable perspective on the value of Erasmus from the view of Christian orthodoxy.

*Kosmokrator* - "the god of this world, the prince of this age"[24] – who has sinister designs upon that which the reader may have heretofore assumed had naught but a Christian purpose and heritage.

## "GAOTU" – "Great Architect Of the Universe"

Early in its history, Masonry developed a hidden nomenclature of religious drivel (in true Gnostic fashion), allowing divine equivalence amongst the gods of all religions, forming the name of a deity intended not to offend – whom they called GAOTU – "Great Architect of the Universe." They are willing to grant that there is a God, he created the universe, and its design testifies to "a great mind." That is the extent of godly attributes that Masonry advocates. It is a much restricted approach to defining the nature of God.

Our first president when writing to the Massachusetts Grand Lodge on December 27, 1792, entombed: "I sincerely pray that the Great Architect of the Universe may bless you and receive you hereafter into his immortal Temple." Of course, for Washington's statement to be internally consistent (logically following from the limited set of divine attributes of *the Great Architect*), GAOTU must have the ability and willingness to choose to bless his creatures and to determine that eternal life lies implicit in "his plan" of action for the universe - if he invites anyone to his temple; after all, this notion betrays a rather anthropomorphic assumption about God being in any one particular place (e.g., a temple). (It seems to make theological statements without im-

---

[24] From Vine's New Testament Dictionary: "Ruler ***kosmokrator*** denotes "a ruler of this world" (contrast *pantokrator*, "almighty"). In Greek literature, in Orphic hymns, etc., and in rabbinic writings, it signifies a "ruler" of the whole world, a world lord. In the NT it is used in Ephesians 6:12, "the world rulers (of this darkness)," RV, AV, "the rulers (of the darkness) of this world." The context ("not against flesh and blood") shows that no earthly potentates are indicated, but spirit powers, who, under the permissive will of God, and in consequence of human sin, exercise satanic and therefore antagonistic authority over the world in its present condition of spiritual darkness and alienation from God."

plying anything about the nature of God stands as quite a conundrum!) Still, humanity innately seeks to achieve such metaphysical magic. Our language often betrays us!

**Figure 19 - Billington's *Fire in the Minds of Men***

We may be assured that Albert Pike did not invent GAOTU. George Washington and the early American Masons were well familiar with GAOTU. Stop your wonderment – George Washington scarcely mentioned Jesus Christ in all his writings (aside from "the religion of Jesus Christ") and that is precisely why his own pastor called him a Deist! But in founding a nation based upon tolerance and not favoring one religion over another, Washington found it necessary to be our first politically correct statesman! [25]

## Illuminati Symbolism

Not to give Illuminists too much fanfare; they are, however, deeply embroiled in what is branded *Pythagorean Masonry*. The Illuminists (we believe to be an inner core of Freemasonry) are an assortment of intellectuals who set themselves apart through obeisance to the teachings of Greek and Roman philosophers – i.e., the "classical authors."

---

[25] Of course, one can be a committed Christian and still believe in religious freedom and the right for all Americans to choose which creed they wish to affirm. After all, faith derived from pressure isn't in line with New Testament teaching. God only wants willing followers. Coercion is not consonant with the nature of Jesus Christ.

Pythagorean philosophy[26] was embraced by our Revolutionary heroes, the Founding Fathers. Indeed, the Pythagorean Theorem and its *right triangle*, provides rationale, according to Masonic

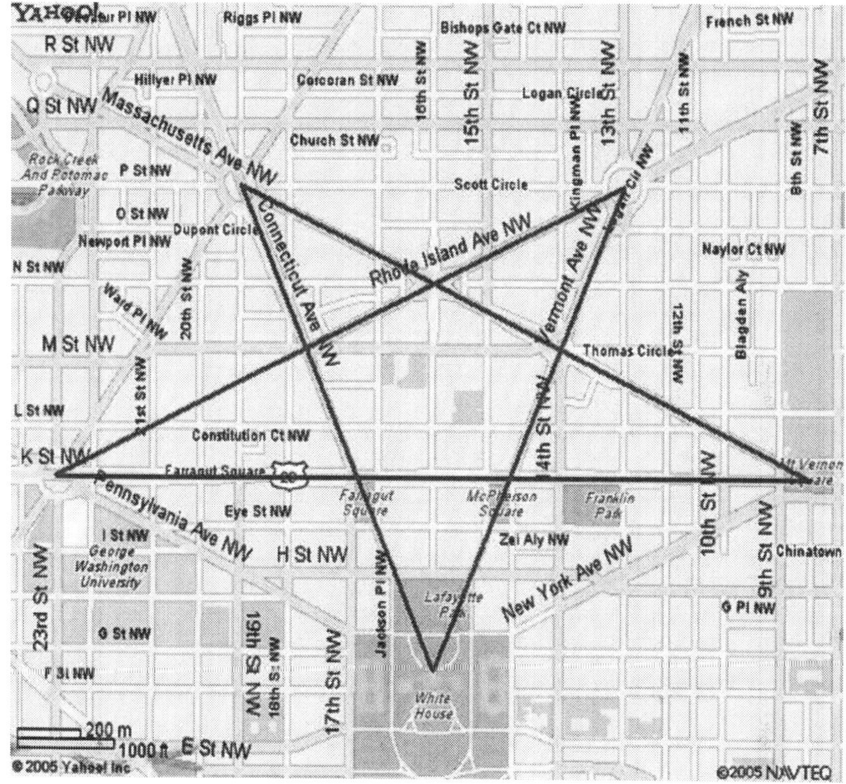


**Figure 20 - The Layout of the Pentagram in Washington DC**

author David Ovason,[27] for the design of the Federal Triangle in Washington DC. Chris Pinto provides a fine summary of James H. Billington's pertinent book:

> Dr. James H. Billington, in his book, *Fire in the Minds of Men*, writes about the revolutionary faith that was inspired by the Bavarian Illuminati. Bear in mind that Billington is not a 'conspiracy writer,' but the thirteenth Librarian of Congress and

---

[26] See plato.stanford.edu/entries/pythagoras/ for an extended discussion.

[27]See www.freemasonry.bcy.ca/anti-masonry/washington_dc/ovason.html.

> a friend of the Bush family. He is as official a historian as you can find. President George W. Bush quoted Billington's book in his 2005 inaugural address after he was elected for his second term. In his exhaustive work, Dr. Billington presents a whole section titled, 'The Pythagorean Passion,' in which he says: 'A vast array of labels and images was taken from classical antiquity to legitimize the new revolutionary faith...
>
> Pythagoras, the semi-legendary Greek philosopher, provided a model for the intellectual-turned-revolutionary. He became a kind of patron saint for romantic revolutionaries.

There should be no surprise that the founder of the Bavarian Illuminati, Adam Weishaupt, named his "final blueprint" for politicized *Illuminism*... ***Pythagorus***.

Billington claims "Revolutionaries... repeatedly attached importance to the central prime numbers of Pythagorean mysticism: one, three, seven, and above all five" (i.e., the Satanic "pentagram"). Interestingly enough, Pythagoras called the pentagram the *pentalpha*, which may account for many Masonic lodges called *Pentalpha lodges*.

There really isn't any controversy as to whether or not the layout of Washington DC has embedded within it such a Pentagram – aerial photos make it obvious. Masons may deny its existence and their responsibility for it and claim that the Rhode Island Avenue's extension which truncates the Pentagram has not occultic meaning. However, we affirm there is more to it than street design merely for traffic purposes. We ask: (1) was the Pentagram intentional or a coincidence in the geometric scheme of things; or (2) why was the Pentagram designed incomplete?

The answer appears to be (2) in that Manly P. Hall, Masonry's greatest philosopher explains: "The pentagram is used extensively in black magic, but when so used its form always differs in one of three ways: The star may be broken at one point by not permitting the converging lines to touch.... When used in black magic, the pentagram is called the 'sign of the cloven hoof' or the 'footprint of the devil.'"

But wasn't Hall writing from the vantage of the Twentieth Century? Were the Founding Fathers familiar with this symbolism? In fact, they were. The greatest Master Mason of all times was *Johann Wolfgang von Goethe.* In his play, *Faust*, he summons Mephistopheles (the Devil) to conclude a pact with him (the infamous "Faustian bargain"). When the Devil tries to depart, he is delayed – leading to the following dialogue between Faust and the devil by another name:

**Figure 21 - A Satanic Pentagram**

> ***Mephistopheles**:*
>
> Let me go up! I cannot go away; a little hindrance bids me stay. The Witch's foot upon your sill I see.
>
> ***Faust:***
>
> The pentagram? That's in your way? You son of Hell, explain to me, If that stays you, how came you in today? And how as such a spirit so betrayed?
>
> ***Mephistopheles:***
>
> Observe it closely! It is not well made; one angle, on the outer side of it, is just a little open, as you see.

There you have it; the "open" or "broken" pentagram is used in *Faust* to summon the Devil as part and parcel of a black magic ceremony. Goethe was not only a Mason but a major player in the Bavarian Illuminati. Moreover, Freemasons are proud to claim Goethe's Masonic symbolisms as their own.

In 1790 the first edition of *Faust* was made – two years later Pierre L'Enfant (no doubt with Thomas Jefferson assisting) designed the streets of Washington DC (1791-1792). It's no quantum leap to suggest that these designers were knowledgeable regarding the "broken pentagram" and its hidden meaning well before the street layout was completed. Perhaps this does not intentionally prove the pentagram's design in Washington DC, but is it such a coincidence that *Faust* and the DC street layout were done in such close chronological proximity? American and European Freemasonry were intertwined – the connection is altogether plausible – L'Enfant and Jefferson could, therefore, have conspired and placed the pentagram at the heart of our nation's Capital!

**Figure 22 – Lord Francis Bacon on Newfoundland Postage Stamp**

Again, David Barton and other Masonic apologists who delight the History Channel repeatedly deny that neither L'Enfant nor Thomas Jefferson were Masons – then they strike out at the "conspiracy theorists" who "slight" the Masons (viz. the Satanic symbol of the pentagram is simply too much for them to admit).

## America: The New Atlantis

Pinto's documentary series, *Secret Mysteries of America's Beginnings*,[28] connects Freemasonry and Rosicrucianism; confirms their origins in Elizabethan England and clearly traces their involvement in the colonization of America. Yes, Christians in the form of the Puritans and Pilgrims made it to our shores, but they were not alone... the "secret societies" saw in America "the New

[28] See http://www.informationliberation.com/?id=12389.

Atlantis" which had been originally envisioned by Sir Francis Bacon. Pinto's discoveries astound: "There is even a 1910 Newfoundland six-cent stamp (with three sixes on it, no less) sporting the image of Bacon that reads: 'Lord Bacon, the Guiding Spirit in Colonization Scheme'."

Sir Francis Bacon's impact upon the New World is unmistakable. He helped organize the Virginia Company and invested some of his wealth in it (Jamestown was financed by The Virginia Company). His occultist philosophies are interwoven into the American experiment. Have you ever wondered who coined the phrase: Knowledge is power? You guessed it, your friendly Rosicrucian-Mason, Sir Francis Bacon, the man from New Atlantis. That knowledge would be pursued through scientific discovery – scientific discovery which has guided and propelled America into the New Atlantis – a society described in Bacon's prescient *The New Atlantis* whose structures reached to the heavens, wherein flying machines and weapons of mass destruction would be built (and incessant pleasures and entertainment abounds). Bacon's vision, if not blueprint, has many remarkable dreams (some not so pleasant) that have come true, including the magnification of sounds and animal experimentation for the benefit of humanity.

Mather Walker entitles Bacon's *New Atlantis* as *The Land of the Rosicrucians* (See: *Mather Walker's Light on Bacon's New Atlantis*).[29] Have these secret societies not achieved many of their most wretched goals? Alas! Rising up out of the sea – the New Atlantis! Tragically, except for the Puritans and other souls seeking freedom from persecution, this was the strategy for our great land developed by its financiers and intellectual godparents.

## Conclusion

Remember well, the "innermost doctrine of Masonry" is *Rosicrucianism.* And the "intrinsic mingling" (where two ele-

[29]See http://www.sirbacon.org/mwlightatlantis.htm.

ments are indistinguishable) of *Christianity with paganism* takes place within the crucible of the so-called American experiment – an instance of political alchemy to be sure.

Recall also that a Rosicrucian can quote the Scriptures and point to Jesus and His salvific qualities while simultaneously extolling the virtues of Plato, Aristotle and any number of Greco-Roman celebrities – gazing upon their pantheon of gods in the same way that Alice Bailey's followers of "The New Age" speak of the "Great Ascended Masters" and their Lord Maitreya, the Buddhist Messiah, as merely differing incarnations or avatars that, according to their statements, seek to lead humanity to a better day! From their sayings, Jesus was but one of them!

Christians, who see discernment a requisite duty, know better.

We wrestle not against "flesh and blood" (Ephesians 6:12). *Our archenemies are not terrorists, communists, or liberals, but unseen forces which wage their warfare against the one true God and His saints.*

The Mystery Religions of Babylon have been incorporated into the New Atlantis! Yet we are but Pilgrims and Strangers who seek a *City Whose Builder and Maker is God* – not a Masonic Lodge amidst the New Atlantis as envisioned by Sir Francis Bacon.

Our Christian commitment, rightly understood (assuming the reader is a Christian), comes first. As such, the Bible teaches us that we remain today a stranger and a pilgrim – *we have here no continuing city (a place to feel 'at home',* Hebrews 13:14) – but we seek such a safe haven – for our citizenship is in heaven from whence comes our salvation.

From the pen of Paul, the Apostle to the Gentiles – especially to one, most accomplished of intellect, Thomas Jefferson, and to all who carelessly embrace our Founding Fathers as stalwart purveyors of the Christian faith, a warning:

> *Howbeit we speak wisdom among them that are perfect: yet not the wisdom of this world, nor of the princes of this world, that come to naught:*

> *But we speak the wisdom of God in a mystery, even the hidden wisdom, which God ordained before the world unto our glory:*
>
> *Which none of the princes of this world knew: for had they known it, they would not have crucified the Lord of glory. (I Corinthians 2:6-8).*

Hal Lindsey shares a personal anecdote upon visiting a seaside prison in Rome (the Mamertine Prison, *Carcere Mamertino*). Lindsey witnessed a plaque that commemorated the circumstances surrounding the death of Paul the Apostle there. When Paul was beheaded, he was put to death in the company of many from the Pretorian Guard, Caesar's personal bodyguards. We do not mean that they witnessed his death. We mean that they died alongside him. *They were Romans as few citizens of Rome could claim.* And yet, no doubt after one to two years of his preaching and teaching, they committed their lives to Christ and elected to die alongside Paul.

May their identification with Paul's vision of that heavenly city (Hebrews 11:10),[30] be our own – for we should not dream of the New Atlantis as envisioned by Francis Bacon and the secret societies which flourished among our Founding Fathers. It is appropriate to aspire to governance that institutes the separation of Church and State, and which protects the free pursuit of religion by the governed. Nevertheless, striving for utopian government is an ill-conceived objective which denies the fallen state of humanity. Believers in the God of revelation and authority must come to terms with what Paul undoubtedly taught the Praetorian guards, his disciples and fellow martyrs. In the words of his the apostle John: *"We know that we are of God, and that the whole world lies in the power of the evil one"* (I John 5:19, NASV).

---

[30] *"For he [Abraham] looked for a city which hath foundations, whose builder and maker [is] God."*

# Chapter 5:
# Why America IS the Final Babylon

## The Most Compelling Arguments

THE VARIOUS AUTHORS PARTICIPATING IN THIS VOLUME IDENTIFY MANY REASONS WHY AMERICA APPEARS TO BE THE SUPREME AND FINAL BABYLON. SOME RATIONALES ARE BASED PRIMARILY on scripture; some, on the basis of logic or reason. The Daughter of Babylon possesses dozens of qualities identified in the books of Jeremiah and Revelation. In light of the teaching of numerous competent forebears as we mentioned at the outset of this work (especially R.A. Coombes to whom we are in debt), almost seventy citations can be enumerated by the authors who provide detailed characteristics of the most evil dominion of the last days by examining the Scriptures.

In this chapter, our intention is to focus on what amounts to be *the most compelling arguments that America* – at the very least – plays a pivotal role in creating the conditions for the Antichrist. While we occupy ourselves in this book predominantly with biblical reasons to see America as THE FINAL BABYLON, in this chapter we emphasize a series of logical reasons why it is highly unlikely that any other geopolitical power base will arise to overtake America in this decade or the decades which lie ahead.

To repeat the premise at the beginning of this book, the standard prophetic scenario of Hal Lindsey, Tim LaHaye, and Grant Jeffrey, assumes that Europe – a revived Roman empire—will host the Antichrist and his evil empire. The contrarian prophetic scenario suggests that it will be America (aligned with European states) and not Europe (absent America or for that matter a confederacy of Islamic states) that serves as the power base for the future Führer; for he will arise as the latter-day King of Babylon. The United States of America will be THE FINAL BABYLON of the Bible, the whore hated by the Beast (Revelation 17:16) and the Kings of the earth; but upon whose powers and dominion they rely to achieve their end – to build a single, global empire – the desire of occultists and mystics down through the ages. This coming king of Babylon will be *the Eleventh Horn*, arising from among the original ten (Daniel 7:8, 20-21, 24-25, 8:9-12).

## One: America's Historical Religious Aspirations Reflect Babylonian Religion

In *Power Quest, Book One: America's Obsession with the Paranormal*, Woodward laid the groundwork for the identification of America with the Daughter of Babylon by tracing how America's "natural" spiritual inclinations have influenced the world toward paganism. The influences of "Anglo-American" authors were enormously influential in the formation of Adolf Hitler's occult worldview which grounded the Vril, the Thule Society, the return to Germany's "Hyperborean" and Teutonic myths, and even the Atlantean cult of racial theory contributing to Anti-Semitism.

America's spiritualism was rampant throughout the nineteenth century from the "burned out district" in rural New York (a region constantly "burned with the fire of religious revivals"); to the pietism of the German Johan Kelpius predicting Pennsylvania to be the locus of Christ's Return in 1694; to the *Transcendentalism* of Emerson, Hawthorne, and Alcott in mid-nineteenth century Concord, Massachusetts; to the hundreds of mediums and channelers which became a national obsession of "parlor tricks" and crystal ball gazing all across New York and New England; to the high-water mark of the 1880's founding of the Theosophical Society by Madame Helena Petrovna Blavatsky and her charmed companion, Henry Steel Olcott at their "Lamasery" at 47th and 8th in Manhattan. [1]

But the biggest factor was the growth and development of the Freemasons in America. Freemasonry grew from the very begin-

---

[1] Together, they led the effort to give an Americanized version of Buddhism as a gift back to the Asians (India) and Africans (Sri Lanka) where it was actually "on the way out".

ning with the Founding of Jamestown. The Founders of our country, particularly Benjamin Franklin and George Washington, were at the center of Masonic beliefs and influence. Some scholars even believe the English lost the Revolutionary War with America because, in part at least, they couldn't put their heart into fighting fellow Masons.

At the heart of these religious affirmations was the primacy of personhood. Unlike eastern Buddhism which denied the importance of the individual, Theosophy and Freemasonry both emphasized *personal power quests* achieved through occultic rituals and beliefs. Combined with a penchant for scientific understanding, America blended these and concocted a perfect "religion" for the last days—the philosophy which interpreted the miraculous in light of modern physics' theories along with occultic teaching (minus the devil's horns and hoofs of course). It is our argument that this pagan-oriented philosophy is well-reflected in the so-called New Age Movement of the twentieth century and the 2012 "movement" of today. Furthermore, it is our considered opinion that it is primarily this "religion" (and not Islam) which becomes *the one-world religion of the last days.*[2]

## Two: America's National Symbols Reflect Egyptian Paganism

Our friends and fellow writer/researchers, Tom Horn, Rob Skiba, and many other contemporary authors have pointed out the many and amazing references built into our Nation's capital

---

[2] This religion places humankind at the center of things, but calls upon the individual to learn how to interact with spiritual forces "on the other side"—often through the exploitation of drugs, tantric sex, and physical means to put oneself into a trance where the spiritual encounter can take place. The core element is the seeking of "transcendence"—the hope to prove the validity of spiritual experience at the risk of doing battle with superhuman beings who seek our destruction, not our benefit despite what many proponents argue (see Graham Hancock's book *Supernatural* (2007) to explore this dangerous agenda). Today's "contemplative movement" within the "Emergent Church" is indicative of this transcendence, opening the door to the "spirit world."

city. Dan Brown makes his fictional Symbologist Robert Langdon take a guided tour of many buildings in Washington D.C (albeit "with a gun to his head" so to speak) in his book, *The Lost Symbol.* This "tour by force" (forgive the pun) educates the reader on the many aspects of how the Nation's seat of power was conceived by George Washington and Charles L'Enfant to reflect the great capitals of Europe, particularly, Rome and Athens, connecting America's ideals with the "Great Work" of Freemasonry and the symbols of Egypt.[3] *The Capitol Building* mirrors Rome's Pantheon while the world's largest obelisk, *The Washington Monument*, reflects Egypt's Heliopolis (the City of the Sun) with its temples and monuments to the sun god, Ra or

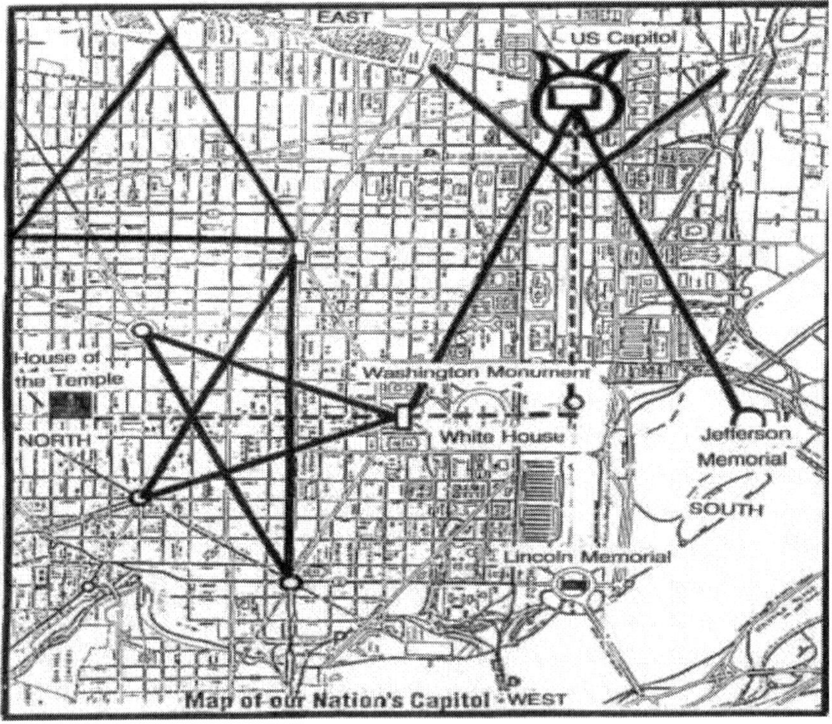


**Figure 23 - The Original Layout of Washington DC**

---

[3] Robert Bauval and Graham Hancock in their recent book, *The Master Game (2011),* document how Paris was also a modern day "City of the Sun" in its street structure, reflecting Heliopolis in many details. Washington D.C. is not alone as architectural symbol for the cult of Rosicrucians and Freemasons.

Atum (the single creator god at the helm of the nine gods of the Ennead).[4] That its height is 6,660 inches and its width 666.0 (555' x 55') inches hardly seems coincidental. The phalanx (and phallus) of the obelisk adjacent to the Capitol dome (the not-so-divine feminine counterpart) isn't missed on Horn who recognizes the distinctly sexual symbolism intrinsic in this architecture. It reflects ancient religions which believed our connection to the divine was best achieved through sexual rituals. Specifically, "hooking up" sexually put us in touch with the supposed divinity "natural religions" believed was intrinsic to "humankind".[5] By engaging in ritual sex, humans would encounter the divine. More specifically, one could "communicate with the gods" via the prophets of BAAL for commercial fees and receive economic insight for a price paid to temple prophets (aka "prostitutes") whose "prophetic services" were designed to make merchants

---

[4] Of course, the Washington Monument wasn't completed until after the Civil War (built between 1848 and 1884) and its original design was necessarily to be a "free standing" obelisk. However, it is significant that in the end, this is exactly what was constructed. The "Powers that Be" seemed to arrange this—it seems unlikely it was accidental.

[5] It is indeed the pinnacle of misinterpretation (if not blasphemy) that the physical encounter and intimacy between man and woman should be seen as a substitute for the relationship between God and the singular human being. No doubt, it is the exhilaration of the sexual experience that causes the "natural man" (as Paul depicts humans apart of God) to sense an "out of the ordinary" event mistaken for divine ecstasy (as the mystics would characterize the interaction). But it is also the false assumption that a spiritual union between the divine and human simply implies ecstasy as is typified in sexual experience. Others (Martin Buber, the Jewish Philosopher), discuss the "I-Thou experience" and (Schleiermacher) the "feeling of absolute dependence". Likewise, there is "dread" that comes from encountering the "holiness" of God—God as absolutely distinct and different from human beings; another sentient experience more appropriate and fitting for the Judeo-Christian encounter with God. The whole subject of mysticism (the confrontation between human and the divine) is not really well expressed in the evangelical's standard phraseology of "having a personal relationship with Jesus Christ". And yet, it is somewhat contained within the Psalmist expression of the "soul which yearns for God as a deer pants for the water brook". But we're afraid that now we've wandered too far from the topic!

rich or feel that their deals would ingratiate the commercial enterprise, while pleasing the gods.

David Ovason, a Freemason, has written the definitive work on this topic (*The Secret Architecture of Our Nation's Capital*). There are those who dispute these arguments and believe we are reading too much into the lay-out of the streets with the implied "compass and square" and various other features seen in the city street map. Then again, if you ask the leaders of the Freemason's National House of the Temple exactly 13 blocks north of the White House (often featured on Discovery and History Channels discussing Freemasonry and denying the conspiracy behind this secret society), they ignore the testimony of their greatest teachers and philosophers, Albert Pike and Manly Hall. In their writings it is clear these designs were intentional. They were certainly symbols to provoke the imagination. They might have even been talismans, providing triggers for the invoking of a divine presence in Washington D.C. Without question, Pike and Hall "made no bones about it" (there is a pun in there somewhere): Freemasonry was on a mission to liberate humankind from religion and dogma; to establish a nation governed by men of reason with democratic ideals; and to implement *The Great Plan* to which we alluded at the outset.

Tom Horn, in his landmark book, *Apollyon Rising: 2012*, addresses the meaning behind the *Great Seal of the United States*, featured on the back of the one-dollar bill. Complete with the many "thirteens" populating *The Great Seal,* is the "eye of Horus" – a long-standing symbol of secret societies and Egyptian mysticism – as well as the Great pyramid itself, a not so-subtle reminder of the land of Egypt and its religion from which the cult of Freemasonry is derived.

If America isn't the Daughter of Babylon, at the very least it certainly deserves the appellation *the daughter of Egypt*. However, as any good mythologist knows, when you work your way backwards from Roman and Greek mythology, you stop in Egypt only briefly; eventually you wind your way back to the land of the Chaldeans. All mythology has Babylon as it singular parent. Babylon stands as the "Mother of all Mythology." Hislop's book, which we have reviewed in detail already, was dedicated to this proposition. More recently, researcher Rob Skiba's first book, *Babylon Rising* (2012), provides substantial support to this thesis too. Skiba provides a sound (and conversational) study on the development of ancient mythology in its modern forms.

## Three: America's Inclusion of Nazi Socialism Corrupted Our Government

*Power Quest, Book Two: The Ascendancy of the Antichrist in America*, centers on the incursion of German national socialists (Nazis) into the United States (and more broadly, the entire Western hemisphere) after World War II. The thesis stated succinctly: *America knowingly and intentionally invited the spirit of Antichrist into our land.* Out of fear, we were motivated to fight Soviet Communism and stave off atheistic Marxism.

However, in our drive to safeguard our society we enabled the occultic (even satanic) powers of the Nazis to infest many of our most vital governmental institutions. Our leaders determined that we could not afford to allow Nazi technology to be superintended by the Soviets. Consequently, as the war ended not only were the allies racing to Berlin to conclude the colossal world-wide fight, they were vying for specific outposts of vaunted German technologies to grab this knowhow and the great minds of Nazi science before "the other guy" got them. The American population today has little idea how much was at stake. Technologies exceeding our wildest imagination (at least for the average citizen, not for most of our military intelligence apparatus) were available for the plunder.

Additionally, *Power Quest, Book Two* documents how deals were cut with noted war criminals to obtain select intelligence and science assets. Reinhard Gehlen, the head of the Soviet desk for Nazi intelligence, made a pact with Allen Dulles (the future head of the CIA), bringing his entire eastern front intelligence operation into America's OSS (the forerunner of the CIA). Gehlen did much to heighten the intensity of the Cold war, most likely overstating the threat to enhance his status and to build his organization. Likewise, Werner von Braun, along with other notable German rocket scientists, brought their entire 100-man plus rocket science team to the U.S. to lead the way in our race into space. This illegal immigration process was the major coops of Project Paperclip.[6] It just so happens that this deal may have involved Clay Shaw, the indicted subject of Jim Garrison (the New Orleans Prosecutor) who brought Shaw to trial in the purported conspiracy to kill John F. Kennedy. This intriguing link was only a foreshadowing of many more associations between the Nazis, the CIA, and the plot to kill the President as documented in Woodward's book.

Also covered in Woodward's *Power Quest, Book Two* were the many intelligence operations employed by our government to exploit Nazi science. These "ops" ranged from controlling the minds of "Manchurian Candidates" to controlling the opinion of the population at large by manipulating the media (if not outright purchasing it). Many other diabolical tasks are laid out in detail – actions that are as dastardly as they are disturbing.

The bottom line was that America leadership aided and abetted the Nazi goal of establishing "the Fourth Reich" by infiltrating the nations of Europe and the Americas. The story of the "ratlines" was another highlight of the book, a path to freedom developed at War's end by the Catholic Church enabling the escape of Nazi war criminals. Like the United States, the Catholic Church was apparently motivated by its fear of atheistic communism and found in the Nazis a suitable partner to fight Marxism; although author Dave Hunt in his classic *The Woman Rides the Beast* (1994) argues that other self-serving motivations were in play.

---

[6] So named because false dossiers were paper-clipped over the true biographical records of the Nazis we brought into our country—breaking the rule President Harry Truman demanded—that no Nazi with a criminal record be allowed in.

In the final analysis, America demonstrated a horrific shortfall in morality. We put war criminals into major leadership roles. We utilized occult practices to fight the communists (namely the esoteric technique known as *remote viewing*). We employed torture on our own citizens to gain leverage in the intelligence "war." And we facilitated the murder of our own President (Kennedy) to ensure that our military-industrial complex would flourish – all in the name of fighting "godless communism." In so doing, we grew as evil as the enemy we feared. In this fiendish pursuit, America lost its way and sold its soul.

So it is that the United States of America appears to have chosen, on its own accord, to become the Bible's *Daughter of Babylon.*

## Four: America's Financial Dominance Unlikely to be Usurped before the Lord Returns

America is the most dominant financial powerhouse in the world. There really is no contest. It is certainly true that the City of London (the center of British financial influence) has been a major player throughout the past two centuries. However, it is England's colonial offspring – sitting pretty on Wall Street in Manhattan – which calls the shots in the world. America's economic power is awesome and unequaled. To bring our economy to its knees requires more than financial crisis alone.

The Babylon of Revelation 17 and 18 stands for many things. But above all else, it exists as a dominating economic center with which all the "kings of the earth" cooperate. *"For all nations have drunk of the wine of the wrath of her fornication, and the kings of the earth have committed fornication with her, and the merchants of the earth are waxed rich through the abundance of her delicacies"* (Revelation 18:3). When she is destroyed suddenly and absolutely it brings the economy of the world to a precipice it will never bridge: *"And the merchants of the earth shall weep and mourn over her; for no man buyeth their merchandise any more"* (Revelation 18:11). John, the author of

Revelation describes the extent of Babylon's financial hegemony with extensive colorful images emphasizing how complete is its control:

> [11] *The merchandise of gold, and silver, and precious stones, and of pearls, and fine linen, and purple, and silk, and scarlet, and all thine wood, and all manner vessels of ivory, and all manner vessels of most precious wood, and of brass, and iron, and marble,*
>
> [12] *And cinnamon, and odours, and ointments, and frankincense, and wine, and oil, and fine flour, and wheat, and beasts, and sheep, and horses, and chariots, and slaves, and souls of men.*
>
> [13] *And the fruits that thy soul lusted after are departed from thee, and all things which were dainty and goodly are departed from thee, and thou shalt find them no more at all.*
>
> [14] *The merchants of these things, which were made rich by her, shall stand afar off for the fear of her torment, weeping and wailing (Revelation 18:11-14).*

This city sits on many waters, controlling peoples, multitudes, nations and tongues. *"And the woman which thou sawest is that great city, which reigneth over the kings of the earth"* (Revelation 17:18). Author Patrick Heron comments:

> So this great city is just that; a city. It is not a country or a Muslim empire or a religious denomination. Scripture repeatedly informs us that it is a great and powerful city. This city does two things here. It reigns over these kings or rulers... and the waters it sits amongst represent a multitude from every nation and tongue and people and language. This clue means that the citizens of this city are multi-cultural and have arrived to live in this metropolis from the four corners of the globe." [7]

As Heron infers, the city is unequaled in many categories. But its reign over the kings of the earth begins with its financial clout. Heron, like these authors, believes the final Babylon of the

---

[7] Heron, Patrick, *Return of the Antichrist and New World Order*, Kindle Location 1560.

Bible's prophets is New York City while the land of Babylon (Chaldea) is the United States of America. New York with her Statue of Liberty standing like a sentinel in its harbor fulfills the stark and ominous symbol of Babylon (aka The Daughter of Babylon).

As mentioned earlier, John Price author of *The End of America* (mentioned earlier) writes, "In this regard, the biggest shock to this writer, in beginning to re-study what the Bible calls the 'mystery' of the identity of the Daughter of Babylon, was that, contrary to the formerly prevailing general belief that America is not in Biblical prophecy, America, as it turns out, is a major player on the prophetic end times world stage."[8]

Price continues with this striking analysis:

> As we enter further into the end times, we can rationally conclude, that America has a major, even a pre-imminent role in the events of the last days, before the return of Christ. Sadly, though, America's role appears to come to an abrupt end before the final years of the end times. Surprising as it may seem to some, the Author of the Word has provided to us a great deal of detail about the United States of America in the end times. Frankly, that's what we would expect from the Creator of the Universe. Daniel described God, as *"the revealer of mysteries" and "a God in heaven who reveals mysteries"* (Daniel 2: 28 and 29). The following prophetic verses all deal with a nation described directly and implicitly as the "Daughter of Babylon" or "Babylon the Great" ... These are the prophetic verses describing the end of a rich and powerful end times nation: Psalm 137: 8; Isaiah 13; 21: 1-10; 47 and 48; Jeremiah 50 and 51; Zechariah 2:7; [and] Revelation 17 and 18.
>
> These prophecies total 223 verses–223 amazing verses. Some who have seriously studied these prophetic verses have concluded they refer to events to take place on the site of ancient or historical Babylon, even concluding that the ruins of Babylon, which Saddam Hussein partially restored, will be the Daughter

---

[8] Price, John (2011-05-15), *The End of America - The Role of Islam in the End Times and Biblical Warnings to Flee America,* Christian House Publishing, Inc., Kindle Locations 506-509.

> of Babylon. Some, on the other hand, have interpreted these verses as referring to an end times Church or denomination. In the years since the 17th century authors interpreted the verses, primarily those from Revelation, as referring to the Roman Catholic Church. The clash of interpretations is quite stark: do these end times verses, yet unfulfilled on their face, refer to modern day Iraq, do they describe modern day America, or is there another possible nation to which they could refer?

Price believes the answer to his hypothetical question isn't Iraq and it isn't another unnamed country yet to emerge from the sea of nations thrashing to and fro (the analogy often used by Bible prophets to depict political tumult). It is America.

Until exactly 11 years ago, few Bible scholars would have considered the possibility that the infamous "Mystery – Babylon" could have been New York City. The United States homeland seemed secure. But everything changed in a matter of a few hours on that fateful, late summer morning.

With the lethal destruction of the World Trade Center on September 11, 2001, and the murder of over 3,000 persons, most of them Americans, the unthinkable happened. As a result of the attack, the world economy took a massive nose dive. Unquestionably, the stock markets were already suffering before this event. But the Twin Towers collapsed in less than two hours. After the airplanes struck the Towers, the financial world fell almost as fast. In March of 2000, the NASDAQ Exchange had hit 5048. After 9/11, NASDAQ fell to under 1500, a drop of almost 70%. After a slow recovery to over 2500, with the failure and debacle of newly engineered *derivatives* (assets based on leveraging high-risk mortgage loans and even the "insurance" set up to protect such investments), eight years later the house of cards buckled yet again. This second assault (likely also caused by Al-Qaida through massive short-selling of Lehman Brothers[9]) plunged the world into an economic crisis from which it still staggers.

---

[9] See Kevin Freeman's book, *Secret Weapon: How Economic Terrorism Brought Down the U.S. Stock Market and Why it Can Happen Again*, 2012, for an

Next up in the economic house of horrors: the current-day degrading of sovereign debt – with a number of nations across Southern Europe on the precipice of default. Greece is in desperate straits and could soon sink. But Spain, Portugal, Italy and even Ireland are also at risk. However, compared with much of Europe, despite its $16 trillion in federal debt, the United States still appears to be a safe haven for very large-scale investors.

While many politicians in the heat of a Presidential election bemoan the rise of China as an economic powerhouse, it still represents only a fraction of the value of the United States' economy. It is important to note that China is investing in us. China wouldn't be investing in the United States if it believed America was bound to fail. Consequently, any theory (even if based on a different biblical interpretation to ours) that suggests America and Wall Street will soon be displaced by the power of Europe – which the standard prophetic scenario does – only needs to study what has happened in the European community over the past few years. America's credit may have dropped from a rating of "A+" to "A" and our debt may have soared to heights previously unimaginable, but the U.S. still towers above all other nations in our ability to produce and consume. According to author Price, the gross national product (GNP) of the world is $48.25 trillion. The U.S. amounts to over 27.3% of this, or $13.19 trillion. China is a distant second, coming in at $2.64 trillion. In other words, the GNP of the U.S. is five times that of China. Many would guess that Saudi Arabia with its vast oil revenues would be a major player in the GNP game. Not so. Its GNP amounts to only $349 billion. The U.S. is fifty (50) times that of Saudi Arabia.

This financial engine, despite concerns expressed by partisan politicians, likely will only be tamed by *destructive forces beyond economics* – which is exactly what the Bible predicts.

---

extensive argument that an economic attack led by Muslim enemies of America were to blame for the woes of 2008.

> "The merchants of these things, which were made rich by her, shall stand afar off... saying, 'Alas, alas, that great city, that was clothed in fine linen, and purple and scarlet, and decked with gold, and precious stones and pearls. For in one hour so great riches is come to naught.' And every shipmaster, and all the company in ships, and sailors, and as many as trade by sea, stood afar off... And cried when they saw the smoke of her burning... saying, *"alas, alas, that great city, wherein were made rich all that had ships in the sea by reason of her costliness, for in one hour is she made desolate"* (Revelation 18: 3, 11-13, 15-19).

There are many doomsday prophets who continue to predict that the rich and powerful *Illuminati* are ready to make a power play to intentionally destroy our economy to force the country into Martial Law and lead the world into global government. However, to these authors such a pathway to globalism seems unlikely – even if it has been envisioned by such a cabal. Besides being summarily illogical, it is inconsistent with what the Bible predicts if this interpretation of the Daughter of Babylon is correct. Instead of a self-imposed financial crisis by elites, it appears instead that some manner of cataclysmic destruction will be the cause of Babylon's downfall. The enemies of Babylon will be summoned by the God of the Bible: "... a sword is upon her treasures..." (Jeremiah 50: 37b). It will be a judgment – truly of biblical proportions – that will be the undoing of Mystery – Babylon.

If the Lord tarries for another 50 years, another nation, city, and economic center may arise and overcome New York City and Wall Street. As we have already pointed out, many continue to believe that the historic Babylon will be rebuilt and become a literal fulfillment of the prophecies of Babylon. But if we live in the "last days of the last days" as most prophecy scholars now affirm – and the Lord returns soon – there is only one city which bears any resemblance to Babylon as depicted in Jeremiah, Isaiah, Zechariah, and Revelation: That city is named New York City. And the "land of the Chaldeans" is the United States of America.

## Five: America's Military Dominates the World – We Remain the One and Only Superpower

Ultimately to completely upset America's fiscal applecart takes more than a mere economic crisis. According to the Bible, it will take war on our soil to end our financial dominance: "And [they] cried when they saw the smoke of her burning, saying, *"What [city is] like unto this great city!"* "*And a mighty angel took up a stone like a great millstone, and cast [it] into the sea, saying, 'Thus with violence shall that great city Babylon be thrown down, and shall be found no more at all'*" (Revelation 18:18, 21).

In today's geopolitical situation, who would dare make war against America on the battlefield?[10]

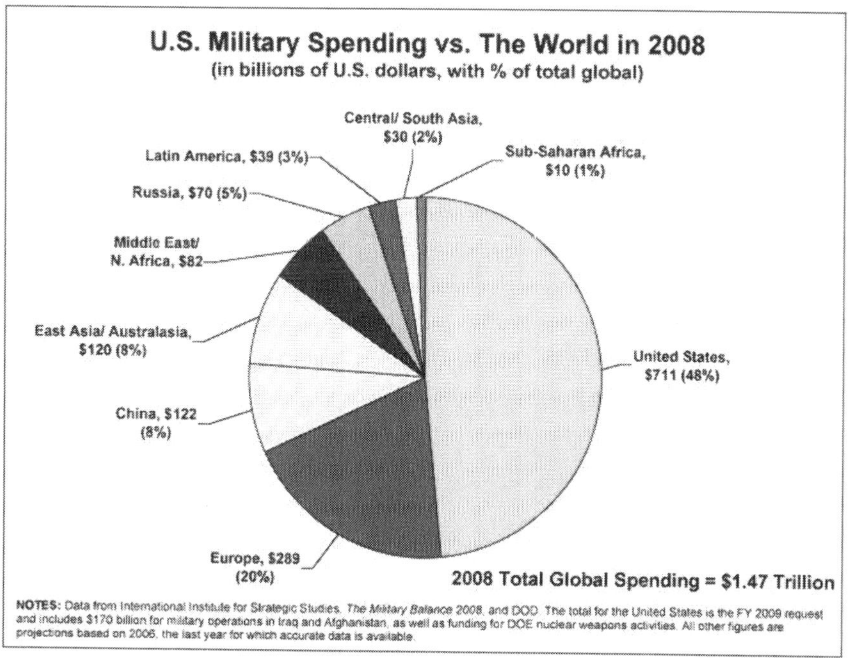


**Figure 24 - The U.S. Military Spend compared to the Rest of the World**

---

[10] *"And they worshipped the dragon which gave power unto the beast: and they worshipped the beast, saying, Who* [is] *like unto the beast? Who is able to make war with him?"* (Revelation 13:4)

In 2003, when we invaded Iraq it took the U.S. military only about two weeks (along with a few enlisted nations in a "coalition of the willing") to take apart the world's fifth largest military. Moreover, as daunting as our economic hegemony is, our military power stands even more supreme. America's military prowess reigns unequaled. We spend six times what China spends on defense. We have 11 carrier groups to 1 for Russia and 1 for China.[11] We have almost 80 submarines compared to 48 for Russia, China at 58 (and surprisingly, North Korea at 53). Our sophistication in nuclear weapons remains capable of destroying our enemies before they could unleash a counter-attack. However, as impressive as these capabilities are, the real advantage is dispersion. Because of our global presence, we have logistical advantages in every way over our closest rivals.

Few citizens of our great country realize that we maintain over 865 bases (according to the Pentagon[12]) and this is before the count is updated with bases in Iraq and Afghanistan. Including those bases, counting both large and small, the U.S. possesses over 1,000 military bases at a cost exceeding $102 billion annually. [13] Remarkably, we continue to maintain 227 bases in Germany consisting of 6,000 plus buildings amounting to over one million square feet. [14] This footprint may have made sense during the Cold War. But does it still seem like a good thing to do when our country is choking on enormous debt?

Clearly, something else must be going on here – much more than the U.S. looking out for American-only interests. There must be larger reasons for serving as the global military power. And – of course – there is. There are profits to be made, there

---

[11] See http://www.globalfirepower.com/countries-comparison.asp for detailed comparisons of the many different military elements composing the world's armies, navies and air power

[12] See the Pentagon's data http://www.defense.gov/pubs/ BSR_2007_ Baseline.pdf.

[13] Professor Hugh Gusterson, "The Bulletin of Atomic Scientists," March 18, 2009. See www.globalresearch.ca/PrintArticle.php?articleId=12785

[14] Ibid., Pentagon's data.

are stock targets to be hit, and there are the lifestyles of the rich and famous to be maintained – not just for America, but for England, France, Germany, our other European allies, including Japan and South Korea. To achieve corporate economic goals, military power is essential. In 1991, after the fall of the Soviet Union, V.P. Dick Cheney, then head of the Defense Department, requested Paul Wolfowitz develop a strategic plan for U.S. world domination as the sole remaining super power.[15] Although implemented partially by Bill Clinton's regime, upon his election George W. Bush along with V.P. Cheney drew upon the Wolfowitz plan placing neo-cons Donald Rumsfeld and Wolfowitz at the Department of Defense fully implementing the kinder, gentler strategy for world domination. No doubt this included a larger force strategically positioned in the middle of the Middle East.

In essence, the big brush strokes to the plan were plain: American influence must be continued – ad infinitum – by the simple tactic of quartering our soldiers (almost 1.5M total persons in all branches of service) in every key region in the world. Despite infractions precipitated by the presence of our service personnel in the respective venues where they are stationed, local economies become addicted to our servicemen and women. Municipalities, states, and even foreign countries protest when any threat arises to eliminate our military bases. Establishing permanent bases isn't the stated strategy. Until our military becomes accepted and part of the "way of life" for the local economy where it resides, our presence is "provisional" – i.e., not set in concrete.

According to our government, we attacked Iraq to ensure weapons of mass destruction weren't used by Saddam's obviously heinous regime. According to Vice-President Dick Cheney, we would be greeted as *liberators* (so he told the late Tim Russert

---

[15] See the film, *Why We Fight* (2006) by Eugene Jarecki, for a telling documentary on the role of America's military. This directive by VP Dick Cheney to Paul Wolfowitz is discussed in the film.

on *Meet the Press* on March 16, 2003, 13 days before we invaded Iraq). Likewise, then Defense Secretary Donald Rumsfeld assured us that our military bases would never be permanent, because we wouldn't be *occupiers*. But what does history actually teach us about the contrast between our official policy and the reality of what we do? While 9/11 was a blatant inducement to remove our military from Saudi Arabia (remember, it was the stated reason Osama bin Laden promised to attack America and so hated his own Saudi government for allowing us to be there), we found it opportune to solidify and expand our military bases just across the border in Iraq after winning the war there.

Journalist Tom Engelhardt wrote this concise analysis in 2006, "There are at least four such 'super-bases' in Iraq, little American islands of eternal order in an anarchic sea. Whatever top officials and military commanders say – and they always deny seeking 'permanent bases' – facts on the ground speak with another voice." He continues:

> Unfortunately, there's a problem in grasping the import of any of this, since American reporters apparently adhere to a simple rule: The words "permanent," "bases" and "Iraq" should never be placed in the same news report. A *LexisNexis* search of three months of press coverage produced examples of those three words in British reports, but US examples occurred only when 80 percent of polled Iraqis (obviously unhinged by their difficult lives) agreed that the United States might want to remain permanently in their country, or when "no" or "not" was added to the mix via any official American denial – as when Brig. Gen. Mark Kimmitt said recently: "It is not only our plan but our policy that we do not intend to have any permanent bases in Iraq." (In other words, in the media such bases, imposing as they are, generally exist only in the negative.) [16]

Besides, should we change our mind about this policy (which we did) isn't that our right as a conquering force provoked by the

---

16 "Can You Say "Permanent Bases" [in Iraq]?" by Tom Engelhardt, *The Nation Magazine*, March 27, 2006.

attacks of 9/11? Whether it was accurate or not, we decided that Saddam was partially responsible for the 9/11 attacks (not true) and that he had weapons of mass destruction (possibly true) and that he would use them against Israel (highly unlikely given our stated policy to nuke anyone that would attack us or Israel if they dared use WMD against either of us).

In a similar use of misdirection, we denounce the possible attack on Iran by Israel all the while clandestinely covering Israel's flank should that course of action become necessary. After all, most Americans support the nation of Israel and its quest to live peaceably in its homeland. Therefore, shouldn't we support Israel

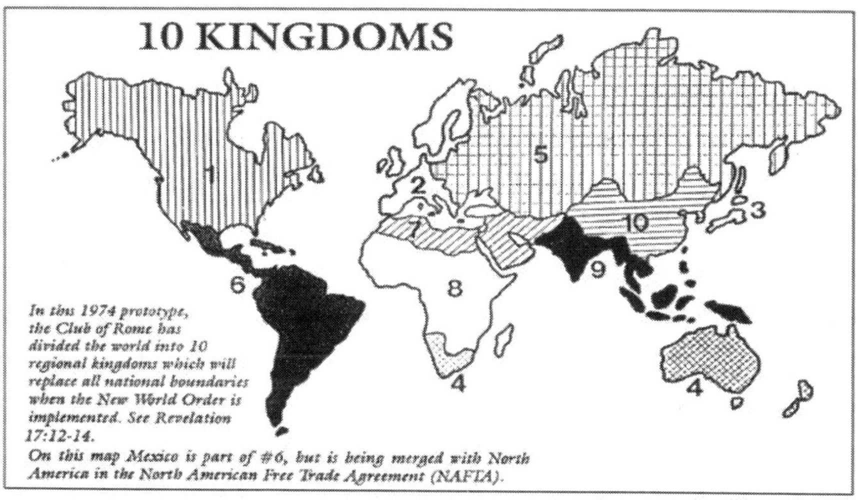


**Figure 25 - The 10 Kingdoms of the Club of Rome and the U.N.**

even if we aren't entirely honest about how and when we do so? Furthermore, if the government of Iran is overthrown during this process, shouldn't we station troops there too – just like Iraq – to make sure we can keep the peace throughout the region? Since American military power has become a permanent fixture everywhere else, why should the Middle East be any different? From the militarist standpoint, who else will take on the responsibility to "bear the white man's burden" as Kipling asked in his 1899 seven-stanza poem?

Consider for a moment how long it might take another power to commit a $100 billion annual budget to post almost one and a half million troops around the world in 1,000 different places. This is surely no easy feat. For those who believe that Christ is soon to return and will come forth to conquer within the next decade or two, does it seem probable another World Empire could arise during this time and replace America in its "peace-keeping role"? Despite the end of the Cold War (perhaps because of it) little has been done to increase the capacity for Europe to handle its own military burden.[17]

In particular, the late (Pre-Wrath) prophecy pundit Herbert Peters[18] supposed that one military corps especially created for quick response, the *Eurocorps,* would form the basis for what was destined to become the replacement for America's military power world-wide. And yet years later, Peter's argument still lacks hard data to support it. In 1988 *Eurocorps* was formed with a force of 40,000 persons. By 1998, it had been expanded to "a force which consists of up to 60,000 soldiers drawn from the armies of Belgium, France, Germany, Luxembourg and Spain. It is independent of any other military command, although it can be placed under the command of international organizations."

So is Europe really going to field an army that causes its enemies to shudder at the thought of their attack? Only months ago in 2012, the European military demonstrated a spectacular lack of capability when lending support to Libyan rebels. America had to "lead from behind" to facilitate the revolution there – temporarily at least – protecting Europe's economic interests.

## Will America Relinquish the Geopolitical Reins?

Evangelical authors who believe in the demise of America "to make room for Antichrist in Europe" may be unwittingly assisting in the Evil One's arrival. They may be masking what is really

---

[17] See Krieger, http://www.the-tribulation-network.com/new_tribnet /articles2.html#the_american_empire.

[18] See the article at http://en.wikipedia.org/wiki/Eurocorps.

happening in the world. Their eschatological position results from a mistaken interpretive heuristic owing to the fact that nowhere in the Bible is America mentioned by name. After all, arguments from silence are a double-edged sword. The name “Antichrist” is never used in the Book of the Revelation despite the fact he is a central character.

As we have argued in previous articles and books, the view that America is absent from prophecy ignores the obvious attributes of “the Daughter of Babylon” and “Mystery Babylon” as disclosed in the Scriptures and convincingly connected to America’s current status in world affairs. Moreover, the connection is rather obvious once the patriotic blinders are removed. As unpopular as this argument is amongst the evangelical community, *America stands as the primary suspect to be the base of operations for the world’s future führer*. This does not mean that other nations play no part. The theme of “the kings of the earth” is laced throughout the Bible and appears consistently in Revelation. The Beast's seven heads (continents?) and the ten horns (nations, regions, kingdoms, economic entities?) are images central to the apocalypse expressing the global nature of “gentile world power” (the revealing of the Beast in Revelation 13 points out the amalgamation of all former gentile empires into this ultimate power that reigns over all peoples and tongues).

But if we look at the current world crisis in the Middle East today we see how the actions of the United States support a misguided strategy for “global leadership” (aka “Democratic Globalism”) setting up the United States to be the catalyst for the coming of Antichrist. Consider what is happening right now in the Israeli-Iranian confrontation.

A blog post from September 16, 2012 from evangelical author Joel Rosenberg recounts that 25 warships including three American carrier groups were then in the Persian Gulf, to ensure the strait of Hormuz remained open even if war broke out between Israel and Iran. Of course, the threat to close the Strait continues to be Iran’s ace in the hole, hoping to forestall military action by the West. One year later, as this is penned, Western nations, along with Israel, continue to worry that the goal of Iran's nuclear program is building atomic weapons of war and not peaceable atomic power.

A review of various articles easily obtainable by searching for "Israel/Iran ready for war" demonstrates that both countries have assumed since the beginning of August (2012) that war is virtually inevitable. For example, one report filed on August 15, 2012, "JERUSALEM (AFP) – Israel is prepared for a 30-day war on multiple fronts should it decide to strike Iran, and is "ready as never before" for such a clash, the outgoing home front defense minister said Wednesday." [19] The number of articles on the subject is rife—*except in the mainline American media.*

Military action may be "covert" in the days ahead, meaning that we have almost assuredly coordinated plans with Israel and several western European nations, including England and Germany to strike at Iran. Some first-hand testimony to supplement our argument: in June, 2012, Woodward spoke with a consultant to the Government at a business meeting in Portland, Oregon (clearly unrelated to this topic) who spoke of the fact that the destructive Stuxnet virus,[20] purportedly placed into Iran's nuclear facilities (via a thumb drive installed by a Russian contractor acting on behalf of Western interests), was in fact a move taken not just by Israel, but by Germany and the United States working behind the scenes together with the Jewish State. (As part of the Edward Snowden "leaks" in the summer of 2013, U.S. involvement has now been confirmed).

Apparently, has become American policy to be thoroughly passive aggressive. We will not *take the lead*; we will "lead from behind" (indeed, it's best if we can act without being detected altogether!)

---

[19] See http://au.news.yahoo.com/world/a/-/world/14562342/israel-ready-for-30-day-war-after-iran-strike-minister/.

[20] This virus was discovered in June 2010 and targets Siemens industrial software.

The violence at American consulates and embassies demonstrates how easy it is to send masses of passionate and undereducated Muslim crowds in the Middle East over the edge (thanks to their activist Imams and ever-lurking Wahhabis terrorists cheering them on). As our diplomats are prone to say, "The political situation is complicated." Unquestionably, that is true. However, we aren't totally without fault when it comes to adding to the complications there. That is especially so since our approach in the international theater appears to be the practice of intentional misdirection – weaving the tangled webs deception famously achieves.

For several reasons, the attacks and threats of attacks on United States' consulates and embassies throughout the Middle East may not be what it seems. Certainly, the Obama administration has attempted to downplay the attacks suggesting that these protests-cum-killing sprees were merely an emotional reaction to a low-budget movie circulating on YouTube that insults the Prophet Mohammed. The initial hope was to downplay any possibility that terrorists were involved. That it transpired on 9/11 must also have been pure coincidence. Consequently, the United States U.N. Ambassador Susan Rice (now National Security advisor to President Obama), took to the Sunday talk shows to minimize assertions the attacks were planned. Much more recently, former Secretary of State Hillary Clinton, testifying before Congress on the attack at Benghazi (Libya) which killed Ambassador John Christopher Stevens on 9-11-12, asked rhetorically, "What difference does it make (who killed him)?" Thus, we suppose if the Secretary of State asks such a question, it clearly doesn't make any difference who should be held to account or what steps should be taken to keep it from happening again.

However, since the State Department went on record five days after the attack with misinformation (it was spurred by "spontaneous acts of religious zeal"), there is little that logic can do to refute their explanation. Forget the fact that spontaneous zeal has never before included "lying in wait" to assassinate an U.S. official. Likewise, it seems useless to bring up the fact that it isn't customary for Muslim zealots (or zealots of any religious affiliation) to come packing heavy weapons (rocket propelled grenades – RPGs) to a prayer meeting. The Obama State Department insisted that the praying "merely got out of control."

**Figure 26 - The Logo for President Obamas Visit, March 20-23, 2013**

After the Susan Rice debriefing to the American people, the new Libyan President had the stomach to say what our government wouldn't: *it is ridiculous to believe these actions of violence were random and unplanned.* But do Americans care?

Americans should realize the pattern of the past. When it's time for war, something happens to fan the flames of national animosity and harden resolve. Therefore, is it an unreasonable bit of conspiracy theory to wonder if the attacks on America's diplomatic missions overseas may be well-timed to influence opinion in support of an attack by the "over-zealous Muslim extremists" who have now done their best to act extreme? After all, the American public is tired of wars in the Middle East. Even when Israel is in dire straits, unless there are events that tie directly to the United States, wouldn't another war be unpopular? Should involvement by our military become necessary, something dramatic must happen to get our populace in the right frame of mind. Recall, we couldn't let Saddam Hussein continue to threaten the oil supply. Neither can we let Iran's radical Imams interrupt the flow of oil through the Strait of Hormuz. The West depends upon "petrol" as our British friends term it. We shouldn't really be surprised that the West has a not-so-hidden agenda to protect its economic interests.

However, that assumes our real policy is to stand by Israel. As this is being written, President Obama announced an "Unbreakable Alliance" between Israel and the United States, in Jerusalem during Holy Week, 2013. For those who watch prophetic matters closely, the parallels with the most common interpretation of Daniel 9:24-27 of a covenant between the "the people of the prince to come" that is broken half-way through the final seven years of Hebrew history (according to Daniel's famous Seventy Weeks of prophecy) is more than unsettling. Many expositors of the Scripture interpret this accord as a "Defense Pact" and therefore, simply a re-affirmation of the same.

Despite who wins presidential elections, political leaders worldwide know what America will do when "push comes to shove". Since World War II, our military-industrial complex has dominated our foreign policy and our decisions to make war when economic matters matter most. Working on behalf of our biggest mega-corporations, "American interests" are defined by our government acting in concert with what's best for the economy; thus, *these bellicose decisions are actually easy to explain.* Only tactics require careful planning and debate at the highest levels in the darkened corridors of power. Otherwise, as far as our public relations program is concerned, we must position ourselves carefully regarding the official diplomatic statements we make. The way it has been for the past six to seven decades isn't showing any real signs of changing.

## Our Failure to Make America Accountable

In short, because our country serves as the sole global superpower, Americans should recognize our obvious but unspoken responsibility. Our post-Cold War policy has become to guarantee the realization of an elitist political and financial strategy on behalf of the Free World. America's military is the dominating force ensuring the world's richest nations stay rich. And yet, as demanded by God's Word, Christians should be calling our government to account when it steps outside time honored guidelines for upholding truth and justice. Instead, we join in the chorus for patriotic wars of retaliation or preemptive military action against radical Islam. Indeed, Christian leaders usually offer little complaint. The more conservative they are, the more likely they are to capitulate.

Thus, it should be no surprise that Christian congregations remain focused on minimizing disruptions to personal peace and accumulating wealth as a sign of God's favor. As evangelicals, we too easily lapse into a position assuming our government acts in the best interests of its citizens and takes the moral high ground. To protect the financial interests of our mega-corporations, mistakenly regarded as bastions of free-market capitalism, it seems apparent to our critics we care much more about condemning homosexuality than condemning warmongering. No doubt, we fall into this pattern because it seems connected to the *patriotic* point of view. "Keeping America strong" means keeping American corporations ahead of foreign competition. It means supporting an indomitable military. After all, what does America stand for if it isn't capitalism and free-enterprise? Where would be we if we didn't police the world? Communism and National Socialism are abject failures. Their turpitude was obvious. So the American Way must be the right way, not merely the best of bad options.

But on the other hand, perhaps we should consider the economics implied in Jesus' advice to His opponents on the question of taxation and obeying the civil authorities: *"Render unto Caesar the things that are Caesars and unto God the things that are God's"* (Mark 12:17). We argue that, from the Bible's point of view, there isn't one pat answer to what is THE acceptable economic theory. What is clear: a "love of money" disproportionate to our love for God stands condemned. Likewise, Jesus cautioned *"He who lives by the sword, dies by the sword"* (Matthew 26:52).

Evangelicals often seem unaware of numerous American shortcomings in the financial and political realms that might otherwise cause vigilant defenders of the faith to stand up, take notice, and call for repentance. Our *eschatology*, surely a surprise for many who wish to ignore the "arcane" subject altogether, should make a difference in how we witness our faith in the world. If it doesn't, we have every reason to question its value.

Since nowadays American citizens benefit from our global superpower status as a matter of due course, we might be wise to consider why other nations could have a problem with our behavior (to say nothing about policy) since affected nations might be losing more than just a modicum of national sovereignty in the process. Indeed, for many third-world countries, their natural resources just might be subject to seizure. Could this be part of why so many nations in the Middle East resent us? Is it actually something more than just a difference in religious affections? Is it not a part of the legacy of the "ugly American" (the now-dated pejorative denouncing an all too frequent display of national arrogance)?

We assume their hatred lies with the fact they are Muslim and we are "Christian". But is this really the issue? Is religion to blame? Or is it because Muslim nations feel we act as if their lands are mere colonies for Anglo-Americans and the other rich nations of the world to exploit? We might even go further in our introspection and consider Washington's warning about entangling alliances with Europe and the Monroe Doctrine mandating we pay attention to our own backyard rather than worrying excessively about the "old world." To be more specific, we should ask whether we want the burden of continuing to be one and only nation who has the military muscle to back up the collective demands of the "first-world". The English eventually had to recognize they couldn't afford their empire. So did ancient Rome. Why does America suppose we can be any different?

In the final analysis, our decision as a nation to continue managing geo-political events on behalf of the West, may amount to whether or not we regard true patriots as those that stand opposed to America becoming Babylon. If we allow our country to continue its steady march toward being the Bible's final Babylon, we inevitably invite Antichrist to assume his seat at the controls, bringing twilight to our republic and soon thereafter the culmination of the present age.

## *Chapter 6:*

# The Colossus of Commercial Babylon

## What Does the Dollar Sign Symbolize?

THE ORIGIN OF THE DOLLAR SIGN PROVIDES AN IMPORTANT CLUE TO THE IDENTITY OF THE FINAL BABYLON. THERE ARE MANY THEORIES ABOUT ITS BEGINNING, BUT THE MOST FASCINATING lies with the Spanish. The story goes that in 1492, Ferdinand and Isabella adopted the symbol of the Pillars of Hercules (the mountains lying on either side of the Strait of Gibraltar) for their coat of arms. Added to the symbol was the Latin phrase, *Non Plus Ultra* which meant "nothing further lies beyond." However, after Columbus discovered America (at least as far as Western Europeans were concerned), the phrase was changed to *Plus Ultra*: "Further beyond." The symbol historically had two vertical lines with an "s" shaped element "wrapping around them." Later, coins minted for the colonies in the New World used this symbol. We see this in the Spanish coin, the *Real*, illustrated in the figure following.

Others have suggested that the two vertical lines and the "**s**" element represent a *caduceus*, a symbol of Hermes, the god of merchants, gamblers, liars, thieves and as a surprising *non-sequitur*, shepherds. Hermes carried a staff, really a magic wand, with a snake curled about it.

Yet another possibility: this symbol may refer to the two pillars of the Freemasons and the serpent of knowledge.[1] The two pillars are thought to represent "heaven" and "earth" and the connection or reflection each one of the other hints at the famous

---

[1] The symbol was first used by "the second most powerful man in America" from 1781 to 1784, Robert Morris, Liverpool born but later a signer of the Declaration of Independence and the Constitution. He chaired the "Secret Committee of Trade" and was the superintendent of Finance for the United States. Despite his power and prestige he wound up in debtors prison toward the end of his life. See http://en.wikipedia.org/ wiki/Robert_Morris_ (financier).

hermetic aphorism "as above so below." Given the history of Freemasonry surrounding the founding of America, this theory is not without merit. If so, it would seem some manner of mysticism may be implied in the symbol of American money, a Masonic mysticism that coincides with the Freemason's plan for *The Great Work* to be instigated in America.

**Figure 27 - The *Plus Ultra* and the Spanish REAL of 1768**

At the very least, our money reflects the mercantile motive in our founding, the mystery of a "utopian" country beyond the great sea, and a possible New Atlantis beckoning Europeans. This symbol reinforces the plan for America and in its own way, America's fate. And contrary to popular opinion amongst political conservatives and most eschatologists, the Dollar, portrayed with stout pillars in its emblematic form, may remain as strong as Hercules almost to the very end.

## More than a Mere City?

Revelation Chapters 16 to 19 deal with the judgment of a great religious, commercial, and political empire known as "the Great City" Babylon. However, a reading of these chapters readily indicates it refers to much more than a city, but to an apostate Christian system (Chapter 17), a commercial empire that the nations of the earth trade with (Chapter 18), and a great military power headed by none other than the Antichrist himself (Chapter 19).

Our focus in this chapter is the mercantile colossus of the nation beyond the Pillars of Hercules, foreshadowed in ancient times by Canaan, Tyre, and Tarshish. A giant in economic affairs, this stands as one of the three facets of the final Babylon in the Scripture. However, of all three aspects of Babylon, the Book of Revelation provides more clues to the identity of the final Babylon through its descriptions of "Babylon's" financial dominance. Hence, a close look at this subject seems more than justified.

To be sure, Revelation 18 delivers a very detailed description of a great commercial nation. The entire world produces merchandise which Babylon consumes (Revelation 18:91). The nations of the earth must trade with this Babylon by sea, for she is a nation surrounded by many waters (Revelation 17:1, 18:19, 21). The many waters themselves also represents multitudes of different peoples, languages, and nations (Revelation 17:15). This is made explicit when we learn that she is destroyed in the space of a single hour causing the merchants to panic. From Revelation 18:

> [18] *Every shipmaster, and all the company in ships and sailors and as many as trade by sea, stood afar off [exclaimed] when they saw the smoke of her burning, saying, What city is like unto this great city!*
>
> [19] *And they cast dust on their heads, and cried, weeping and wailing, saying, Alas, alas that great city, wherein were made rich all that had ships in the sea by reason of her costliness! for in one hour is she made desolate.*
>
> [20] *Rejoice over her, thou heaven, and ye holy apostles and prophets; for God hath avenged you on her.*
>
> [21] *And a mighty angel took up a stone like a great millstone, and cast it into the sea, saying, Thus with violence shall that great city Babylon be thrown down, and shall be found no more at all. (Revelation 18:19-21)*

It would appear that taken in the context of Revelation 16 to 18 we are dealing with a nation or an empire but not a single metropolis. This can also be inferred from many references in Jeremiah, Isaiah, Daniel (verses we have cited elsewhere) and other sacred books in which Babylon (aka Daughter of Babylon) is also known as "the land of the Chaldeans" and not merely a single city. Given its world-wide ascendancy, this is not surprising. Furthermore, we should recall the context of the Bible: ancient powers were "city-states" and referenced by the major city at the heart of the "kingdom." We see this with the land Phoenicia (present day Lebanon) referred to principally in the Bible as Tyre and Sidon (aka Cydonia)[2] which appeared to give rise to the merchants of Tarshish much further west, likely referring to the city of Tartessos in ancient Hispania (the Iberian peninsula), on the coast of what is now Spain (note the connection with Spain and the Pillars of Hercules).

| 2005 | | |
|---|---|---|
| Rank | Land | GNP* |
| 1 | USA | 11,351 |
| 2 | Japan | 4,366 |
| 3 | Germany | 1,966 |
| 4 | United Kingdom | 1,647 |
| 5 | China | 1,529 |
| 6 | France | 1,455 |
| 7 | Italy | 1,212 |
| 8 | Kanada | 728 |
| 9 | Spain | 655 |
| 10 | Mexico | 642 |

| 2050 | | |
|---|---|---|
| Rank | Land | GNP* |
| 1 | China | 44,453 |
| 2 | USA | 35,165 |
| 3 | India | 27,803 |
| 4 | Japan | 6,673 |
| 5 | Brasil | 6,074 |
| 6 | Russia | 5,870 |
| 7 | United Kingdom | 3,782 |
| 8 | Germany | 3,603 |
| 9 | France | 3,148 |
| 10 | Italy | 2,061 |

* In Billion US$; Source: Goldman Sachs

**Figure 28 - Gross National Product (GNP) by Rank Comparing Actual Data from 2005 with 2050 Forecasted Data**

But what clues are we given to expose who the subject of these prophecies is? Could it be America? John indicates it is *"that great city, which reigneth over the kings of the earth."* (Revelation 17:18).

As we've noted from the beginning of this book, most Christian scholars dismiss America as even a possible candidate for Babylon because they contend the Scriptures fail to mention it. But unlike Egypt, Israel, and Persia (Iran), the future Babylon did not exist at the time the prophecies were envisioned and written down. Consequently, we must rely upon symbols and images to provide its identity.

---

[2] Phoenicia is also known as *Canaan*, a word meaning *merchant* or mercantile. This will be discussed in detail in a later chapter.

Nevertheless, we must ask, "Why haven't popular authors and biblical scholars considered that America is nothing more than an extension of Europe in terms of peoples, culture, language, literature, politics, economy, law, etc.? Why don't they see America as *the little horn* (of Daniel 7) arisen to dominate the other ten horns/nations?"

By the turn of the twentieth century, America had surpassed Britain as the biggest economy of the world. At the end of the twentieth century, it surpassed all of Europe. Today it remains the world's largest economy in spite of China's spectacular growth in recent years with almost five times China's GNP. According to Goldman Sachs, China will surpass the USA within the next 30 years. However, this assumes no wars and likely doesn't take into account the major shift occurring in energy, with the U.S. becoming the main beneficiary of new technologies like *fracking*, natural gas liquefying, and production of oil from oil shale that will make the U.S. energy independent before the end of this decade, AND a major exporter of both oil and gas, not to mention coal.

## The Rise of America's Commercial Empire

During the past century America has built a vast global empire. By the end of WWII, it was the undisputed leader with only Russia and its satellites standing in the way of total global hegemony! But to understand the emergence of our empire, we must understand the nature of waging war in the modern era. Warfare just isn't the same today as it was 100 years ago. There were two wars, in particular, that taught us this harsh lesson and reshaped our behavior ever since.

Our "police actions" in Korea and Vietnam showed the futility of fighting by conventional means. For America to influence the world and bend it to its will, we learned the hard way that neither bullying with threats nor fighting unsustainable wars with "boots on the ground" could be effective any longer – "projecting power" and getting our way in the world requires a more subtle approach (especially in light of media coverage which brings the horror of war into our living rooms – war has grown increasingly unpopular nowadays!)

The "war" effort was redirected to turning most of the "free world" effectively into client states of America – tied to us by our apparent generosity and good will. We must still carry a gun in one hand, while we now carry a checkbook in the other. Why this approach?

The end of World War II left Europe and Japan in shambles. To rebuild capitalist democracies there, we opened our consumer markets for them to sell their goods and services here. We opened our capital purse strings to make strategic investments there. We invested in complementary businesses, development of their labor force, and their national transportation and communication infrastructure. Eventually (along with the British) we would supersede World War II combatants, now our allies, and invest in the *underdeveloped* world. In true American form and efficiency, we launched a multi-pronged attack encompassing both money and a "para-military" force of sorts, able to be our eyes and ears "on the ground."

The Peace Corp sent out young people throughout the world to identify and develop infrastructure projects. These volunteers were some of our best and brightest. They were bilingual, sensitive cross-culturally, and became the source for great expansion of international business, international aid, and they created a great source of intelligence for the CIA in the process (a not unforeseen dividend). Along the way, the Peace Corp spawned the birth of companies known as "the beltway bandits" – consulting companies eager to help the government spend USAID, World Bank, IMF and other monies. One of the authors, McGriff, worked on and off for these consulting companies over 25 years of his career. Likewise, Christian relief and development agencies also got involved in the act (*World Relief, Catholic Relief Services, World Vision, Food for the Hungry,* etc.). McGriff also worked for *World Relief* putting on seminars on project development and for *Food for the Hungry* as Country Director and head of a project to resettle Southeast Asian refugees in Bolivia.

Minions of American "do-gooders" (among whom McGriff counts himself), fanned out across the globe developing relationships, identifying needs, writing grants and business plans to bring economic development to the "undeveloped" world.[3] All this time, like most others, he had no idea he was an unwitting part of the strategic machine not only to develop but to exploit the developing world for America's benefit.

### Phase I

As the Marshall Plan wound down in the years that followed World War II, the developed world – Europe, Japan, America and Canada represented about 20 percent of the world population. Latin America, Africa and the rest of Asia, India, Pakistan and Southeast Asia represented the other 80 percent. These countries desperately needed infrastructure – water, power, transportation, industry, bridges, dams, and other "high" technology. Many people were dying from diseases caused by drinking bad water. Cholera, typhoid, malaria – so many diseases could be taken care of just by improving sanitation. Agriculture could be improved, natural resources exploited, industry developed, housing improved, etc. American aid usually helped in these important respects.

The same capital foundation that was used to rebuild Europe and Japan – the IMF and World Bank, the United States Agency for International Development (USAID), the Inter-American Development Bank, the Asia Development Bank, etc., would be leveraged for the "rest of the world." USAID is a part of the State Department but surreptitiously works closely with the CIA. Indeed, the "political" and "economic" officers and attachés of our embassies were almost always CIA. Reports produced by aid

---

[3] McGriff worked all over Central and South America, the Far East (Thailand, Indonesia and the Philippines), Africa, and the Middle East.

workers – whether on health care, agricultural development, education, population control (known as "woman and child health") – all would up as data points in CIA reports too. Eventually, USAID tended to phase out and the World Bank took over while "bilateral relationships" were established with developing country governments. However, a key issue that was seldom raised was, "How can these countries ever service their debt?"

When one looks at the billions of dollars spent in these different countries, it's easy to see that less than 10 per cent of these dollars were grants and 90 or more percent were in the form of loans – loans that had to be paid back! Given this uneven structure, it was best when a natural disaster happened (an earthquake, typhoon or flood – not to be cynical) for it led to greater cooperation and bigger, fully-funded projects to rebuild what was destroyed. This meant more money came in the form of aid and less in loans.

The bottom line: the debt became an unbearable load to these developing countries. The infrastructure projects were sold based on optimistic estimates of GDP growth that almost never happened. A few of the elites in the government and businessmen got wealthy, but there was far less benefit for the people than we would hope. A history of default and restructuring of loans followed, but seldom if ever were these loans repaid. Just like personal credit card debt, debtor nations were lucky to keep up with the accrued interest much less retire the principal. They often worked off some debt by concessions to American business, voting with the U.S. in the United Nations, or providing other benefits to America. In a few cases, the situation grew so critical debts had to be written off. However, the strategy was always the same: the American Empire spread by enticing the developing world into projects with extremely high costs. Our government knew our "clients" would usually default on the loans. When the loans came due, the IMF would restructure the loan and tie them tighter into America's Commercial Empire.[4] Money became more powerful than the military in maintaining the American empire.

### Phase II

The first phase had been to complete basic community and infrastructure development. The second phase expanded the global empire by exporting jobs to cheap labor markets such as Indonesia, the Philippines, and Nigeria (this began in the 1980s). Consultants like McGriff sought to convince the plant managers how they would get better productivity if they provided health and family planning services to their workers. While this was true, American business benefitted.

Another aspect of this strategy was *privatization*. The concept presumes the private sector can do a better job than the public sector (since they operate under "the profit motive"). Whole sectors would thus be privatized – transportation, health, utilities, etc. However, instead of being "privatized" by local business, mul-

---

[4] Christians played an unknowing role in this first phase of development. The role of *Summer Institute of Linguistics* or *Wycliffe Bible Translators* is well known and documented. Missionaries were used by the CIA and promoted American business interests. (See Dennet, Charlotte Please, Thy Will be Done, New York: Harper Collins, 1996). McGriff's supplies this personal anecdote: "In 1979, I went to work for *World Relief of the National Association of Evangelicals (NAE*). I wrote the first grant funded by USAID to start our development activities (in contrast to relief). I worked for Cleo Shook who had just left the Carter administration as an Under Secretary of State. Cleo, like many missionaries, in the 1950s had gone to Afghanistan but couldn't stay as a "Christian Missionary." He became the CIA eyes and ears in Afghanistan and later Iran, started the Peace Corps with Sergeant Shriver, and though a wonderful Christian, was an emissary for the empire.

In Bolivia, I was debriefed by the CIA – by an assistant "political officer" named Greg. When I found out that our conversation had been telexed to every embassy in the world, I was furious. These are just two of many experiences I had as a missionary with the intelligence community as I traveled around Latin America putting on conferences for missionaries on how to develop and get funding for projects, mainly from USAID."

tinationals (many of course financed and run by Americans) would take over the service usually resulting in much higher costs than before. McGriff saw such projects in Brazil, Argentina, Colombia, Jamaica, Indonesia, Nigeria, and elsewhere.

Today we see jobs going overseas by the boatload. Our development efforts have been successful in part because there is a relatively healthy, well-fed, educated work force willing to do jobs Americans often don't want to do – especially given the fact it's for one tenth the wage. However, do American financial and corporate elites really care when they displace American workers? Let's just say that this isn't a significant cause for any sleepless nights they may experience.

Author John Perkins writes about this sad situation (like McGriff, he worked in many of these same organizations):

> A whole new class of soldier was emerging on the world scene and these people were becoming desensitized to their own actions...
>
> Today, men and women are going into Thailand, the Philippines, Botswana, Bolivia, and every other country where they have to find people desperate for work. They go to these places with the express purpose of exploiting wretched people – people whose children are severely malnourished, even starving, people who live in shanty-towns and have lost all hope of a better life, people who have ceased to even dream of another day. These men and women leave their plush offices in Manhattan or San Francisco or Chicago, streak across continents and oceans in luxurious jetliners, check into first-class hotels, and dine at the finest restaurants the country has to offer. Then they go searching for desperate people.
>
> Today, we still have slave traders. They no longer find it necessary to march into the forests of Africa looking for prime specimens who will bring top dollar on the auction blocks in Charleston, Cartagena and Havana. They simply recruit desperate people and build a factor to produce the jackets, blue jeans, tennis shoes, automobile parts, computer components, and thousands of other items they can sell in the markets of their choosing. Or they may elect not even to own the factory

> themselves; instead, they hire a local businessman to do all their dirty work for them.
>
> These men and women think of themselves as upright. They return to their homes with photographs of quaint sites and ancient ruins, to show to their children. They attend seminars where they pat each other on the back and exchange tidbits of advice about dealing with the eccentricities of customs in far-off lands...
>
> The old-fashioned slave trader told himself that he was dealing with a species that was not entirely human and that he was offering them the opportunity to become Christianized... The modern slave trader assures himself (or herself) that the desperate people are better off earning one dollar a day than no dollars at all and that they are receiving the opportunity to become integrated into the larger world community... desperate people are fundamental to the survival of her company..."[5]

Looked at from a high perch, we see that America has encouraged the rest of the world to make things for us to buy. Italy and Spain made shoes, Japan made cars, electronics and just about everything else. Clothing was often made in sweatshops all over the world. America bought this merchandise and in exchange, foreign countries bought ours. It now appears this strategy worked so well that we now buy far more than we are sell (creating the trade deficit). In fact, now the Chinese and other countries loan us money to help fund our excessive consumerism and government programs. America once enjoyed a significant trading surplus. But it has been decades since this was the case. As a result, our wealth is transferred overseas.

In summary, the Marshall Plan worked. The IMF and World Bank strategies have worked too. This isn't all bad: we can't create endless "give-away programs" for the third world – but we can open our markets to them (and "encourage" them to open their markets to our consumption). This stimulates economic development by flowing U.S. Dollars into the underdeveloped

---

[5] Perkins, John, *Confessions of an Economic Hitman*, San Francisco: Berrett Koehler Publishers, 2004, p. 180.

world and making "western democracies" rich at the same time. As we've pointed out here, the system isn't perfect, but neither is it without some redeeming quality.

But back to the main point of this chapter: The Final Babylon of Revelation 18 is such a great commercial empire that all the nations of the earth get wealthy trading with her. One of the downsides, however, is that we have been blinded to what we have done. No matter where one goes today, it is easy to find Coke, MacDonald's, Proctor and Gamble toothpaste and soap, Hollywood's movie and television videos and every kind of American consumer item you can think of! We have *Americanized* the world. Many hate us because of it. But the majority loves us and would choose to be smack in the middle of our consumer economy if they had the choice.

*Note: A nation of such economic might, with tentacles reaching into every corner of the world can't develop this kind of empire overnight. Replacing such power doesn't happen overnight either.*

## Don't Count America Out

However, don't count America out. Amateur financial observers often condemn questionable government economic policies and fiscal mismanagement. But America survives; it usually thrives. It is crucial to keep things in a comparative perspective. America is rich in natural resources and surpasses all other nation's economies by a large margin. America has never defaulted on foreign debt. Plus, when we issue bonds to raise more capital, there are three times as many buyers as there are "Treasuries" to sell (i.e., Treasury Bonds – America's I.O.U.). Buyers are willing to loan us money even though we pay nothing more than zero to two percent interest on five, seven, and ten –year bonds. America remains the safe haven for the world's money. We are not like Argentina that runs up debt and stiffs creditors (a country we love despite this short-coming!) But almost everyone (except our current administration, apparently) realizes we can't keep adding to our debt indefinitely. Eventually the assets and liabili-

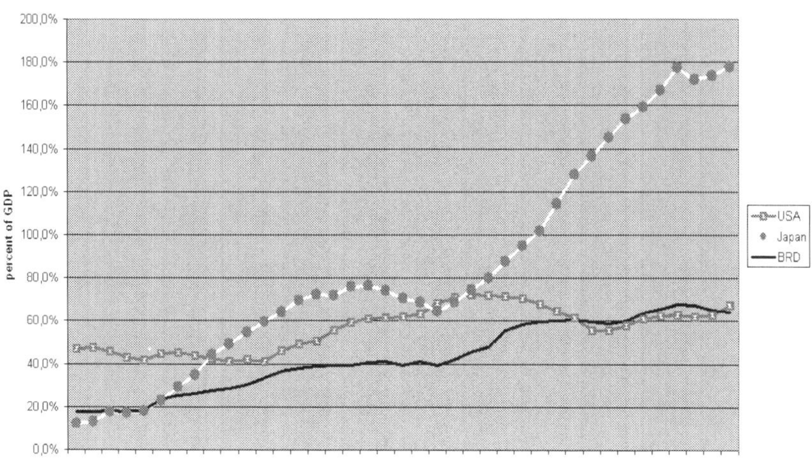


**Figure 29 - Debt as a Percent of GDP: USA, Japan, & Germany**

ties must be balanced. Printing more money and retiring debt with cheaper Dollars spurs inflation (reducing our debt by the same percentage the Dollar declines in value), and eventually causes creditors to raise interest rates or stop loaning money altogether.

Like the U.S., Japan is another country leveraging their economy with "quantitative easing" (creating money to stimulate economic activity). We have been following their playbook for five years now. Even though Japan has been in a slump for over twenty years, it remains the third largest economy in the world. In the 1980s it was the miracle economy – everyone expected it to overtake America claiming the number one slot. Then in 1989 something happened. Almost overnight its stock market and real estate lost three-quarters of its value. The government responded by deficit spending, bank bailouts, and even government works projects. Fortunately for the Japanese government, the Japanese people were "savers," so Japan was able to fund government deficits leveraging their people's savings funneled into Japanese financial institutions. But Japan's savings is down while their national debt will reach 245 percent of GDP in 2013 (compared to US debt to GDP ratio of 101 percent). In spite of all of their spending, they have been in a deflationary cycle (another word for depression) for over 20 years with no end in sight. Stimulus, bailouts, and printing currency haven't led to hyperinflation but these have caused stagnation. The government refuses to let banks fail, bailing them out instead. Japan is "maintaining." However, analysts are predicting this is about to change. What does this foretell for the U.S.? Will Japan collapse and will the U.S. be right behind?

The mistake lay people often make is thinking a crash is imminent and America will become a third-world country within a few years. Take a lesson from Japan, England or even Rome. *Things don't change that quickly.* America still has plenty of national resources, including oil and gas that is just beginning to come on line. It is still a bread basket for the world; still a serious consumer of the world's best "junk"; and still has the most powerful military to help protect our economic interests. The one-and-a-half billion "problems" (known as people which both China and India must satisfy in the decades ahead), will be a difficult burden to bear. China and Japan could fall because of their unfavorable demographics (not enough productive young taxpayers exist to pay benefits for unproductive elders).

Then there is Europe. Even though a deal has been struck to save Greece, it is only a matter of time before the highly leveraged "sovereign debt" of other European countries causes the *Eurozone* to collapse. Cyprus is the latest casualty. Italy and Portugal may be next. The "odds-on bet" is that Europe will decline because it can't pay the bill for early retirements, free health care, and long vacations to which their people are accustomed. With citizen "have-nots" and immigrants screaming for their "fair share," we predict European business will continue to decline under increased demands from the State.

As we have illustrated, while the U.S. has a tough row to hoe, it looks easy compared to the inevitable and overwhelming situations other countries face.

## Getting Deeper and Deeper in Debt

America's National Debt was about $10 trillion when President Obama took office. In five years it increased to nearly $17 trillion. But some pundits ask, "Does it really matter?" We can sell Treasury Bonds for 1.5 to 2 percent interest right now so the interest on our debt is only about $225 million annually. Of course, should it increase to historic levels, this amount could double or triple. Then there is the debt we don't register on today's "balance sheet." This is our *unfunded liability* (mainly Social Security and Medicare benefits that the government has to pay in the future if it honors its "statutory commitment" to its citizens); this liability raises the real amount of our National Debt to an amount closer to $50 or 60 trillion. But the fact is the Federal government collects more in taxes and fees because of increased oil production. The amount of the Budget deficit is decreasing as is the Trade Deficit. Newly found oil and gas is fueling (pun not intended) a new boom. America will become the energy giant of the world! Consequently, the rest of the world feels safe buying American debt.

The relevant point here is that any time tax dollars are diverted to pay for interest on debt or any other governmental activity, it takes financial resources from the private sector which could have been used to buy more equipment or hire more laborers to produce more goods, which allows the business world to sell more, make more money, and pay more taxes. But when you force businesses to pay more taxes, you eventually lower tax revenue and decrease economic growth. It's a double whammy too, because they don't hire wage earners, so individuals don't pay personal income taxes either. So as governments increase taxes, they push down economic productivity, decreasing tax revenue even more. Can you say, "It is a vicious cycle?" It is a case of cutting off your nose to spite your face. As we will see below, all the austerity in the world in Greece just dampened the economy more resulting in lower government tax revenues and increased government debt.

Debt, debt creation, loans, bailouts, money being printed represents a systemic cancer that is eating the world monetary system alive and will inevitably result in death – at least for somebody. However, Rome wasn't built overnight and it didn't fall overnight either. Neither will the western economies all fail at once. But if they don't rekindle productivity, their economies will eventually collapse. Five-hundred years ago, the problem was solved when the peasants revolted. Not because they rioted – but because the government slaughtered the peasants and decreased the liability the government had to feed its people. Ironically, in today's world, politicians benefit most of the time from making the problem worse, not solving it. And like the frog in the pot of water beginning to boil, the average person won't become aware until it is too late.

Whether we like it or not, we are a global economy. If you take our basic situation and multiply it to both developed and developing countries around the world, you have an unsolvable problem, especially in Europe among those nations with all-encompassing safety net social programs. But it's not just limited to there. Asia and Africa historically suffer as well but mostly due to having too many mouths to feed and not enough food to sustain uncontrolled population growth. Unfortunately, these problems don't stay isolated. When countries around the world implode, they often take their neighbors with them. In Europe today, neighboring countries hold an incredible amount of "Sovereign Debt." Remember, the EU countries can't just print money so they issue "Sovereign Debt" which banks buy.

So who is bailed out? When we look at the Greek bailout for example, Greece didn't receive a single penny in "bailout" money. Only the banks who loaned out money were "bailed out." This money didn't "trickle down" to the government and certainly not to the citizens who were counting on retirement and health care benefits to continue on indefinitely. The wealthy are protected. The poor aren't. As the old song "God Bless the Child" laments, "The rich seem to get more while the weak ones fade. Empty pockets don't ever make the grade."

So here is the thesis. The entire world is living beyond its means, printing too much money which leads to currency inflation, hyperinflation, devaluation, a complete loss of all savings, and the eventual destruction of currencies. Only the "last man standing" wins, because he can collect what everyone else leaves behind. Right now, the bet is that the United States will most likely be "the last man standing" (along with whoever else we allow to remain alive and well).

We live in an interdependent world. Just think about it. The GDP of the U.S. is $15 trillion and the whole world is about $50 trillion. The amount of debt out there is beyond a quadrillion (a thousand trillion dollars).

These numbers are so big we can't comprehend them. Do you know how long a million seconds is? Eleven and a half days. How about a billion seconds? 31.7 years. How about a trillion? 31,709 years. And a quadrillion seconds? 31.7 million years! Okay, so back to earth.

If global GDP totals $50 trillion, how on earth could you ever pay off debt that exceeds a quadrillion dollars? That is 200 times total revenues produced. To appreciate how impossible the situation is, this is akin to Joe Schmoe who makes $50,000 a year attempting to pay back a $10,000,000 loan, 200 times the amount Joe makes. So, 1% interest amounts to $100,000 annually. Joe needs to double his salary just to pay interest on the note – and that's an interest rate that Joe could never obtain. In fact, since Joe is such a loan risk, his rate will likely be 20% or more. Anyway you do the math, Joe's loan will never be repaid. Neither will the world's debt.

Not only that, the amount of currency and debt continues to grow so that the debtors will either default or become impoverished (off to debtor prison they go!) or the whole financial system will collapse and currency will be worth nothing. The stark truth is this: No one has the guts to find real solutions to these hard problems. The issue isn't who can keep up with paying their debt, but who can't keep up. Just like in a heavy-weight fight lasting 15 rounds: The winner is the fighter who can outlast his opponent and keep on his feet. The loser is the guy that falls to the canvas first and doesn't get up.

This is the reality of the world's economic situation. The U.S. has debt levels that are unsustainable. But so does almost everyone else. And when push comes to shove, the crucial point is, "Who has the 'biggest/baddest' military in the world to grab somebody else's lunch when their lunch is gone?" That's right: the United States of America. That's why the medieval theory to achieve and sustain prosperity ("Mercantile economics") may become popular again real soon.

To explain: Economics in the Old World was really simple. There were two options: (1) Make it yourself if you were so inclined, had the resource, the labor, and the capital to finance its development; or (2) steal it from someone else who already built it or bought it and had it on the shelf.

Spain did a great job of gathering gold in the New World (by stealing it from Native Americans). The infamous English sailor, Sir Francis Drake did an even better job of raiding Spanish Galleons to steal this "Spanish" gold for Queen Elizabeth I (the first and best QE1!). However, there eventually comes a point when the debt collector needs muscle to collect the debt. And yet, that collector runs out of luck when the guy from which the debtor is trying to collect possesses 11 aircraft carriers and while you only have one (which is the current ratio of U.S. aircraft carriers to China's).

When the going gets tough, the tough keep what they already got – whether they paid for it with their own money, by borrowing someone else's, or just plain stole it.

Unfortunately, we could arrive at that state of affairs.

## Sure We're in Bad Shape, but Compared to Whom?

For four decades the traditional prophetic scenario has predicted the U.S. will collapse or fade away, enabling Europe to come to the forefront. How does this prediction stack up today?

Is the U.S. really going to decline? Is Europe likely to rise to the top of the heap?

First off, remember that Europe relies almost totally on the U.S. for military resources. The U.S., even when it doesn't officially take the lead, still has to "lead from behind" because Europe has too little military to sustain most military operations. Given that truism, surely Europe has its financial house in order at least – *doesn't it?* Isn't Europe capable of matching the U.S. economically? After all, Europe has "tons of money" left over since she doesn't have to spend it on defense. Therefore, Europe can just "go on holiday" and still deliver its citizens a social safety net surpassing what the U.S.A. provides to its patrons.

When we look at the facts, the reality of what has happened in Europe suggests the opposite. Europe overtaking Uncle Sam in military might or financial prowess stands the same chance of happening as a top-tier NFL team losing to a small-town seven-man squad. For all the fuss about a unified Europe, it amounts to more hype that heft.

### Greece

In contradiction to the reporting of the mainline media, there never was a bailout of "Greece" – just a bailout of the bankers who had purchased their "sovereign debt" – another way of saying those unfortunate "saps" who bought Greek Bonds. Greece doesn't have a central bank and can't print money, so governments like Greece borrow from big banks. The loaning banks took a haircut on their principal but received interest payments for many years. In return, the Greeks got nothing back other than austerity – budget cuts, program cuts, and increased taxes which only made matters worse – leading to more unemployment, a declining GDP, and reduced tax revenues. They voted out the Prime Minister put in office by the IMF and elected a socialist in his place. If he can form a government, he will cancel all agreements, default on debt, and leave the EU.

No surprise that European leaders agree: Greece will be the first to drop out. The GDP of Greece is about the same as the city of Philadelphia. We should ask, "If Europe can't save a small country the size of a city, how is it going to be able to save larger countries?" Greece earned the distinction as the biggest sovereign debt defaulter ever – but it will be dwarfed by Portugal, Spain, Italy and possibly France! Talk about too big to fail! These countries are too big to even think about bailing out!

Greece first received $200 billion which was to be followed by another $700 billion in three installments. However, the bankers have been rewarded in billions of low interest loans they will never be able to repay. (The operative practice is delay, avoid, and postpone). Meanwhile, the Greek economy decreased in size by 10 percent. Unemployment is near 20 percent. People are sleeping in the streets. Those who still have houses can't afford to have the utilities turned on. Only the rich have electricity. You don't read about this in the news. Everyone, especially the banks, just hope to stretch out the inevitable default until it becomes someone else's problem.

## Portugal

Portugal is the next country to go broke. The bankers there have already received $300 billion. Nevertheless, Portugal GDP has dropped every quarter for over a year. Unemployment is 15 percent and rising. The housing bubble has collapsed and a fourth of all homes went into default in 2011. Personal bankruptcies are soaring into record territory as government, private and corporate debt exceeds four times the country's GDP. And what's the government's response? Really quite predictable: *increase taxes!* Of course, this only makes matters worse. Then there's the latest news full of even more wishful thinking: a proposal has been put on the table for a few hundred billion more in banker bailouts which hopes to solve a mere few hundred trillion problems! Meanwhile the EU is pressuring the Portuguese government to make even more cuts in social programs. However, these mandates just make the problems worse and leave the people with next to nothing. Remember how the medieval Kings used to solve peasant revolts – eliminate as many mouths as possible, then there will be enough food to go around. That way the Lords and Ladies will live to oppress the poor another day.

### Spain

Spain is facing Depression Era unemployment – 25 percent for the country as a whole and over 50 percent for adults under 25. In a country of only 38 million people, over 5 million have lost their jobs and are no longer paying taxes, but they are burdening the "safety net". Once the EU and IMF impose their own "austerity" program, we will see unemployment go from bad to worse. Housing prices have plummeted by 40 percent and a third of all houses are "under water." The practice of having several people co-sign for the home loan puts a lot of people on the hook and lets the bank book the old value without ever writing it off. And so the financial elite push the same formula onto Spain that they did on Greece and Portugal. Bail out the banks, raise taxes, cut services and allow the Spanish government to run greater deficits. Spain is the ninth largest economy in the world and a bailout will be twice the size of Greece, Portugal and Ireland combined. Who is going to put up the money? No one. When Spain falls, it will create a shockwave felt world-wide.

### Italy

According to its own rules, the IMF will not allow any country to have a debt-to-GDP ratio of greater than 60 percent – but Italy's stands at twice that, now 120%! Once the ratio gets this out of kilter, the risk premium goes way up – so interest rates rise and Italy follows Greece and the unlucky others into a debt/death spiral from which they never recover. When Silvio Berlusconi was kicked out as Prime Minister (he resigned on November 12, 2011), the EU replaced him with a central-bank lackey named Mario Monti. Monti quickly raised taxes and cut spending, imposing the standard Eurozone austerity program. Italians do not like such strong medicine and will reject it just as Greece and France did.

### Europe Overall

Remember, downfalls don't happen overnight. These economies unravel slowly. But downward momentum grows in Greece, Portugal is hot on its heels, and Spain crumbles as we go to press. Once Spain collapses, Italy will be sure to follow. By then, Europe's central bankers – mainly those who call Germany home – will have no stomach for trying to save another country – particularly one that doesn't want to be saved. Last year, France voted out conservative President Nicolas Sarkozy in favor of a left-wing socialist. This amounts to a resounding slap in the face to the EU. Perhaps the French haven't changed all that much in the past two hundred years. Some say the French populace still demands "cake and circuses." So here comes more big government, higher debt, and reckless spending.

Say a final good bye to the EU. Uniting Europe was such a noble idea! Napoléon thought so and so did Hitler. But it takes a lot more discipline (and a commitment to a true market-based economy), something that Europe seems unwilling to muster.

Germany is the last hope. However, this time Germany will likely just save itself and let the rest of Europe go pound sand. For Germany not only can't bail out all its neighbors, it doesn't much want to either. Why give away its nation's considerable wealth (which has taken 60 years to replenish), especially if it's just to bailout greedy bankers in countries of "undeserving and non-productive" people?

## Where is the Global Economy Going?

As we have stated from the beginning, most eschatologists are unwilling to see America fulfilling Bible prophecy, although the U.S.A. still stands as the 800-pound gorilla lurking in the middle of the room. It boasts the leading economy, military, and perhaps, at least for the time being, *remains the only legitimate friend of Israel.* That is no small factor in considering from what country or grouping of nations the Antichrist will arise. But since America as Babylon doesn't fit into the "standard" (Lindsey-LaHaye-Jeffrey) scenario, most eschatologists assume the U.S.A. must decline and enter the trash bin of history so an acceptable candidate for the Antichrist (and his powerbase) may emerge... even if it should be the Assyrian-Dan-Islamic Antichrist which some propose. We hate to say it, but many authors stand to get too much egg on their face should they admit to misunderstanding the Scripture for so many years.

On the other hand, most biblical scholars are correct when they see economic calamity coming, citing Revelation 6:5-6, picturing the black horse of the apocalypse and the great disparity between the haves and have-nots (those who "work a whole day just to buy their daily bread" and the rich with their "pure oil and fine wine" that isn't spoiled). One day, there will be an overwhelming collapse of the world economy. When that happens, the "Mark of the Beast" will emerge as a defining element of Antichrist's economic "fix" which all must accept in order to buy or sell in his "new deal" (Revelation 13:15-17). Indeed, this will be the ultimate "offer which no one can refuse."

What is the answer which the world will eventually embrace to solve its economic maladies? We believe it is yet another version of an old economic model tweaked especially for the end times. Actually, it's proven to be the most efficient form of economic management ever invented: a method for corporations and governments to work together. Sometimes it's called corporatism; but it's better known as *fascism* (i.e., "International Socialism" or as we will label it later, "Democratic Globalism").

We Americans shouldn't really be that surprised by this economic theory (that is, fascism) so named by Benito Mussolini and practiced by him along with Adolf Hitler. For the reality is that America has been growing fonder of fascism for the past sixty years, ever since a Republican president and World War II hero, Dwight David Eisenhower warned us to beware of the "Military-industrial Complex" (a warning which we didn't hear). In our day, most economic pundits believe that what's good for big business (e.g., Exxon, Shell, Bechtel, Halliburton, Monsanto, even Wal-Mart) must be good for America. It doesn't matter if jobs are outsourced to other countries. The upside is worth it: corporate America makes more than ever with cheap labor. For it appears that "growing shareholder value" trumps increasing worker's wages and the oft-repeated goal of populist politicians calling for the stabilization of the middle-class. You see: corporate boards like Chinese labor and Indian help desks. They blithely surmise that Americans don't want those jobs anyway.

If fascism leads us into a few wars, not to worry! After all, who benefits from the new spate of regional wars? American corporations do, especially those that specialize in transportation, technology, and aerospace. Likewise, who benefits from any oil shortage that could result? It's the oil companies and the oil servicing enterprises like Halliburton who are making dollars hand over fist. In fact, last year oil conglomerates made a record $150 billion in profits! What programs are being funded (military) and what programs are being cut (social safety net entitlement programs, health, education, retirements, even veteran's benefits) provide real insight into the nation's true agenda. All you have to do is follow the money to see where our real priorities lie. Do we sound like socialist liberals? We aren't! But we are Christians who read the Bible.

So just how "fascist" is America's economic and political structure today? Take a look at the following checklist of what constitutes Fascism as your guide to answer that question. A country dominated by fascism possesses the following characteristics:

1. It is highly nationalistic with slogans, patriotic symbols and mottos heard from its administrative leadership. The fascist nation often champions a righteous cause which places it at the head of other nation states.

2. It often characterizes its opposition both internally and externally as enemies. Dissent is discouraged, increasingly restricted, and eventually outlawed completely.
3. Human rights are reduced in importance; the desire for security replaces human rights as the people's top priority. Consequently, to keep law and order, most civil liberties are willfully sacrificed.
4. The mass media ceases to be independent; people are led to believe the opposite of the truth. The media tells the populace what it should believe and intimidates those who don't agree.
5. The military is glorified and the government spends an inordinate proportion of money on weapons and military campaigns.
6. "Church and state" lose their distinction from one another. Religion provides legitimacy to the government. Religious belief bolsters the State – it's no longer okay to challenge it.[6]
7. Power and perks for corporate and governmental elite are protected at the expense of the average citizen.
8. Society becomes obsessed with "criminals and punishment." *Note: America has more incarcerated prisoners per capita than any country in the world. What is the growth industry of the future? The military, law enforcement, and managing prisons!*
9. Cronyism and corruption are widespread (as we have seen in the case of Enron and other scandals); not to mention influence peddling (e.g., Abramoff, Tom DeLay), election fraud, etc.
10. Political options are minimized. The differences between candidates are reduced; the contrast between political par-

---

[6] That is, the Church "separated" from the State in order that the State might have it both ways: The Church provides it moral covering while being registered by the State for legitimacy, (i.e., non-taxable status), and told not to interfere in the "body politic."

> ties is diminished. No matter who wins, the elite and the status quo are maintained.

Does this resemble America today? We think it fits us to a tee.

## How to End America's Dominance? Sack the Dollar!

The war in Iraq was not about WMD (weapons of mass destruction) or retaliating for 9/11. Nor was it just about oil. No, that's a common but overly-simplistic view. In reality, it was about the Dollar. To be more specific, it was about keeping the world using U.S. Dollars as the reserve currency. The most valuable item which can only be bought in U.S. Dollars is petroleum. And guess what Saddam Hussein was getting ready to do? He was going to use his control of oil to force a switch from U.S. Dollars to Euros. And the U.S. financiers, oil companies, acting in conjunction with our government could not let that happen. The ONLY thing that keeps the world on *the Dollar standard* is that everyone has to have Dollars to buy oil. No dollars – no gasoline! No gasoline – no go!

However, the world has gotten wise to our game. That's why China, Russia, Brazil, India and most recently, South Africa (known as the BRICS association) are attempting to create a new world currency that doesn't rely upon the Dollar. These nations believe that the U.S. has an unfair advantage with our money serving as the world's currency. Since we print the Dollar, we can create as much as we want and repay our debts with inflated (devalued) currency. This is a clever way to discount what we owe the rest of the world! The BRICS want a level playing field. How unfair of them to demand it!

Likewise, we should ask, "Why are we upset with Iran at this moment in 2013? Does it have anything to do with their possessing nuclear weapons?" The answer is "probably not as much as we have been led to believe." However, the "bomb" is the emotional image our leaders want the public to visualize, because this fear will make another predictably unpopular war apparently necessary – whether most Americans want it or not.

No, the real truth of what is happening behind the scenes: Iran is setting up a "Bourse" (a European-based stock exchange, stemming from the French word for "bag") – an exchange where buyers can purchase Iranian oil in Euros rather than U.S. Dollars. Is this a big deal? It is an enormous deal. America simply cannot allow this to happen. It is a big step toward eliminating the Dollar as the *de facto* world currency. So whether our leaders have to use Israel as our proxy or we have to do it ourselves, Iran must be stopped at all costs, even if it means we must declare war (unofficially of course). If the Dollar falls, the corporate elite fall, and old-guard politicians' careers could end.

Consequently, the "currency war" is the real fight... not whether we should be using fossil fuels to sustain the world's economy... or how we can ensure a steady stream of oil flowing through the Strait of Hormuz.

But there is a possibility this crisis could be moot.

## The Remarkable Rebound of America

As long as we can remember, naysayers have been predicting America's demise via hyperinflation, lenders calling our loans, or the unbearable weight of our debt (the increased likelihood we would default on what we owe others). We have been told time and again that "Peak Oil" occurred back in the 1970s and it is downhill for oil-based economies ever since.[7] Likewise, we have become too dependent on expensive imports and the resulting imbalance that implicitly transfers our wealth to other nations. But rumors of America's demise, at least economically, are greatly exaggerated.

On January 10, 1901 oil was discovered in Texas at the famous *Spindletop*, which eventually produced 100,000 barrels of oil a day. This and subsequent discoveries catapulted America

---

[7] *Peak oil* amounted to a point in time in which growth built on petroleum would cease because oil was running out. Supply could not keep up with demand.

into a position as the leading producer of energy in the world. It facilitated our becoming the greatest industrial and military power in the world. Then in the 1970s, oil production began to decline and the Middle Eastern suppliers realized they literally had America "over the barrel." The price of energy soared and the Middle East became birthplace to terrorism as Arab nations used their new found wealth to advance Islam across the globe.

But the tables are about to turn again. America (in spite of the Obama Administration's generally anti-oil company policies and predilections), will return once again to the number one oil producer in the world (*Reuters*, November 12, 2012). This reversal of fortune may happen sooner than many experts think. In fact, America is already a net energy exporter. Whether Obama opens Federal lands and offshore locations to drilling, production is already booming on private lands. Old, thought to be played out oil fields in places like Texas and California, are coming back on line as new technology ("fracking") enables oil companies to extract twice, even three times as much as they did originally. New lands in North Dakota and across America are creating boom towns and areas of full employment, increased wages, and new supplies of oil every day. Plus, the emerging development of oil shale promises to provide fossil fuel for more than a century.

In the past, producers could only get oil from large underground pools; but most oil is trapped in tiny pockets in rock and shale. New fracking technology and horizontal drilling allows literally trillions of barrels of oil to be freed that were previously inaccessible. This is not only widely found in the US but in Canada, Europe, Venezuela, Mexico, Brazil, etc. The amount of oil available in the world will increase by 20, 40 or a hundred times, making the oil in the sands of the Middle East a cheaper commodity. Oil prices should drop as greater supply comes on line. (It is interesting that fracking only works in shale and rock but not in sand. Some might say this is poetic justice – but to be sure those commentators wouldn't be sheiks in Saudi Arabia or Kuwait!)

We don't know exactly how much oil there is, but any *one* of the oil fields in Alaska, the Baken field in the Upper Midwest Plain States, in Monterey Bay, the Gulf of Mexico or the Rocky Mountains may hold as much oil as the whole Middle East. This could also be true of Venezuela, Brazil, Australia, and even places thought to be played out such as the North Sea. Literally, trillions of barrels (compared to Saudi Arabia reserves of 267 billion) will be available in a few short years. But that's not all. *Fracking* releases natural gas as well as oil and this alone could make the U.S. energy independent before the end of this decade.[8] Boone Pickens has privately campaigned for natural gas to be transformed into *liquefied natural gas* (LNG). The U.S. is quietly building huge tankers and expanding its ports to be able to export LNG around the world making us once again the largest exporter of fossil fuels in the world.

Once the Administration realizes this fact (and it is safe to assume it already does), the U.S. government can obtain billions in tax revenues from leases and shipping concessions. American deficits will shrink and then disappear. America will once again be capable to do whatever she wants in the world without having to worry about being a second-class debtor nation. America will rebound and remain number one.

This is no pipe dream (pun intended). This is happening right now.

## Isn't Hyperinflation a Real Threat?

Some economists see our biggest threat stemming from Federal Reserve policies of printing money and implementing the so-called Quantitative Easing programs. They suggest this will cause hyperinflation and result in the utter ruin of the Dollar. Recall, if you will, that *inflation is the result of money creation* while *deflation is the destruction of money*. All of the debt we have been fixated on in America the past decade and the mystical

[8] See the article by Bernice Napach in *Yahoo Finance,* March 5, 2013

"derivatives" we hear about continue to increase debt. A great deal of debt has been written off but derivatives continue to grow. Money is being destroyed through the continued loss in asset value. That is the opposite of hyperinflation.

Look at what happened to the housing and stock markets over the past twenty years. Housing is going up again because of low interest rates. Once rates go up, prices will drop yet again. Markets go up and then they go down. Pension funds, fund managers, and speculators are cash rich with a new infusion of capital once or twice a month. They put new money into stock markets and commodities, and that makes its way into more derivatives; but the real value isn't there. So it's just a matter of time before these investment vehicles crash, losing half or more of their value. Meanwhile, the managers placing these bets have paid themselves big bonuses while the average Joe who made the investments in the first place takes a bath losing his retirement and savings. Take a look at what just happened in Cyprus. This

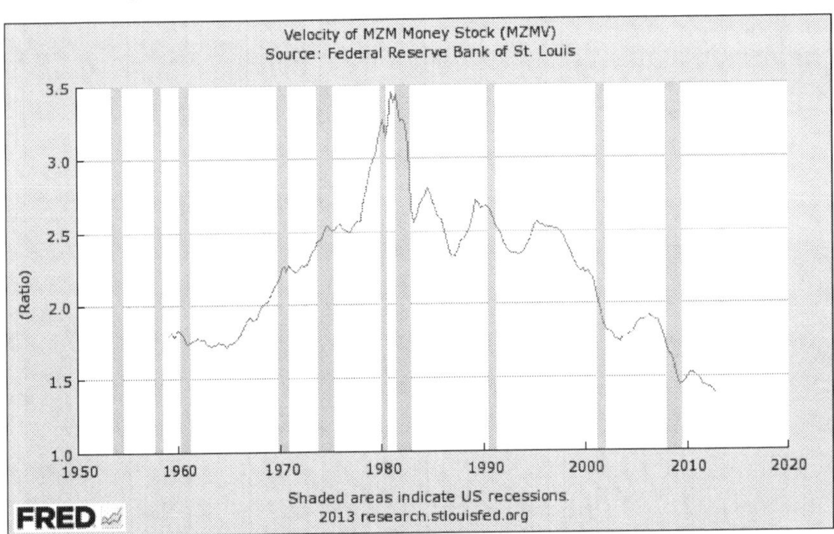


**Figure 30 - The Velocity of Money as a Measure of Inflation**

"asset grab" of private deposits to fund the government had the blessing of the European Community and IMF. Consequently, these draconian maneuvers to making government solvent may soon be coming to a mega-bank near you!

So is there really a threat of hyperinflation destroying the Dollar? Stephen Hank provides this assessment in the *Daily Reckoning* from April 8, 2013:

> ***Is hyperinflation coming to the U.S.?***
>
> No. Hyperinflation arises only under the most extreme conditions, such as war, political mismanagement, or the transition from a command economy to a market-based economy. If you compare the U.S. to countries that have experienced hyperinflation — think Iran, North Korea, Zimbabwe, and the former Yugoslavia, for example — the U.S. doesn't even come close.
>
> "Hyperinflation begins when a country experiences an inflation rate of greater than 50% percent per month — which comes out to about 13,000% per year. Although it experienced elevated inflation around the time of the Revolution and the Civil War, the United States has never passed this magic mark. At present, the U.S. inflation rate, measured by the consumer price index (CPI), is less than 2% per year. So, to say that the U.S. is on its way to hyperinflation is just nonsense. [9]

He points out that *Quantitative Easing* is "state money" and an insignificant part of our *true money supply* (which is what constitutes "bank money"). If you think money is abundant, just try and get a car or house loan if you have "so-so" credit. The Money isn't there. Therefore, conditions for hyperinflation don't exist.

Also, we should remember that it isn't just the amount of money available but the "velocity" or turnover of money (how many times it is spent and spent again). Notice in the chart above, in the early 1980s when there was double-digit inflation, the velocity of the money supply was at almost a 3.5 ratio. Today it is below 1.5. Banks are holding onto their money. People are holding onto their money. Businesses are holding onto their money. This leads us to economic stagnation.

---

[9] Hank, Stephen, "Is Hyperinflation Coming to the US?" *The Daily Reckoning*, April 8, 2013.

This does not take away the seriousness of inflation. Even a small amount like 3 or 4 percent inflation rapidly devalues any currency. Since the Federal Reserve was created 100 years ago, the value of our currency has dropped by 95 percent. Remember the nickel candy bar, the dime coke or coffee, or the 25 cent movie or haircut? The same house in LA purchased 65 years ago for $10,000 is "worth" several hundred thousand today. Why such a difference? In a word: Inflation.

Yes, inflation does destroy the value of currency; but we live now in a deflationary period. Prices for housing, commodities and all goods and services continue to fall. Why? Because all of the debt (government deficits, unfunded liabilities such as Social Security, Medicare and pensions, business debt, state, city and county, business debt, student loans, bad mortgages, etc.) exists both in its essential form, and also multiplied through so-called *derivatives*. There isn't enough money in the entire world to pay off all the debt. The amount of debt world-wide already "on the books" far exceeds the potential for income growth to satisfy the debt service of such massive debt. Money is more likely to shrink rather than grow.

Eventually the financial system will demand that someone with a really bright idea, faster supercomputers, and an ability to control fraud, will come up with an electronic system that is virtually failsafe. This will identify a person's income and track all of his or her expenses leading to a "Brave New World Order." Hyperinflation might happen someday. But we should realize it is not a necessary precondition or prelude to "the Mark of the Beast" and his New World Order. The flames of fear are inappropriately fanned by well-meaning but lightly educated financial "advisors" who are alarmists, perhaps for the right reasons, but nonetheless drawing the wrong conclusions. After all, we should realize that for the rest of the world, the U.S. Dollar already IS *the Mark of the Beast*! For when it comes to buying or selling oil, the fundamental commodity that underlies the world's economy, only Dollars will do!

## Conclusion

There have been other fiscal giants down through history, but no nation before now meets the attributes of the great commercial empire and consumer nation described in Revelation 18 as well as the United States of America does today. Still, the idea that America could be "Commercial Babylon" of the last days remains anathema to American evangelicals for a variety of reasons. Whether for purposes of biblical interpretation or because of the unjustified premise that America remains a Christian nation (therefore, not subject to playing host to Satan's seed), designating America as Babylon is inconceivable to most Bible-believing Christians. And yet, any honest appraisal of world nations surfaces no other candidate and leads to no other reasonable conclusion.

The standard prophetic scenario regards Europe as the powerbase for Antichrist. An alternative today, relatively new, sees Islam as the possible power lurking to become the haven for *"the Assyrian"* (as Antichrist is sometimes referenced in the Old Testament). However, any reasonable appraisal of either Europe or the Muslim World reckons them unfit to dominate the world and unable to manage it if such a role were suddenly thrust onto either.

Instead, it is far more likely the "revived empire of Rome" is a revitalized and vast, dominating Gentile Empire, without Semitic heritage. True, Babylon isn't Rome, but it is Gentile. And Babylon is the allusion invoked by John, Isaiah, and Jeremiah. Also true: Babylon is not an American city *per se*, but neither is it European! It is reasonable to assume that Babylon, like Tyre, Sidon, and Tarshish, provides a historic symbol of the future Gentile world power which winds up seeking to destroy the Jewish people and ultimately opposing their God, Jehovah.

The nations of Europe historically founded and formed America. There are thousands (if not millions in some cases) of immigrants from each European country which came here, learned our language, and have been assimilated. Even the recent so-called Hispanic Invasion remains a mixture of mostly European bloodlines. In contrast, Europe most certainly exists without a bona fide unifying principle (neither religion, nor language, not even currency as several countries do not base their economy on *Euros*). Conflicting interests, cultures and language divide the continent into mish-mash that lacks cohesion. Supposing Europe "homogenized" by a single government has two world wars and centuries of regional wars that prove otherwise. Furthermore, the greatest part of Europe is on the verge of total financial collapse. Europe has nothing approaching America's military might, few common interests, and lacks unified goals and domestic policy. Europe is thoroughly post-Christian. Astonishingly, anti-Semitism still lurks in Europe. Achieving an "about-face" in which Europe rushes to the aid of Israel (an undisputed attribute of Antichrist as he establishes a covenant with Israel – see Daniel 9:24-27), stretches credulity to the breaking point.

Therefore, for almost every reason America should be the resounding choice to play this most undesired and unwanted role of THE FINAL BABYLON. It boasts the world's largest economy. It possesses the world's largest military. There is a cultural identity that runs throughout our nation. There is a consensus of sorts regarding national goals and statutory policies for domestic issues. Plus, no other nation remains a friend and defender of Israel, even if our alliance is on shaky grounds at the present moment (despite the hosted "celebration" engineered by the Israeli government – *The Unbreakable Alliance*, so-called, of March 22, 2013).

When one goes in search of the great consumer nation that "all the world trades with by sea" (recall we are an ocean away from either Asia or Europe – or anywhere else for that matter), what other nation comes to mind? Three-quarters of the U.S. economy is based on consumption! No other marketplace comes close.

Ours is a land that was discovered 500 years ago (a New World of which Europe formerly denied its existence), only when motivated by its mercantile interest, did explorers such as Columbus quest beyond the Pillars of Hercules. Their pecuniary motive, characteristic of the ancient Phoenicians, the inhabitants of Canaan (which means, we remind the reader once again, *merchant*), provides the foreshadowing of that future Babylon at the center of world trade. Primarily, through its fiscal power, it will come to dominate the affairs of the whole world and eventually incarnate all manner of rebellion that inevitably evokes God's judgment.

It's a conclusion that the authors of this book take no joy in proclaiming. Nonetheless, it is our collective, studied, and reluctant opinion: America is THE FINAL BABYLON.

# *Chapter 7:* The First World Empire

*"Now it shall come to pass in that day that Tyre*
*will be forgotten seventy years,*
*according to the days of one king.*
*At the end of seventy years it will happen to Tyre*
*as in the song of the harlot:*

*'Take a harp, go about the city, You forgotten harlot;*
*Make sweet melody, sing many songs,*
*That you may be remembered.'*

*And it shall be, at the end of seventy years,*
*that the LORD will deal with Tyre.*
*She will return to her hire, and commit fornication*
*with all the kingdoms of the world on the face of the earth."*

*(Isaiah 23:15-17)*

## The Many Methods of Empire Building

AMERICA IS AN EMPIRE. TRUE, IT IS NOT AN EMPIRE IN THE COLONIAL TRADITION OF BRITAIN OR ANCIENT SENSE OF BABYLON, GREECE, ROME, OR EVEN THE EMPIRES OF THE LAST millennium like Mongolia (Genghis Khan) or the Ottoman Empire of Turkey. Pertinent to our study, the United States of America is most like the most ancient empire of Tyre and Sidon, aka *Phoenicia*, a vast commercial enterprise expanded by her creativity and culture as well as her commercial expertise and her technical skills (in whose time the key technologies were navigational and mathematical, as applied to shipbuilding and sailing).

Indeed, Tyre teaches us that it is possible to rule the world in more ways than one. Ancient Tyre dominated by developing money, commercial exchange, and trading partnerships. The Phoenicians surpassed all others in their ability to circumnavigate large continents (not just sail "around" the Mediterranean). They may have brought North America into its commercial empire, exploiting finds of precious metals. Some scholars argue that the Bronze Age[1] was actually facilitated by large finds of copper in the region now known as the Great Lakes.[2] Vast amounts of copper are also associated with recent discoveries of giants in America, 2,500+ year-old skeletal remains unearthed in full armor made with pure copper.[3]

**Figure 31 - A 9' Giant with Full Copper Armor, discovered in 1925 in Walkerton, Indiana (1 of 8 co-located skeletons)**

Phoenician culture was spread far and wide through developing the ancient alphabet that served as the basis for world trade and would eventually be taught to the Greeks, who would create an alphabet that was literally a mirror image of the Phoenician

---

[1] Bronze is made of copper and tin. The Bronze Age began in the fourth millennium BC and continued to nearly the end of the second millennium BC (3500 BC to 1200 BC). It was superseded by the Iron Age. If true, the Phoenicians were active in America 3,000 years before Columbus "discovered it."

[2] Discussed in the documentary on the Discovery Channel, *America Unearthed, Episode 3: The Great Lakes Copper Heist*. See http://www.amazon.com/Great-Lakes-Copper-Heist/dp/B00AX4EKFE to view the episode.

[3] See Fritz Zimmerman's work, http://www.thetruthdenied.com/news/2012/02/11/fritz-zimmerman-author-of-the-nephilim-chronicles-interview-re-giant-skeletons/.

one.[4] Eventually Greek would become a world language, after Alexander the Great "Hellenized" civilization replacing the language of Tyre with its Grecian derivative.

Phoenicia lives on in many of our modern words: *Phonics*, *phone* (as in telephone), *phonemes*, to name but a few. However, the point of this chapter is that Phoenicia supplies a legacy which summarizes the history of humankind, from the beginning of civilization to its conclusion. Indeed, the Bible proffers a portrait of Phoenicia suggesting it foreshadows the final great Empire, an Empire that dominates the world through commerce, culture, and unfortunately, corruption. While Phoenicia no doubt had military capacity, it appears that its empire was built upon civilization not barbarism. Civilizing influences, not military threats, provided the carrot rather than the stick, motivating other peoples' cooperation rather than inspiring conflict.[5] That itself is a noteworthy accomplishment. It also provides a clue why the Daughter of Tyre and the Daughter of Babylon are offspring from the same unsavory father we know as Satan, and why the Bible's prophets connect them both to the same image of a harlot, a woman "returning to her hire," a woman that rides the beast.

---

[4] It is likely that the Phoenicia alphabet was actually a modification of the Hebrew alphabet. As we will see, Phoenicia was also known as Canaan, the inheritance of Abraham, and destined to be the land of Israel. Which came first, Hebrew or the Phoenician alphabet remains a controversial subject scholars' debate. Biblical scholars likely argue that ***Enoch*** was the first to be taught the art of writing as he was known as scribe to the "watchers" in the tradition of the Book of Enoch. *Thoth* (the Egyptian god of knowledge and writing), *Hermes* (the Greek god of knowledge and the messenger to the gods) and *Teuton* (the Norse god of knowledge) were all derived from Enoch. "*Djehuty* is sometimes alternatively rendered as Jehuti, Tahuti, Tehuti, Zehuti, Techu, or Tetu. *Thoth* (also Thot or Thout) is the Greek version derived from the letters *ḏḥwty*. Not counting differences in spelling, Thoth had many names and titles, like other goddesses and gods..." See *http://en.wikipedia.org/wiki/ Thoth.* For a discussion on the age and origins of the alphabet, see http://news. bbc.co.uk /2/hi/middle_east/521235.stm.

[5] Perhaps America surpasses Phoenicia's empire building techniques in one demonstrative way: *It possesses the most powerful military in the history of the world.* If our competitors don't wish to adopt a compatible economic and political arrangement, there are other ways to compel their compliance.

## A Short History of Canaan (Tyre and Sidon, aka the Phoenicians)

To understand why the Bible identifies the land of Tyre and Sidon as illustrative of a corrupt Gentile world system (and particularly its commercial aspect – i.e., "commercial Babylon"), it's essential we learn its remarkable history in relationship to God's plan through the patriarchs of Israel: Abraham, Isaac, and Jacob. This story begins in the first one-fourth of Genesis with Abraham, his calling, and the destinies of his offspring.

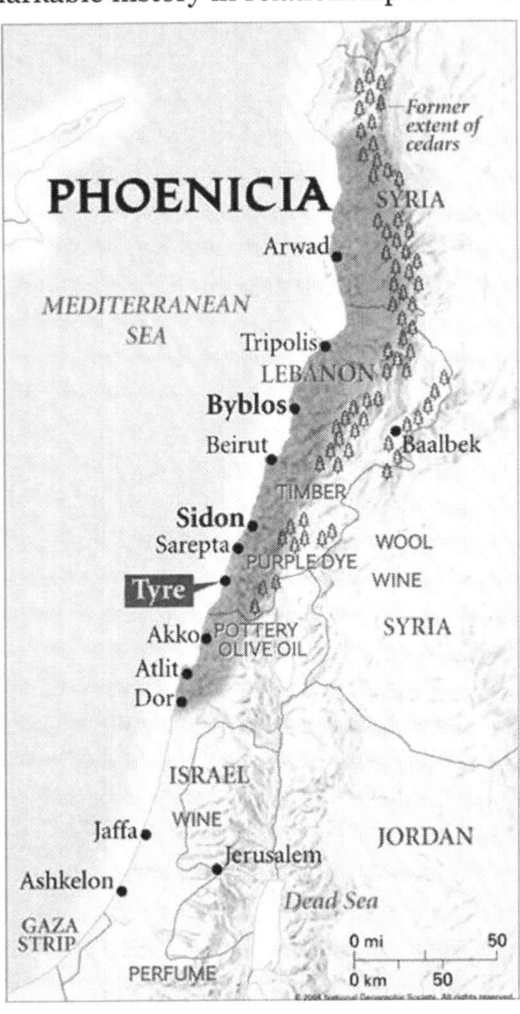

Figure 32 - Phoenicia and its Key Cities

We begin with Abraham's origin. We read that Abraham (aka *Abram*) in Genesis 11:31; 12:5-6, left the land of Ur of the Chaldeans (aka Babylon, so please note that the tale of two Kingdoms, Babylon was always at the heart of the story), "to go to the land of Canaan." In Genesis 13, we find that the Almighty promises to Abraham he would inherit the land of Canaan (Genesis 13:14-18)... "Arise, walk in the land through its length and its width, for I give it to you." (vs. 18)

The first question to consider isn't, *"where is Canaan?"* but rather, *"what does Canaan mean?"* And it literally means *"mer-*

*chant*" – so the derivative, *Canaanites,* means *merchants* or *merchandisers.* The connection to "commercial interests" and commercial Babylon seems, at the very least, extrapolative, if not blatantly obvious.

Now, of great interest to us in our study is the "coincidence" that *Canaan* (a name derivative of Cain, the first child of Adam and Eve who was cursed after murdering his brother Abel), happens to be the second human referenced in the Bible to be cursed. Almost everyone knows Cain was cursed for spilling his brother's blood. But why was Canaan cursed?

Recall Noah had three sons: Shem, Ham, and Japheth. We see in Genesis 9:18 after introducing these three sons, the Scripture says: "And Ham was the father of Canaan." It appears that the Scripture emphasizes this immediate connection for a particular reason. For immediately after this familial introduction comes the story of how ark-builder and captain, Noah, became a farmer upon planting a vineyard, "Then he drank of the wine and was drunk, and became uncovered in his tent (i.e., naked)...and Ham, the father of Canaan, saw the nakedness of his father, and told his two brothers outside...but Shem and Japheth took a garment, laid it on both their shoulders, and went backward and covered the nakedness of their father...Their faces were turned away, and they did not see their father's nakedness... So Noah awoke from his wine, and knew *what his younger son had done to him*" (Genesis 9:18-24).

Commentators – especially among Jewish commentators[6] – contend that Ham's son, Canaan, was involved in some kind of sexual exploitation of his grandfather while Noah was drunk. This conclusion might be excessive; however, at issue was the fact that "Noah awoke from his wine, and knew what his younger son had done unto him" (Gen. 9:24). The phrase "younger son" could refer to either Ham as the younger son of Noah, or to Canaan, Ham's youngest of four sons. In fact, although oft-called the "curse of Ham," most scholars regard the reference *to Ca-*

---

[6] See http://en.wikipedia.org/wiki/Curse_of_Ham.

*naan* not Ham, since Ham was younger than Shem but older than Japheth. It appears that Canaan was responsible and engaged in the "act." However – whatever happened – Ham did not bear the curse; Canaan did. "Ham...saw the nakedness of his father." Thus it appears Canaan was the primary culprit in the incident after which Ham saw "Noah's nakedness" and reported this to his brothers. Ham did not participate with his two brothers in covering his father just as the Scripture says. Ham may have "sat that one out" being despondent for the shame of what his youngest son had done to his father.[7]

We believe the critical iniquity committed was defaming Noah, insulting him, and by implication a DEFAMATION UPON ALL HUMANKIND; for this man Noah, whom God greatly esteemed, was a righteous man of great faith. From that point forward, recall that he was the father of all humankind. *Canaan had ridiculed what God treasured.* THE IMAGE OF MAN, who is made in the image of God, was besmirched by an act of desecration – a "line had been crossed, a border had been bridged, broken, severed" – and Canaan's curse resulted.

It is most interesting that embedded within the curse was Canaan's servitude to Shem (the eldest of Noah's sons). In times past, theologians conjectured that this "Hamitic curse" implied slavery. Because Ham was reputed to have black skin (as we recall from an earlier chapter), through this curse slavery was affixed to the black race. However, we reject this "traditional" and repugnant interpretation outright. There is something more profound and provable from the biblical history about the curse and its prophetic implications. Predicted here was a future conquest of the descendants of HAM (that is, Canaan) by the descendants of SHEM (that is by the Semites, specifically, the *tribes of Jacob/Israel*).

---

[7] We can readily put ourselves in Ham's shoes. What would we feel if our child disrespected his or her grandfather with what must have been an act with sexual innuendo or worse?

"The sons of Ham were Cush (Ethiopia), Mizraim (Egypt); Put (Libya or North Africa), and Canaan" (Genesis 10:6). A few verses later the 11 sons of Canaan are mentioned – and that number *eleven* is important. The first of Canaan's sons being #1 *Sidon* (as in *Tyre and Sidon*) – Genesis 10:15 – then #2 Heth; the #3 Jebusite; #4 the Amorite; #5 and the Girgashite; #6 the Hivite, #7 the Arkite, #8 and the Sinite; #9 the Arvadite, #10 the Zemarite, and #11 the Hamathite (Genesis 10:16-19).[8]

The "borders of Canaan" were also given: "And the border of the Canaanites was from *Sidon* as you go toward Gerar, as far as Gaza; then as you go toward Sodom, "Gomorrah, Admah, and Zeboiim, as far as Lasha (which is roughly today's Israel and about half of Lebanon and parts of Jordan and Syria).

It is history as well as custom that there were the twelve tribes of Israel – i.e., the twelve sons of Jacob/Israel (who were Reuben, Simeon, Levi, Judah, Issachar, Zebulon, Joseph, Benjamin, Dan, Naphtali, Gad and Asher) – Genesis 35:13-26.

The significance of "the Canaan Eleven" is this: The *Twelve Patriarchs of Israel* were told to go in and possess the Land of Canaan – *the Canaan of 11 sons.* We recall the number "11" is associated in Scripture with the "little horn" of Daniel 7 and that in Revelation, the beast arises with seven heads and ten horns, but the future king arises from the ten, *making it the 11th horn* (Daniel 7:24-25). It is not coincidental that with the betrayal of Jesus by Judas Iscariot, the number of the **12** disciples was reduced to **11**. Biblically, *twelve* is regarded as a sacred number while *eleven* is most profane. Numbers, as we will continue to see in our study, are extremely "telling" in regard to biblical prophecy, especially so considering Antichrist (who we famously associate with the number 666) and Babylon, a city in three parts, and associated with the "11th horn" of the beast.

The curse of Canaan continues through all his sons, but one in particular, *Sidon* (his first-born). Tyre is normally mentioned in conjunction with Sidon when referencing Phoenicia – as "Tyre

---

[8] But no *troglodytes*. Humankind wasn't living in caves anymore.

and Sidon" – its principal cities in the ancient world (see the map earlier). To be sure, Tyre lies "beneath" Sidon; therefore, these two sit solidly within the borders of the Land of Canaan – hence, the people of this land were known as *Canaanites.* These two cities may date as far back as 2000 B.C. For comparison, archeologists regard Ur of the Chaldees (in southern "Babylon" the land from which Abram hailed), the world's oldest city dating from 2400 B.C.

It is *significant* that Joshua's entry into "Canaan Land" although successful, *did not include the complete conquest of Tyre and Sidon.* These cities were never conquered by Joshua (Joshua 13:3-6). In effect, this implies the tribes of Israel never realized the final subjugation of Canaan. It remains a future accomplishment to be achieved near or within the time of Messiah's return. Whether Israel achieves this conquest literally or figuratively, (or in both fashions) remains to be seen.

Additionally, the famed Phoenician seafaring prowess seems to have been derived from an even earlier source of capable "sea people"[9] originating from the Aegean Sea area who, as marauders, attacked settlements along the eastern edge of the Mediterranean. This seafaring folk made peace with the Canaanites of Tyre and Sidon while undoubtedly mingling with their DNA as well as their nautical skills, becoming "cultured seafaring Phoenicians." The timing of this connection likely transpired before 2,000 BC.

Soon the Phoenicians combined a penchant for "making money" with unsurpassed *sailing skills* attaining unprecedented commercial exploits throughout the Mediterranean Basin and beyond. (It should be noted that the cultured Greeks considered them the scum of the earth – mere "deal makers" – the same way we speak of "used car salesmen" today).

---

[9] http://ngm.nationalgeographic.com/print/features/world/asia/lebanon/phoenicians-text.

## The Sidonians

At this point, we must draw attention to the noteworthy work of the late David Flynn and his thesis on "Sidonia," a land to the north of Israel, but within Israel's covenant borders. This is the land where Mt. Hermon resides; and Mt. Hermon serves as source of the Jordan River.

Based on both Scripture and ancient text, Flynn conjectures that this land, well before it was Canaan, held a dark and dramatic secret from the time before Noah; an extraordinary phenomenon as the root cause for the watery judgment of the Earth "that then was." Flynn argues, as have many evangelical authors over the past three decades, that "The antediluvian Earth was contaminated by super-human [i.e., angelic] beings who descended upon the crest of Mt. Hermon (an "ancient gate" [or portal]) and "created hybrid offspring with human women, the 'Nephilim' and mighty men of renown preserved in ancient myths."[10]

Writing several years ago (before 2012), Flynn conjectured:

> The source for the dispersion of angelic 'alien' technology, and the Hermetic knowledge that influenced human civilization since the days of Noah, was Sidonia/ Cydonia. The symbolism surrounding the coming End of the Aion in 2012 suggests perhaps another 'descent' is approaching. The time & location should not be a mystery as it has been looked for, advanced & ardently pursued by the Mystery Schools for centuries, from its earliest advocacy in the *Edfu* Texts to the current wizardry going on at NASA. At the very least, could there be a revelation that alien intelligences left evidence of their civilizations on Mars?[11]

Indeed, although traditional scholars consider any phenomenon implying "the supernatural" farfetched, Flynn's thesis extends well beyond that forbidden threshold. Nevertheless, Flynn doesn't sit on that proverbial limb by himself. His view of "the secret history of Sidon" coincides with that of Tom Horn, Steve Quayle, L.A.

---

[10]See http://www.mt.net/~watcher/.

[11] Flynn, Ibid.

Marzulli, Gary Stearman, and a host of other contemporary writer/researchers. We read: "Phoenicia was the first place where beings from heaven came to the earth. The union of these (alien) beings with the daughters of Adam produced hybrid offspring; Nephilim (translated *giants* but literally the *fallen ones*)."[12] According to the pseudepigraphic *Book of Enoch*, the *Book of Jubilees* and many other ancient texts, the exact point of descent of the Sons of God was *Mt. Hermon in Phoenicia*. The history of angelic incursion, a mixing of their "seed" (DNA) with human seed, has become a subject for considerable titles in the past thirty years. But Flynn's contribution to this collection of "alternate history" stands out, in its attention to detail and reach, across no small number of mythic records.

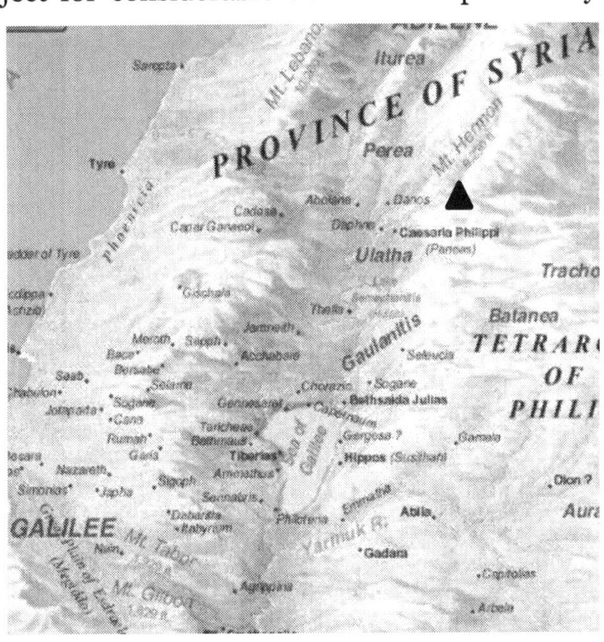


Figure 33 - Mt. Hermon, Near Caesarea Philippi

The later stories associated with the Tribe of Dan and "the Danites" adds to *the occult history* of this land, but these Danites (or *Danaans* of Homer's *Iliad*) did not originate that history. As Flynn indicates, this angelic incursion reaches farther back still into the dark mists of time. If we take the Book of Enoch to reflect a true history of the anti-diluvium world (at least in part), we should consider that the locus of evil down through the centuries was precisely in this place. From this "gate" at Mt. Her-

[12] See http://www.biblestudytools.com/bible/passage.aspx?q=ge+6:4&t=kjv.

mon, we link the evil which (1) gave rise to the flood; (2) to that which persisted through Canaan's descendants including Nimrod; and (3) only later expanded after Israel took possession of the land from the Canaanites by settlements of the tribe of Dan and the other ten tribes of Northern Israel.[13] The wickedness of the Danites continues to the time of the great Hebrew prophets, specifically we think of Ezekiel's conflict with King Ahab (including the infamous Jezebel and her god from Tyre – Baal), followed by the continued worship of such gods "in the high places" of Israel.[14]

---

[13] One source provides this comment: "In the division of Canaan by lot, under Joshua, the whole of the country as far north as Sidon was apportioned among the tribes. The coastal towns of Sidon, Tyre, Akka and Dor are particularly mentioned as being awarded to the tribes of Asher and Manasseh. It is definite, however, that some localities were never occupied at all by the tribes, and others only partially so. The Bible record makes it clear that the Israelites came to some sort of unauthorized "live-and-let-live" arrangement with the existing inhabitants, possibly because the task of complete conquest seemed too formidable. The narrative positively states that the cities of the Phoenician seaboard and the immediate hinterland were not cleared of their inhabitants and that, in these areas, the Israelites *"dwelt among the Canaanites, the inhabitants of the land"."* *See* http://www.ensignmessage.com/archives/*tarshish.html.*

[14] From *Fausset's Bible Dictionary*, we read about the high places:

> Archaeological and scientific researchers have made it evident that in the varying forms of early religions, and in lands far distant from each other, high places were selected for worship of a sacrificial character. This was so especially among the Moabites (Isaiah 15:2; Isaiah 16:12; Numbers 23:28). The three altars built by Abraham at Shechem, between Bethel and Ai, and at Mamre, were on heights. Such sites consecrated of old would naturally be resorted to in after times as sanctuaries. Not only these, but heights originally dedicated to idols (Numbers 33:52; Leviticus 26:30). The law forbade sacrificial worship elsewhere save at the one national sanctuary. Old usage however strove against the law, and too frequently reasserted itself. The high places polluted by idol worship (2 Kings 23:9) were condemned by all the kings that worshipped Jehovah.
>
> But those sacred to Jehovah (2 Chronicles 32:12; 2 Chronicles 33:17) were tolerated by less thoroughly reforming kings; and sacrifices and burnt incense were offered on them (1 Kings 12:3; 1 Kings 14:4; 1 Kings 15:35). Hezekiah and Josiah removed them utterly, as opposed to the letter of the law and mostly to the spirit of it too (2 Kings 18:4; 2 Kings 23:5 margin; 2 Chronicles 34:3). In the time of the judges (Judges 6:25-26; Judges 13:16-23; 1 Samuel 7:10; 1 Samuel 16:5), and while the temple

If Jerusalem was then and still remains the geographical center of God's Kingdom, just a few hundred miles to its North abides the center of the kingdom opposed to God. It is this evil kingdom, enlivened by demi-gods from ancient days, and, through their descendants at the present time (perhaps genetically, but certainly symbolically), which still opposes God and seeks to thwart His plan. The fact the name of this land was known as *Canaan* (and that the word literally means "merchant") makes plain no incidental point. The opposition to the Kingdom of God, in part, *festers upon unrivaled commercial exploits.* Tyre[15] and Sidon, Canaan, and Phoenicia (essentially synonymous) all provide symbol and foreshadowing of this great commercial empire, identified also *as financial Babylon in chapter 18 of Revelation. Together these images represent the "Kingdom of fallen humanity" – the Gentile world – opposing the God Yahweh and His people from both Old Testament and New.*

## Phoenicia, the Merchants of Tarshish, and the Celts

"Phoenicia" is derived from Greek designation– although, to the core, the Phoenicians were definitely Canaanites. The name itself derives from *the purple dye of mollusks* found along the

---

was yet unbuilt (1 Kings 3:2), and in the Israelite northern kingdom where religious order could not be preserved, owing to the severance from Judah (1 Kings 18:30), greater latitude was allowed. But the strict rule was against it, except where God especially (1 Chronicles 21:26) sanctioned sacrifice on some one occasion at a place (Deuteronomy 12:4-11; Leviticus 17:3-4; John 4:20).

See http://www.bible-history.com/faussets/H/High+places/.

15 Listed amongst Shakespeare's plays is *Pericles, Prince of Tyre* (see http://www.william-shakespeare.info/shakespeare-play-pericles-prince-of-tyre.htm). His spirit and quest for greater riches and the mystery of his whereabouts are well documented in the works of Maria Eugenia Aubet, Glenn E. Markoe and the editing work of the late Sabatino Moscati in his work, *The Phoenicians*; who, in his legacy found in the *New York Times*, is quoted as saying that the Phoenician culture "*is one that we must confront in order to understand ourselves*" (New York Times, Sept. 10, 1997, emphasis added). We can only wonder if this Italian Semitic linguist and archeologist fully *knew the profundity of his remark!*

shores near Tyre; hence, the term literally means "purple people." [16] Tyre seemed driven to extend her commercial seafaring enterprise throughout the ancient world within the Mediterranean region (with her religiously-based harlotries of Baal and Astarte coming along for the ride) – into such places as Carthage (modern Tunisia) and the Iberian Peninsula (Portugal/Spain), from whence we derive the phrases "Ships of Tarshish," "Merchants of Tarshish," and "Daughter of Tarshish." Tarshish itself refers to a city in southern Spain, *Tartessos*. The Canaanites or Phoenicians became known in Rome as the *Punic Peoples* (the *Purple People* as translated into Latin). [17]

Therefore, we anticipate the reader might inquire, "So how did the Phoenicians refer to themselves?"

> It doesn't seem that the Phoenicians ever used [only] a single word to refer to themselves. It was the Greeks who gave them the global name of Phoinix[18], "red" (for the dye they produced [or "purple"]), rendered as Fenkhou in Ptolemaic Egypt.

---

[16] The Phoenicians and the Carthaginians expanded all across North Africa and Western Europe. They pushed past the Straits of Gibraltar and founded the city of Gades (present day Cadiz) in Spain. While active in Spain, these Phoenician/Carthaginian descendants are called "Celtiberians" by archaeologists. Later, some sailed away from Spain and colonized the British Isles, where they are simply called "Celts" by archaeologists. In their migrations throughout the Mediterranean, these Celts assimilated a number of different languages and alphabets. These languages and writing systems were in use by different Celtic groups at different times. Memories of some of these scripts were retained up until the medieval period in Ireland. *The Book of Ballymote*, believed to have been composed about 1200 A.D., gives an alphabet, described as "African". Until recently, scholars considered that this "African" script was some sort of cryptic monkish secret alphabet, or maybe just gibberish, but since 1960 this alphabet has been shown to be an actual ancient North African one in use about 1000 B.C." [Fell, America B.C.] - Michael Bradley, *Holy Grail Across the Atlantic*. (See Family Finder, Ancestor.com, http*://freepages.genealogy.rootsweb. ancestry.com/~donegalstrongs/u6b.htms*).

[17] As a comic aside, this reminds us of the 1958 Billboard #1 pop song by Sheb Wooley, "Purple People Eater." It gives an entirely new slant on the nature of the beast. Was it a 1950s rock-and-roll prophetic warning?

[18] Note the spelling correlation to *Phoenix*, the bird that rises from the ashes. Could the Phoenix (and eagle in the America seal, which originally was intended to be a Phoenix, bespeak of America's connection to Phoenicia?

> The earlier Egyptians referred to them as Kinahni, the people of Canaan. [They] themselves used the names Tyrians, Sidonians, Berytians, Giblites, Aradians – the names of their cities. The Phoenician cities never formed a single political entity; they were always fiercely independent but shared their culture, language, art and religion. Each city worshipped its own deity independently from the others and had its own history. Therefore, rather than trying to define Phoenicia as a territory within borders, it is more pertinent to consider it as the land around a string of nuclei cities: from North to South Arwad, Byblos, Beryte, Sidon, Tyr [Tyre], and Akk™. [19]

Despite this ambiguity in self-identity – Phoenicia's "commercial culture" formed a societal bond, a hardened cohesion; and actually gave rise to a sort of "mysterious people" which had its own peculiar DNA but purposefully seemed to proliferate via colonization for commercial reasons – although we should emphasize they toted along *their religious point of view for good measure* (a familiar tactic for imperial colonization of both new world and the old, e.g., America, India, Africa, the Middle-east, and Southeast Asia during the past 400 years). God condemns Phoenicia's/Tyre's wealth and "commercial empire" (poetically expressed in Ezekiel 28:11-19 and other portions of Scripture, e.g., Isaiah 23:1–18; Jeremiah 25:22; 27:1–11; Ezekiel 26:1–28:19; Joel 3:4–8; Amos 1:9,10), for it *suppresses the dignity of human freedom in the name of commercial accomplishment.* At first glance, this prophetic passage (familiar to most evangelicals), seems to refer to a singular human king; but scholars generally see in this passage a description of the adversary – that is, Satan himself. Unquestionably, Tyre is the recipient of some of the strongest prophetic condemnations in the Bible. Given that near explicit connection, the condemnation takes on added meaning while its prophetic nature becomes all the more explicable.

---

[19] See http://freepages.genealogy.rootsweb.ancestry.com/~donegalstrongs/ u6b.htm.

History tells of the famed Punic Wars around 200 B.C. with the famously capable Punic General Hannibal nearly defeating Rome by invading her through the Swiss Alps, having led a sub-

**Figure 34 - The Kensington Runestone in Alexandria, MN, discovered there in 1897 (dating circa: 1100 AD)**

scripted army of professional militarists riding elephants to intimidate their enemy. Hannibal achieved substantial and sustained victories on the Italian Peninsula for 15 years. His good fortune was reversed after Rome determined they couldn't defeat him on their home field in Italy, so they attacked his capital in Carthage, drawing him back to Northern Africa to provide for its defense.

It is another no small "coincidence" that Hannibal allied himself as an advisor to *Antiochus III Epiphanes* (a Seleucid Ruler in what Rome called "Syria" – the Middle East) and father of the perfect archetype of the future Antichrist, *Antiochus IV Epiphanes*. Afterwards, Hannibal fled to Armenia, and thence to the court of Bithynia, where he achieved an outstanding naval victory against a fleet from Pergamum. Finally, he was betrayed to the Romans and committed suicide by poisoning himself.

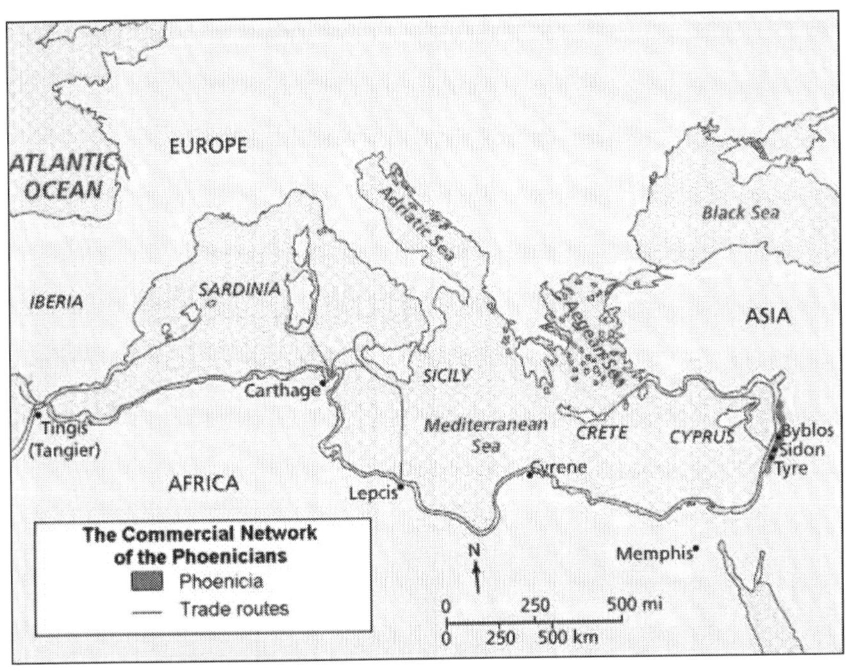


**Figure 35 - Tyre's Commercial Empire**

Rome was so outraged over Hannibal's machinations – devious but brilliant general though he was – they determined to abolish all traces of Punic culture and society. After they had destroyed the massive war ships of the Punic fleet (some transports being over 200 feet long), Carthage was demolished and salt plowed into their ground. All that remains of the ancient glories of the Phoenician-Punic-Tartessos peoples are accounts from their enemies.[20] Thus, Rome subsumed Tyre into its "collective" – assimilating Phoenicia into its highly divergent Roman Empire.

But all was not lost.

Rome inherited the Phoenicians vast commercial expertise, and no doubt benefitted from their remarkable sailing skill. Their "early" circumnavigation around the horn of Africa is well known – likewise, it appears evident to open-minded scholars that "the Merchants of Tarshish" trafficked in North America 2,500 years before Columbus. There are numerous discoveries of their script (their alphabet) on our continent before the time of Christ.

> The possibility that the Phoenician's may have made a pre-Columbian voyage or voyages to the Americas has been explored by several scholars from as early as T. C Johnston's 1892 book, *Did the Phoenicians Discover America?* Work on Phoenician coins carried out by Mark McMenamin suggests that gold coins minted in Carthage between 350 and 320 B.C.E. may depict a map of the Americas.[21] [See Mark's intriguing interpretation of this coin adjacent]
>
> Some have speculated that the Phoenicians may

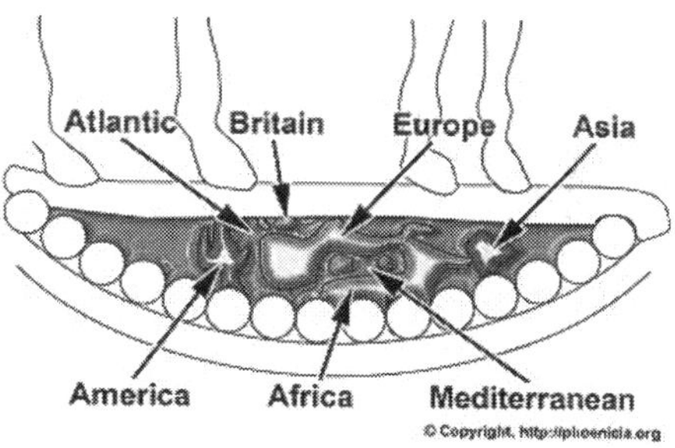


**Figure 36 - A Gold Coin from Carthage with a World Map?**

[20] See http://www.lost-civilizations.net/phoenicians-history.html for a brief history of Phoenicia and Canaan.

[21] See http://www.newworldencyclopedia.org/entry/Phoenician_Civilization # cite_note-4.

> even have colonized the Americas. Thor Heyerdahl's Ra I and Ra I expeditions were designed to prove that Egyptian ships could have crossed the Atlantic but could also be applied to the Phoenicians, who were renowned for their seamanship and who were often employed as sailors and explorers by the Egyptians. Some first century Peruvian pottery resembles Phoenician pottery. Wreckage of Phoenician ships and an inscription on a rock in Brazil suggests Phoenicians had visited there.[22]

We find it altogether remarkable then, that the colonization of the Americas in earnest was initiated in 1492 by the Spaniards,[23] and subsequently thereafter by Celtic peoples of the United Kingdom, both of whom had ample ancestry derived from ancient Canaanite/ Phoenician /Punic peoples whose ancestral roots can be readily traced. The custom of Celtic warriors to dye themselves purple/blue before they faced their enemies may hearken to their "Punic" origin. [24]

Given this lineage, it should be little wonder the renowned "colonizers of the earth" have such deep roots in seafaring and commercial empire building. Indeed, archeology substantiates that the *Phoenicians* originated colonization for purposes of commercial enterprise not the Greeks, Egyptians, Babylonians, Assyrians or other peoples of the ancient world as traditional historians generally speculate.

Furthermore, the ability to amass wealth originated in Tyre. The first actual stock and/or commodities market was founded there, with Tyre being the first city in the ancient world to strike its own city coinage.[25] It is no exaggeration to proclaim that money was invented by Tyre. No wonder then that *Canaan means merchant.*

---

[22] Ibid.
[23] http://en.wikipedia.org/wiki/Tarshish.
[24] Discussions abound on the subject. One small reference: http://wiki.answers.com/ Q/ What_is_Blue_Celtic_war_paint
[25] http://www.usc.edu/dept/LAS/arc/profilecoin/html/page1.htm.

## God's Disdain for Corrupt Commerce

However, we should now allow the Scripture to proclaim its absolute condemnation upon Tyre and from God's perspective, its metaphorical counterparts:

> [1] *The word of the Lord came again unto me, saying,*
>
> [2] *Son of man, say unto the prince of Tyrus, Thus saith the Lord God; Because thine heart is lifted up, and thou hast said,*
>
> *"I am a God, I sit in the seat of God, in the midst of the seas"; yet thou art a man, and not God, though thou set thine heart as the heart of God:*
>
> [3] *Behold, thou art wiser than Daniel; there is no secret that they can hide from thee:*
>
> [4] *With thy wisdom and with thine understanding thou hast gotten thee riches, and hast gotten gold and silver into thy treasures:*
>
> [5] *By thy great wisdom and by thy traffick hast thou increased thy riches, and thine heart is lifted up because of thy riches. (Ezekiel 28:1-5)*

The poor, as Jesus said, "*You have with you always*" (John 12:8). But we also have the unabated growth of riches among America's wealthy 1%! Today, in America, this 1% owes almost half of our wealth.[26] The destruction of the middle class and the disparity between rich and everyone else, strikes at the heart of the principles of democracy; moreover, it attacks the freedom afforded America's "common man."

*However, making money is not evil.* In itself, *wealth does not inevitably corrupt just as poverty does not inexorably en-*

---

[26] Forbes breaks it down for us in this rather shocking set of data points: "The 1 (one) percent are executives, doctors, lawyers and politicians, among other things. Within this group of people is an even smaller and wealthier subset of people, 1 percent of the top, or .01 percent of the entire nation. Those people have incomes of over $27 million, or roughly 540 times the national average income. Altogether, the top 1 percent control 43 percent of the wealth in the nation; the next 4 percent control an additional 29 percent." (See http://www.forbes.com/fdc/welcome_mjx.shtml).

*noble.* But riches do lead to the quest for power, and absolute power does corrupt absolutely. The 1% has a natural habit of striving for as much of the total wealth of a nation as the 1% can amass. *Enough* is not a word in its vocabulary.

So is there anyone in particular that is plainly and painfully aware of "monetary and commercial excesses" of the rich? Yes – the Almighty is. For through His prophets He inspired stinging metaphors culminating in Revelation 18 which depicts in copious detail the destruction of that great commercial city, Babylon – aka, the *Daughter of Tyre and Tarshish* – wherein the power brokers of the earth have participated "luxuriously" in this disparity of wealth – bewailing her demise when they see her literally go up in smoke:

> 9 *And the kings of the earth, who have committed fornication and lived deliciously with her, shall bewail her, and lament for her, when they shall see the smoke of her burning,*
>
> 10 *Standing afar off for the fear of her torment, saying, Alas, alas that great city Babylon, that mighty city! for in one hour is thy judgment come.*
>
> 15 *The merchants of these things, which were made rich by her, shall stand afar off for the fear of her torment, weeping and wailing,*
>
> 16 *And saying, Alas, alas that great city, that was clothed in fine linen, and purple, and scarlet, [*purple and scarlet may harken to the purple people*] and decked with gold, and precious stones, and pearls!*
>
> 17 *For in one hour so great riches is come to naught. And every shipmaster, and all the company in ships, and sailors, and as many as trade by sea, stood afar off,*
>
> 18 *And cried when they saw the smoke of her burning, saying, What city is like unto this great city!*
>
> 19 *And they cast dust on their heads, and cried, weeping and wailing, saying, Alas, alas that great city, wherein were made rich all that had ships in the sea by reason of her costliness! for in one hour is she made desolate (Revelation 18:9-10, 15-19).*

Babylon's demise described in the Revelation demands comparison to the semblance of texts in Ezekiel 26-28, pertaining to the King and Kingdom of Tyre, as well as Tyre's future (and symbolic offspring): *The Daughter of Tarshish and the Daughter of Tyre.* However, the commercial colossus of the last days contemplates "no restraint" in her unbridled consolidation of wealth. No, there is more here than a literary attempt to connect poetic metaphor – as may be rightly discerned in the sublime prose of Isaiah, Jeremiah, Daniel, Joel, Zechariah and Ezekiel – with John the Revelator's recasting it in the powerful image of a woman riding a seven-headed beast with ten horns.

We feature this prophetic linkage for the reader's careful consideration as a most *potent expression of a vital prediction yet to be realized*; indeed it stands as a suspension of a pivotal prophecy dating from antiquity, quietly left unfulfilled until our present time. We conclude that this future Babylon's commercial exploits, as well as her multi-faceted apostasies, are metaphorically expressed in the terms and *prophetic language incriminating Tyre.* Simply put, the two are linked. The Final Babylon's administrative, political and military empire testifies to its unmistakable imprimatur of power from Ezekiel's *King of Tyre, and the hidden malevolent force which undergirds his kingdom.*

Indeed, how could we dismiss Isaiah's excoriation of this "marketplace for the nations" and denounce Tarshish "whose antiquity is from ancient days" without connecting the dots to the "land of the Chaldeans" (the enchanters, diviners, astrologers, magicians, channelers, soothsayers of Babylon – Daniel 2:2; 4:7; 5:7, 11)? How could we avoid the obvious metaphor which binds these ancient empires together, that rehearses its destruction by singing the "song of the harlot" wherein at the "end of seventy years...the LORD will deal with Tyre," though "her feet carried her far off to dwell"? How could we miss the underlying comparable imagery: *"She will return to her hire, and commit fornication with all the kingdoms of the world on the face of the earth"* (Psalm 45:12; Isaiah 23:3, 7, 10, 13, 15, and 17)? Finally, how could we consider this as yet unconsummated future incarnation of "commercial harlotry" not wholly merged with the apostasy of the city we know as Babylon?

## Other Witnesses against Modern Tyre and Tarshish

It has been necessary for us to uncover the roots of "the first empire" (predating the first Babylon by 1,400 years) – to explore the outer reaches of Tyre's merchandising – its origins, influence, disrepute and ultimate judgment (Isaiah 23:7), because it is intrinsically intertwined with THE FINAL BABYLON. For despite Rome's cruel annihilation of all things Canaanite, Phoenician and Punic, the symbol of Tyre and Sidon lives on in its clandestine descendants. And so does its closely related sister, the Daughter of Tarshish, with her seafaring vessels, whose identity with a future Western trading empire abides as more than casual inference. We read in Ezekiel 38:13 and Ezekiel 27:25-29: "After many days you (the Merchants of Tarshish)...*in the latter years*" will question Gog and Magog's ulterior motives to "take a spoil" and abscond with the "booty" of the Middle East (Ezekiel 38:13) when they descend upon the "unwalled villages" of Israel, who by this time, has committed its security to (we believe) those same Merchants of Tarshish under the command of the King of Tyre's alter ego, the "prince who is to come" – the Antichrist (Daniel 9:26).

This humble trio of authors hardly stands alone in drawing this conclusion. Dr. Thomas Ice, a noted eschatologist, conjectures America's engagement in the Gog-Magog War is *consequential,* unlike Lindsey, LaHaye, and Jeffrey who consider America out for the count.

> First, merchants of Tarshish refer to the Phoenician maritime and trading community located in Spain during the general time of King Solomon, 3,000 years ago. Second, *the merchants of Tarshish, during the last 500 years, developed into the modern mercantile nations of Western Europe like Spain, Holland, and Britain.* Third, the phrase "with all its villages" or the variant rendering "with all its young lions," would be a reference to its trans-Atlantic colonies, *which would include America.* Thus,

> *it is reasoned, because America is the most dominant of these Western nations, this must be a reference to America.*[27] [Emphasis added]

Ice continues....

> This view is strongly espoused by Steuart McBirnie, who concluded: "'In the light of such conclusive scholarship, coming to light most significantly at this time when the nations indicated by Ezekiel to be involved in a great Middle Eastern war, we can now say with definite assurance that the merchants of Tarshish and "the young lions (colonies) thereof" must include the Western nations of Europe and the Americans, particularly the United States." [28]

The late David Allen Lewis agrees: "So the young lions of Tarshish would definitely refer to the North American colonies as well as the European colonies, and hence bring the U. S. into this prophecy as one of the nations that will strongly protest the Russian invasion of Israel in the last days."[29]

---

[27] Dr. Thomas Ice, "Is America in Bible Prophecy?" Rapture Ready, accessed 6/6/13, see http://www.raptureready.com/featured/ice/AmericaInBible Prophecy.html.

[28] Ibid. Another slightly less credentialed source provides this comment: "There are recently discovered pointers to trade with both Celts and Indians who had by then established themselves in North America. Mysterious inscriptions have been discovered, deep in the interior of the United States showing that a thousand years of commerce was carried on between Tarshish in Spain and their Celtic colonies in what is now the United States. Their ships regularly traded with the northeastern coastland: inscriptions on rocks have been found with Tarshish lettering. Even more; these ancient mariners entered the Mississippi from the Gulf of Mexico, penetrating inland to Iowa and the Dakotas and westward along the Arkansas and Cimarron Rivers to leave behind inscribed records of their presence there. In 1975 an inscription was found at Union, New Hampshire with excellently preserved Tarshish letters: "Voyagers from Tarshish this Stone proclaims." See http://www.hope-of-israel.org/tarshish.html.

[29] Ibid. Note: Not all authors agree that the invaders are Russians. Recently, numerous scholars suggest it may be a Muslim alliance headed by Turkey. This opinion waxes and wanes based upon the changing strength of Russia and her leadership.

Ezekiel's message finds support in Jeremiah's prophetically stated judgments – against that yet future and ultimate manifestation of the King of Babylon, his empire and the supernatural "Destroying Mountain" (Jeremiah 51:26, 27 – *Bel* of Babylon – "founder of Babylon"). Behind these earthly metaphors and adumbrative language, lie numerous warnings and denunciations:

> *Babylon was a golden cup in the LORD's hand, that made all the earth drunk...the nations drank her wine; therefore the nations are deranged... Babylon has suddenly fallen and been destroyed... for her judgment reaches to heaven... O you who dwell by many waters, abundant in treasures, your end has come, the measure of your covetousness...Though Babylon were to ascend up to heaven... I will punish Bel in Babylon...and the nations shall not stream to him anymore... Behold, I am against you,* ***O destroying mountain,*** *who destroys all the earth... and I will stretch out My hand against you, roll you down from the rocks, and make you a burnt mountain" – Behold: The "City of Confusion [i.e., Babylon, Babel] is broken down"* (Isaiah 24:10; Jeremiah 51).

Regrettably she has indeed returned to her hire! She who makes all the kings and their merchants to drink of the wine of her fornications where apostate religion (especially the "mingled Christian religion" whose chic flirtations with ecumenism and "post-modern culture" accelerates our own "great apostasy"), mercantile pursuits and political power converge – yes, she, the Daughter of Tarshish (which phrase encompasses her worldly and commercial enterprise), returns to her bed of iniquity with her partners, one final time, in a vain attempt to ascend unto the Mountain of the Most High God.

## Conclusion: The Final Condemnation of Tyre, Tarshish, and Babylon

No, the comparisons between the Hebrew prophets Isaiah, Jeremiah, Daniel, Zechariah, Joel and Ezekiel with John's Revelation *"doth demand a verdict"*, an unquestioned judgment soon to descend upon this earthly emperor who, like his Punic predecessor, bears the markings of his ancient prototype: THE KING OF TYRE!

Is this not the crafty culprit, the King of Tyre from Ezekiel 28 (being the archetype), one and the same with that incarnation of Satan we know as the Beast? The evidence confirms that he:

(1) Voiced the idolatrous statement: I AM A GOD! And so declared this "before Him who slays" by setting his "heart as the heart of a god" – a most reckless claim (Ezekiel 28:9, 2)?

(2) Asserted a most obnoxious soliloquy: *"I sit in the seat of gods, in the midst of the seas."* He sought, through force of his own will, to ascend into heaven, exalt his throne above the stars of God, that he might sit on the *"mount of the congregation on the farthest sides of the north,"* above the heights of the clouds, and, finally, in outlandish and idolatrous design: *"Be like the Most high."* (Ezekiel 28:2; Isaiah 14:13-14)?

(3) Is charged with rampant materialism on such a grandiose scale as to defy all human propriety; to wit: *"With your wisdom and your understanding you have gained riches for yourself, and gathered gold and silver into your treasuries; by your great wisdom in trade you have increased your riches, and your heart is lifted up because of your riches."* (Ezekiel 28:3-5)?

(4) Epitomizes mercantile extravagance most especially in our day; whose heart is set "as the heart of a god" and Scripture declares *"The most terrible of the nations"* using *"terror to be on all (its) inhabitants."* Other nations should *"draw their swords against the beauty of (his) wisdom, and (have full liberty to) defile (his) splendor"*—throwing him *"down into the Pit...in the midst of the seas"* – the abyss, from whence he shall ascend in the latter days as the Beast – even *"in places desolate from antiquity, with those who go down to the Pit"* – an eternally *"uninhabited"* place (Ezekiel 28:7; 26:17, 20; Revelation 11:7; 13:1)?

Furthermore, the Scripture heightens its condemnation – speaking to the *evil one* behind the King of Tyre, whose merits were forever unparalleled amongst all created beings. He was:

(5) Accorded *"the seal of perfection – full of wisdom and perfect in beauty"* (Ezekiel 27:3b, 11; 28:7, 12, 17).

(6) *"The anointed cherub who covers"* this symbolic King of Tyre was *"in Eden, the garden of God"* and that he possessed *"every precious stone"* as his "covering" – even *"sardius, topaz, and diamond, beryl, onyx, and jasper, sapphire, turquoise, and emerald with gold" and that his "workmanship of timbrels and pipes was prepared for (him) on the day (he was) created"* leading us to affirm this counterfeit and superlative imposter was designed to lead the angelic hosts in the worship of the One and only True God – making the charges of his forfeiture, which we as children of the most High God hold against him, all the more cosmic in their scope and universally egregious (Ezekiel 28:13-14, 16).

(7) Once allowed full access to *"the holy mountain of God"* and the ability of having *"walked back and forth in the midst of fiery stones"* (all the more traitorous in so far as he was *"perfect in (his) ways from the day (he was) created"* – Yet, no trace of repentance was found in him – so taken was he with his own perfection, obtained without pain and tested without suffering – as vindication of his unworthiness. *"O, how have the mighty fallen?"* (Ezekiel 28:14-16; Isaiah 14:12).

(8) The one whose "crowning city" – Tyre, Babylon, Rome (and we argue New York/ Washington) – has been ever moving (unlike the Almighty's Jerusalem) *to hide his intrigues* – awaits final sentence (no matter how hidden are his intentions and pursuits). For he stands apart as one who has "become a horror, and shall be no more forever for the LORD of Hosts has purposed it, to pollute the pride of all glory, to bring into contempt all the honorable of the earth" (Isaiah 23:8; Ezekiel 28:19; Isaiah 23:9).

For the Scripture testifies of the inevitable outcome:

*15 The merchants of these things, which were made rich by her, shall stand afar off for the fear of her torment, weeping and wailing,*

*16 And saying, Alas, alas that great city, that was clothed in fine linen, and purple, and scarlet, and decked with gold, and precious stones, and pearls!*

*17 For in one hour so great riches is come to nought. And every shipmaster, and all the company in ships, and sailors, and as many as trade by sea, stood afar off,*

> [18] *And cried when they saw the smoke of her burning, saying, What city is like unto this great city!*
>
> [19] *And they cast dust on their heads, and cried, weeping and wailing, saying, Alas, alas that great city, wherein were made rich all that had ships in the sea by reason of her costliness! for in one hour is she made desolate (Revelation 18:15-19).*

And how presumptuous of the Daughter of Tarshish – the Whore of Babylon – the Harlot of Tyre – to declare:

> *"I sit as queen, and am no widow, and will not see sorrow" – Oh, you "Lady of Kingdoms" ... for it is you who said, "I shall be a lady forever"* (Revelation 18:7; Isaiah 47:5, 7).

However, her judgment is sure – being declared from antiquity:

> [1] *Come down, and sit in the dust, O virgin daughter of Babylon, sit on the ground: there is no throne, O daughter of the Chaldeans: for thou shalt no more be called tender and delicate.*
>
> [2] *Take the millstones, and grind meal: uncover thy locks, make bare the leg, uncover the thigh, pass over the rivers.*
>
> [3] *Thy nakedness shall be uncovered, yea, thy shame shall be seen: I will take vengeance, and I will not meet thee as a man (Isaiah 47:1-3).*

And there are, yet, more divinely sanctioned charges spoken against her:

> [8] *Therefore hear now this, thou that art given to pleasures, that dwellest carelessly, that sayest in thine heart, I am, and none else beside me; I shall not sit as a widow, neither shall I know the loss of children:*
>
> [9] *But these two things shall come to thee in a moment in one day, the loss of children, and widowhood: they shall come upon thee in their perfection for the multitude of thy sorceries, and for the great abundance of thine enchantments.*
>
> [10] *For thou hast trusted in thy wickedness: thou hast said, None seeth me. Thy wisdom and thy knowledge, it hath perverted thee; and thou hast said in thine heart, I am, and none else beside me.*

> [11] *Therefore shall evil come upon thee; thou shalt not know from whence it riseth: and mischief shall fall upon thee; thou shalt not be able to put it off: and desolation shall come upon thee suddenly, which thou shalt not know (Isaiah 47:8-11).*

Therefore, we rehearse this final diatribe against the city Babylon and its king, King of Babylon, King of Tyre – who is also called the Daughter of Babylon and Daughter of Tarshish – *NO ONE SHALL SAVE YOU!*

> [12] *Stand now with thine enchantments, and with the multitude of thy sorceries, wherein thou hast laboured from thy youth; if so be thou shalt be able to profit, if so be thou mayest prevail.*
>
> [13] *Thou art wearied in the multitude of thy counsels. Let now the astrologers, the stargazers, the monthly prognosticators, stand up, and save thee from these things that shall come upon thee.*
>
> [14] *Behold, they shall be as stubble; the fire shall burn them; they shall not deliver themselves from the power of the flame: there shall not be a coal to warm at, nor fire to sit before it.*
>
> [15] *Thus shall they be unto thee with whom thou hast laboured, even thy merchants, from thy youth: they shall wander every one to his quarter;* ***none shall save thee*** *(Isaiah 47:12-15).*

All those willing to speak out against that Great City – this woman made "drunk with the blood of the saints and with the blood of the martyrs of Jesus" – who dares mix the religion of YHWH with her abominations; we testify against you King of Tyre, King of Babylon – his kingdoms and his cities. The kings of the earth with whom you conspire, like you, are destined to sample His justice and call down His insatiable wrath:

> [21] *And it shall come to pass in that day, that the LORD shall punish the host of the high ones that are on high, and the kings of the earth upon the earth.*
>
> [22] *And they shall be gathered together, as prisoners are gathered in the pit, and shall be shut up in the prison, and after many days shall they be visited.*
>
> [23] *Then the moon shall be confounded, and the sun ashamed, when the LORD of hosts shall reign in mount Zion,*

*and in Jerusalem, and before his ancients gloriously (Isaiah 24:21-23).*

Strikingly, the prophet affirms:

> *"In that day there shall no longer be a* ***Canaanite*** *(or merchant) in the house of the LORD of hosts"* (Zechariah 14:21, emphasis and parenthetical comment added).[30]

Although we have not used the traditional phrase, the "Judgment of the Nations" up to this point, what we are describing provides the backdrop to this penultimate event. It is the "great and powerful" DAY OF THE LORD, when Babylon the Great is burned with fire and her smoke ascends and is seen by all from afar, especially the *Merchants of the Earth.* It is the time of His Coming – the fulfillment of Joel 2:30-32, Matthew 24:29-31 and the vindication of the saints of the Most High (Revelation 14:17-20; 16:16; 19:17-21). The same winepress portrayed so vividly by the prophet Joel, runs at capacity. But we see how it overflows in the language of Revelation 14:17-20.

> [17]*And another angel came out of the temple which is in heaven, he also having a sharp sickle.*
>
> [18]*And another angel came out from the altar, which had power over fire; and cried with a loud cry to him that had the sharp sickle, saying, Thrust in thy sharp sickle, and gather the clusters of the vine of the earth; for her grapes are fully ripe.*
>
> [19]*And the angel thrust in his sickle into the earth, and gathered the vine of the earth, and cast it into the great winepress of the wrath of God.*
>
> [20]*And the winepress was trodden without the city, and blood came out of the winepress, even unto the horse bridles, by the space of a thousand and six hundred furlongs.*

---

[30] This may be a clear prophetic reference to the "cleansing of the Temple" when Jesus chased the merchants (aka "moneychangers") out of the Second Temple. When Messiah Jesus builds the Temple as described by Ezekiel at the outset of the Millennium, there will be no *Canaanites,* no *merchants* to cheat the worshippers.

Apart from God, these symbolic cities face certain death. Children of God: Flee from them! Doom remains their allotted destiny. Only in His Kingdom will eternal life be found. Once inside the city of the New Jerusalem, only then will God's children be comforted, be "at home," and receive their ultimate and eternal reward. Whoever fails to enter this city, whoever chooses to stay on its outskirts, whoever fails to call God their Father and Jesus Christ Master and Lord, will know no comfort. Their destiny is dark, being without the light of God.

The Kingdom of "Earthlings"[31] has been warned. The dwelling place of devils is condemned already. Be that city Tyre, Tarshish, Babylon, Rome, or even the cultural, financial, and political capitols of these United States, only a few more ticks of the clock remain to sound. Indeed, the final grains of sand run through the hour glass as the Children of Darkness continue to stare in disbelief. But awareness of history's climax grows and those without begin to tremble in fear. How many more ticks will sound; how many more grains will drop until the end comes? Just how much time do we have left?

We will explore that mercurial question in the next chapter.

---

[31] The great evangelical pastor and author, Ray Stedman chose to use the word, "earthlings" in short, for earth dwellers. It is a pejorative for carnal earth inhabitants. He provides this commentary on Revelation 13:8, which reads as follows: *"All inhabitants of the earth."*

> Verse 8 should actually read, "All the *earth dwellers* will worship the beast." We have seen this term before in Revelation, and it is a reference not to those who live on planet Earth, but to those who live only for this world, the materialists and humanists who have no use for heavenly things, no heavenly citizenship, no life except the so-called "good life" here on earth. In contrast to these materialistic "earth dwellers" are "those who tabernacle in heaven," whose names are "written in the book of life belonging to the Lamb that was slain from the creation of the world." FROM: *GOD'S FINAL WORD, Understanding Revelation* by Ray C. Stedman, p. 249, Discovery House Publishers, Grand Rapids, MI, 1991

*Chapter 8:*

# Prophecy and the Powers of Seven

## Seventy (70) and the Perfection of Judgment

AS A "PROPHETIC VEHICLE" THE REPETITION OF THE NUMBER *SEVEN, MULTIPLES OF SEVEN,* AND SEVERAL *POWERS OF SEVEN* (SPECIFICALLY, 49, 70, 490, 777, 7000) ASTOUNDS THE ASTUTE student of eschatology. Certainly, "7" is the number of completion, perfection, Sabbath, the day of God's rest. *But it has a special use in Bible Prophecy.* Consequently, we propose here how the prophetic *sevens* are used in relationship to "God's plan of the ages," to reinforce the future destiny of His people (both Christians and Jews) and their greatest foe, *THE FINAL BABYLON (aka "The Great City"),* as discovered by author Krieger[1].

As preface, we should pause and say a few words about "where we are going" with this chapter. It is a bit different from previous ones. Here we will set forth an argument that Biblical numerology, nothing occultly mystical, but the usage of numbers in Bible prophecy, provides an important confirmation of our overall thesis: The ancient empires of *Tyre and Sidon* (Phoenicia), their descendants – the *Merchants of Tarshish,* and *Nebuchadnezzar's Babylon*[2] are all prophetically identified as the same entity. In other words, the Bible sees all three empires as a singular archetype for the final, great, but horrifically destructive Gentile Empire

---

[1]Author Krieger is a genuine expert in Sacred Geometry, a legitimate study of the sacred employment of numbers in the Bible, God's creation, and ancient history. For instance, Daniel 8:13 speaks of the "messenger," "another holy one said to that certain one who was speaking" which literally in Hebrew is the Angel *Palmoni*: "The Wonderful Numberer of Secrets, *Palmoni* "that certain saint"" in disclosing to Daniel the vision of the 2,300 "evening-mornings" – see Daniel 8:9-14, *Young's Literal Translation.* As angel Gabriel interprets Daniel's dreams and visions, the angel Michael serves as Israel's protector; even so, the angel Palmoni appears as the "Wonderful Numberer of Secrets."

[2] The culprits of Ancient Babylon begin with Nimrod, then Nebuchadnezzar, and conclude with Belshazzar. The first two, in particular, embody Antichrist attributes.

of the last days, *Mystery Babylon*. In the spirit of E.W. Bullinger (1837 – 1913), the Anglican dispensational scholar in biblical numerology, we are eager and pleased to share these insights here.

When Scripture employs "70" in its most primordial portions – we find its initial use, in Genesis 4:19-24 regarding Lamech, who was of the father of Noah.[3] Lamech had two wives (incidentally, he was the first recorded polygamist). He confessed to his two spouses (or perhaps he bragged– we suspect the latter) that he "slew a man for wounding me – even a young man for hurting me." It is possible his statement was a pitiful excuse (in the best case claiming that he killed in self-defense or in the worst case, in a rage), to set the record straight that this murder wasn't in cold blood (as even in ancient times "premeditated murder" demanded greater recompense than manslaughter). Indeed, he must have had in mind the notion of justifying himself. For given the lack of remorse he showed in the aftermath, we can't help but think the less of him.

Lamech composed a little two-verse musical ditty (perhaps the first "rap") to impress us with his victory. First off, within his lyrics, he implies an arrogant boast that he's a lot more valuable than his ancestor Cain. He recounts for us – in case we had forgotten God's promise to Cain – that if anyone slew Cain, God would avenge Cain's death sevenfold – i.e. seven times).[4] However, after Lamech killed the "young man" (possibly for merely bloodying his nose in a fight), Lamech pledges: "*If Cain shall be avenged sevenfold, then Lamech seventy-sevenfold*" (Genesis. 4:24), that is, 70 * 7 or 490 times. It seems Lamech holds many firsts: *polygamy*, *poetic expression*, and... *putting words into God's mouth*! We think the Lord could remark, "Speak for your-

---

[3] The lineage of Lamech may have been through Cain or through Seth. There is some difference of opinion regarding whether Lamech in Genesis 4 is the same Lamech in Genesis 5. See http://en.wikipedia.org/wiki/Lamech_(father_of_Noah) for a tracing of the genealogy of Cain and of Seth.

[4] Some sources say Lamech slew Cain – but there's little evidence to support this conclusion.

self, Lamech" (as apparently Lamech did). Indeed, we notice God remains silent regarding Lamech's chant – there is no confirmation the world should be wary of doing harm to Lamech despite his self-pronounced judgment on anyone who messed with him, akin to the warning God had covenanted with Cain by "marking him" (apparently along with a public notice broadcast far and wide) lest he be subject to a vengeful act accomplished "on Abel's behalf." Moreover, Lamech's tirade may have motivated the Almighty towards retribution – but in the "long run."

Lamech's statement seems outrageous. But is it possible that Lamech was onto something? Was he actually prophesying about what lay ahead? What was it as Noah's father that made "490" so immediately significant? Was his dirty little ditty setting the stage for world affairs, millennia into the future?

The Scripture often has a marvelous way of making something out of what seems like nothing. When patterns emerge, better take careful note. Indeed, we have such an observable pattern here – but it takes a keen eye to discern its form.

## Seventy Years of Gentile Judgment

Now, seventy (70) and seven (7) are linked in Lamech's poetic pledge. They put forth, at least in his mind, a "standard" for perfect judgment. If he is harmed by someone trying to "get even" for dispatching the aforementioned "young man" to the hereafter, 490 persons must be slaughtered as recompense for Lamech's hypothetical execution. If this "avenging" seems excessive to the reader, we heartily concur. However, his hasty words appear to haunt us all.

"In the beginning" *seven* had already been established as the threshold for completion or fulfillment by the Almighty; He having rested on the *seventh* day after six days of creative effort. Almost any "man on the street" knows that there are seven days in our week because of this divine precedent and commandment to keep the Sabbath Day. Furthermore, it seems striking, to say the least, that Lamech's age is recorded as "seven hundred and seventy-seven years" (Genesis 5:31), laying stress upon the three sets of 7 (i.e., a series of sevens), incidents of "sevens" or powers of seven that we will soon see relate to prophecies pertaining to Tyre, Babylon and the Beast of Babylon... in relation to the "perfection of divine judgment." As we proceed, we will present to the reader a series of time periods or events each relating to sevens, multiples of sevens, or powers of sevens. We assert that these "coincidences" in the use of such sevens are not coincidences at all (coincidence has no equivalent word in Hebrew). Our belief in the providence of God and His inspiration of His Holy word lead us to affirm that these numbers are not mystical in an occult sense, but they are VERY meaningful.

As Genesis concludes and Exodus begins, we find there were

**Figure 37 - *Palestra* ruins (athlete training center) in Ancient Tyre**

"70 souls" in the loins of Jacob who went into Egypt and 70 elders of Israel (Exodus. 1:5; 24:1, 9). More could be said of these "early 70s" (but we won't digress here), for its first use remains the most prominent, and constitutes the forerunner of 70 as an expression *of completeness, consummation,* and sometimes the *fullness of judgment.* Scholars have been puzzled (downright perplexed actually) by the statement from the prophet Isaiah, who proclaimed (almost from out of nowhere):

> *Now it shall come to pass in that day that Tyre will be forgotten* ***seventy years****, according to the days of one king. At the end of* ***seventy years*** *it will happen to Tyre as in the song of the harlot: 'Take a harp, go about the city, you forgotten harlot; make sweet melody, sing many songs, that you may be remembered.' And it shall be, at the end of* ***seventy years****, that the LORD will deal with Tyre. She will return to her hire, and commit fornication with all the kingdoms of the world on the face of the earth.* (Isa. 23:15-17)

Did the Assyrians or King Nebuchadnezzar (both of whom laid siege to Tyre but never overcame her) start a 70-year clock? Not exactly – at least not a clock that ran a contiguous length of 70 years. History records that Tyre may have paid tribute to the King of Babylon (in the sixth century BC or earlier) but was not subdued until Alexander the Great[5] laid siege nigh unto *seven* months (in the fourth century BC) building a famous rock rampart or causeway out to the Island upon which Tyre was situated.[6]

And yet, Tyre rebounded time after time until the Romans destroyed the principal city of the Punic peoples about 125 years later. Recall from the prior chapter the Phoenician dye was made for royal ware near Tyre from beached mollusks (and likely many more "under the sea").[7] But in case you missed it, we expand on

---

[5] See http://en.wikipedia.org/wiki/Tyre,_Lebanon.

[6] "In 332 BC, the city was conquered by Alexander the Great, after a siege of seven months in which he built the causeway from the mainland to within a hundred meters of the island, where the sea floor sloped abruptly downwards. The presence of the causeway affected local sea currents causing sediment accumulation, which made the land connection permanent to this day and transformed the erstwhile Tyre Island into a peninsula." See http://en.wikipedia. org/wiki/Tyre,_Lebanon.

[7] The reader might conclude (rightly we believe) that since the infamous "harlot was arrayed in purple," and this color appears in the text in the final judgment of Babylon (Rev. 17:4; 18:12, 16), it is a metaphoric *link to Tyre.* Note also the first convert to Christ in Europe was Lydia the "Seller of PUR-

this point again as it provides a graphic backdrop to the clothing of the Great Harlot, draped as she is in purple decking, foreshadowed by Tyre's penchant for purple – the color of royalty:

> The Phoenicians also became famous for their discovery of purple. History says that the inhabitants of the City-State Tyre would have been these who discovered the color of purple. The purple was extracted in almost all Phoenician cities. The Phoenicians were the first ones who began to extract purple and to dye wool and linen with it.
>
> The purple was a natural color which came from a small shell (murex), distributed on the coasts of Syria and Lebanon, but which the Phoenicians made to vanish in that region because of their extensive use. This small shell includes three tinctorial species, from which two are the most common: *murex trunculus* and *murex brandaris*.
>
> When the flesh, which is inside the shell, dies and rots, it secretes a yellow liquid. This juice applied on a white cloth, when dried, produces the color, violet. When the cloth is exposed much more to the sun, the color becomes more intense. The color doesn't fade or disappear over time. Through mixing, using an intensive or diluted color of this small shell, gives different shades: rose, light or dark violet. [8]

The words of Ezekiel 26:2–14 warned that the Hebrew God would cause Nebuchadnezzar to utterly destroy Tyre because its residents gloated over the fall of Jerusalem. Tyre held off Nebuchadnezzar's siege for thirteen years, resupplying the walled island city (with walls that reached 150 feet high) through its two harbors. The siege ended when Tyre agreed to pay tribute – but Tyre survived to trade another day.

Was God mistaken about the Seventy Years before judgment would occur? Was the judgment nullified? Or was Nebuchadnez-

---

PLE" (Acts 16:14). There was only one source of supply – Tyre. Such *little* details might seem inconsequential, but they testify to the preciseness and providence of God in a *big* way!

[8](From *"Influences of Phoenicians on Hebrew Civilization," The Reformation Messenger*).

zar a "placeholder name, a fore type, for a future beast"? (It is another no small fact that Nebuchadnezzar, had developed a bout of *lycanthropy*... thinking he was a wolf, the animal "type" associated with Apollo, Apollyon, and Antichrist... *for a seven-year period no less!*) More about that later.

## Why Tyre and Babylon Are Prophetically Identical

And, what should we make of this verse: "*She will return to her hire, and commit fornication with all the kingdoms of the world on the face of the earth*" and then "*It shall be, at the end of* ***seventy years*** *that the LORD will deal with Tyre*"? What connects *this seventy* with the timing of Tyre's final destiny (its ultimate demise), jumps out from the very next chapter in Isaiah. It amounts to nothing less than the "Day of the Lord"– the Apocalypse and the final Wrath of God directed at "the kings of the earth" – the kings that give over their power to the Beast of Babylon (Revelation 17:12, 17). For consider the Prophet's assertion: "*The CITY OF CONFUSION is broken down*" (recall that Babylon literally means *confusion*) - and afterwards when judgment has fallen, all that remains: "*THE CITY OF DESOLATION.*" This passage in Isaiah 24, following the prophecy against Tyre in Isaiah 23, provides a distinct linkage between Tyre and Babylon. Thus, its fate could hardly be clearer: The FINAL BABYLON runs headlong towards judgment:

> "*It shall come to pass in that day that the LORD will punish on high the host of exalted ones, and on the earth* ***the kings of the earth.*** *They will be gathered together, as prisoners are gathered in the pit and will be shut up in the prison; after many days they will be punished. Then the moon will be disgraced and the sun ashamed; for the LORD of hosts will reign on Mount Zion and in Jerusalem and before His elders, gloriously*" [that is, the Glory of God outshines the lights "ruling" humankind, thus "shaming" them] (Isaiah 24:21-23).

Again, we contend the student of Scripture would be mistaken not to see Isaiah 24 as that "Great and Terrible Day of the

Lord" following hard on the heels of Isaiah 23. Consequently, the 70-year judgment of that "forgotten harlot" Tyre at the end of Isaiah 23 coincides with Babylon's ultimate judgment apocalyptically depicted in Revelation 17-19.

**Figure 38–The stele of BAAL, the god of Tyre holding a Thunderbolt (found in Ugarit)**

Isaiah must have spoken his prophecies around 680 B.C., since Isaiah mentions the death of the Assyrian king, Sennacherib, who died in that year (Isaiah 37:37-38); and Isaiah must have outlived another prophet, Hezekiah, by just a few years. Jeremiah, on the other hand prophesied beginning in 626 BC through about 586 BC – during the reigns of Josiah, Jehoahaz, Jehoiakim, Jehoiachin, and Zedekiah. In the same era, Daniel was taken captive into Neo-Babylonia as a teen in 605 BC and lived there for about 60 years (Note: The deportation of the royal descendants into Babylon had been prophesied by Isaiah to Hezekiah in Isaiah 39:7; this is relevant as Daniel possessed "royal blood").

Scholars agree Scripture indicates Judah, the remaining Hebrew tribes of Southern Israel, would be held in captivity for seventy (70) years. In fact, Jeremiah 25:11-12 is the very scripture Daniel read which caused him to realize, only a few years before this period would end, that God would soon restore a remnant of the Hebrew nation to its capitol city, Jerusalem. Daniel read from Jeremiah the following:

> [11] *And this whole land shall be a desolation and an astonishment, and these nations shall serve the king of Babylon* ***seventy years****.*
>
> [12] *Then it will come to pass, when* ***seventy years*** *are completed, that I will punish the king of Babylon and that nation, the land of the Chaldeans, for their iniquity,' says the Lord; 'and I will make it a perpetual desolation."*

However, whereas the Jewish nation was made desolate being judged for seventy years as prescribed by Isaiah, Bible students often slide past the seventy years of *Babylon's judgment* and how Babylon would be made a total desolation – *perpetually*. Daniel 5 records the demise of King Belshazzar, descendent of King Nebuchadnezzar. However, this Neo-Babylonian Empire lasted longer than 70 years – lasting 87 years from 626 B.C. to 539 B.C.[9]

Therefore, could this prophecy make explicit what is implied in Genesis 4:19-24 and expressly stated regarding Tyre in Isaiah 23:15-17? Do the prophets (Jeremiah and Isaiah) connect Babylon and Tyre *by means of prophesying judgment upon each after seventy years*? We would emphasize that while the Hebrew people were judged over a literal 70-year period, the judgment of the Gentiles was not realized in the same way. So make note: one prophecy was *literally* fulfilled and one was not. Like Tyre, *Babylon was not judged within a sequential seventy year timeframe*. Perhaps this *seventy*, in the case of Tyre and Babylon, is symbolic and not to be taken literally; or more likely, is to be seen ***not*** *as seventy sequential years*. This is the conclusion we draw – because both are "metaphors" of Gentile dominion due to their commercial clout, and because both are to be judged *after a seventy-year period*. The Bible's use of *seventy* as a "deferment

---

[9] See http://empires.findthedata.org/q/92/2515/How-long-did-the-Neo-Babylonian-Empire-exist.

of judgment" links the two implicitly. More so, the very *seventieth* Week of Daniel's ultimate prophecy of the *seventy* weeks bespeaks of the final week of Gentile World Powers and the ultimate judgment of the Final Babylon the Great.

**Figure 39 - Jehu Bowing Before the Assyrian King, Shalmanessar III, 827 B.C. from the Black Obelisk of Shalmanessar**

Staying with the theme of the judgment of Babylon and Tyre, we would underscore how they pre-figure THE FINAL BABYLON. The one, Tyre, signifies "Commercial Babylon;" whereas Babylon, "that Great City," speaks to its global political and military influence, having fornicated with all *the kings of the earth* (who signify the leaders of humanity in conscious rebellion against God!).

Perhaps it is a poorly chosen expression in a biblical exposition, but we cannot resist making a play on words by noting how that the ancient Kingdom of Tyre (the first commercial world empire) is associated with Babylon, a symbolic city-state opposed to "the City of God" (representing as it does the City of God's adversary), which is judged for fornicating with the *kings of the earth.* Thus, we find both Tyre and Babylon in bed together!

Moreover, the "perfection" of the *judgment of seventy* wrought upon Tyre for her apostasy is more than sentencing for *commercial exploitation.* Tyre poisoned the ten tribes of Northern Israel through its worship of BAAL.

This apostasy was made concrete, about 240 years before Jeremiah, Hezekiah, and Daniel, with the princess/prostitute Jezebel's marriage to Northern Israel's King Ahab. Surely it made for a "marriage of commercial convenience" with profits to be shared between the two Kingdoms. But the union of Jezebel and Ahab conveyed an additional matter of infidelity between Israel and Yahweh. When Tyre aligned with Israel, it formed a most wicked institution: RELIGION, POLITICS, AND COMMERCE INCORPORATED. The sacred was mixed with the profane, contaminating the religion of YHWH. Recall this meets the criteria for religious apostasy as described at the outset of our study (in citing Hislop's historical analysis of Nimrod/Semiramis and Hunt's conviction concerning Mystery Babylon).

## The Annihilation of Ahab and Worshippers of BAAL

Furthermore, it yields context for why the judgment against King Ahab was so severe. And note once more, in the lengthy passage we cite below, how we see the number *seventy* deliberately expressed in God's act of judgment through Jehu, whom Elisha's servant anointed to be the new King, thereby replacing Ahab.

After his anointing, Jehu went on a "slaying" excursion (not *sleighing* as in sleigh ride, forgive the pun), in which he rounded up everyone associated with Ahab. As one result, there was a most demonstrative death of Ahab's Queen Jezebel (a remarkable demise befitting her crimes against Yahweh that we discuss in our final chapter). Next, Jehu sent a letter to the "great men of the city" who were "jointly and severally" raising Ahab's *seventy* sons, whereupon he called for a ghoulish act of loyalty. He commanded they lop off the heads of Ahab's sons and bring them to a designated meeting place in Jezreel, Northern Israel's capitol under Ahab. There, he had the seventy heads stacked in two heaps at the city gate, and let them stay the night there. No doubt the resulting stench was nigh unbearable; but it was as a testimony or witness (for "2" is the number of testimony) against Israel's apostasy and "70" as the perfection of the Almighty's judgment thereof.

> 5 *And he that was over the house, and he that was over the city, the elders also, and the bringers up of the children, sent to Jehu, saying, "We are thy servants, and will do all that thou shalt bid us; we will not make any king: do thou that which is good in thine eyes."*
>
> 6 *Then he wrote a letter the second time to them, saying, "If ye be mine, and if ye will hearken unto my voice, take ye the heads of the men your master's sons, and come to me to Jezreel by tomorrow this time."Now the king's sons,* ***being seventy persons****, were with the great men of the city, which brought them up.*
>
> 7 *And it came to pass, when the letter came to them, that they took the king's sons, and* ***slew seventy persons,*** *and put their heads in baskets, and sent him them to Jezreel.*
>
> 8 *And there came a messenger, and told him, saying, "They have brought the heads of the king's sons. And he said, "Lay ye them in two heaps at the entering in of the gate until the morning."*
>
> 9 *And it came to pass in the morning, that he went out, and stood, and said to all the people, "Ye be righteous: behold, I conspired against my master, and slew him: but who slew all these?*
>
> 10 *Know now that there shall fall unto the earth nothing of the word of the Lord, which the Lord spake concerning the house of Ahab: for the Lord hath done that which he spake by his servant Elijah."*
>
> 11 *So Jehu slew all that remained of the house of Ahab in Jezreel, and all his great men, and his kinsfolks, and his priests, until he left him none remaining.* (2 Kings 10:5-11).

So, in spite of their murderous acts accomplished in direct response to his request, Jehu promptly slew all of *the great men* (the political leaders, maybe not so great), their families, their priests, until he had vanquished every last one. His declaration at the city gate implied he had the right to commit murder in the name of God, but the great men didn't; they committed a heinous act of murder merely to appease him! Jehu had had the "unsuspecting sons" killed by their masters to make sure none

**Figure 40 - The view from Mount Megiddo, looking northeast across the Jezreel Valley in Israel (Mount Tabor arises on the horizon)**

escaped. Then he killed the "unsuspecting masters" after they had completely purged the offspring of Ahab... "what goes around comes around." From the human point of view, it was a most astonishing act of treachery! However, without condemning– let alone justifying the actions of Jehu (although we stipulate Yahweh declared to Jehu He would smite and destroy "all the King's men"), we should make note that where this occurred, its location – the city of Jezreel – is where God will judge the Gentile nations at the time of Messiah's return. For this place is also known as the *Valley of Jezreel* – being near Mount Megiddo

– which is more commonly referred to as *Armageddon*. The symbolism of the "seventy" (signifying the judgment of the Gentile Kingdoms as well as the rebellious amidst Israel) remains joined to the location where Jesus Christ will conquer all his enemies (referenced in Psalm 2, in which the *kings of the earth* are advised to "kiss the son" lest they be destroyed)... "And they gathered them together to the place called in Hebrew, Armageddon" (lit. "Mountain of Megiddo") (Revelation 16:16) – so concludes the *seventieth* week of Daniel's prophecy, the same place where the *seventy* sons of Ahab were slain.

Was this thorough purging of Ahab's progeny and the priests of BAAL foreshadowing the judgment of God? Yes indeed. Plus, since Scripture wove "seventy" into the story, it prefigured the judgment of the Gentile nations. The mention of *seventy* would certainly appear to be no incidental comment to add "color" (purple or otherwise) – as if the story needed more graphic detail. Indeed, we should recite the following truism until we are sure never to forget: *the Bible wastes no words.*

> *And it shall come to pass, when* ***seventy years*** *are accomplished, that I will punish the king of Babylon, and that nation, saith the Lord, for their iniquity, and the land of the Chaldeans, and will make it a* ***perpetual desolation***.(Jeremiah 25:12)

Now, one can weasel wondrously in his exegesis or eisogesis of Holy Writ; however, whatever historical revision one may find satisfactory, Babylon did quite well for hundreds of years after the Medes and Persians conquered her, in fact, for over 1,000 years, right up until 700 AD. To be sure, it's little more than a pitiful tourist trap today, for when the radical Iraqis aren't killing each other, even the men and women of the 82nd Airborne aren't much interested in the place. However, can we really label historical/physical Babylon "*a perpetual desolation*?" That fate appears to await a future fulfillment.

Indeed, we argue it occurs in both a *different time and place* – for we assert that the Babylon referenced in Jeremiah's prophecy is *The FINAL BABYLON*, not the Babylon of Nebuchadnezzar or Belshazzar. Furthermore, we read in Jeremiah 29:10: *"For thus says the LORD: After **seventy years** are completed at Babylon, I will visit you and perform My good word toward you, and cause you to return to this place [i.e., Jerusalem*]." As to the Jews, the LORD did fulfill His promise of redemption in *exactly seventy years.* Again, His prophetic promise to the Jews was literally fulfilled; however, the prophetic "perfection of judgment" of the Final Babylon's ultimate" in the language of prophecy occurs "at the end of ***seventy*** years..." which did not equate to seven literal decades.

## The Lesson from Another Ahab: Get Out Quick!

As a pertinent aside, in Jeremiah 29 we see two false prophets, (a different) Ahab and Zedekiah, caught committing adultery with their neighbor's wives,who advised the Hebrews to "*build houses*" in Babylon (Jeremiah 29:23, 28), claiming they spoke in the name of the LORD... "*Because you said, 'The LORD has raised up prophets for us in Babylon.*" We read of their sordid tale of APOSTASY IN BABYLON throughout the whole chapter wherein they were "roasted in the fire" by King Nebuchadnezzar to be a "curse" – for these prophets "*have spoken lying words in My name, which I have not commanded them... Indeed I know, and am a witness, says the LORD*" (Jeremiah 29:21-22).

Why is their tale worth telling? Despite arguing for an eventual literal fulfillment, nevertheless, we assert that "Babylon" always stands symbolically as "God's opposition party." Hence, the story of these false prophets has application down through the ages – especially now. Therefore, we must ask, "Are there Ahabs and Zedekiahs to be found in the *City of Confusion* – in Apostate Babylon – today?" If so, their advice would be along the lines of these two false prophets who counseled: "*This captivity is long; build houses and dwell in them, and plant gardens and eat their fruit*" (Jeremiah 29:28). In other words: "Acculturate! Blend in! Quit being so *chosen*!" Moreover, "Forget about Jerusalem and the City of God! Where are you going? Don't flee Babylon!"

Consequently, as a spiritual application of this truth, we feel compelled to ask, "Are we who call ourselves God's people getting a bit too comfortable in the CITY OF CONFUSION, soon to be no more than the CITY OF DESOLATION?"

Without a doubt, false prophets like Ahab and Zedekiah abound today. There are those who believe that the "Church Triumphant" means that the Church will, in this present age, overtake the forces of evil and transform the world – without the direct physical intervention of Jesus Christ. We consider those who proclaim this false eschatology (denying the impending Second Coming and the future earthly reign of the Messiah), to be false prophets, however well-intentioned they may be. True: the Church can withstand the Gates of Hell. Yet, it is also evident through two millennia of history that the ultimate "makeover", the renewal of this world, will not come to pass until Jesus Christ transforms His church through its resurrection and rapture; and soon thereafter begins a reclamation program that transforms the world (i.e., the creation). The universe longs for this redemption. As of this moment it *groans*, awaiting its full recovery. Paul tells us in his epistle to the Romans that this makeover connects the creation's redemption to the liberation of God's children, that is, their physical glorification in the next aeon.

> 18 *For I reckon that the sufferings of this present time are not worthy to be compared with the glory which shall be revealed in us.*
>
> 19 *For the earnest expectation of the creature waiteth for the manifestation of the sons of God.*
>
> 20 *For the creature [or creation] was made subject to vanity, not willingly, but by reason of him who hath subjected the same in hope,*
>
> 21 *Because the creature itself also shall be delivered from the bondage of corruption into the glorious liberty of the children of God.*

[22] *For we know that the whole creation groaneth and travaileth in pain together until now.* (Romans 8:18-22)

Make no mistake: Bible prophecy consistently bespeaks a future judgment of "*Babylon the Great – Mystery Babylon*"– the FINAL BABYLON, which has grown dark and dominant in our world. Moreover, this comeuppance involves more than symbol. And yet, Babylon still signifies the rebellion of humankind, living apart from the dwelling place of God, in a world of "man's own making."

## The Prophetic Principle of Postponement

Historically, God did not deal with Tyre in a literal sense "after seventy years." The meaning of this prophecy must be understood as an adumbrative[10] expression akin to the "70 Weeks" ("heptads" of years, i.e., seventy sevens or "weeks of years" – analogous to our decade – but *seven years in length* instead of ten), as found in Daniel 9:24-27. Note: This seventy remains distinct (not parallel) from the seventy years of Hebrew servitude to the King of Babylon.

The Evangelical theologian, Robert Duncan Culver, made an outstanding reflection on the way Bible prophecy was written by the prophets (clueing us in on how it should be understood too!):

> To one acquainted with the technique of the prophets this will not appear strange (i.e., How that the careers of Antiochus and of Antichrist seem to intertwine –in that Antiochus' career (Daniel 8:11-21-35) is adumbrative of Antichrist's...it also appears that the prophecy of Antichrist (Daniel 11:36-45) may be reflected back toward Antiochus). It is one of the commonest of phenomena to find events of similar nature, but separated widely in time, *united in one prophetic oracle*. Barnes calls it the "law of pro-

---

[10] A great word for prophetic assertions, according to the *Encarta Dictionary*, it means a "faint outline", a vague indication, or forewarning of what will come.

phetic suggestion." Delitzsch said that prophecy is *"apotelesmatic."*[11]

"Telesmatic" refers to something that is magical or *supernatural*, rather than natural or normal, i.e., literal. "Apo" is from the Greek and can, according to *Dictionary.com*, mean the following: "In modern scientific coinages in English and other languages, **apo-,** marks things that are detached, separate, or derivative." Hence, Franz Delitzsch (1813 – 1890), that great scholar of Hebrew, sought to convey through this term how prophetic words are *derived from supernatural origins* – they are "detached" or distinct from "normal" discourse; hence, they cannot uniformly be taken literally – although in many cases they can and should. Just as Jeremiah's prophecy had a *literal* sense (as it pertained to the Jews), it had a *different* sense as it pertained to the Gentiles. To say "it isn't intended to be taken literally" is only one aspect of the story – and may in fact be misleading. Prophecies are, if you will, given within "inspired spurts" – sometimes without reference to exactly when they will be fulfilled. However, that doesn't necessarily mean prophecies will never be historically fulfilled. In fact, just the opposite is true: They are always fulfilled in space and time – one way or another. Jesus said, the *Word of the Lord cannot be broken* (John 10:35). In fact, this is the proper evangelical interpretive method.

Evangelical scholar Randall Price offers an articulate summary of this principle, consistent with *dispensational* interpretation:

> The technical expression for this delay in the fulfillment of the messianic program for Israel is derived from the Greek verb *apotelo* meaning, "to bring to completion, finish." The usual sense of *telos* as "end" or "goal" may here have the more technical idea of "the consummation that comes to prophecies when they are fulfilled" (Luke 22:37). With the prefix *apo*, which basically

---

[11] See Robert D. Culver, ***Daniel in the Latter Days***, *A Study in Millennialism* (1977) p. 167.

has the connotation of "separation from something," the idea is of a delay or interruption in the completion of the prophetic program. Therefore, *apotelesmatic* interpretation recognizes that in Old Testament texts that present the messianic program as a single event, a near and far historical fulfillment is intended, separated by an indeterminate period of time. Dispensational writers have referred to this as an "intercalation" or a "gap." However, prophetic postponement better expresses this concept. *Prophetic,* because we understand a purposeful, preordained act in the divine program, and *postponement,* because it retains the original idea of an interruption in fulfillment, while supplementing it with the notion that such a delay is only temporary. [12]

We assert *context is the key.* In biblical prophecy, there is "adumbrative and apotelesmatic" language (in other words, *particularly paranormal paragraphs!*) which cannot be understood as mere historical narrative – but rather as predictive assertions (not simple poetry, mind you) *to be fulfilled in space-time,* sometimes far into the future. To superficially assume – and that's what it is –that Israel (the Jews) would be "scattered among the nations" and then re-gathered (and that this re-gathering took place with the return from Babylon of a "remnant" after the 70-year Babylonian captivity), ignores the "adumbrative intent" of the prophets prior to that "great and terrible Day of the Lord." (See *Ezekiel 37*) Logically, Israel's final scattering must follow the destruction of Jerusalem in 70 AD, to fulfill the words of Jesus.[13] If so, it will be prophetically by her re-gathering at the "end of days." The final week of Daniel's prophecy is yet to be fulfilled. It is substantiated by a modern-day Israel re-gathered to form *Eretz Israel.* Furthermore, the Abomination of Desolation, mentioned by Daniel the prophet, and affirmed by Jesus in the gospels, also assumes a final "en-gathering" of Israel's exiles as the "end of the age" scenario unfolds.

---

[12]See http://www.raptureready.com/featured /price/13rp.pdf.

[13] Jesus prediction of the Jewish diaspora happens over 500 years after the return to Jerusalem of Zerubbabel and Joshua and a remnant of the Jews (Matthew 24:15-20).

In one instance, Jeremiah predicted a literal *seventy years* of Jewish captivity over *seventy consecutive years.* But the seventy-year prediction *he posed for Babylon* was neither literal nor consecutive! Needless to say, to make sense of Jeremiah's differing predictions, requires a more sophisticated "hermeneutic" (method of interpretation) than what most students of the Bible would prefer. That is where Price's perspective comes into play. Invoking the methodology of "prophetic postponement" to properly interpret passages, such as Jeremiah's, makes perfect sense. Jewish prophecies, even those within the same verse, often refer to events that are separated by hundreds and sometimes thousands of years.

As an illustration, imagining a "viewpoint from eternity" may be helpful here. That is, if we were to view a parade from a helicopter high above, the whole parade could be seen in one instant rather than observed from a ground-level vantage point, i.e., from "street-side bleachers," seen over a two-hour period in which one "act" follows another. Like the "hypothetical" helicopter parade watcher, from God's perspective events are seen all at once - everything happens simultaneously. That is the way the predictions of the great Hebrew prophets were recorded, and that is how they should be interpreted.

## Daniel's Prophecy of the 70 Weeks

We do well to compile these phrases surrounding *seventy*, for there are many which speak in one consistent prophetic voice, telling of *The Last Days* when Gentile judgment transpires and God redeems His people: Recall these phrases from Jeremiah, Isaiah, and Daniel which we have touched upon:

- The "end of 70 years"
- "serve the King of Babylon 70 years"
- "when 70 years are accomplished"
- "he would accomplish 70 years"
- "70 weeks are determined"
- "even those 70 years"

However, it is Daniel's famous prophecies of "70" that arguably contains the most famous of the prophetic "70's." We recount once more Daniel 9:24-27 for the reader's convenience:

> [24] ***Seventy weeks*** *are determined upon thy people and upon thy holy city, to finish the transgression, and to make an end of sins, and to make reconciliation for iniquity, and to bring in everlasting righteousness, and to seal up the vision and prophecy, and to anoint the most Holy.*
>
> [25] *Know therefore and understand, that from the going forth of the commandment to restore and to build Jerusalem unto the Messiah the Prince shall be* ***seven weeks****, and threescore and two weeks: the street shall be built again, and the wall, even in troublous times.*
>
> [26] *And after threescore and two weeks shall Messiah be cut off, but not for himself: and the people of the prince that shall come shall destroy the city and the sanctuary; and the end thereof shall be with a flood, and unto the end of the war desolations are determined.*
>
> [27] *And he shall confirm the covenant with many for* ***one week****: and in the midst of the week he shall cause the sacrifice and the oblation to cease, and for the overspreading of abominations he shall make it desolate, even until the consummation, and that determined shall be poured upon the desolate.*

For these authors, our focus rests on the fact that these seventy heptads come at the conclusion of *seventy years of prophecy* spoken by Jeremiah about the desolations of BOTH JERUSALEM *AND* BABYLON. *One key instance of seventy is stacked upon another significant instance of seventy.*

We should also realize that the meaning of the famous incident of "the handwriting on the wall" occurred during Neo-Babylonian King Belshazzar's feast in Babylon.[14] The timing of the event in 539 BC is important. It came near the beginning of

---

[14]Belshazzar (and Babylon) was defeated on October 12, 539 BC; therefore, the first Jews who returned to Jerusalem did so under the decree of Cyrus of the "Medes and Persians" in 538-539 B.C. (See Ezra 2:64-70).

Daniel's annunciated 70 prophetic weeks of years for the Jewish people, delivered to Daniel by the Angel Gabriel. Not coincidentally, this event happened near the completion of Jeremiah's prophecy of Jewish captivity for seventy years (ten heptads). It seems clear these THREE SEVENTIES *are inextricably linked.* God's judgment upon Belshazzar's Babylon may have commenced Babylon's judgment, but it didn't complete it. And yet, it was this event which would lead to one of history's most important milestones: Cyrus's declaration emancipating the Jewish captives, facilitating those that would "go up" to Jerusalem; thusly, to get the ball rolling as it were; that is, to "start the clock" for the 70 Heptads.

Perhaps we should pause, for the reader to catch his/her breath and recap these matters: Daniel references Jeremiah's "70 years" and connects it to the failure of Israel to allow the land to "keep its Sabbaths." From II Chronicles 36:20-23, we read:

> 20 *And them that had escaped from the sword carried he [Nebuchadnezzar] away to Babylon; where they were servants to him and his sons until the reign of the kingdom of Persia:*
>
> 21 *To fulfill the word of the LORD by the mouth of Jeremiah, until the land had enjoyed her Sabbaths: for as long as she lay desolate she kept Sabbath, to fulfill threescore and ten years.*
>
> 22 *Now in the first year of Cyrus king of Persia, that the word of the LORD spoken by the mouth of Jeremiah might be accomplished, the LORD stirred up the spirit of Cyrus king of Persia, that he made a proclamation throughout all his kingdom, and put it also in writing, saying,*
>
> 23 *"Thus saith Cyrus king of Persia, All the kingdoms of the earth hath the Lord God of heaven given me; and he hath charged me to build him an house in Jerusalem, which is in Judah. Who is there among you of all his people? The Lord his God be with him, and let him go up."*

Jeremiah prophesied after seventy years of Jerusalem's desolation, God would pardon His people. *"For thus says the LORD: After* ***seventy years*** *are completed at Babylon, I will* *visit you and perform My good word toward you, and cause you to return to this place* [i.e., Jerusalem – Jeremiah 29:10].”

And earlier in the same book bearing his name, Jeremiah predicted seventy years of desolation upon Babylon. *“And it shall come to pass, when seventy years are accomplished, that I will punish the king of Babylon, and that nation, saith the Lord, for their iniquity, and the land of the Chaldeans, and will make it a perpetual desolation.”* (Jeremiah 25:12).

Probing a bit deeper, we remember the rationale for the desolation for Jerusalem: over 490 years the land never enjoyed its Sabbath rest – all told, 70 Sabbaths were missed (one every seven years). Subsequently, in II Chronicles 36, Jeremiah declared on behalf of the LORD that Jerusalem would experience *70 years of desolation* as a direct result of skipping the land’s Sabbath rest – of failing to honor the Mosaic Law. In contrast, the rationale for why Babylon (and Tyre) will someday become desolate seems very different; indeed, it’s quite concise if not precise: Babylon’s judgment results from God’s response “for its iniquity.” That’s plain enough.

Why this judgment does *not* take place until *after a period of seventy years* has elapsed, is not made clear in Jeremiah’s prophecy. This is also true of Isaiah’s prediction (in Isaiah 23) – Tyre’s judgment will also be forestalled *for seventy years*. What’s up with that?

Since Israel remains part of God’s people, we venture He doesn’t conclude His judgment against the Gentile nations until the very end, the last of the “last days” because He primarily concerns Himself with His people: Israel (its redemption) and His Church (its sanctification). In other words, the LORD remains preoccupied with his “Beloved” before He addresses the issues outside His brood.

While judgment (at least in part) may occur at any time in accordance to the Providence of God, the Scripture appears to convey that the ultimate judgment spoken of by His prophets against Tyre and Babylon, although separated in distinct books and directed to two geographically distinct locations, are actually related to the same entity and completed in "the Day of the Lord" or the "Day of His wrath" – that measured period of judgment immediately prior to the coming of God's Son, Jesus Christ, to establish His Kingdom...specifically, at the terminus of the ***seventieth week*** of Daniel's ***seventy week*** prophecy.

While God's prophets speak of Tyre and Babylon, their judgments aren't fully realized until God unleashes His wrath upon THE FINAL BABYLON and a bit later, the Gentile nations at Armageddon. In fact, there are noteworthy occasions where the Lord mentions, almost as an aside, that there is to be a full realization of unrighteous actions before the LORD lowers the boom! In scriptural terms, their cup of iniquity is not yet full! *"And he said unto Abraham, know of a certainty that thy seed shall be a stranger in a land...and they shall afflict them four hundred years* [this is the prediction of Israel's lengthy sojourn in Egypt]*...but in the fourth generation they shall come here again* [after Moses delivers them from Pharaoh]: *for the iniquity of the Amorites is not yet full"* (Genesis 15:13-16). Once again, as to the Jews, the Lord set forth a principle of literal, consecutive timing to fulfill a plan for his people, while the retribution against the "Gentiles" (Amorites, residents of Canaan no less!) would not be accomplished until their sin reached a full measure allowed by God's "permissive will." The timing for both would coalesce at that moment. The Jews would reside in Egypt for 400 years – then return to "Canaan-land." Their return would be bad news for the Amorites (after the 40-year delay of "wandering in the wilderness"), for this is when Joshua leads the Hebrew army in conquest of "the promised land" and brings judgment to Canaanites of all kinds.

This same principle, the coalescing of the separate plans for Jew and Gentile, for the believing and unbelieving, seems to be in force for THE FINAL BABYLON and the redemption of God's people in these final years! Indeed, the literal, space-time fulfillment of God's prophecy is precisely timed for Jew and Gentile alike, when the two distinct "programs" come together in history's concluding heptad, i.e., seven years, aka 2,520 days specified by Daniel and repeated by John the Revelator multiple times, culminated as it were in the return of Jesus Christ. As history's concluding event, we see why Daniel's Seventy Weeks are so pivotal for all of humanity.

## Why Did the Seventy Years of Captivity Happen?

At the beginning of Daniel's prophecy of 70 Weeks, resides a Bible-based "backgrounder" supplying a crucial *context* to *underscore* the prophetic import of what was about to happen to Daniel:

> *"In the first year of his (Darius the son of Ahasuerus, the Mede) reign I, Daniel, understood by the books the number of years specified by the word of the LORD through Jeremiah the prophet that He would accomplish* ***seventy years*** *in the desolations of Jerusalem" (Daniel 9:2).*

Prophesied by Jeremiah, these 70 years of judgment were foundational to Daniel's subsequent prayer (comprising most of the chapter – Daniel 9:3-23). Daniel provided a powerful prayer of intercession on behalf his people, identifying himself with them, in order to mediate between them and their God.[15] His intense prayer continued until an angelic visitation interrupted him. *"Yea, whiles I was speaking in prayer, even the man Gabriel, whom I had seen in the vision at the beginning, being caused to fly swiftly, touched me about the time of the evening oblation"*(Daniel. 9:21). Note the intersection of "history" with the eternal. Daniel specified exactly when a *supernatural event* happened in the *natural scheme of things.*

Daniel recalled Jeremiah's prophecy of 70 years captivity – how there would be 70 years in which the land would lie fallow. Therefore, this prophecy, *"When seventy years are completed,*

---

[15] Daniel, despite his righteous life, identified with the sinful Hebrew people, not declaring himself above them before God to whom he prayed.

*[God] will punish the king of Babylon and that nation...and I will make it a perpetual desolation,"* must speak of a future destruction of Babylon – THE FINAL BABYLON – which would occur outside of 70 consecutive years tied to the events in the sixth century BC. Even the words used in the 70 Weeks prophecy hint at a "non-linear" sequence of events: We read: "[at the] *end of the war desolations* [more than one] *are determined"* and *"on the wing of abominations* [suggesting an indefinite commencement date] *shall be one who makes desolate, even until the consummation, which is determined, is poured out on the Desolator"* (Daniel 9:26-27).

Moreover, this period of seven years is employed numerous times in respect to what is known as *the seven-year Tribulation* in Daniel's writings (with the final 3.5 years as the *Great Tribulation*), found in the Gospels, as well as in the Book of Revelation. *"And he shall confirm the covenant with many for one week: and in the midst of the week he shall cause the sacrifice and the oblation to cease, and for the overspreading of abominations he shall make it desolate, even until the consummation, and that determined shall be poured upon the desolate" (Daniel 9:27).* While the supernatural is intertwined with the natural – the normal and the paranormal interact – the emphasis here remains how the ultimate evil will transpire at a specific moment in the future. It is not symbolic. And the culmination of history will involve a most horrible period of peril, centered around the most evil man to ever live. *These authors believe he is alive today – and he is an American.*

## The Anti-Hero of Daniel – the Antichrist

One of the most important aspects of this final verse found in Daniel 9:27, is the mention of the "he." This "he" is *he who confirms the covenant* and *causes the sacrifice and oblation* (the Temple rituals) *to cease* – whose actions culminate in the desolation of a rebuilt Jewish Temple – right up to the moment of the consummation; that is, the arrival of Messiah to His Temple.

This "he" is none other than the Antichrist, the Beast, and many other names by which he is known in Scripture – indeed, so many are provided by Daniel that it would not be inaccurate to say that Daniel seems obsessed with the final Antichrist.

Jesus referred to this event as the ABOMINATION OF DESOLATION. *"So when you see standing in the holy place 'the abomination that causes desolation,' spoken of through the prophet Daniel – let the reader understand... For then there will be great distress, unequaled from the beginning of the world until now – and never to be equaled again"* (Matthew 24:15, 21, NIV). In fact, the "he" (depending upon interpretation) within himself represents *the abomination.* He is "*the prince who is to come*" (Daniel 9:26) – and is most definitely connected to the theme of the *Willful King* found in Daniel 11:36: *"And the king shall do according to his will; and he shall exalt himself, and magnify himself above every god, and shall speak marvelous things against the God of gods, and shall prosper till the indignation be accomplished: for that that is determined shall be done."*

Earlier in Daniel Chapter 2, we see his cloaked presence in the very image within King Nebuchadnezzar's dream, and the smashing of that image by the stone "*cut without hands*" (Daniel 2:45). We speak also of the "worship of the Golden Image" found in Daniel 3 and of the foreshadowing of the wolf-like *Beast*[16] embodied in Nebuchadnezzar's lycanthropic madness for ***seven years***: *"And they shall drive you from men, and your dwelling shall be with the beasts of the field. They shall make you eat grass like oxen; and* ***seven times*** [most likely as in

[16] Classical mythology connects the wolf to the god Mars, considered by the Romans as their divine father, pre-dating Aeneas. Likewise, it is noteworthy that Romulus and Remus, twins descended purportedly several generations from Aeneas, were the mythical (but possibly actual) founders of Rome (*Rome* of course derives from *Romulus*). They were "suckled" by a she-wolf. The wolf itself can be seen to be a symbol of Antichrist, and not coincidentally, Mars is the god of war; thus, it says of the Antichrist-Beast: "Who is like the Beast? Who is able to make war with him?" (Revelation 13:4)

"years"] *shall pass over you, until you know that the Most High rules in the kingdom of men, and gives it to whomever He chooses"* (Daniel 4:32).

This same "one" is revealed in the "2,520" days (recall 360 days comprise a prophetic year while the final 7 years equals the $70^{th}$ Week). Now, his image denotes the Beast revealed as the "little horn" (the $11^{th}$ Horn – undoubtedly having allusions to the "11 sons of Canaan" as mentioned early on), and as the "fourth beast" revealed in Daniel 7:7-8 and 7:19-28, wherein his judgment is pronounced in the heavenly court and executed by the "Ancient of Days" - aka the Son of Man. Indeed, the vision of this deceitful figure is clarified by the label "*little horn*" of Daniel 8:9-14, in which we see the vision of the Transgression of Desolation. For the vision includes *the abomination* (a topic of great speculation today), which in some manner involves Satan incarnating himself into the body of the Antichrist. This embodiment of Satan – his direct incursion into humanity whereby the "he" becomes the Beast reigning during the latter half of Daniel's $70^{th}$ Week – is conveyed in yet another name, "the king of fierce countenance" which constitutes a recap of the tribulation the Antichrist shall himself foment:

> 23 *And in the latter time of their kingdom, when the transgressors are come to the full,* ***a king of fierce countenance****, and understanding dark sentences, shall stand up.*
>
> 24 *And his power shall be mighty, but not by his own power: and he shall destroy wonderfully, and shall prosper, and practise, and shall destroy the mighty and the holy people.*
>
> 25 *And through his policy also he shall cause craft to prosper in his hand; and he shall magnify himself in his heart, and by peace shall destroy many: he shall also stand up against the Prince of princes; but he shall be broken without hand.*
>
> 26 *And the vision of the evening and the morning which was told is true: wherefore shut thou up the vision; for it shall be for many days.* (Daniel 8:23-26)

This same king is the "Vile Person" of Daniel 11:21 and we should realize "*the king who shall do according to his own will*" (Daniel 11:36) "'*till the wrath has been accomplished.*"

Additionally, there can be but little doubt that the personification of this Antichrist-Beast is the "him" against whom the King of the North and the King of the South shall come against in Daniel 11:40-43. Dwight Pentecost of Dallas Theological Seminary in his classic work, *Things to Come*, asserts that this conflict is the very Gog-Magog War of Ezekiel 38-39). Then the same "him" shall commence immediately thereafter the Armageddon campaign found in Daniel 11:44 when he shall hear of rumors from the east and north which shall "*trouble him and he shall go out and annihilate many.*" He will then place his tabernacle between the Mediterranean Sea and the Holy Mountain in Israel.

It appears he locates his final headquarters in this most auspicious place toward the climax of the 70th Week. "*Yet, he shall come to his end, and no one will help him*" – notwithstanding, recall his desolations commenced "*in the middle of the week*" (Daniel 9:27) which will continue unto the 1,290th Day of Desolation (Daniel 12:11) but at the "*brightness of His coming*" shall the Messiah DESTROY THE DESTROYER as the Wrath of God and the Lamb are poured out upon the Desolator until the end of desolations on the 1,290th day (Daniel 12:11) which is 30 days beyond the terminus of Daniel's 70th Week indicating that these 30 days most likely shall be the very Wrath of God and the Lamb - then the Messiah shall bring in the "time of blessing" unto the 1,335th Day as found in Daniel 12:12.

## Conclusion: Tying it All Together

We began this chapter with the story of Lamech, his wives, and the killing of a young man for beating up Lamech; a bit in a fight. We asserted that the Bible doesn't waste words. There is something of import in this passage that is in fact mysteriously encoded regarding Lamech's infamous boast, if not demand, that

God must avenge anyone who harms him as recompense for his act of shedding blood.

Alas! Lamech's wishful curse of vengeful judgment (for anyone attempting retribution), amounted to doing some math: 7 * 70 = 490 "times" that he must be avenged. This brash statement was made in reference to Cain whose curse (sanctioned by Yahweh) was seven-fold or a mere seven times. Lamech's bold contention called for divine sanction; but, as we argued here, may be fulfilled as a sort of "unintended consequence," aka perhaps "in reverse." His request for a curse on those who harmed him may have broad and distant repercussions against globalist gentile empires– which Lamech appears to represent as "legal agent" from the beginning of Genesis.

Jesus said in John 8:44 in speaking of the Devil: *"He was a murderer from the beginning..."* The connection between sin and Satan, between the mayhem of man's rebellion and the first murders carried out in the sordid history of mankind, appears to have had vast implications. The first murder – Cain killing his brother Abel – led to God's protective promise of vengeance against those harming Cain. *Cursed be any murderer of Cain* – sevenfold.

Lamech murdered a young man (whose identity we would be eager to know) and then demanded seventy times more vengeance from God than Cain merited. It is likely not incidental that Lamech lived to be 777 years old (a long age but about 200 years less than a number of his contemporaries!). Lamech's self-proclaimed decree of 490 times, which appears reflected in several seventies, including Daniel's 490-year prophecy of the seventy-sevens (70 * 7 = 490 years), wherein the final week, the 70$^{th}$ Week, highlights the Abomination of Desolation (the Antichrist/Beast/Little Horn/etc.) at the conclusion of the 490 years of Hebrew History as foretold by the Angel Gabriel.

Judgment in "denominations of seventy" also plays out in the story of Jehu and Ahab, whose wife was the daughter of a King of Tyre, leading to an unholy alliance between Tyre and Israel, which then encouraged the BAAL apostasy to contaminate the Hebrew religion in Northern Israel. Judgments enunciated by the prophet Isaiah against Tyre and later Jeremiah (and Daniel implicitly) against Babylon are all timed "telesmatically" to 70 years.

In summary, *seventy is a number of completion, culmination, and conclusion* in respect to God's providential plans, of which judgment for iniquity (and especially for the Jew in transgressing God's commandments as given through Moses) plays no small part. *The scripture's use of seventy provides a numerological means to "connect the dots" between the evil empires, combining them metaphorically, to identify THE FINAL BABYLON.*

In conclusion, we provide a summary chart (following) developed by author Krieger (with a little help from his friends) to put all of these seventies into perspective, along with a summary analysis of what the chart attempts to capture for the readers benefit:

- The chart begins by tying the three aspects of Babylon as depicted in Revelation (Babylon, a city divided into three parts) – a subject to be discussed also in the final chapter.

- It assumes the case we've argued for *seventy tied to judgment,* and that this principle applies to Babylon (beginning at the end of seventy years of Jewish captivity – 536 B.C.), but not concluding until THE FINAL BABYLON – until the final week of Daniel's 490 years of Hebrew history; which concludes during the final "week", the seventieth heptad, or the final seven years preceding the return of the Messiah Jesus Christ, to judge the nations and establish His Kingdom (in space-time), upon this earth.

- The 490 years of Jewish history builds on 70 "sevens" or heptads. The curse demanded by Lamech (from God for his protection) pencils out to 490 years. We have noted the pattern and believe it is not coincidental.

- There are three Babylons which have been represented through history by different "empires" at different times.

However, ultimately, there is a FINAL BABYLON which comprises all three and is the power base of the Antichrist. Like Nimrod's Babylon (the first archetype of Antichrist), and Nebuchadnezzar's Babylonian empire (whose lycanthropy for seven years pictured the "madness" of Antichrist); Babylon represents an empire opposed to the true God. America reflects the Final Babylon. It combines spiritual apostasy, commercial despotism, with globalist political and military domination in the name of the State, destroying the liberty God intended for all His children.

- There are numerous related connections in the sacred numbers of Scripture. This is especially so in regard to the *sacred cubit*, a unit of measurement of 25.20 inches (2.1 feet) devised by God, and given to the Hebrews for sacred measurement (employed in the dimensions of the Ark of the Covenant). We invite the reader to explore these in more depth at Krieger and McGriff's website (see especially http://www.the-tribulation-network.com/new_tribnet/ebooks/year_ of_ jubilee/ TOC.html and within the late David Flynn's wonderful book: *The Temple at the Center of Time.*

| THE FINAL BABYLON<br>"Now the Great City was divided into **THREE PARTS**" - Rev. 16:19<br>"When 70 years (605 B.C. – 536 B.C.) were completed, I will punish the king of Babylon" – Jer. 25:12 | | | |
|---|---|---|---|
| **Principle of "70" used in Judgment** | Genesis 4:19-24 – "If Cain shall be avenged sevenfold, then Lamech seventy-sevenfold" or 7 * 70 = 490 times (LXX) (Contrast with Matthew 18:22 - "Forgive 7 * 70" = 490). Note: the first example of "70" as a number for retribution or judgment. | | |
| **THE THREE SETS OF 70 AS JUDGMENTS AGAINST BABYLON** | | | |
| **70 – Harlot of Tyre Apostate Babylon**<br>Revelation 17 | Isaiah 23:15-18 | "Now it shall come to pass in that day that Tyre will be forgotten **70 years**...at the end of **70 years** it will happen to Tyre as in the song of the harlot...and it shall be, **at the end of 70 years, that the LORD will deal with Tyre**. She will return to her hire, commit fornication with all the kingdoms of the world on the face of the earth" - (Note: 3 sets of 70s) | Note: "Commit fornication with all the kingdoms of the world on the face of the earth" |
| **70 – King of Babylon Commercial Babylon**<br>Revelation 18 | Jeremiah 25:11-12 (Ref. Jer. 29:10; II Chron. 36:21-23) | "Serve the King of Babylon **70 years**...then it shall come to pass, **when 70 years are completed, that I will punish the King of Babylon** and **that nation**, the land of the Chaldeans, for their iniquity,' says the LORD; 'and I will make it a **perpetual desolation'**...." | Note: "Perpetual desolation" begins when? |
| **70 – Antichrist-Beast Political Babylon**<br>Revelation 19 | Daniel 9:2, 24-27 | "...accomplish **70 years** in the desolations of Jerusalem"...**70 weeks** (lit. "sevens") "confirm a covenant/treaty for one week" or the **70th Week** of the 70 weeks prophecy – the focus in Daniel is upon the Antichrist-Beast and his Image, aka *Little Horn/Willful King* and the *Abomination of Desolation*<br>NOTE: Visions delineated in 7 weeks or 7 * 7 = 49 years; 62 weeks or 62 * 7 = 434 years and 1 week or 7 years.<br>Thus, 49 + 434 + 7 = 490 years. This reflects Lamech's 7 * 70 = 490 times.<br>This reflects the "full"measure of judgment: 7 * 70 = 490 times = 490 years. | Note: 3 Separate 70s : 70 years, 70 weeks, & 70th week |
| **CONCLUSION OF THE 3 SETS OF 70**<br>Other numerological mysteries:<br>3 * 70 = 210, while 70 + 70 + 70 = 210, and 210 is 1/12th measure of the 2,520 Days of Daniel's Final Week (i.e., 210 * 12 = 2,520)<br>7 * 360 = 2,520 Days, which also reflects the Measurement of the Sacred Cubit (25.20"/12" = Exactly 2.1 feet)<br>2.1 is also a fractal of the number 210<br>Also reflected in the "*Hand writing on the wall*" with the words "Mene, mene, tekel, upharsin" (1,000+1,000+500+20) | **(1) Apostate Babylon** (Tyre) arises at the end of 70 years to fornicate with all the Kingdoms of the World on the face of the Earth (i.e., the Great Harlot who rides the Beast) – these are the last days of the Final Babylon, i.e., "Apostate Babylon".<br>**(2) Commercial Babylon** – afflicted by Tyre, as well, is the Great Commercial Empire of the Last Days: "When 70 years are completed I will punish the King of Babylon and I will make it a perpetual desolation." At the "End of the Age" – the last days of THE FINAL BABYLON, i.e., "Commercial Babylon".<br>**(3) Political Babylon** – the Beast will be judged at the end of the "70" *(70th Week) unto the "1,290th Day" to be precise – found in Daniel 12:11 – the last days of the Final Babylon, i.e., "Political Babylon".<br>***"Come out of her My People" – Revelation 18:4*** | | |

**Figure 41 - Recapping the Seventies in Judgment**

*Chapter 9:*

# When Antichrist Reveals Himself in America, Will We Recognize Him?

## Political Professions of Faith

TO THE SURPRISE AND THE DISMAY OF CHRISTIANS, IT IS PROBABLE NO REPELLENT POLITICAL FIGURE IN MODERN TIMES EVER PROFESSED FAITH IN CHRISTIANITY MORE THAN ADOLF HITLER. No public official ever championed the separation of Church and State more fervently than the Führer. And it is unlikely any religious leader promoted putting faith into action with more exuberance than the leader of the National Socialist Party. Consider a small sample of Hitler's words:

> "This 'Winter Help Work' [a social "outreach" program] is also in the deepest sense a Christian work. When I see, as I so often do, poorly clad girls collecting with such infinite patience in order to care for those who are suffering from the cold while they themselves are shivering with cold, then I have the feeling that they are all apostles of a Christianity – and in truth of a Christianity which can say with greater right than any other: this is the Christianity of an honest confession, for behind it stand not words but deeds." [1]

For these substantive reasons and many more (not always so warmly swaddled in biblical ideals), the German Catholic as well as "Evangelical" Church failed to discern a glaring and provocative manifestation of Antichrist in their midst. The best and the brightest, the priests and the theologians, all were caught up in the rush to support the cause of National Socialism. German leaders, both spiritual and political, stood side-by-side to bring the Fatherland back from the brink. And Adolf Hitler inspired them to come together for the common cause.

---

[1] Adolf Hitler, speaking of the Winter Help Campaign on 5 Oct. 1937.

Certainly, more than "mass psychology" was influencing 1930's Germany.[2] Christian intellectuals, from the middle ranks to the upper echelons, professed faith in the Führer. In hindsight, we could be justifiably aghast how the experts wholly missed the most obvious incarnation of the Antichrist since brutal first-century Roman emperors fed thousands of Christians to the lions.[3] How, pray tell, could this happen?

Indeed, this particular "mystery of iniquity" (2 Thessalonians 2:7) astonishes us because Hitler not only convinced the hungry and unemployed masses – he gained the favor of the theologically sophisticated. Despite his outspoken rancor and the suspected occultism amongst his accomplices, opposition from the Church never materialized in any meaningful way until almost War's end. He promoted what Germans wanted to hear – that God was on their side. He provoked patriotism by calls to revere the old ways. He assured the nation that the disgrace of losing "the Great War" (World War I) had nothing to do with the Kaiser's blatant imperialism. And despite outrageous anti-Semitism, Adolf Hitler was hailed as "God's man of the hour." The servants of God were simply witless in detecting the malevolent motivating force behind Adolf Hitler.

---

[2] "The main idea of Sigmund Freud's crowd behavior theory is that people who are in a crowd act differently towards people from those who are thinking individually. The minds of the group would merge to form a way of thinking. Each member's enthusiasm would be increased as a result, and one becomes less aware of the true nature of one's action." See http://en.wikipedia.org / wiki/Crowd_psychology.

[3] The study of who understood Hitler and fled and who didn't is an intriguing study in itself. Walter Stein, student of Rudolph Steiner whom Trevor Ravenscroft credits with the story behind The Spear of Destiny fled to England. Paul Tillich who later became a major voice in American Theological Liberalism supposedly looked into the eyes of Hitler and saw the demonic and left for Switzerland. Dietrich Bonheoffer is the most noteworthy theologian who saw Hitler for what he was – a mass murderer. Eventually he lost his life for participating in an assassination attempt on Hitler. He is perhaps the most famous Christian martyr of the twentieth century.

Behold the uniqueness of Adolf Hitler! With contagious conviction he voiced what the German soul could be in its manifold creative genius! His carefully orchestrated words disclosed complete commitment and utter brilliance as a leader of the people. With rapturous expressions, he invigorated a dejected Germany. He guided the rediscovery of its powerful but pagan roots, illuminating who they were and what they could become, with Almighty God guiding their steps (he saw no conflict between Odin and Jehovah!) Hitler injected into nearly every German heart a DIVINE IMPRIMATUR, which justified an inferno of destruction and death unmatched in human history. Its pristine message created a new Reich of *DAS VOLK*, a people destined by the triumph of their collective will to be the consummation and commencement of the Kingdom of God – DAS THOUSANDE JAHRE REICH (the millennial reign, a one thousand year kingdom initiated in the German spirit of Charlemagne, the emperor of the FIRST REICH, the Holy Roman Empire inaugurated at Christmas 800 AD).[4]

**Figure 42 – Luther's cover to the 1543 edition, *The Jews and Their Lies***

This infamous would-be Kaiser/Caesar/Antichrist arose in Germany over a ten-year timeframe, from the end of 1924 until he became Chancellor in March 1933, and soon thereafter the supreme leader – having combined upon the death of President

[4] Recall his true name was German, *Karl the Great*, in the line of Peppin, representing the dynasty of the Carolingians.

Paul von Hindenburg the offices of President and Chancellor into "Führer and Reichskanzler."

There were those who possessed the ability to discern the real meaning of National Socialism. They possessed the necessary time and skill to analyze the political, social, and spiritual events leading up to the Nazi takeover. No doubt their failure in part stemmed from a latent (and all-too-often blatant) anti-Semitism wide-spread amongst the German population, arguably stimulated by Martin Luther's strong anti-Semitic perspectives.[5] However, even the dramatic incidents of hate expressed toward Jews (one thinks of *Kristallnacht, Crystal Night* or *the Night of the Broken Glass,* 9-10 November 1938) failed to supply the spiritually astute with insight into what was going to happen. The appeal of Hitler satisfied a number of concerns related to national pride, providing simple answers to very complex questions, economic rebirth to a nation dead in its fiscal tracks, and the rehashing of the nation's favorite Teutonic folk myths stirring the soul of its people.

However, we don't have space to concern ourselves with *all* the causes for the *apokalypsis* of Antichrist in Germany.[6] Instead, we will focus on the spiritually-based sentiments Hitler explicitly expressed, promising that his ideology and his government supported the Christian faith – that there was no conflict between National Socialism and Christianity. It was this relationship – an overtly rank expression of "religio-political apostasy" – which so disturbs us. In his countless statements made directly to Christian audiences, we will learn why Adolf Hitler was so extremely dangerous. Surprisingly (we think you'll agree it isn't the standard interpretation), it was not because he could scheme so treacherously. To the contrary, the key to Hitler's

---

[5] Luther's *The Jews and Their Lies (1543, Von den Jüden und iren Lügen*) stands as the seminal statement on anti-Semitism. According to friend and scholar, Gary Stearman, Luther makes his hatred for the Jews crudely plain.

[6] The Greek word, *apokalypsis,* means the revealing, particularly the revealing of deep secrets, from whence the word *Apocalypse* derives.

sleight-of-hand was due to his own self-delusion: he possessed unwavering faith that his was a righteous calling from God above – wrought by "providence."

Our point in this chapter: Beware! Similar circumstances are present in our land today. Americans must be on guard – especially at this most portentous time – with depressed economic conditions, a high unemployment rate, and smooth talking politicians long on promises and short on accomplishments. Our vigilance can't be dulled even by the most sincere sounding statements of faith and vision from prominent public figures. Our observations must be focused on not just what has been said, but what is being done. A superficial assessment won't suffice. We must consider all the evidence carefully and draw conclusions in pious contemplation.

**Figure 43 - "*Gott Mit Uns*" - God With Us**

We begin by proposing a troubling issue for the reader's consideration: If Antichrist were to be revealed in America, would the faithful recognize him? Would Americans committed to spiritual values miss the same clues disclosing Antichrist's true nature as did the Germans with Hitler?

There is little doubt that if a figure paraded himself in front of the American people resembling an easily stereotyped leader of the Third Reich – with a mousy moustache, an armband with hypnotic logo, and wearing a brown shirt – his character and agenda would be obvious to almost everyone. Mounting the podium with an emotional appeal to our national loyalty, the adamant display of venom and vitriol against the enemies of the State, the promise of the restoration of our American "empire" through a continuing buildup of military might, the stark name calling identifying an appropriate scapegoat to fault for our problems – all of these factors would, at best, betray a would-be antichrist figure as a false messiah – or at worst, spotlight an artless actor who undoubtedly took us for fools.

However, we can be certain the *apocalypse* of (that is, the *revealing* of) Antichrist in America, an event we believe will transpire in the years just ahead, will be a one-of-a-kind challenge requiring spiritual discernment worthy of only the most circumspect and attuned "code breakers" whose specialty is exposing wolves in sheep's clothing.

## Orchestrating the Madding Crowd

Remember Hitler achieved a meteoric rise to prominence and power because he understood the soul of his people. He could relate. He knew what made them tick. He realized how to couch his message in the context of the political situation and how to engage those who would be but mere spectators by relating to their financial pain and anxiety over the future. Hitler understood crowd psychology and how to manipulate it. To mesmerize his audience, he learned the power of emphatic facial expressions and energetic hand gestures. He compelled unquestioning allegiance by conveying solutions plainly and confidently no matter how oversimplified or extreme his answers might be. In fact, the more oversimplified and uncompromising his solutions were – the better to persuade the people of their usefulness. His greatest weapon was that "wretched Treaty of Versailles" and its national humiliation – its guilt-ridden condemnation upon the German people, coupled with horrific war reparations.

**Figure 44 - *Reichskirche* Flag, circa 1936, Nazi Germany**

What is the lesson for us? If the Antichrist were to arise in America at this moment, we would be foolish to expect him to be anything but a consummate American. He would look like us. He would talk like us. He would think – for the most part – like us. And with a straight face he might even assert a profession of Christian faith – and why he believes the teaching of Jesus Christ is so well suited for society. Following Adolf Hitler's lead, he would appeal to the most devout class of Christian – the Evangelical. He would offer opportunities to bring biblically-based believers "out front" – to escape the shadows of social disdain and distance themselves from the hackneyed portrait affirmed by the intelligentsia and showcased by the media; supposing that those who call themselves Evangelical are intellectually bankrupt. He would convince Bible-believing conservatives that they should no longer see themselves as simple *plebeians* (the common folk). Their self-image should be elevated so they regard their value no less in status than the progressive patricians of sophisticated national institutions.[7] Not that he would identify himself with the elite nor propose that the common man should be ashamed of his laborer status. Rather, he would argue he remains a man "of the people" yet holds himself sufficiently apart to sanctify his status as our formidable if not *fearless* leader.

This *positioning* reflects the example of Herr Hitler in many respects. Likewise, the tone and substance coming from the mouth of the Führer, although etched in the *zeitgeist* of that age, begs for comparison to what we hear today from select political leaders promoting the American version of The New World Order;[8] especially those who were, are, or would be our President. Consider for a moment: Might it not be a factor in the false Christ's persuasiveness – the fact that he could "*deceive, if possible, even the elect*"? (Matthew 24:24).

---

[7] We might even have one of our most noteworthy evangelical leaders be asked to give the prayer at a Presidential Inauguration!

[8] Hitler spoke of bringing about the New Order as did Franklin D. Roosevelt.

However, the sham to fool Evangelicals will make use of more than patronizing remarks. It will turn the words of our most popular preachers against us. The ideology that should prohibit the arising of Antichrist – the Christian religion and its worldview – will be a powerful tool co-opted to capture the "believing" masses and to encourage, through a moral veneer and political resolution, an agenda resonating within the heart of the "folks" in these United States. Indeed, the future philosophy of Antichrist will convince us we should resolve to be nothing less than what our most prominent spiritual leaders teach us to be – successful, healthy, and committed to classic American ideals (although our most noble notions of individual liberty, a la Henry David Thoreau and Thomas Jefferson, have long since quietly departed for destinations unknown).

In like manner, Antichrist would deftly implore citizens to follow his lead. He would criticize Christians for failure to follow the most "positive" aspects of our faith. Indeed, similar to Hitler's "Positive Christianity" – a Christianity that is proactive, expressed in "unselfish service" to others, characteristic of true Americans.

He would call us to be the best Americans we can be – a worthy aspiration for the greater good of all Americans. The health of our nation, he would argue, depends upon living productive lives that contribute to economic prosperity for all. Morality, like ethics, should be shaped to improve our communities in light of standards established by the majority. Religion, true religion, will instill these values. It will not conflict with political objectives because *positive* faith goes hand-in-hand with constructive political ideology. The manifesto of "the public good" will brand any substantial opposition worthy of elimination. True believers will be activists – but for causes that comply with the will of the many – all the better to reflect his "image", with "*great signs and wonders to deceive*" (Matthew 24:24).

On the surface, the nature of these ideals will seem consistent with the Bible. After all, who would argue that the spiritually inclined should be unproductive, immoral, unethical, a burden on the public's well-being, and incapable of contributing to the community's economic health? And yet, upon a more cautious objective inspection, there will emerge a thin but distinctive line between a laudable social compact (built upon beneficial principles for both the individual and the nation) with an overreaching "State" that demands unquestioned obedience (aka *cooperation*) – commanding allegiance above all other causes no matter how worthy.

Moreover, the challenge to discern the agenda of the Antichrist will be difficult for many reasons, not just intellectual. Social pressure to conform will be "maxed out." The path to achieve clarity will be a lonely path, for our peers will be only too ready to encourage complicity. Any complaint and disparagement will be interpreted as unpatriotic, a threat to social order, and harmful not only to our own health, but to those we love and care about. An "untoward behavior" viewed as "self-alienation," first frowned upon, and then doggedly condemned since it benefits not the whole. One's consciousness raising must be done in stealth not to draw attention to an expressed awareness that the enemy of Christ speaks profanely in our presence. It will not be easy to resist even if we come to the realization we have been asked to serve Antichrist. Our peers will plead with us not to rock the boat, not to question falling in line, not to label the State as anything but what is best for one and all. To be "the best Christian one can be" will appear synonymous with being the perfect U.S. citizen. Fear will

**Figure 45 - The Cross and the Swastika**

lead families to betray one another: brother will betray brother, children will betray their parents, and all in the name of doing what is "for the common good of all."

As a harbinger of the evil one to come, study the words of Hitler below. Consider just how difficult our task to discern the voice of Antichrist when it reverberates in America:

> "We demand liberty for all religious denominations in the State, so far as they are not a danger to it and do not militate against the morality and moral sense of the German race. The Party, as such, stands for *positive* Christianity, but does not bind itself in the matter of creed to any particular confession." [9] [Emphasis added]
>
> "The National Government regards the two Christian Confessions as the weightiest factors for the maintenance of our nationality. They will respect the agreements concluded between them and the federal States. Their rights are not to be infringed... It will be the Government's care to maintain honest co-operation between Church and State; the struggle against materialistic views and for a real national community is just as much in the interest of the German nation as in that of the welfare of our Christian faith. The Government of the Reich, who regard Christianity as the unshakable foundation of the morals and moral code of the nation, attach the greatest value to friendly relations with the Holy See and are endeavoring to develop them." [10]

The partnership of Church and State constructed by Hitler was remarkable in many ways for he appealed to Christians' proclivity to self-righteous aspiration, beguiling them through awarding accreditation as possessors of the very "moral soul" of the nation. To enhance his appeal, he vowed without a Christian moral foundation, there would be no German morality. In light of this, the reader of the Gospels can stop wondering why Jesus (in Matthew Chapter 24) was so repetitious regarding "deception

[9] Item #24 of the German Worker's Party "Program" circa 1920s.

[10] Adolf Hitler, in his speech to the Reichstag on 23 March 1933

and being deceived," "false prophets and false messiahs," and the like in reference to the "state of society" at the end of the age.

At the time his audience was Catholic, but his announcement of the *Concordat* with Rome (the papal agreement, 5 July 1933) had meaning to Protestants as well. The message was obvious and clear: friendly relations – relations that are inclusive of the Church – must be the norm in a resurgent Germany. "The fact that the Vatican is concluding a treaty with the new Germany means the acknowledgement of the National Socialist state by the Catholic Church. This treaty shows the whole world clearly and unequivocally that the assertion that National Socialism [Nazism] is hostile to religion is a lie." [11]

Hitler was even more effusive about the value of Nazism to benefit the Church:

> "While we destroyed the Center Party [a Catholic political party [12]], we have not only brought thousands of priests back into the Church, but to millions of respectable people we have restored their faith in their religion and in their priests. The union of the Evangelical Church in a single Church for the whole Reich, the Concordat with the Catholic Church, these are but milestones on the road, which leads to the establishment of a useful relation and a useful co-operation between the Reich and the two Confessions."[13]

---

[11] Adolf Hitler, 22 July 1933, writing to the Nazi Party (quoted from John Cornwell's *Hitler's Pope.*)

[12] "The **German Centre Party** (German: *Deutsche Zentrumspartei* or just ***Zentrum***) was a Catholic political party in Germany during the *Kaiserreich* and the Weimar Republic. In English it is often called the Catholic Centre Party. Formed in 1870, it battled the *Kulturkampf* which the Prussian government launched to reduce the power of the Catholic Church. It soon won a quarter of the seats in the Reichstag (Imperial Parliament), and its middle position on most issues allowed it to play a decisive role in the formation of majorities. "When the Nazis came to power the party dissolved itself on 5 July 1933 as a condition of the conclusion of a Concordat between the Holy See and Germany." See en.wikipedia.org/wiki/Centre_Party_(Germany).

[13] Adolf Hitler, in his New Year Message on 1 Jan. 1934

## The Division of Labor in the Third Reich

Furthermore, it was essential *to separate the realms of personal faith and political action.* Hitler's "spheres of function" were altogether essential insofar as the Church's dominion was concerned, for without the spiritual health of Germany, there would be no political health. But he also took a hard line to distinguish their responsibilities: The Church was to look after the spiritual and moral health of the flock – the State would tend to its material need:

> "The German Church and the People are practically the same body. Therefore there could be no issue between Church and State. The Church, as such, has nothing to do with political affairs. On the other hand, the State has nothing to do with the faith or inner organization of the Church."[14]

> "The National Socialist State professes its allegiance to *positive* Christianity. It will be its honest endeavor to protect both the great Christian Confessions in their rights, to secure them from interference with their doctrines (*Lehren*), and in their duties to constitute a harmony with the views and the exigencies of the State of today." [15] [Emphasis added]

> "So long as they concern themselves with their religious problems the State does not concern itself with them. But so soon as they attempt by any means whatsoever – by letters, Encyclical, or otherwise – to arrogate to themselves rights which belong to the State alone we shall force them back into their proper spiritual, pastoral activity."[16]

In other words, both Church and State must reassure its citizens they abide to provide for their well-being. But it is necessary they split duties. Keep the Church's message personal and positive while the State should keep promises of economic welfare.

---

[14] Adolf Hitler, answering C. F. Macfarland about Church & State (in his book, *The New Church and the New Germany*).

[15] Adolf Hitler, on 26 June 1934, to Catholic bishops to assure them that he would take action against the new pagan propaganda.

[16] Adolf Hitler, in a speech delivered in Berlin on the May Day festival, 1937

Of course, the primacy of the State was unquestionable. The State dictated the role of the Church. Furthermore, it mandated any criticism of the State would not be tolerated.

Moreover, upon close inspection, Hitler would "gerrymander" the territory of the State when it suited him. For some theological modifications would be necessary. In a Germany liberated from the "old-fashioned" faith, the Church should dismiss any talk of humankind's sinful inclinations and its need for repentance. Evil must be mitigated – more specifically, downgraded – and reduced in substance to "mistakes" and not the more menacing notion of sin. Defects in human behavior amount to little more than "poor choices." Thus, with sin redefined and evil eliminated as a "metaphysical reality"[17] the Gospel was compromised and the Church complicit. It could then pray reverently with the Führer:

> "We want honestly to earn the resurrection of our people through our industry, our perseverance, and our will. We ask not of the Almighty, 'Lord, make us free!' – we want to be active, to work, to agree together as brothers, to strive in rivalry with one another to bring about the hour when we can come before Him and when we may ask of Him: 'Lord, Thou seest that we have transformed ourselves, the German people is no longer the people of dishonor, of shame, of war within itself, of faintheartedness and little faith: no, Lord, the German people has become strong again in spirit, strong in will, strong in endurance, strong to bear all sacrifices.' 'Lord, we will not let Thee go: bless now our fight for our freedom; the fight we wage for our German people and Fatherland.'" [18]

Furthermore, while the Führer did not directly confront Christian sensibilities, his prayer led one to conjecture what "positive Christianity" involved and exactly what its opposite –

---

[17] By this we mean a reality in its own right, although C.S. Lewis was likely on to something by describing *evil* not as essential to reality as "good" is, but akin more to "spoiled goodness" – lest we inadvertently fall into the conundrum of a Zoroastrian dualism in which good and evil are on equal footing.
[18] Adolf Hitler, giving prayer in a speech on May Day, 1933

"negative Christianity" – would entail. No doubt his listeners let the matter drop without questioning his meaning behind the exhortation for accentuating a "positive Christianity". However, we suppose if such a loaded phrase lies dormant for too long, like a lit firecracker failing to pop, the listener will worry more than a bit about when it *will* detonate.

To the wary hearer, Hitler's statement anticipates a pause "for the other shoe to drop." And yet, assuming nothing but good intent from the Führer, the audience didn't worry one iota that another shoe would hit the floor (or worse, the fecal matter would collide with the oscillating rotor!) Instead, they were enraptured by Hitler's acclamation:

> "MY LORD AND SAVIOR... IN THE BOUNDLESS LOVE AS A CHRISTIAN... HE HAD TO SHED HIS BLOOD UPON THE CROSS. My feelings as a Christian point me to my Lord and Savior *as a fighter*. It points me to the man who once in loneliness, surrounded only by a few followers, recognized these Jews for what they were and *summoned men to fight against them [Peter should take up his sword, rather than put it away]*. This is God's truth! He was greatest not as a sufferer *but as a fighter*. In boundless love as a Christian and as a man I read through the passage which tells us how the Lord at last rose in His might and seized the scourge to drive out of the Temple the brood of vipers and adders. How terrific was His fight for the world against the Jewish poison. Today, after two thousand years, with deepest emotion I recognize more profoundly than ever before in the fact that it was for this that He had to shed His blood upon the Cross. As a Christian I have no duty to allow myself to be cheated, but I have the duty *to be a fighter* for truth and justice..."[19] [Emphasis added]

The notion that the Messiah was himself NOT Jewish was a view propounded by Richard Wagner, the famous German composer whose operas were expressions of the nineteenth-century German *Zeitgeist* (the "spirit of the age"). Unquestionably, Hitler's favorite composer, Wagner, stirred Hitler's soul to envision

---

[19] Adolf Hitler from his speech of 12 April, 1922.

a revived, irrepressible, and vengeful Germany. During World War II, Wagner's legacy lived on as his music filled the putrefied air of Holocaust death camps. As a result, survivors would forever associate Wagner with Auschwitz. This was no disservice to Wagner – for he believed that Christ was Aryan, not Jewish. And like Friedrich Nietzsche, the "*Philosopher Emeritus*" of the German people (a good friend of Wagner until their falling out), he believed the German soul must not be dragged down by the "slave mentality" of the Jew. Consequently, it logically followed that Jesus could never be considered a Jew. To the aspiring German mindset, the Jews were a millstone about their necks. The Hebrew religion bestowed nothing but restrictive laws and depressive guilt. It was time for Germany to cast aside the Jewish mentality and its stifling effect upon the soul of humankind, especially the Aryan race!

As to Nietzsche, he famously asserted a philosophy known as *the will to power*. To the extent Jesus allowed himself to be crucified, to that same extent Jesus was Himself the anti-Christ. For Nietzsche, Jesus' commitment to die for the sin of the world was nothing but a *death wish* to be condemned and repudiated. Jesus' willingness to lay down his life remains the source of so much nonsense contaminating the true purpose for religion. Instead, a "true confession" encourages struggle! (*Mein Kampf* of course means, *My Struggle*) Suffering saves no one. Moreover, this must be the stalwart creed of all true believers. The gospel of Wagner, Nietzsche, and especially Adolf Hitler held in common disdain for the Jew.

The duty to be a fighter for truth, justice (and the German way) comprises, of course, the motto of *Superman*, the quintessential American superhero. Indeed, less feted translators often seek to convey the meaning of Nietzsche's *Übermensch* with the expression, *Superman*. However oversimplified this one-word translation (especially vulgar to the sophisticated), nonetheless, it likewise urges those loyal to Old Glory – the red, white, and blue – to stand and be counted! America boasts the greatest military ever assembled. Any concept of redemptive suffering preached from the Bible by ignoble vicars of Christ, surely misses the mark. Turning the other cheek (Matthew 5:39) can't be what Christ actually meant. "Fight back! Don't get mad – get even!" Of course, the German people in the 1920s and 30s were a frustrated, defeated people, wearing anger on their sleeves right below their swastikas.

Americans don't feel compelled to take such overt military action. Discretion is the better part of valor. We much prefer to keep our battles on the "down low" equipping our intelligence services to act covertly (witness the current, 2013 conflict regarding NSA's [National Security Agency] mining of private phone and Internet data, spying on multiple foreign (friendly) governments, accessing and cataloguing private data of one hundred million Americans, as well as the intrusive behavior of the Treasury Department's Internal Revenue Service), our special forces to operate in darkness, and U.S. sorties of the aeronautical kind be carried out in stealth mode. As the military is wont to say, "We own the night." Unlike the saints to whom Paul addressed his letters, it never sought to be Children of the Day.

## Hating in the Name of Christ and Country

The unity of the Church was important to Hitler. He could not consummate his grand plan without the support of the Church. He required his back side be covered. Consequently, it was crucial that disputes in the Church be silenced, if for no other reasons, than quarrels not bubble over into matters of State nor distract the populace from the bellicose but sacred duty before them.

> "It will at any rate be my supreme task to see to it that in the newly awakened NSDAP, the adherents of both Confessions can live peacefully together side by side in order that they may take their stand in the common fight against the power, which is the mortal foe of any true Christianity." [20]

---

[20] *Adolf Hitler, in an article headed "A New Beginning," 26 Feb. 1925*

> "This is for us a ground for satisfaction, since we desire that the fight in the religious camps should come to an end... all political action in the parties will be forbidden to priests for all time, happy because we know what is wanted by millions who long to see in the priest only the comforter of their souls and not the representative of their political convictions." [21]

Furthermore, Hitler required that the Church's energy contribute to the Fatherland's fighting spirit. Religious fires must burn on his behalf.

> "So far as the Evangelical Confessions are concerned we are determined to put an end to existing divisions, which are concerned only with the forms of organization, and to create a single Evangelical Church for the whole Reich... And we know that were the great German reformer [Martin Luther] with us today he would rejoice to be freed from the necessity of his own time and, like Ulrich von Hutten [1488 – 1523, an outspoken German scholar, poet and reformer], his last prayer would be not for the Churches of the separate States: it would be of Germany that he would think... and of the Evangelical Church of Germany." [22]

After all, to Hitler, the real enemy was the "International Jew." Christianity must unite, Catholics and Protestants, laity and priesthood – "against the power" – i.e., the international Jewish conspiracy that [he argued] warred against the Church of Jesus Christ and the German people. Not that this tactic was especially risky. His approach was tried and true – unite around a well-defined mutual foe. Foment hatred against them. Exaggerate images to make plain their villainess ways. Build the faithful into the "hammer of God" – make it an instrument of *righteous indignation!*

---

[21] *Adolf Hitler, in a speech to the men of the SA at Dortmund, 9 July 1933, on the day after the signing of the Concordat (Agreement with the Roman Catholic Church, the Papacy).*

[22] Adolf Hitler, in his Proclamation at the *Parteitag* at Nuremberg on 5 Sept. 1934.

## Impulse for a New Christian Ecumenism?

In comparison, today's political leadership in America and Europe has it somewhat easy; it doesn't need to manufacture a fanatical enemy. RADICAL Islam has served itself up as the despicable lunatic fringe fighting against Christendom and the State. Our message must be made plain to the public: The radical Muslim is not at war not with the actions of the American government. They hate us because of our "way of life." Their enmity is personal. It is not due to protectionism of American corporations, supervised by the political system and safeguarded by the military. It is not because we have military bases in their land. Nor could it be because we have helped ourselves to their petroleum. It is our sacred values of freedom and faith in the Bible of both Old and New Testaments. This is a primary reason why Islam hates Americans. Islam views the Church's toleration with secular society as an abhorrent mixture of the *sacred and profane* – not so much an expression of political unity, but a compromised expression of religious weakness.

Subsequently, the more Islam frightens the free world, the more its enemies (secular and religious) unite. Other than twisting its ulterior motive (making it about the difference in religion as the root cause for animosity),[23] why create falsehoods about the opposition when of its own accord it provokes with carefully crafted words of hate, carries out cowardly acts of terror, and callously celebrates death when it completes its missions of murder?

No, the pathway to coopt the Church in our day first likewise requires encouraging unity within the varied hallowed institutions, then secondly, aligning them according to the political

---

[23] Not that we believe Islam is a religion of peace as many of its followers maintain. Allah appears merciful only to his devout followers. Those who reject Islam deserve to lose their heads, at least according to a large segment of the Muslim faithful. Tolerance is not a strong suit of Mohammed's teaching. If you doubt it, just express the fact that Islam is intolerant and see how much intolerance it beckons.

agenda. The broad strategy hasn't changed – although selected tactics may differ.

So what is the method to achieve an ecumenical union? It involves reconstructing the Christian message. Building unity in the contemporary church comprises a modern day equivalent of building the Tower of Babel. The most relevant message, what will really bring us together as one, requires we substitute the content of the gospel with a message of confusion, which is what Babel means. How can this be? By creating confusion over the nature of good and evil. We could say that reaching new heights in cooperation isn't based upon clear communication and seeing things eye-to-eye. *It's about not seeing things at all.* "Coming together" necessitates closing one's eyes to see no evil, hear no evil, and speak no evil. The less said the better. We must dispense with controversial matters, uniting against intolerance, epitomized in militant Islam. We can do no less. Indeed, the nature of sin and the reality of evil stand out like sore thumbs. Therefore, we must paper over them with platitudes about self-improvement, overcoming self-doubt, as well as proclaiming health and wealth to magically make them come to pass. In today's Evangelical Church, it is most certainly about a positive Christianity! Hitler would feel especially vindicated.[24]

Depleting doctrine as an essential element in a confessing Christianity is hardly new.

---

[24] Indeed, Evangelical spiritual sentiment may be content to connect with nothing more than the name "Jesus." Without specific assertions, we possess nothing distinct or definite. Thus, the name of Jesus may stand for nothing. It is the ultimate use of the Lord's name in vain. There are those in leadership within the Church that would prefer to pray only to Jesus and talk about nothing but Jesus, to avoid any sectarian debate. After all: *dogma divides; love abides.* Of course, that adage presumes *intuition* replaces *reason* as the sole religious faculty or means to discover reality. As Francis Schaeffer once conveyed, Evangelicals have their own form of religious mysticism that is just as elusive and ineffable as Buddist koans.[24] However, in the final analysis, only *true truth* prevails (an awkward *Schaefferian* tautology meant to convey truth that is objective and universal – i.e., the opposite of relative "truth" or truth that is "caught" not "taught"). "Doctrineless sound bites" bite us all in the end.

Liberal Christian Churches dispensed with any meaningful theological content decades ago. They embraced a social gospel, replete with platitudes of pluralism, while promoting the practice of social good works, unwittingly leading to greater government intervention. When they sentenced God to death in the 1960s, they assigned their own ecclesiastical institutions to death row. Fifty years ago, they reduced the Gospel to what was left over after so-called science ravaged the Bible. Theology became nothing more than existential philosophy. The meaning of being Christian amounted to little more than repeating holy words in ritual. It didn't matter however far out (i.e., supernatural) the notions of the original creeds or "Psalters" were. Theology became applied psychology. It was reconstructed to be a frame of mind or better yet, a mental state. Once the Creeds had been ransacked of all calls to spiritual transformation and relieved of all miracles, what remained was Schleiermacher's "feeling of absolute dependence," Tillich's "grounding" in the "ground of being," or Karl Jasper's "ultimate experience." Consequently, today's mainstream churches are now so emaciated it is a wonder they haven't given up the ghost altogether.

In contrast, today's Evangelical churches (that proclaim that oh so positive message) swarm with believers. But the question is, "What do they believe in?" To be sure, there are many assemblies of faithful, believing Christians that keep science in its place and esteem spiritual reality; who regard the Bible as God's Word; and rely upon the Spirit of Christ to be ever-present in their lives, not so much as an emotional impulse stimulating a mystical faith, but as an enabling power to conquer the challenging circumstances of daily life. On the other hand, as we contend, the most well-known churches appear guilty of depriving their congregations of meaningful content – biblically-based content. It's almost as if the Gospel so successfully preached today is derived from aphorisms in *Poor Richard's Almanac*: "Early to bed and early to rise makes a man healthy, wealthy, and wise." Or to misquote a famous mega-church preacher: "It IS about you!" Or worse yet, the Evangelical message transforms spirituality into a transaction: You do "x" and God does "y." "Give and it shall be given to you" – *not out of need but out of greed.* God *guarantees* our destiny to be healthy, wealthy, and wise (although the last item in this threesome isn't

**Figure 46 - The Pope's Nuncio, Archbishop Orsenigo with Hitler and Joachim von Ribbentrop**

always requested). At issue is only whether you count yourself entitled to merchandise from the Heavenly commissary, stocked wall-to-wall to assure your material needs are met in full.

## Betraying the Meaning of the Kingdom of God

After the death of Pope Pius XI in 1939, the electoral procedure to seat another Pope began. The election favored Eugenio Pacelli (1876 – 1958) and four days later, Pacelli made it clear that he would handle all German affairs personally.

He proposed the following to Hitler:

> "To the Illustrious Herr Adolf Hitler, Fuhrer and Chancellor of the German Reich! Here at the beginning of Our Pontificate

> We wish to assure you that We remain devoted to the spiritual welfare of the German people entrusted to your leadership.... During the many years we spent in Germany, We did all in Our power to establish harmonious relations between Church and State. Now that the responsibilities of Our pastoral function have increased Our opportunities, how much more ardently do We pray to reach that goal. May the prosperity of the German people and their progress in every domain come, with God's help, to fruition!"

Pacelli was crowned Pope on March 12, 1939 (becoming Pius XII). The following month on April 20, 1939, at Pius XII's express wish, Archbishop Orsenigo, the nuncio (ambassador) in Berlin, opened a gala reception for Hitler's fiftieth birthday. The birthday greetings thus initiated by Pacelli immediately became a tradition; each April 20 during the few years left to Hitler and his Reich, Cardinal Bertram of Berlin would send "warmest congratulations to the Fuhrer in the name of the bishops and the dioceses in Germany," to which he added "fervent prayers which the Catholics in Germany are sending to heaven on their altars." [25] The walls of the Kingdom of God were thoroughly breached. The homogenization of Church and State was complete.

In the context of today's megachurch, we must ask, "What does the Kingdom of God mean?" It is a most unwelcomed question since almost all our ministers and theologians in America do not proclaim a "coming Kingdom" – such prophetic assertions implies a negative message. If the Kingdom exists at all, it is up to us to "take dominion" and bring it about ourselves. Like Hitler, we "struggle" (the meaning behind *mein kampf*) to make it real. How odd, then, that we who foresee the Kingdom to be before us (in the future) to proclaim America could truly be that "City on a Hill" beckoning the "huddled masses" (yearning to be free) to come be a part of our melting pot.

---

[25] Cornwell, John, *Hitler's Pope: The Secret History of Pius XII*, Viking, 1999, p. 209.

This phrase, "The Kingdom of God" was the theme of Jesus' ministry. It was his "call to action" – his byword, his catchphrase. Despite that being so, given what appears to be the *modus operandi* of megachurches, we question whether the coming of the Kingdom of God resides at the center of today's preaching. No, the preaching of our most celebrated churches resounds with a different message.

We believe its common creed is rather crass. It is at least as material as it is spiritual. It's about getting the most out of life – or better yet, making the most (money) you can! In fact, one's financial independence indicates your spiritual status. The manner of making your life count is measured in denominations of $20s, $50s, and $100s. Jesus' blunt injunction about deciding between two masters: God and mammon (material prosperity) seems intentionally withdrawn. *God wants you to have all the mammon you can muster*! If the Apostles showed up in the megachurch today, chances are they would wonder what the message proclaimed has to do with the faith for which they died. Jesus told them (much to their astonishment) that it is virtually impossible for the rich to enter into the Kingdom of God. It is easier for a camel to pass through the eye of a needle (Matthew 19:24). The real truth couldn't have been more out of step with their colloquial tradition. In their day, it was just common sense: prosperity meant God's affirmation – if you were rich, you were "in like Flynn." You were as valuable in the Kingdom of God as your net worth – and not a penny less. That's why Jesus' message crashed his disciples' worldview like a brick landing on a paper airplane. Or better yet, a margin call on an over-leveraged portfolio.

Is it any wonder that the topic of prophecy is so taboo in most megachurches today? The apocalyptic message of Jesus Christ guarantees that private property means next to nothing – the world is passing away! Riches are of no value. Wealth will be consumed in the fire of the last days!

To be sure, Jesus taught many parables based on the priority of keeping one's eyes peeled – the parables of readiness (Matthew 24:32-51 and Matthew 25) resoundingly affirm such a prescient posture: the "wise and foolish virgins;" the "sheep and the goats;" the traveling "master of the vineyard" (to name but a few). Nevertheless, His point was consistent: (paraphrasing, but only slightly): "*Watch! For you know not when the Son of Man cometh.*" (Matthew 25:13) All too often, those weary of prophetic teaching cite those they deem obsessed with its message for failure to remember what Jesus said, "*For you do not know the day or hour of my return... wherein the son of man cometh*" as if His words were a concession to the impossibility of living life in light of His charge – or as if His intent was granting license to ignore the *temporal* implication in the apocalyptic message since we can't tell when it will happen. But that is most assuredly the opposite of what Jesus taught. His words could not have been more plain – or provocative. "The world is ending! Be ready. Don't focus on wealth. Don't sequester treasure for yourself! Don't build bigger barns! Live one day at a time."

Indeed, the strategic plan for Kingdom members amounts to remembering "You can't take it with you" – so better to share the wealth with your brothers and sisters (not waste it on your every whim!) To quote our Lord in His own words:

> *19 Lay not up for yourselves treasures upon earth, where moth and rust doth corrupt, and where thieves break through and steal:*
>
> *20 But lay up for yourselves treasures in heaven, where neither moth nor rust doth corrupt, and where thieves do not break through nor steal:*
>
> *21 For where your treasure is, there will your heart be also. (Matthew 6:19-21)*

The point of prophecy and why it is indispensable to the Gospel: to keep life and material things in proper perspective.

## Justification by the Providence of God

In 1939 Adolf Hitler summarized why he was so confident the Third Reich was imminent: "The National Socialist Movement has wrought this miracle. If Almighty God granted success to this work, then the Party was His instrument."[26] In retrospect the reader would be hard pressed to find a historical leader who levered faith, however skewed, more effectively as a power tool for REALPOLITIK. Hitler was almost unparalleled in the annals of leadership as a champion for the relevance of spiritual belief. He saw man created by God, rewarded for his reliance upon God, and sustained when cooperating with Him on a grand scale. In Hitler, we confront a leader who abandoned all self-consciousness – he was so tightly coupled with his constituency that they became of one mind. Yes, he learned the craft of public speaking like few others – maybe better than anyone. But we are dangerously mistaken if we regard his fervor as an act. He believed in what he was doing. He lost himself in his cause.

He was not tepid in faith, darting hither and thither, equivocating whenever the opportunity afforded itself. To the contrary, the leader of the Third Reich was a champion of conviction that was so "in your face" it was contagious. If faith wavered, Hitler reinstated it, bolstering public confidence in his program for a new Germany. His power hinged on claiming a brilliant destiny lay at Germany's feet. God's providence guaranteed success. In every darkened pathway, he claimed God would enlighten the path, keeping National Socialism on track because it fulfilled the Almighty's Plan. Hitler pleaded it, believed in it, and "owned" what he stridently confessed. All doubt concerning Germany's mission fled from his presence because, as far as he was concerned, God mandated that the German people be ultimately victorious. History would demon-

[26] Adolf Hitler, in his proclamation to the German People on 1 Jan 1939.

strate divine preference. God would honor Hitler's unfeigned devotion to his people. Listen to his confident faith:

> "In this hour I would ask of the Lord God only this: that, as in the past, so in the years to come He would give His blessing to our work and our action, to our judgment and our resolution, that He will safeguard us from all false pride and from all cowardly servility, that He may grant us to find the straight path which His Providence has ordained for the German people, and that He may ever give us the courage to do the right, never to falter, never to yield before any violence, before any danger... I am convinced that men who are created by God should live in accordance with the will of the Almighty... If Providence had not guided us I could often never have found these dizzy paths... Thus it is that we National Socialists, too, have in the depths of our hearts our faith. We cannot do otherwise; no man can fashion world history or the history of peoples unless upon his purpose and his powers there rests the blessings of this Providence." [27]

In the final analysis, the Antichrist may be dangerous not because he is the best actor ever to mount the world stage or since he will hide insincere intent and cloak satanic motive. He will be exceptionally treacherous because, like Adolf Hitler, he will be utterly convinced that defeat is inconceivable. Convinced of his invincibility and even more, his infallibility, the deception characterizing the man of lawlessness will be utterly commanding because he is himself deceived, believing that God is evil and Satan good.

> Only so you can appeal to your God and pray Him to support and bless your courage, your work, your perseverance, your strength, your resolution, and with all these your claim on life." [28]
>
> "In this world him who does not abandon himself the Almighty will not desert. Him who helps himself will the Almighty

[27] Adolf Hitler, in a speech at Wurzburg on 27 June 1937.
[28] Adolf Hitler, in a speech at Frankfurt on 16 March 1936.

always also help; He will show him the way by which he can gain his rights, his freedom, and therefore his future." [29]

Such sentiments cannot be dismissed because they are disingenuous. It would be preposterous to suppose Adolf Hitler was consistently inauthentic. He believed in an "active cooperation" with the divine – his was a form of perseverance strengthened by a Calvinist-like conviction. Echoing the adage of the common man in America – *God helps those who help themselves!* Can we imagine a more *positive* way to express Christian faith?

Perhaps it is to our advantage to listen to the words of Adolf Hitler and believe we must struggle and fight against our enemies. Perhaps we should put ourselves first. Perhaps we prioritize worldly riches, personal health, and not the Kingdom of God.

Maybe we would be wise to forget the self-effacing teaching of the Master: *"He that findeth his life shall lose it: and he that loseth his life for my sake shall find it."* (Matthew 10:39) If so, it would also follow we should ignore the testimony of the aging Apostle Paul who was tormented by all manner of physical and emotional distress: *"Therefore I take pleasure in infirmities, in reproaches, in necessities, in persecutions, in distresses for Christ's sake: for when I am weak, then am I strong."* (2 Corinthians 12:10)

For if we believed those things, we would be willing to stand opposed to the State, be willing to sacrifice ourselves in the cause of the old-fashioned faith *"once delivered unto the saints"* (Jude 3), and find affliction, famine, peril, and suffering a way to draw close to God and be remade anew from the inside out. Surely that is a confession differing in kind and color.

Of this one thing we can rest assured: the Führer would not approve.

Beware the false flag operation, the burning of the Reichstag, the diminution or even elimination of the People's Assem-

[29] Adolf Hitler, in a speech at Hamburg on 20 March 1936.

bly (our Congress), and the coming of the Imperial leader in the name of heightened security and peace.

*"Those who cannot remember the past are condemned to repeat it."* (Santayana)

*Chapter 10:*

# The Judgment of Babylon

## The Stage is Set

WE ARE IN HEAVEN STANDING WITH THE MULTITUDE BEFORE THE THRONE OF GOD. A MOMENTOUS EVENT HAS JUST TRANSPIRED. THE LORD HAS SEALED 144,000 – 12,000 from each of the Tribes of Israel upon the earth – while in heaven, "*After this I beheld, and, lo, a great multitude, which no man could number, of all nations, and kindreds, and people, and tongues, stood before the throne, and before the Lamb, clothed with white robes, and palms in their hands; and cried with a loud voice, saying, 'Salvation to our God which sitteth upon the throne, and unto the Lamb*'" (Revelation 7: 9, 10).

John the Revelator is puzzled. An angel standing with John asks him, "Who is this innumerable assembly?"

> 14 *And I [John] said unto him, "Sir, thou knowest." And he said to me, "These are they which came out of great tribulation, and have washed their robes, and made them white in the blood of the Lamb.*
>
> 15 *Therefore are they before the throne of God, and serve him day and night in his temple: and he that sitteth on the throne shall dwell among them.*
>
> 16 *They shall hunger no more, neither thirst any more; neither shall the sun light on them, nor any heat.*
>
> 17 *For the Lamb which is in the midst of the throne shall feed them, and shall lead them unto living fountains of waters: and God shall wipe away all tears from their eyes."* (Revelation 7:14-17)

Back on earth, a time of great tribulation has thundered and raged, a time unlike any in world history. Six seals of Revelation Chapter Six have already all been opened. But then the seventh seal is broken. "*And when he had opened the seventh seal, there was silence in heaven about the space of half an hour*" (Revelation 8:1). Utter silence, a noiseless time in heaven lasting for only "about a half hour." The silence is deafening – for those in heaven know that what is about to happen on earth will mean the destruction of most of the planet and death for a majority of its inhabitants. The contrast between what has happened in heaven (the salvation and reception of the Saints with the sealing of Israel upon the earth) with the judgment below on humankind ("*they that dwell on the earth*"), is beyond imagining. The anticipation of what will soon come to pass, from an earthly perspective, could not be more distressing.

And then is heard a glorious shout – the voice of the Archangel sounding through seven trumpets (or perhaps a single, final seven-fold trumpet), as seven angels come forth, each with a trumpet to blare. "*Then another angel, having a golden censer, came and stood at the altar.*" It is here in Revelation 8 that this angel receives incense to offer along with the abundance of the prayers of the Saints. For the suffering under the Devil's Wrath during this time of great tribulation has been intolerable. Now, however, the smoke ascends, saturated with saintly prayers. It is brought forth by the "Angel-Priest" – the mediator between God and man, *The Man Christ Jesus.*[1]

Then the very censer filled with the sweet smell of the persecuted ones is filled with the fire off the altar from whence the incense is mingled. The multitude so vast that no man could number – those who came out of such great tribulation – they know now that their "number is complete" and that Almighty God has heard their prayers. Suddenly they witness the same angel take the fire-filled censer and in great dramatic effect throw it to the earth. With the terrestrial crash (we assume here what is envisioned is symbolic), there is seen and heard "noises, thundering, and lightnings" and suddenly a great earthquake such as had never occurred before shaking the whole world and all its inhabitants. The earth cries out in terror... for the Devil's wrath (which was it-

---

[1] As designated by the famous evangelical scholar Harry A. Ironside in his *Revelation – Ironside Commentaries*, pp. 101-2.

self most dreadful) is now to be superseded by the Wrath of God and the Lamb!

This vivid scene is like no other from time or eternity. The saints of the Most High find themselves before the throne of God via the resurrection from the dead and through the *harpazo* (i.e., the snatching away from Babylon's clutches – a physical translation from mortal to immortal) before Babylon's fall (Revelation 18:4).

Before the rapture, the Devil's wrath (Revelation 12:12) has been aimed at these believers. But now his wrath is concluded. Now is the judgment of the LORD. The seven-fold trumpet sends alarming tones of thunderous judgment upon humankind. The earth had been warned. The two witnesses had testified until they were murdered by the Beast (Revelation 11:7). After three and one half days, they were resurrected. They had been snatched away to heaven while the whole world watched. Those remaining on the earth exchanged gifts in raucous partying, rejoicing that the two witnesses who tormented them with the Testimony of Jesus, had at long last been crushed, their witness concluded, and the torments they instigated brought to an end.

But now, in recompense, the sevenfold trumpet blast proclaims the DAY OF THE LORD (Revelation 11:15), a proclamation with no attenuation. The DAY OF THE WRATH of our God has come. There is no further delay. And there is no escape. Babylon is to be judged – the final Babylon, the epitome of all gentile empires in its most corruptible and despotic form. "*And the great city was divided into three parts, and the cities of the nations fell: and great Babylon came in remembrance before God, to give unto her the cup of the wine of the fierceness of his wrath.*" (Revelation 16:19)

(Following is a summary chart to graphically place the three "WOES" of Revelation in context of the seven phases of the Trumpet or Seven Trumpets, depending upon interpretation.)

| SEVEN-FOLD TRUMPET & THREE WOES | | | | |
|---|---|---|---|---|
| **Phase** | **Scripture** | **Method** | **Consequence** | **Fraction/ Time Frame** |
| First | Revelation 8:7 | Hail, fire – mingled with blood | Trees, all green grass burned | 1/3 |
| Second | Revelation 8:8-9 | Burning Mountain thrown into the sea turned to blood | Sea creatures die and ships destroyed | 1/3 |
| Third | Revelation 8:10-11 | Burning Star Wormwood fell from the heavens | Rivers and springs made bitter – many men died from the water | 1/3 |
| Fourth | Revelation 8:12-13 | Striking and Announcement | Sun, Moon and Stars struck and darkened – day and night darkened – 3 woes announced | 1/3 – sun<br>1/3 – moon<br>1/3 – stars<br>1/3 – day/night |
| Fifth & 1st Woe | Revelation 9:1-12 | Locust from Bottomless Pit - Smoke as Scorpions led by Apollyon/Abaddon | Sting/hurt all not having seal of God on foreheads – cannot die | 5 Months or 150 days (Symbolic) |
| Sixth | Revelation 9:13-21 | Released – 4 angels bound at Euphrates - 200-million army hour/day/month/year – 3 plagues – fire, smoke and brimstone | Humanity did not repent of its murders and sorceries, still worshipping demons and idols of gold, silver, brass, stone and wood – kept practice of sexual immorality | 1/3 |
| 2nd Woe | Revelation 11:14 | Great Earthquake – 2nd Woe is in the midst of the Day of the Wrath of God and | After the 3.5 Days of the Open Persecution of the Two Witnesses – Their | 1/10 of the City Fell 7,000 were killed |

| | | | | |
|---|---|---|---|---|
| | | the Lamb | Resurrection and Rapture (Rev. 11:11-12) | (Symbolic) |
| 3rd Woe | Revelation 11:14 | Battle of Armageddon – My Sacrificial Meal – Supper of the Great God | The Finale of the Winepress of the Fierceness of the Wrath of God – Judgment of Tri-partite Babylon the Great | THE DAY OF THE LORD |
| Sev-enth | Revelation 11:15 | Second Coming of Messiah, Jesus with All His Saints – Direct Intervention | The Kingdom of this World has become the Kingdom of our Lord and of His Christ – Messiah Unveils Himself to Israel | 45 days – between the 1,290th Day unto the 1,335th Day – Daniel 12:11-12 |
| | Revelation 20:4-6 | Millenarian Rule & Reign of Messiah | Optimal Societal Harmony upon the Earth | 1,000 Years on the Earth |

***CHART: A SUMMARY OF THE SEVEN TRUMPETS AND TIMING OF THE THREE WOES***

The *tripartite nature of the Great City, GREAT IN THREE PARTS as explicitly stated in the text,* is also reinforced via the *three woes.* We see Babylon's final judgment in chapters 17, 18 and 19 of Revelation. Revelation 17 addresses Babylon's religious apostasy; Revelation 18 deals with Babylon's commercial exploitation; while Revelation 19 concerns the destruction of her political ascendancy and administrative structure.

THE THREE WOES (within the final three phases of the sevenfold trumpet) are accorded special recognition and transpire within the fifth trumpet: *"Woe, woe, woe, to the inhabiters [inhabitants] of the earth by reason of the other voices of the trumpet of the three angels, which are yet to sound!"* (Revelation 8:13).

## The First Woe

Under the FIRST WOE the Harlot can been seen symbolically as the locusts had "hair like women's hair" (Revelation 9:8) – they are led – as Jezebel, the ancient and despicable Queen of Israel was led – by the one who is "the angel of the bottomless pit, whose name in Hebrew is *Abaddon* (literally *Destruction*), but in Greek he has the name of *Apollyon*" (i.e., *Destroyer*).

The *Oracle of Delphi* – a woman who "channeled the spirit of *Apollyon*" and attended by maidens – was the pagan prophetess of a religious system that dominated the ancient world for hundreds of years. Since she was the mouthpiece for *Apollyon*, her words were his words; and her "wisdom" his wisdom. It was sought after by everyone from Alexander the Great to the most erudite philosophers of Greece; to wit:

> The Delphic Oracle exerted considerable influence throughout Hellenic culture. Distinctively, this female was essentially the highest authority both civilly and religiously in male-dominated ancient Greece. She responded to the questions of citizens, foreigners, kings, and philosophers on issues of political impact, war, duty, crime, laws—even personal issues. Nevertheless there was a catch. *The Pythia* (as in *Python*), when about to deliver, would chew leaves from Apollo's sacred laurel tree and would then sit on her holy tripod, seated in the innermost sanctum, over a crack on the rock from where noxious volcanic fumes emanated. Dazed and disoriented, she would then be 'possessed by the voice of Apollo' and utter inarticulate sounds before fainting. Only the priests were present there, and they had the task of 'translating' her utterances in plain speech. The priests were extremely well versed on the various matters of state, as part of their work was to debrief pilgrims about all that they knew. In addition, no question to the god was ever dealt with immediately. After the query was submitted, several days of prescribed ceremonial had to be observed before Apollo was so satisfied as to speak through his priestess, which gave the priests precious time for research.[2]

---

[2] See http://en.wikipedia.org/wiki/Oracle.

The parallel implicit in the Book of Revelation is that its FALSE PROPHET (i.e., the Second Beast) serves as Jezebel served Ahab and religious apostasy in ancient Israel. The False Prophet, on behalf of the Antichrist-Beast creates an IMAGE of the Beast to whom he gives *life* so that it speaks. Whoever does not worship the Image of the Beast is put to death (Revelation 13:11-17).

Earlier at the outset of Revelation, the woman Jezebel was foreshadowed. *"Notwithstanding I have a few things against thee [the Church in Thyatira], because thou sufferest that woman Jezebel, which calleth herself a prophetess, to teach and to seduce my servants to commit fornication, and to eat things sacrificed unto idols." (Revelation 2:20)*

Thus, the FIRST WOE targets the harlot (Jezebel) of Revelation 17 – the judgment of Babylon's apostate religious system, which is the Great Whore of Revelation 17._ There can be little doubt with this insertion of *Apollyon* into the account that his connection with the False Prophet parallels the ancient prophetess who channeled the spirit of the Antichrist. Indeed, *Apollyon* is "king over them – the angel of the bottomless pit!"[3]

---

[3] Insofar as the chronological issue of the 5 months taking place within the span of 30 days – are meant to be comprehended in a fashion that, in this particular instance, is overtly "signified" (Rev. 1:1) in symbolic terms. The 5-month equals 30 days, as postulated by author Krieger, is resolved (Rev. 9 under the 5th trumpet) in that humankind (*"they that dwell on the earth"*) are within this First Woe held "responsible" (the meaning ascribed to the number 5) for their own iniquitous behaviors. They cannot die. All the forces of hell are released during this period (symbolically "five months") with their amassing more a matter of sentencing than final demonic fratricide. All the hosts of the abyss, and those in rebellion, are gathered together for "My Sacrificial Meal" (Ezek. 39:19) or "the Supper of the Great God" (Rev. 19:17) during the same time frame. Five months is equal to 5 * 30 (30 days in a prophetic month) = 150 days * 24 hours (1 day = 24 hours) = 3,600 hours * 60 (60 minutes in 1 hour) = 216,000 minutes * 60 (60 seconds in 1 minute) = 12,960,000 seconds or 1296/144 (144 being the dimensions the Wall of the New Jerusalem) = 9 = the Arising of the Omega, the End, the Last, in that He is the "1" and He is the "9" (all "numbers") – the Beginning and the End, the Alpha and the Omega, the First and the Last – "The Wrath of the Lamb has come."

The description of the locust/scorpions befits the Great Harlot's motif. *"And the shapes of the locusts were like unto horses prepared unto battle; and on their heads were as it were crowns like gold, and their faces were as the faces of men. And they had hair as the hair of women, and their teeth were as the teeth of lions."* (Revelation 9:7-8) Babylon's religious apostasies, her "commercial fornications," and her perverse practices whereby she traffics in the "bodies and souls of men" comprise the circumference of "*demonic worship.*" However, Babylon's false auspices of prosperity, undergirded with avarice supplied by the merchants of the earth who were made rich off the "*wrath of her fornications*" curiously appear as "horses prepared for battle." We must ask, "Why the military allusion?" The answer is really quite sim-

---

These are ALL the numbers, derived from the Indian sub-continent via Arabic influence and are called the "Arabic Numerals" starting from "0" – however, all that can be summed, added, constituting all the numbers and their combinations in the universe or 1, 2, 3, 4, 5, 6, 7, 8, 9... added together the numbers 1 through 9 sum to "45" which comports to the 45 days of the Sun of Righteousness (Daniel 12:11-12, "unto the 1,335th day" or 45 days beyond the 1,290th day of desolation) – in other words all numbers ultimately display the coming of the Son of Man. As factors to each other as in (1*2*3* 4*5*6*7*8*9) they equal to 362,880 or "36288" which is the perimeter in inches of the base of the Great Pyramid of Giza (756' * 4 base edges = 3,024' * 12" = 36,288" or "36288" and both these can be seen as "36" and "288" which is the Eternal God as in 360° of a circle without beginning or ending and the two sets of "144" (i.e., 288/2 = 144) seen in the New Jerusalem in Revelation 7 (Israel) and the Church found atop the heavenly Mt. Zion in Revelation 14 with both constituting the Wall of the New Jerusalem as in 144 Sacred Cubits (i.e., 12 * 12 = 144 and 36/2 = the "18" of the New Jerusalem) or 144 * 2.1' (i.e., 25.20") = 302.4' which in turn gives us "324" which hearkens back, once again, to the base perimeter of the Great Pyramid of Giza at 3,024' or 1/10th the size of the perimeter of the GPG or "324" = "324" and 18 (New Jerusalem's 18,000-mile 12 edged perimeter) * 144 = 2,592 or the fractal of the garland of victory over the Woman's head in Rev. 12 = to the 25,920 years/12 constellations of the Great Precessional of the Equinoxes/Zodiac/Mazzaroth.

The point to be made (and the chronology of 5 months isn't the literal point here) – at the terminus of the 5 months is the "45 days" of the Second Coming of Messiah – Jesus, the Son of Man – who comes as the "Sun of Righteousness with Healing in His wings" (in fulfillment of Malachi 4:1-2), and there will be such a need for healing after 5 months of the scorpion's sting!

ple: you cannot institute apostasy on a global basis without military might to enforce it.

The "crowns of something like gold" upon their heads indicate political authority and military might – both mandatory to instigate this *religio-commercial* system; for while the city of Babylon consists of three parts, the *three elements are inextricably intertwined although the distinctions are necessarily and distinctly noteworthy.*

To fully appreciate the biblical allusion which supplements this Babylonian metaphor, we must certainly return to ancient Israel, to the time of Elijah the prophet and his enemies, King Ahab and his wife Jezebel. Ahab was perhaps the most evil King in the history of evil. To recite the text:

> 28 *So Omri* [the previous King] *slept with his fathers, and was buried in Samaria: and Ahab his son reigned in his stead.*
>
> 29 *And in the thirty and eighth year of Asa king of Judah began Ahab the son of Omri to reign over Israel: and Ahab the son of Omri reigned over Israel in Samaria twenty and two years.*
>
> 30 *And Ahab the son of Omri did evil in the sight of the LORD* ***above all that were before him.***
>
> 31 *And it came to pass, as if it had been a light thing for him to walk in the sins of Jeroboam the son of Nebat, that he took to wife Jezebel the daughter of Ethbaal king of the Zidonians, and went and served Baal, and worshipped him.*
>
> 32 *And he reared up an altar for Baal in the house of Baal, which he had built in Samaria.*
>
> 33 *And Ahab made a grove; and Ahab did more to provoke the LORD God of Israel to anger than all the kings of Israel that were before him.* (I Kings 16:28-33)

It is a frightening thing to provoke the LORD God of Israel more than any other Israelite King in the legion of dishonor! The tongue in cheek words of the writer of 1 Kings ("as if it were no big deal to walk in the sins of Jeroboam and Nebat") put Ahab's action in perspective. Ahab chose to marry Jezebel to spite the LORD. This was the *coups de gras* – the finishing stroke! So why was it such brazenness to marry her? Who was Jezebel?

Jezebel's history begins with her connection to the King of Tyre and its priest *Ethobal*, Jezebel's father. Ethobal, the High

**Figure 47 - Ahab, Jezebel, and Elijah**

Priest of Tyre, usurped the kingly crown by assassinating *King Phelles* (of Tyre, ancient Phoenicia). He therefore became Tyre's "combo-dictator" – a Priest and King (much like Julius Caesar, the first *Pontifex Maximus,* a king and high priest). As Jesus Christ is both a King and a Priest (Hebrews 7, 8), and as His Saints are to be kings and priests with Him (Revelation 1:6, 5:10), the Antichrist and his prophetess (Ahab and Jezebel) mimicked this combined office. And as we discussed in the opening of this book, an essential characteristic of Babylon is the despotism that comes *when political control and priestly power fuse into one.* [4]

The phrase in the text "something like gold" is another way of saying "fool's gold" – which conveys a counterfeit reality. This High Priest of Astarte assassinated King Phelles and became an illegitimate, counterfeit king. Likewise, Jezebel followed in her mentor's footsteps! In a not altogether dissimilar way, she seized the crown (for all intents and purposes) from King Ahab, her mostly bamboozled lesser-half. By combining this weakling King with the wicked Priestess, the Old Testament story foreshadows the False Prophet and Antichrist. Indeed, the fruit of their marriage gave rise to myriad apostate male and female prophetic prostitutes[5] (ultimately *pulverized* by the prophet Elijah!)[6]

Yes, their faces were like the expressions of the "faces of men" – for, though their "hair" was "like women's hair" they, like the Oracle of Delphi, the Prophetess of Apollo, expressed the image and voice of Apollyon/Abaddon. (Incidentally, this particular double name connotes a Greco-Hebraic heritage – a mixture

---

[4] See http://en.wikipedia.org/wiki/Ithobaal_I. "Primary information related to Ithobaal comes from Josephus's citation of the Phoenician author Menander of Ephesus, in *Against Apion i.18.* Here it is said that the previous king, Phelles, "was slain by Ithobalus, the priest of Astarte, who reigned thirty-two years, and lived sixty-eight years; he was succeeded by his son Badezorus (Baal-Eser II)." Ithobalus or Ithlobaal I as Ethbaal seen in I Kings 16:31 slew King Phelles, thereby usurping the crown – thus, he became Tyre's King-Priest – it was his daughter, Jezebel, who married Israel's King Ahab…she was indeed totally versed in the rituals of Astarte (Greek) or Ashtoreth (Hebrew) whereby "Church and State" were enmeshed in a relationship combining commercial interests with sexual immorality in "temple worship."

[5] *Myriad* infers ten thousand or "too many to count," but the exact number to be 450. Krieger points out the number "45" connotes the WRATH OF THE LAMB as the Sun of Righteousness on that Great Day of God Almighty (i.e., the Second Advent) who will again slay the "prophets of Baal" (Ref. I Kings 18:20-40; Daniel 12:11-12 unto the 1,335th day or 45 days beyond the 1,290th day of desolations to the Second Coming and the subsequent 1,335th day, or 45 days beyond the 1,290th day).

[6] Note: we were tempted to say "caramelized" as the famous contest between the false and true prophet took place on Mount Carmel. But the play on words doesn't quite work.

of Phoenician/Israelite nomenclature, which mirrors the marriage of Jezebel and Ahab).

Moreover, it evokes a memory of Jezebel's fury consummated by King Ahab's slaying of *Naboth* (a vineyard owner, "the *Jezreelite*") in a distorted exercise of "imminent domain." For those unfamiliar, the story goes this way: the evil Jezebel conspired with the "sons of Belial" and proclaimed a feast in honor of the noble vinedresser Naboth. (The "sons of Belial" were two perfect *scoundrels*; literally the phrase means the "sons of worthlessness" – although this phrase would later grow synonymous with a more fiendish foe, *Beelzebub*). Then at the "Banquet of Belial" the worthless pair arose and accused the guest of honor, Naboth, of committing treason through "blaspheming God and Country" – i.e., Yahweh and King Ahab. Finding no opposition to their false accusation from the audience, the sons stoned the guest of honor. [7] Jezebel couldn't have been happier. She had what she wanted, the vineyard Ahab coveted (no doubt enhancing his palatial view, where looking out Ahab could boast, "Look at all that's mine!"

Yes, Jezebel, operating behind the political power and military might of King Ahab had the "face of a man" but the "hair of a woman." Ahab and Jezebel in their acts were as one – both Priest and King. But remember, underneath her marital disguise was the FALSE PROPHETESS who schemed and spoke in the place of Ahab. Like the False Prophet who conspires with Apollyon, Jezebel embodied the "hair of the harlot" with the "mouth of a lion" – and that "lion" as Peter said is, *"your adversary the devil, [who walketh about] as a roaring lion... seeking whom he may devour"* (I Peter 5:8).

---

[7] And therewith supplied us with the first recorded instance of someone (forgive the jest) being stoned at a banquet!

## The Second Woe

When we reach the SECOND WOE (at the blast of the sixth trumpet or sixth phase of the seven-fold trumpet), we hear these words: *"Loose the four angels which are bound in the great river Euphrates."* (Revelation 9:14). Here – as in Revelation 16:12 is the pouring out of the Sixth Vial or Bowl of Wrath. Note the connection. The River Euphrates refers implicitly once again to BABYLON: *"Then the sixth angel poured out his bowl on the great river Euphrates...."* Notwithstanding the other descriptions under the sixth phase of the sevenfold trumpet it appears that the Second Woe has much to do with this remarkable situation: *"And the rest of the men which were not killed by these plagues yet repented not of the works of their hands, that they should not worship devils, and idols of gold, and silver, and brass, and stone, and of wood: which neither can see, nor hear, nor walk"* (Revelation 9:20)

Today's rampant materialism is but as an idol to humankind who worships it without waver! Indeed, Revelation 18 presupposes that the "Mark of the Beast" and its commercial mandate evoked the severity of God's wrath – for without the MARK, a symbol of loyalty to the Beast, one could not "buy or sell." This commercial imprimatur is an analogue which signifies the King of Tyre in ancient times. In other words, the descriptions of judgment against Babylon's commercial wickedness relate to *the destruction of the King of Tyre;* for the Kingdom of Tyre represents the Great Commercial Empire, an empire which extended *throughout the Mediterranean.* Just as Jezebel provides a portrait of the Harlot and *religious (apostate) Babylon*, the King of Tyre provides a historical representation of *financial Babylon.* And, not without significance is the fact this King was Jezebel's father in crime!

The comparison to financial or commercial Babylon described in Revelation 18 connects with the Second Woe found in Revelation 9:13-21. It lies within the Sixth Trumpet and supplements those accounts within the Sixth Vial/Bowl of Wrath found in Revelation 16:12-14. Again, recall the reference to the River Euphrates provides the linkage. This River provides the nexus to Babylon the Great – the same destruction of Babylon described in Daniel which relates to the fall of the post-Nebuchadnezzar Neo-Babylonian Kingdom, well documented by historians and of course, the Bible, to wit. "*In that night was Belshazzar the king of the Chaldeans slain. And Darius the Median took the kingdom, being about threescore and two* [62] *years old.*" (Daniel 5:30-31).[8] Of interest too: Author Krieger lays "Messianic emphasis" upon Neo-Babylonia's demise at the hand of the Medo-Persian King Darius, being *62 years of age* (a fact he considers of no small import as the Bible makes careful note), as the Messiah Price came during the segment of the 62 weeks of Daniel's vision of the 70 weeks (recall the 70 weeks are separated into three segments: 7 weeks, *62 weeks*, and the final week of seven years – yet future, Daniel 9:24-27).

One-third of mankind is killed during the "Sixth-phase of the Trumpet" – the on-going destruction of Babylon the Great is the target and, specifically, financial or commercial Babylon, aka the King of Tyre… the annihilation of the final Gentile World Commercial Empire. Listen to the unrepentant response from humanity during the Sixth Trumpet's sounding and the pouring out of the Sixth Vial:

> [20] *And the rest of the men which were not killed by these plagues yet repented not of the works of their hands, that they should not worship devils, and idols of gold, and silver, and brass, and stone, and of wood: which neither can see, nor hear, nor walk:*

---

[8] It was the lowering of the River Euphrates which permitted the Medes to cross over waste deep in water to interrupt the party of dignitaries and their King Belshazzar who had just heard the interpretation by Daniel of the numerical-monetary "hand-writing on the wall" which MENE (1,000), MENE (1,000), TEKEL (20), UPHARSIN/PERES (500 or ½ a MENE) summed to 2520 (1,000 + 1,000 + 20 + 500 = 2,520) or the Sacred Cubit as in 25.20".

> [21] *Neither repented they of their murders, nor of their sorceries, nor of their fornication, nor of their thefts.* (Revelation 9:20-21)
>
> [13] *And I saw three unclean spirits like frogs come out of the mouth of the dragon, and out of the mouth of the beast, and out of the mouth of the false prophet.*[9]
>
> [14] *For they are the spirits of devils, working miracles, which go forth unto the kings of the earth and of the whole world, to gather them to the battle of that great day of God Almighty.* (Revelation 16:13-14)
>
> [2] *And he cried mightily with a strong voice, saying, Babylon the great is fallen, is fallen, and is become the habitation of devils, and the hold of every foul spirit, and a cage of every unclean and hateful bird.*
>
> [3] *For all nations have drunk of the wine of the wrath of her fornication, and the kings of the earth have committed fornication with her, and the merchants of the earth are waxed rich through the abundance of her delicacies.* (Revelation 18:2-3)

The Scriptures treat this rampant materialism as idolatry – the worship of idols made of gold, silver, brass, stone and wood – a "tangible demonstration" behind which is the "worship of demons" wherein this "dwelling place of demons" is a drunken stupor from whence ALL the nations have become drunk via the "wine of the wrath of her fornication." This rank form of materialism from whence "the merchants of the earth have become rich through the abundance of her luxury" constitutes FORNICATION in a very real sense – a demonstration of *infidelity to the God of Heaven* characterized by the writer of the Revelation as a perverse practice. John summarizes the whole activity as nothing more than *"the kings of the earth, who have committed fornication and lived deliciously with her, shall bewail her, and lament for her, when they shall see the smoke of her burning"* (Revelation 18:9).

---

[9] We believe the three frogs are yet another reference to the three-fold nature of THE FINAL BABYLON, the thrice sinful City opposed to God.

The "worship of demons" is precisely what Jezebel's "religious-commercial-political" fabrication with King Ahab wrought when she, as Princess of Tyre (aligned with the King-Priest of Tyre), united in a "religious-economic" enterprise. This partnership commercialized Tyre's "worship with prostitutes." Realize please that "Temple Worship" wasn't just religious, it was financial. It filled the coffers and treasure chests of the King. The point we must make is this: Why be concerned with the "Daughter of Babylon" when you should beware of both the "Harlot of Tyre" and her "Daughter of Tarshish"? Implied in the prophecies of Isaiah, in Chapters 23 and 24, is the mercantile nature of Tarshish and thus, the gentile financial empire which is at enmity against God. Just as Jeremiah described the future Babylon as the *Daughter of Babylon (Jeremiah 50, 51)*, Isaiah calls the *future Tarshish*, the land of Tyre, the *Daughter of Tarshish.*

> 6 *Pass ye over to Tarshish; howl, ye inhabitants of the isle.*
>
> 7 *Is this your joyous city, whose antiquity is of ancient days? her own feet shall carry her afar off to sojourn.*
>
> 8 *Who hath taken this counsel against Tyre, the crowning city, whose merchants are princes, whose traffickers are the honourable of the earth?*
>
> 9 *The Lord of hosts hath purposed it, to stain the pride of all glory, and to bring into contempt all the honourable of the earth.*
>
> 10 *Pass through thy land as a river,* ***O daughter of Tarshish****: there is no more strength.*
>
> 11 *He stretched out his hand over the sea, he shook the kingdoms: the Lord hath given a commandment against the merchant city, to destroy the strong holds thereof.*
>
> 12 *And he said, Thou shalt no more rejoice, O thou oppressed virgin, daughter of Zidon: arise, pass over to Chittim* [ancient Cyprus]; *there also shalt thou have no rest.*
>
> 13 *Behold the land of the Chaldeans; this people was not, till the Assyrian* [Nimrod] *founded it for them that dwell in the wilderness: they set up the towers thereof, they raised up the palaces thereof; and he brought it to ruin.*
>
> 14 *Howl, ye ships of Tarshish: for your strength is laid waste.*

> [15] *And it shall come to pass in that day, that* ***Tyre shall be forgotten seventy years****, according to the days of one king: after the end of* ***seventy years*** *shall Tyre sing as an harlot.*
>
> [16] *Take an harp, go about the city, thou harlot that hast been forgotten; make sweet melody, sing many songs, that thou mayest be remembered.*
>
> [17] *And it shall come to pass after* ***the end of seventy years,*** *that the Lord will visit Tyre, and she shall turn to her hire, and shall commit fornication with all the kingdoms of the world upon the face of the earth.*
>
> [18] *And her merchandise and her hire shall be holiness to the Lord: it shall not be treasured nor laid up; for her merchandise shall be for them that dwell before the Lord, to eat sufficiently, and for durable clothing.*[10]

The continuing saga of Tarshish continues in Isaiah 24. The context clearly is the end of days when "*the moon shall be confounded, and the sun ashamed, when the Lord of hosts shall reign in mount Zion, and in Jerusalem, and before his ancients gloriously*" (verse 23). "*The kings of the earth who committed fornication and lived luxuriously with her will weep and lament for her, when they see the smoke of her burning*" (Revelation 18:9).

And this shall be, according to Isaiah 24:15-23, during the days of the Wrath of the Lamb:

> [15] *Wherefore glorify ye the Lord in the fires, even the name of the Lord God of Israel in the isles of the sea.*
>
> [16] *From the uttermost part of the earth have we heard songs, even glory to the righteous. But I said, My leanness, my*

---

[10] The "Harlot of Tyre" – and her alias, the "Daughter of Tarshish," is found at the end of the Seventieth Week of Daniel – for the Seventy Years is 70 * 360 days = 25,200 as in "252" which is the fractal/resemblance of the Sacred Cubit's 25.20" and is, therefore, the measurement of Divine Judgment for the 7-day encirclement of Jericho was 360° (per day's rotation of the Earth) * 7 (times on the 7th day) = 2,520° and the handwriting on the wall summed to 2,520 (likewise, 2,520 days of Daniel's 70th Week itself – 360 days * 7 years which equals 2,520 days – which is the Sacred Cubit's fractal of 25.20").

*leanness, woe unto me! The treacherous dealers have dealt treacherously; yea, the treacherous dealers have dealt very treacherously.*

17 *Fear, and the pit, and the snare, are upon thee, O inhabitant of the earth.*

18 *And it shall come to pass, that he who fleeth from the noise of the fear shall fall into the pit; and he that cometh up out of the midst of the pit shall be taken in the snare: for the windows from on high are open, and the foundations of the earth do shake.*

19 *The earth is utterly broken down, the earth is clean dissolved, the earth is moved exceedingly.*

20 *The earth shall reel to and fro like a drunkard, and shall be removed like a cottage; and the transgression thereof shall be heavy upon it; and it shall fall, and not rise again.*

21 *And it shall come to pass in that day, that the Lord shall punish the host of the high ones that are on high, and the kings of the earth upon the earth.*

22 *And they shall be gathered together, as prisoners are gathered in the pit, and shall be shut up in the prison, and after many days shall they be visited.*

23 *Then the moon shall be confounded, and the sun ashamed, when the Lord of hosts shall reign in mount Zion, and in Jerusalem, and before his ancients gloriously.*

Even so, the prostitute portrayed as Jezebel will return to her hire, and "commit fornication with all the kingdoms of the world on the face of the earth." Yes, the mixture of religion and politics is a practice well known by the *harlot of Tyre* and the *daughter of Tarshish.* And it will resurface in that day not far away. However, it should be understood, that the APOSTASY which Jezebel brought into the "religion of Yahweh" was not designed to supplant Israel's worship of the One True God. Not at all. It was designed to ingratiate, to blend into the culture, to alter Israel's worship, to "mingle" the perverse practices of Tyre with those of Israel. (See I Kings 16:29-34 through I Kings 22:40)

In no uncertain terms, the Word of the Lord exposes this entire practice as perpetrated by "the spirits of demons" craving the "material" – especially physical bodies – to house their disembodied spirits which are wont to inhabit any creature rather than live disincarnate. (In Luke 8:32-33, the demons named *Legion* beseech Jesus to allow them to possess pigs rather than wonder through the mystical dry places as Jesus called them). Frankly, it is an easy exercise to connect the dots between these passages concerning the Sixth Trumpet, the Sixth Vial, and Revelation 18's account of commercial Babylon, once we recognize the demonic link between the worship of commercial things and the trafficking in the "*bodies and souls of men*" (Revelation 18:13).

Think it not strange then, that the merchants of the earth, symbolized by the merchants of Tarshish, made rich by her seductions, have taken such abstract things of necessity (such as automobiles, fashion, and modern appliances) and made them "sexy" in their commercial displays, that they might entice the public already inclined to purchase such things. Indeed, cravings for merchandise often take on the compulsion of a "sexual object." It should be easily agreed that such salacious enterprise has become an art form where the "worship of demons" excels. No doubt this form of demon worship is perhaps the most costly![11] It is truly a false religion in which no expense is sparred!

---

[11] Author Krieger provides a startling interpretation for the reader's consideration of the 200,000,000 army of horsemen found at the River Euphrates: "Maybe you've never been in the military before – I have – and let me tell you – all the food in the world couldn't suffice that army for one day! Talk about a strategic piece of military insanity. Something else is going on here with those numbers again. Remember, 150 days (prior to this mentioning) ultimately equates to 12,960,000 seconds in 150 days or "1296." Now, taking the "2" from the 200,000,000 (don't let that distract you - first the 1296 is Rev. 9:10 and then the 200 mil. in Rev. 9:16) and combining it with the "1296" from the previous Fifth Trumpet and combining both 5th and 6th trumpets we find: 1296 * 2 = 2,592. Do we see something here? How about the "garland of 12 constellations over the Woman's head in Revelation 12?" You're starring the Great Precession of the Equinoxes straight in the face…5 months in seconds (i.e., 12,960,000 seconds or 1296) times 200,000,000 (i.e., 1296 * 2 = 2,592) = 25,920 Years which is precisely the Zodiacal or Mazzaroth Great Precession of the Equinoxes and equates to the 12 Stars over the Woman's head in Revelation 12:1… "And on her head a garland of 12 stars" (each star/constellation representing 2,160"

But to return to the text, the Second Woe is now passed – financial Babylon has been judged with her subversive and soul-eating form of fornication – a "worship of demons" consisting of financial greed, sexual perversity, and trafficking in the "bodies and souls of men."

## The Third Woe

The final of the Sevenfold Trumpet and the Third Woe are conflated – they appear simultaneous; but realize they are distinct – for the *demise of political Babylon* is the essence of the Third Woe. Now comes to pass the intervention of the King of kings and Lord of lords along with His "armies of heaven." The kingdom(s) of this world have now become the Kingdom of our Lord and of His Christ. While this moment for the impatient saints (who have endured for so long), has seemed always afar off, the people of the earth have been warned repeatedly that it will arrive too soon for those unprepared, for those refusing to heed the admonitions:

> *"The second woe is past; and, behold, the third woe cometh quickly." (Revelation 11:14)*
>
> *"Repent, and do the first works; or else I will come unto thee quickly." (Revelation 2:5)*
>
> *"Repent; or else I will come unto thee quickly," (Revelation 2:16)*
>
> *"Behold, I come quickly!" (Revelation 3:11)*
>
> *"Behold, I come quickly: blessed is he that keepeth the sayings of the prophecy of this book." (Revelation 22:7)*
>
> *"And, behold, I come quickly; and my reward is with me." (Revelation 22:12)*
>
> *"He which testifieth these things saith, 'Surely I come quickly.' Amen. Even so, come, Lord Jesus."* (Revelation 22:20)

---

years or 25,920 / 12 = 2,160 years). Wow! Talk about the ending of the age – and the beginning of a whole new age – yet not in the "New Age" sense but in the Divinely-orchestrated numeric sense!"

Please see that the "Kingdom" or "kingdoms" of this world has to do with judgment upon "political Babylon" – the First Beast and the Second Beast whereof we read in Revelation 19:20:

> *"And the beast was taken, and with him the false prophet that wrought miracles before him, with which he deceived them that had received the mark of the beast, and them that worshipped his image. These both were cast alive into a lake of fire burning with brimstone."*

In reflection, we often sing with great bluster Handel's Messiah most having little idea of its context. But the context is everything: the resurrection, the rapture, and the Wrath of God (poured out upon tripartite *Babylon the Great*). And yet, a simple reading of the Book of Revelation clearly provides, when all the presuppositions are set aside (that is, the traditional prophetic scenarios of popular eschatology writers), an appreciation for this battle between the God of Heaven and His ultimate worldly

**Figure 48 - The Valley of Jehoshaphat**

foe, Babylon. This is the theme of the entire book: the Image of Christ vs. the Image of the Beast – the Holy City, New Jerusalem vs. the Great City, Babylon the Great (The Bible, especially the Book of Revelation is the real "Tale of Two Cities"!) God will ultimately triumph over Babylon! The New Jerusalem will be the capital of a new Kingdom and the old Kingdom will be no more. The "stone which the builders rejected" will crush the empires of the Gentile world into dust, *including the final Babylon* (Daniel 2:44-45).

Lest we forget – the destruction of Babylon by the Wrath of God and the Lamb – is accomplished on behalf of all saints who have "overcome" and come out of great tribulation. They prophesied, testified, and witnessed against that Great City – not loving their lives unto the death (Revelation 12:11). In the cause of Justice, the Judge of all the Earth shall do right by His saints. "The angel thrust his sickle into the earth and gathered the vine of the earth, and threw it into the great winepress of the wrath of God" (Revelation 14:19).

For when we arrive at the THIRD WOE, we witness God's judgment upon political Babylon. The Kings of the earth have conspired with the Antichrist. The woman rides the Beast until the Beast destroys her and the Kings of the earth eat her flesh. But a house divided cannot stand! Truly the "sons of Belial" – the Antichrist and the False Prophet, along with the Kings of the world who once believed they had won the battle – soon come to the realization that their efforts are all for naught. The Lamb of God is coming to avenge His saints.

A clear reading of Revelation 11:11-15 is explicit with heightened focus upon the "Kingdoms of this world" being defeated and Him Who sits on the White Horse whose name is KING OF KINGS AND LORD OF LORDS written upon His robe, dipped in blood. For "*He Himself treads the winepress of the fierceness and wrath of Almighty God*" (See the entire passage, Rev. 19:15-19). The Kings of the earth have drunk fiercely the wine of her fornication, yes, "full of abominations and the filthiness of her fornication." They had their day in the sun. Now they produce utter darkness, cloaking the entire world in gloom and death. It is time for the *Sun of Righteousness* to arise and shine on the Great Day of God (Revelation 17:2; Malachi 4:2)!

This moment is also known by the prophetic labels, "My Sacrificial Meal" (Ezekiel 39:17-20), and the "Supper of the Great God" (Revelation 19:17)! The metaphor of eating vast amounts of food is appropriate, for the LORD OF HOSTS shall entirely consume his enemies. But remember, first He has preserved both the resurrected and raptured – all of His elect from the four winds (Matthew 24:31) – in order that He might be free to release His judgment indiscriminately upon political Babylon and conclude the days of desolation (unto the 1,290th Day as prophesied in the Book of Daniel).[12] For the testimony of Scripture to this final judgment is placed throughout God's Word. It is a warning that cannot be missed! First from the New Testament Book of Jude:

> [14] *And Enoch also, the seventh from Adam, prophesied of these, saying, "Behold, the Lord cometh with ten thousands of his saints,*
>
> [15] *To execute judgment upon all, and to convince all that are ungodly among them of all their ungodly deeds which they have ungodly committed, and of all their hard speeches which ungodly sinners have spoken against him. For behold, in those days and at that time, when I bring back the captives of Judah and Jerusalem, I will also gather ALL NATIONS, and bring them down to the Valley of Jehoshaphat; and I will enter into judgment with them there on account of My people, My heritage Israel."* (Jude 14, 15)

And then from the Old Testament Book of Joel:

> [9] *Proclaim ye this among the Gentiles; Prepare war, wake up the mighty men, let all the men of war draw near; let them come up:*

---

[12] Author Krieger and McGriff believe that the 30 days between the 1,260 days, concluding Daniel's 70th Week, and the 1,290 days unto the end of desolations prophesied by Daniel, equals the 30 minutes ("about half an hour") of silence in heaven.

> [10] *Beat your plowshares into swords and your pruning hooks into spears: let the weak say, I am strong.*
>
> [11] *Assemble yourselves, and come, all ye heathen, and gather yourselves together round about: thither cause thy mighty ones to come down, O Lord.*
>
> [12] *Let the heathen be wakened, and come up to the valley of Jehoshaphat: for there will I sit to judge all the heathen round about.*
>
> [13] *Put ye in the sickle, for the harvest is ripe: come, get you down; for the press is full, the fats overflow; for their wickedness is great.*
>
> [14] *Multitudes, multitudes in the valley of decision: for the day of the Lord is near in the valley of decision.*
>
> [15] *The sun and the moon shall be darkened, and the stars shall withdraw their shining.*
>
> [16] *The Lord also shall roar out of Zion, and utter his voice from Jerusalem; and the heavens and the earth shall shake:* (Joel 3: 9-16a)

Then from Zechariah:

> [2] *For I will gather all nations against Jerusalem to battle; and the city shall be taken, and the houses rifled, and the women ravished; and half of the city shall go forth into captivity, and the residue of the people shall not be cut off from the city.*
>
> [3] *Then shall the Lord go forth, and fight against those nations, as when he fought in the day of battle.*
>
> [4] *And his feet shall stand in that day upon the mount of Olives, which is before Jerusalem on the east, and the mount of Olives shall cleave in the midst thereof toward the east and toward the west, and there shall be a very great valley; and half of the mountain shall remove toward the north, and half of it toward the south.* ( Zechariah 14: 2-4)

And finally, back again to Revelation:

> [16] *And he gathered them together into a place called in the Hebrew tongue Armageddon.*

[17] *And the seventh angel poured out his vial into the air; and there came a great voice out of the temple of heaven, from the throne, saying, It is done.*

[18] *And there were voices, and thunders, and lightnings; and there was a great earthquake, such as was not since men were upon the earth, so mighty an earthquake, and so great.*

[19] *And the great city was divided into three parts, and the cities of the nations fell: and great Babylon came in remembrance before God, to give unto her the cup of the wine of the fierceness of his wrath.*

[20] *And every island fled away, and the mountains were not found.*

[21] *And there fell upon men a great hail out of heaven, every stone about the weight of a talent: and men blasphemed God because of the plague of the hail; for the plague thereof was exceeding great.* (Revelation 16:16-21)

[17] *And I saw an angel standing in the sun; and he cried with a loud voice, saying to all the fowls that fly in the midst of heaven, Come and gather yourselves together unto the supper of the great God;*

[18] *That ye may eat the flesh of kings, and the flesh of captains, and the flesh of mighty men, and the flesh of horses, and of them that sit on them, and the flesh of all men, both free and bond, both small and great.*

[19] *And I saw the beast, and the kings of the earth, and their armies, gathered together to make war against him that sat on the horse, and against his army.* (Revelation 19:17-19)

Without equivocation – the Lord of Glory has now come as a thief before that "great and terrible Day of the Lord" to the recalcitrant earthlings – those Gentiles who have trampled underfoot the Holy City for 42 months – who heard the call to the Two Witnesses, "COME UP HERE!" (Revelation 11). These remaining, who live on the earth, are now subject to prophetic fulfillment of Revelation 16:15: *"Behold, I am coming as a thief."* This is the true meaning of the expressed words of the Lord. They are not in reference to the His raptured bride, the Church; but in response to the indolence and iniquities of those within the apostate Church that fell away and to those outside who are fallen humankind – the "earth dwellers"; for those who are true and faithful are not children of darkness, but of light (I Thessalonians 5:5). Moreover, Christ's coming will shock all those who have continually chosen to live in darkness.

Political Babylon is doomed despite its grand administrators serving that ignoble and GREAT CITY. The great meal of the Almighty is served. "*That ye may eat the flesh of kings, and the flesh of captains, and the flesh of mighty men, and the flesh of horses, and of them that sit on them, and the flesh of all men, both free and bond, both small and great.*" (Revelation 19:18).

Please recall, it is under the jurisdiction of the First Beast and under the religious façade of the False Prophet, the Second Beast, that all the kings of Babylon are condemned. From the famous Messianic Psalm 2, we read:

> 1 *Why do the heathen rage, and the people imagine a vain thing?*
>
> 2 *The kings of the earth set themselves, and the rulers take counsel together, against the Lord, and against his anointed, saying,*
>
> 3 *Let us break their bands asunder, and cast away their cords from us.*
>
> 4 *He that sitteth in the heavens shall laugh: the Lord shall have them in derision.*
>
> 5 *Then shall he speak unto them in his wrath, and vex them in his sore displeasure.*
>
> 6 *Yet have I set my king upon my holy hill of Zion.*
>
> 7 *I will declare the decree: the Lord hath said unto me, Thou art my Son; this day have I begotten thee.*
>
> 8 *Ask of me, and I shall give thee the heathen for thine inheritance, and the uttermost parts of the earth for thy possession.*
>
> 9 *Thou shalt break them with a rod of iron; thou shalt dash them in pieces like a potter's vessel.*
>
> 10 *Be wise now therefore, O ye kings: be instructed, ye judges of the earth.*

> [11] *Serve the Lord with fear, and rejoice with trembling.*
>
> [12] *Kiss the Son, lest he be angry, and ye perish from the way, when his wrath is kindled but a little. Blessed are all they that put their trust in him.*

It is Jesus, the Spirit of Prophecy, and His prophetic Word that now drives fallen humankind, giving heed to their own desire to harden their heart, inexorably to the *winepress of the wrath of ALMIGHTY GOD.* Depraved humanity has chosen this path whether they knowingly acknowledge it or not!

The climax of the ages: the Third Woe, the Seventh-Phase of the Sevenfold Trumpet, the Second Coming of Messiah, the Battle of Armageddon, "My Sacrificial Meal – the Supper of the Great God."

It's all comes down to this, to the climax of the ages: *THE DAY OF THE LORD* – the Winepress of the Wrath of God!

## Summing Up

We shall deliberate at this three-fold discharge of His wrath upon Babylon the Great, for it marks the long-awaited conclusion to the reign of the Beast.

In reprise: The prayers of the martyrs who suffered under the DEVIL'S WRATH (Revelation 12:12) have ascended as sweet incense before the Throne of God. The Angel-Priest takes the fire from that altar of incense which caused that sweet savor (to ascend amidst the smoke thereof) and casts the censor full of these fiery coals to the earth in response to the prayers of the saints. Indeed, now is fulfilled, "[The Father]... hath given him authority to execute judgment also, because he is the Son of man" (John 5:26-27). The MYSTERY OF GOD has been made complete. It is finished (Revelation 10:7).

For the Three Woes utterly decimate Babylon the Great. Her Apostate Religious System so craftily employed by the False Prophet (and reflecting Jezebel's ancient "fornication religion" for profit), *is no more.* No longer will commercial exploits combine with sexual perversion and be exemplified in "demonic worship" –

orchestrated by fallen spirits bent on seducing those who lust for things which content themselves and enrich earth's merchants!

Realize the Book of Revelation is not an assortment of biblically inspired nightmares meant to provoke fear; or mere moral lessons with hope sprinkled in to help us manage the formidable opposition we must face today. Its vision is specific and conclusive. It entails BABYLON THE GREAT put on trial in a "cosmic courtroom" during which time we know as Daniel's Seventieth Week, during the measured time of greatest tribulation, a time of extreme persecution, even death of His witnesses! The evidence has been compiled and is now delivered before the "Heavenly Bar of Justice." The verdict is swift and unmistakable: BABYLON THE GREAT – as the great multitude is witness, you are found guilty as charged! The plan of eternity has been vindicated. Jesus is King and He shall rule and reign with His saints.

To hearken once more to the story we've used as allegory: Babylon is as Jezebel. She had become "*a dwelling place of demons, a prison for every foul spirit, and a cage for every unclean and hated bird*" (Revelation 18:2). The harlot was devoured by her own kings as they turned on the Great Whore, making her desolate and naked, eating her flesh and burning her with fire. Realize that that is precisely what happened to Jezebel:

> 30 *And when Jehu was come to Jezreel, Jezebel heard of it; and she painted her face, and tired* [adorned] *her head, and looked out at a window.*
>
> 31 *And as Jehu entered in at the gate, she said, Had Zimri peace, who slew his master?*
>
> 32 *And he lifted up his face to the window, and said, Who is on my side? who? And there looked out to him two or three eunuchs.*
>
> 33 *And he said, Throw her down. So they threw her down: and some of her blood was sprinkled on the wall, and on the horses: and he trode* [trod] *her under foot.*
>
> 34 *And when he was come in, he did eat and drink, and said, Go, see now this cursed woman, and bury her: for she is a king's daughter.*

> [35] *And they went to bury her: but they found no more of her than the skull, and the feet, and the palms of her hands.*
>
> [36] *Wherefore they came again, and told him. And he said, This is the word of the LORD, which he spake by his servant Elijah the Tishbite, saying, "In the portion of Jezreel shall dogs eat the flesh of Jezebel:*
>
> [37] *And the carcass of Jezebel shall be as dung upon the face of the field in the portion of Jezreel; so that they shall not say, 'This is Jezebel.'"* ( II Kings 9:30-37).

She had contaminated Israel with her "whoredoms." Her fate was just. After adorning herself with cosmetics and fixing her hair, Jezebel was thrown from her bedroom window falling to her death. Then she was eaten by dogs. Her flesh was excised to the bone (although the dogs refused to eat her feet and hands, perhaps due to the poison of [her perfume!). She had combined the materialism of Tyre with the religion of Israel. She sought to dilute and deface the true worship of Israel's God. Babylon, like Jezebel, which had so cleverly trafficked in the bodies and souls of men – making the merchants of the earth so profligate through her wealth (that is, through the excesses of the King of Tyre and his god, Baal) finally finds her end, engulfed in flames from the Almighty Himself. We read: *"And a mighty angel took up a stone like a great millstone, and cast it into the sea, saying, Thus with violence shall that great city Babylon be thrown down, and shall be found no more at all."* (Revelation 18:21). And also,

> [9] *And the kings of the earth, who have committed fornication and lived deliciously with her, shall bewail her, and lament for her, when they shall see the smoke of her burning,*
>
> [10] *Standing afar off for the fear of her torment, saying, "Alas, alas that great city Babylon, that mighty city! For in one hour is thy judgment come."* (Revelation 18:9-10)

And then we hear the shouting of HALLELUJAH – the only HALLELUJAHS recorded in the New Testament. They ring forth at Great Babylon's utter destruction (Revelation 19:1, 3, 4, 6). Yes, four HALLELUJAHS burst forth from heaven throughout the universe – THREE which emanate from the Great Multitude – that Great Multitude which came out of such great tribulation, troubled throughout history by her torment, a throng which no man could number. And as surely as Babylon will smolder, the Holy City will shine. The saints will gleam! Despite the trouble of our day, remember that our destiny is predetermined. Our enemy, THE FINAL BABYLON, will be defeated. The New Jerusalem will be the city of light; with no need of a star we call our sun, for the Sun of Righteousness will be her everlasting light! (Revelation 22:5)

So the next time you hear HALLELUJAH, or the next time you worry about what will become of you, remember this: the only time HALLELUJAH is exclaimed in the New Testament is WHEN BABYLON GOES UP IN SMOKE! The victory is ours through Jesus Christ. The NEW JERUSALEM stands triumphant! Therefore, with boldness let us witness and testify against that Great City – we who comprise the Holy City – so that one day we may stand amidst it as part of that Great Multitude which no man could number and chant the seven-fold adulation:

> *"Saying, Amen: Blessing, and glory, and wisdom, and thanksgiving, and honour, and power, and might, be unto our God for ever and ever. Amen!"* (Revelation 7:12)

*AFTERWORD:*
# Democratic Globalism and the Fate of America

## The World's Commercial Empire

FOR THE MOMENT, THE UNITED STATES OF AMERICA HIDES HER TALONS. HOWEVER, WHEN SPURRED TO ACTION AND DRIVEN TO SPREAD ITS AWESOME WINGS AS A REGAL WARNING TO ITS foes, no rival state, no toothless tiger (such as the UN), and no global consortium like the G8 or the G20 can stare down the daunting hulk appropriately symbolized by the American eagle.

The plain truth: no entity other than the U.S.A. can impose its will politically or commercially upon the entire planet – no nation exists which is beyond our conquest – in the highly unlikely event we decided to take that uncharacteristic action.

However, for the time being, America languishes as the sleeping giant swatting at flies. Twenty-five years ago, the economic disintegration and political demise of the former Soviet Union, established America as the world's sole superpower. This hegemonic empire found herself the inheritor of all that exemplifies civilization, be it the high cultural expression of Egypt, the seductions of Sodom, the international trading empire of Phoenicia, the mystical religion of Babylon, and especially the organizational and military genius of *Pax Romana*.

From a military standpoint, America remains unchallenged by any singular State or alliance of nations. It has been termed the "New Roman Empire" some ten years ago by Russia's President Vladimir Putin when unilateral and pre-emptive action against Iraq was pending. The United States determined it would "go it alone," if necessary, without UN, French, German (or at that time, Russian) support. Furthermore, America has arguably waged her wars for the past half-century, more out of national interest than to diminish the threat of communism or to support the establishment of democratic freedoms in spite of socialist foes. When it came to halting racially or religiously-based genocide, America chose to engage in the former Yugoslavia, but abstained in Rwanda and the Congo.

Indeed, the "Bush Doctrine" or any other canonized foreign policy has never been consistently applied based solely upon its core premises. Today's hesitant "lead from behind" military policy of selective intervention by the Obama administration, supplies a smoke screen to cloak the real party responsible to ensure success in selected military acts. America remains the only power that has the capacity to make good on its political commitments, with the unquestioned military muscle necessary to carry the day.

This bashfully spoken and seldom overtly discussed agenda – protecting American interests, freed from self-righteous rationalizations – has grown more pronounced over the past decade as the U.S. fought against "State-sponsored" terrorism, certainly in Iraq, but even in the war fought in Afghanistan. America's overtly aggressive policy hides cloaked in the guise of what has been termed abstrusely as *geo-political realism* (a perspective suggesting we cannot wage war solely on the premise of differing values). Ultimately, it is motivated by what syndicated columnist Dr. Charles Krauthammer calls "Democratic Globalism" – a term coined during his speech given before the American Enterprise Institute, Annual Public Policy Research Council in February 2004, when he received the Irving Krystal Award for public policy.

## America's True Golden Rule

Democratic Globalism (according to Krauthammer) is the realpolitik of the twenty-first century and the only resolution to the "anti-realism" and self-hate of "liberal internationalism" historically embraced by the Democratic Party, which sees no redeeming attributes within the self-centered "national interest" policies of geo-political realism. Because of its idealistic stance, liberal internationalism could be accused of undermining American national interests, since it argues military action exists as an option only when the moral high ground is available to justify interventionist policy (viz., the Carter Doctrine). What makes matters even more complicated: the "moral high ground" argument has been proven vacuous over the past three years when trying to pick sides in the so-called Arab Spring. We once supposed it was easy to invoke the military option out of "humanitarian intervention" when helpless peoples were being massacred (e.g., Bosnia, Somalia, and to some extent, Libya). Furthermore, defining a foe as a supporter of terrorism, and in the case of Saddam Hussein, a threat to use WMD, certainly made the two longest wars in American history more palatable to the public. However, during the past year (2013), our inability to take action in Syria to protect its innocent populace stands as a prime example of how difficult a decision we have even when the moral choice is "obvious" but what best serves our national interests isn't. For in the end, all "Syrian options" may provoke equally unsavory outcomes; probably doing little more than sucking enemies Iran and Hezbollah (in Lebanon) deeper into the Middle East sinkhole – along with (unnecessarily) nettling the Russians. As we write this *Afterword*, the relationship between presidents Obama and Putin is hardly cordial with "NSA secret leaker" Edward Snowden (aka Benedict Arnold or Daniel Ellsberg – you pick) receiving safe transit through Russia on his way to Cuba and then Ecuador (where he actually winds up nobody knows).

However, looking at the superficial if not misdirected statements made by politicians today, this ignores the real motives and activities driving geo-politics. Both political parties march to the same beat when it comes to leading the country down the path to Democratic Globalism. The goal of creating a *New World Order,* called for by President George Bush the Elder (exactly 11 years before 9/11),[1] smacked of the centuries' old idealis-

---

[1]When George H.W. Bush spoke before Congress, it was September 11, 2000, eleven years to the day before 9/11, a number itself which oozes with occult implications.

tic ambitions of Rosicrucians, Freemasons, and even occultic groups like the Theosophists. For the time being, devious tactics seem apparent in the form of a multi-tiered program of mass media disinformation conjoined with possible false flag operations designed to frighten the American public. But to what end? Many voices claim our "masters" seek greater control of the masses to benefit the "common good". Apparently, such covert programs would decrease resistance to "world government" among most Americans who recognize the erosion of national sovereignty will easily lead to the diminishment of personal liberty while failing to achieve the goal of world peace.

The challenge for those who see what's really happening: *Speak too loudly – one is branded and ridiculed as a conspiracy theorist; speak too softly – one only helps the program further its goals.* For unofficial disclosures, made by unaccredited sources, can do little more than *initiate* the masses to what game is truly afoot. Such ineffectual insurgency against the masterminds of the globalist agenda may even be an element taken into account by such planners – an implicit tactic bespeaking their wicked genius.

The policies of self-interest defining America's globalists in the only recently unipolar world are very pragmatic as American notions often are. Despite waving olive branches, reigning Democrats such as the present Obama Administration (or the Clinton Administration for that matter) are as willing to engage in military action as were the previous Republican regimes of Bush the Elder and the Younger. Indeed, new revelations surface daily in the summer of 2013 regarding domestic surveillance against American citizens, the IRS used as a hit-squad to take down political adversaries, and the press targeted by the White House when it gets out of line (such as wire-tapping the Associate Press and the paranoid surveillance of Fox News' chief Washington Bureau correspondent, James Rosen). These admissions only prove that fascist-like tactics are not the exclusive property of so-called political conservatives drunk with power. Consequently, realism and economic self-interest, though decried by the Democrats, has captured the "nobility" within our current administration. Despite a self-righteous sense of imbuement to the calling of a higher mission, unwarranted self-confidence in its academic acumen, and implicitly holding to a stirring ethical mandate "to look out for all humanity," pre-emptive wars are still fought and justified in the name of domestic tranquility.

Remember Ben Franklin's counsel: *those willing to sacrifice freedom in the name of greater security are worthy of neither.*

Furthermore, listening to the definitive capitalist and über-financial manipulator George Soros patronize the rest of us by chiding how we must give a damn about the rest of humanity (as the justification for why nationalism is so "yesterday"), makes Democratic Globalist motives seem positively messianic. Listen to the arrogance of Soros:

> "The United States is the only country in the world that is in a position to initiate a change in the world order, to replace the Washington consensus with a global open society. To do so, we must abandon the unthinking pursuit of narrow self-interest and give some thought to the future of humanity."[2]

The Globalist, if you believe his or her polemics, seeks to spread "democratic freedoms" through which Western civilization hopes to tame barbaric, medieval religions of the Middle East (and eradicate their meager remains here in the West – the goal of Nietzsche's Übermensch – remnants which survive in too few Judeo-Christian institutions opposing such Orwellian *doubletalk*).[3]

That is where Krauthammer's analysis goes awry. Our current policy of throwing our economic weight around isn't the first time the world has witnessed a mostly "commercial" approach to controlling geo-politics. According to Krauthammer, we are NOT an empire in the classical sense of the term — we are the "custodian of the international system." True enough. How-

---

[2] From Jim Garrison, *America as Empire: Global Leader or Rogue Power? p. 193.*

[3] In 1984, George Orwell introduced us to several new terms like *doublethink* and *newspeak*, but has been inaccurately credited with *doublespeak*... but it's all just *doubletalk*! See http://www.orwelltoday.com/dblspkthennow.shtml.

ever, we are not now exclusively, nor will we be forever bound by what Krauthammer calls "the Gulliver Effect" in which the colossus can only strain at the tethers strapped upon him by international midget organizations like the UN, planning convocations such as the G8, G20, Bilderbergers, Trilateral Commission, or Council on Foreign Relations. America talks a good game about fully cooperating with other industrialized nations, but when the going gets tough, you can bet we will continue to act in our own self-interest (witness our years of *Quantitative Easing* at the expense of those who hold our debt)[4], even while our leaders campaign for more expansive world government as an opiate to assuage our allies who dare to believe we mean what we say.

## Commerce as Empire

Nevertheless, it is true that today's export-driven economies, massive population flows, regional conflicts over resources (like energy, food, and water), and post-9/11 terrorist activities have made American isolationism fall from favor, leaving Democratic Globalism standing as our much preferred normal course. Woodrow Wilson (rest his soul) with his failed League of Nations, and the Rockefeller Family – the impetus behind the United Nations (Kabuki Theater at its best) – should be feeling especially vindicated. For the moment, America exists shackled by chains of its own making (not forged by the *People* of course, but by both our known and unknown leaders who spend most of their time creating fetters that befit us). Again according to Krauthammer, we are a benign, reluctant but powerful COMMERCIAL REPUBLIC, not an exploitive and land-hungry empire of antiquity or recent colonialism. And, as the custodian of the international system, we will decide cooperatively but nonetheless out of our own self-interest, when, where and how to defeat our most immediate problem; that is, *Islamic fundamental-*

---

[4] This program of the U.S. Treasure and Federal Reserve inflated our currency and therefore, reduces our debt in real money terms.

*ism*, which has not only made terrorism an every-day threat to Western cultures, but has radically altered the status quo in the Middle East. The ongoing so-called *Arab Spring* (now in its fourth season)[5] promises many more surprises! Also related, but downplayed for the time being, are the Islamic demographics which tell us Muslims are steadily breeding themselves, as is their right, into majority status across Europe. This back-burner revolution further threatens the dominance of white, Anglo-Saxon, German, and French elites used to manning the helm of their respective governments – as these mushrooming Muslim communities alter societal standards and mores, steadfastly choosing cultural "non-assimilation," at the expense of what's left of Europe's individual national identities.

Then there is our less-than-above-board absconding with the earth's oil reserves in the name of Democratic Globalism – which rewards our Commercial Republic's participation in the Middle East pseudo-democratization process – simultaneously gaining the spoils of territorial conquest as we embed ourselves through building local military bases. *Pax Americana's* military stands ready – in the name of fighting global terrorism – and will remain on indefinitely as a threat to crush those not aligned with U.S. economic priorities.

No doubt the patriotically sensitive reply: "Surely America's economic policies (euphemistically entitled 'Free or Fair Trade') are *not* designed to enslave the bodies and souls of men, *nor* to heap up wealth for the Merchants of the Earth who are made rich through trading with America (Revelation 18:3)? No, America stands for freedom! Of course we mean well in supporting liberty, free enterprise, and espousing democracy – we are, after all, the last and best hope for the world! *American Exceptionalism* is the presupposition that guarantees we will do right in the world!" Bible believing readers might note how such talk is idolatrous to the core. Only Jesus saves.

---

[5] It began in December, 2010.

These ideals comprise what all Americans hope would be true of our conduct. On the other hand, all real patriots not frightened by objective analysis, do keep watch – questioning whether we genuinely attain such worthy aspirations. Unfortunately, those seeking the truth find we are not always so pure in our policies or exemplary in our accomplishments.

Krauthammer's claim that our Commercial Republic bears no resemblance to any empire of the past is actually not accurate. True, America is not Rome, not Medo-Persia, and not Charlemagne's Holy Roman Empire. Neither is she a colonizing empire like the British, French, Dutch, or, less recently, the Spanish. Certainly there remain only faint comparisons to the excesses of the Nazis or the Communists – (although the admissions of the last few weeks during the summer of 2013 are disturbing portents, perhaps of worse things to come).[6] The unipolar world of American hegemony (i.e., with many "foreign benefactors" of her Commercial Republic), does share an uncanny resemblance to another international trading empire some 3,000 years ago – the *Phoenicians;* aka the biblical Kingdom of *Tyre and Sidon* which ruled the Mediterranean and beyond, navigating beyond the Pillars of Hercules, perhaps even into the New World.

In fact, this ancient commercial empire whose influence continues even today in matters of alphabets, religious notions, and commercial inventions (trading pacts, the tool of money, and the creation of commodity markets to manage and create wealth), seems a perfect archetype of America. Given the typology of biblical connections between Tyre, Tarshish, and Babylon explored by these authors in the work before you, America appears particularly well-suited for a run at prophetic fulfillment as the full-fledged Babylon of the Last Days. In fact, the question for the true patriot to consider is this: Does the United States of America fit the description of Tyre and of Babylon that flagrantly summons the Bi-

[6] Such as spying on friendly foreign embassies and countless millions in the European Union, hacking into any computer system of any country in the world we choose to compromise.

ble's condemnation? Does our nation serve as the powerbase for the enemies of the LORD? Could the leader of our country someday become the Antichrist of the Bible in spirit or in reality? Just how close are we today to realizing this dark fate – and how much do the actors on stage and producers behind the scenes really direct the play? Have they made the Faustian bargain? Have they sold their soul (and our fate) to Mephistopheles?

## Who Are the True Agents of Change?

In the name of global democratization, America appears eager to go forth "conquering and to conquer" mounted upon a white horse (often seen by eschatology scholars as an allusion to the Antichrist – see Revelation Chapter 4, and the figure of the "Warrior Beast" of Revelation 13:4, "*Who is like unto the beast? Who is able to make war with him?*"). In the name of liberty (often duplicitously), we seek to extend freedom to all peoples oppressed by political despots that destroy human freedom and misguided religious tyrants which sacrifice the dignity of human thinking. The planet awaits its greatest hour, so we are told, and preemptive aggression (rather, "liberation") by the world's only unipolar power still lurks as a viable alternative "on the table." The third world is almost guaranteed to remain in third place, even though it may be allowed to enjoy some measure of progress to mitigate intermittent threats of social unrest (we surely must keep it around since it remains a cheap source of goods and services, not to mention essential raw materials to fuel our consumerism and militarism).

However, the truth is this: The only thing worse than being irreparably harmed to the point of no recovery (forever put into the place of debtor), is to be made to believe "it's for your country's own good" – although the facts show that only the top-tier of the third-world social order receives the lion's share of economic and social benefit. Despite all claims to the contrary, despite the good-intentions of classic liberalism as well as today's Democratic Globalism, the truth still remains: "*the poor you have with you always*" (Matthew 26:11). Moreover, at least classic liberalism actually thought it could make a difference. Claims made by Democratic Globalists seem at best hypocritical and at worse mere propaganda which misleads not only the common people, but the globalists themselves. For even the smartest people in the room characteristically believe their own hype.

In contrast to the do-gooder mythology paraded before us by American policies and politicians, Democratic Globalism purveys *a policy of greed, not goodwill* – masquerading as a moral crusade of good over evil, freedom over autocracy, and prosperity over poverty. Hence, this covertly commercial resolve demands an interior motivation that can only be supplied by that which espouses, defines, and provides moral covering for "Gulliver in his modern-day travels." Arise, the *New Indefatigable Right*– now inclusive of prosperity motivated evangelical southern Protestants mustered by mega-church celebrity pastors, and coupled with pro-family elements inside religious America – e.g., Mormons, Fundamentalists, and Conservative Catholics – too often blithely in league with secular humanist neo-cons, especially those that glisten with the trappings of success.

Together, these strange bedfellows unwittingly salute the aggressive policies of an Imperial Presidency (more often in Republican garb than Democratic), determined to rid the world of terrorism – and in so doing, quietly rule the earth. Nowadays, both religious and profane conservatives are greeted with enthusiasm by the oft corrupted corporate benefactors – the same ones who guzzle petroleum profits and corner other commodities secured through an aggressive policy of economic domination – i.e., "corporatism." Such control is secured through the threat of military conquest and subjugation, all under the banners of global democratization, freedom, liberty, and the elimination of "evil doers" from the planet.

*Mission Accomplished!*

Consequently, over the past twenty-five-plus years, today's Robber Barons have galvanized the new American vision of a milder, less militant, and more "internationally responsible"

U.S.A. through media complicity, corporate public relations, and financial subterfuge of the world economic system (how does one justify "bankster derivatives" anyway?) while capturing the so-called "value's vote" in America. The old "Moral Majority" – so important to America's "swing to the right" during the era of Ronald Reagan – has been superseded by a milder, less militant evangelicalism. In other words, evangelicals today are much less evangelistic, while they also generally disengaged in serious public discourse and outright disenchanted with politics.

You ask, "What is their highest priority in our day?" All too often, evangelicals, especially their leadership, seek to secure a place in society's status quo or get their names on the list of "up and comers" – both of which are dedicated to the principle of preserving the Old Republic. In so doing – they have masterfully hijacked the "moral high ground" by claiming uprightness remains on their side; and, in the process, performed a "Jesus" makeover, dressing him in commercial clothing. Additionally, they've quieted Jesus' biblically authentic threat to disguised secular hedonism/consumerism... even as he chastens Christians obsessed more with plenty than piety!

Author Krieger was raised in a home where Mom and Dad were stalwart Democrats. Not only were they died-in-the-donkey-hide democrats, they'd vote for a jackass if the democrats ran one for President – and that may have happened on more than one occasion! He remembers when Mom came home from *Blue Diamond* (an association of almond growers) in Sacramento and told him she was fired for trying to organize a union – which to this day does not exist there!

*A labor union* – that's right – Krieger's mom was a *Teamster* and proud of it. Nonetheless, their faith was steeped in social values that mirror those of the conservative right today. And yet, the "Dems" embraced a socialist activism that got real "peculiar" as far as Mom and scores of other old-fashioned democrats were concerned. So what happened? Go to Wichita, Omaha, or Oklahoma City and find out if you don't know. What's happening for blue collar workers happens all over the nation as the working class struggles and the middle class dissolves. The only ones that can't figure it out are leaders of the Democratic Party. Today, it isn't so much the workers who support the Democratic Party – it's those who'd rather not work much at all!

Workers of the world unite! And while you're at it, oust the Democrats who, if the truth be known, could care less about those who have to work for a living! They just want votes.

On the flip side of the political spectrum, the conservative Republican "caucus" has now been thoroughly replaced by the "neo-Con" ideology. Not that its tenets are clearly understood. The traditional symbol of the GOP (that funky elephant) ought to be exchanged for an overweight chimeric "El-if-I-know" because our confusion (and everyone else's) regarding what Republicans stand for today has finally reached its own sort of convoluted singularity! The meaning of being a Republican is lost on us! All we know is that Republicans are more business-friendly than Democrats and they seem to realize that taxing the common man and the not-so-rich can't be justified under the mantra of "paying their fair share" to grow Government – not to mention paying IRS employees bigger bonuses to gouge the rest of us (and most recently, attack those that stand in their way).

Indeed, the "old generation" of Republican Party leadership remains, stifling the possibility that something fresh and magical could bring new life into the Republic. The "old guard" still guards. They continue on as prominent leaders of the choicest metropolitan country clubs. They are diluted only by the newly rich socio-religious conservatives – many of whom are white refugees from the disenfranchised "Solid South." Most evangelicals today filtering into Republican leadership, predictably promote the newly updated *Gospel of Prosperity* (preached so positively by most Mega-Church meta-ministers); and, *ipso facto*, there stand but few amongst us rank and file evangelical patrons of the Constitution that remain willing to challenge the pseudo-spiritual ideology forged by these (1) imbued with new "churchly values", or (2) inculcated by the age-old corporate American values tying liberty to profitability. The classic heresy has arisen again: *judg-*

*ing one's standing with God by the amount of money in the bank.* Paul lays it on the line: such *"people [are] of corrupt mind, who have been robbed of the truth and who think that godliness is a means to financial gain."* (I Timothy 6:5, NIV) And yet, I Timothy 6:6 teaches *"godliness... is a means of great gain"* if combined with *contentment*! (From the verse of singer/ songwriter Sheryl Crow: "It's not getting want you want, it's wanting you got!")

> [6]*But godliness* ***with contentment*** *is great gain.*
>
> [7]*For we brought nothing into this world, and it is certain we can carry nothing out.*
>
> [8]*And having food and raiment let us be therewith content.*
>
> [9]*But they that will be rich fall into temptation and a snare, and into many foolish and hurtful lusts, which drown men in destruction and perdition.*
>
> [10]*For the* ***love of money*** *is the root of all evil: which while some coveted after, they have erred from the faith, and pierced themselves through with many sorrows. (I Timothy 6:6-10)*

Moreover, the new and improved evangelicalism of the American Right[7] hasn't really leavened the loaf of the Republican Party as much as providing a superficial moral casing to cover-up the old Republican stereotype of the "too-rich-to-care." In the end, both Democrats and Republicans alike, whether actively or passively, support efforts which subjugate both U.S. and world economies under plutocrat control. Remember the Golden Rule: *He who has the gold makes the rules* – which the rest must heed.

For those of us who cherish the liberties we hold as unalienable and given by our Creator, we fear we are now much too enfeebled to turn back the momentum of Democratic Globalism espoused implicitly by leaders of both political parties. We will pay for our failure to heed Thomas Jefferson's sage advice (alt-

---

[7] Including the family friendly Mormons like Mitt Romney and pious supporters too theologically naïve to tell the difference between biblical evangelicalism and the Mormon counterfeit.

hough usually ascribed to George Washington)[8] to steer clear of European politics and "entangling alliances." We've allowed ourselves to become the pawns of the financial elite who muster our military to make the world safe for their globalist economic advantage. As the capitalist head of corporate media giant said to his lunatic newscaster in the 1976 movie *Network (paraphrasing a bit),* "This is no U.S., England, France, Soviet Union, or Saudi Arabia... There is only IBM, Xerox, Coca-Cola, Aramco, and GM!"[9] While oversimplified, the point was plain enough. *Fascism* (where governments and big corporations join hands to build an unbeatable economy) stands as the guiding principle of *Democratic Globalism.* Whereas America was the champion of free markets and the rights of persons to engage in profitable enterprise, for too long we've allowed big corporate power players to impose monopolies upon us at home and abroad, established in the name of free markets and "Fair" Trade! Simply put: Politicians are in the tank with Corporate America because corporate contributions keep politicians in power. And any real measure of power seems to corrupt absolutely.[10]

George Washington, Thomas Jefferson, and John Adams must be turning over in their graves. This is not the America we once knew – and *neither* political party stand willing to speak in an attempt to stop the madness!

In the name of freedom and liberty, of democracy and the banishment of terrorism and tyranny, we've unwittingly commit-

---

[8] "Contrary to common belief, the phrase "entangling alliances" was turned by Thomas Jefferson, not George Washington. Washington advised against "permanent alliances," whereas Jefferson, in his inaugural address on 4 March 1801, declared his devotion to "peace, commerce, and honest friendship with all nations, entangling alliances with none." See http://www.answers.com/topic/entangling-alliances#ixzz2Y6TbB5qr.

[9] Ned Beatty played the head of the Network, while Peter Finch won an Oscar for his role as Howard Beal, the Television News anchor, who became "The Mad Prophet of the Airways."

[10] The saying of John Dalberg-Action, "Power tends to corrupt, and absolute power corrupts absolutely in such manner that great men are almost always bad men."

ted ourselves and our posterity to march to the beat of a drum played by the nameless elite and mercurial financial henchmen who manipulate markets, while their spokespersons preach about what is best for the middle-class and the down-trodden. Excuse us if we find all such talk egregiously disingenuous. Indeed, Supreme Court Justice Ruth Bader Ginsberg recently stated that Egypt should not look to the *outdated* U.S. Constitution in drafting a new constitution, but to that of South Africa – since our Constitution is now so flexibly interpreted that it can suit any political regime once it ascends to the Oval Office.

## Conclusion

Perhaps we have been too critical of our fellow Americans, too disdainful of our nation's missteps. Therefore, we should make sure the reader understands we find fault in all manner of economic or political theory supposing utopia can be achieved in this life.

For the United States, even when operating outside its Constitutional moorings, has assuredly *not* cornered the market on failure to detect ones' own shortcomings.

A "crusade against evil" in the mind of either of the last two administrations – launched against the genuinely evil forces of global terrorism and their byzantine networks – reminds us of communism's stupidity, a generation ago when Brezhnev proclaimed the USSR's overt military acts were wholly justified, as its "sacred internationalist duty" to thwart all attempts to subvert socialism's glorious experiment across the globe. Communists are proven just as myopic as the rest of us! This does not mean true terrorists are not real enemies – they are. But it points out how easily our leaders can disguise sheep in wolf's clothing with no more than a home-made costume. Just because our President says someone is our enemy doesn't mean they really are.

Likewise, the Fascists can easily demonstrate their blindness as regards Über-National Socialist shortcomings. Joseph Goebbels' famous dictum holds true today: to tell a believable lie, the bigger the whopper the better – while a cacophony of lies works well too!

Speaking of Joseph Goebbels, hear what Hitler's False Prophet authorized, via Dr. Otto Dietrich, when he declared not all that many years ago in the name of freedom:

> Herein lies the secret of the indestructibility of Adolph Hitler and his work—the guarantee that the road he has taken cannot be altered. For it is no longer the man Adolph Hitler, it is no longer his works and no longer the road he has taken that expresses itself in him. It is the German nation itself that expresses itself in him. In him the nation loves itself; in him it follows its most secret desires, in him its most daring thoughts become reality. Every single person feels this and because of it Adolph Hitler is a stranger to no one, and no one is a stranger to the Führer. Workers and farmers speak with him; Nobel Prize winners and artists, warriors and dreamers, happy men and despairing men speak with him, and each and every one hears his own language, he understands and is understood in return. Everything is natural and self-evident, and no one is shy before this great man. No one is ordered to follow. No one is courted, but everyone is called, just as one would be called by his own conscience. He has no choice but to follow, should he not want to be guilty and unhappy in his own heart. Thus, what must happen happens voluntarily, and *no nation on the face of this earth has more freedom than the Germans.*[11]

Pretzel logic notwithstanding (Goebbels was the Minister of Propaganda after all), a simple faith in a larger-than-life leader appeals to most of us. However, although the speech of an orator may diminish the complexities of political realities (and not just the discourse), the fact remains no simple solution exists to the challenge of human government. Our current President, a master orator with an appealing persona, has certainly learned this lesson well at the beginning of his second term in office: His poll numbers are in steady decline. His recent speech at the Brandenburg Gate in Berlin (June, 2013) demonstrated that the enthusiasm

---

[11] Adolph Hitler, *A Chilling Tale of Propaganda*, Dr. Otto Dietrich, The Third Reich's Press Secretary, p. 20, Typhoon International, 1999.

and "promise" he presented just five years ago has unquestionably waned in the minds of Europeans too.[12]

There is little question that overly-exuberant nationalism led to deadly wars throughout Europe for hundreds upon hundreds of years finally culminating in two world wars primarily begun there.[13] Doubtlessly, this grim reality played no small part in motivating miscreant creations like the United Nations, Trilateral Commission, and Council on Foreign Relations. However, Democratic Globalism promises something even worse: A monolithic government, too unwieldy to manage on a world-wide basis, with no checks and balances to mitigate against the risk that a totalitarian leader will take the helm (a transformation happening today in America as witnessed through the inaction of the Congressional Oversight Committees and their customary ineffectual effort to get to the bottom of any major scandal). The tyranny of the committee will cry out for the efficiency of a dictator, whether benevolent or not so much. For as much as the plutocrats and elitists seek a government ruled *by reason alone* (in the spirit of the *Illuminati* – there, we said it!), unfettered by the tyranny of monarchs, priests, and religious authority – their self-centered agenda of the rich, by the rich, and for the rich – in reality promises little relief from despotism, less freedom for the individual, and diminished economic benefit for the masses.

This is why the Bible warns that the Final Babylon awaits humanity in the days leading up to the Apocalypse – before the Messiah comes literally to win the day and usher in the Kingdom of God. Babylon will be a regime financed by the "kings of the earth" who give over their authority to a solitary figure known in Christian "literalists" parlance as "The Antichrist." Consequently, we believe a dystopian, not utopian, future approaches in the

---

[12] During his first Presidential Campaign, Obama drew 200,000 cheering Germans to the same spot and received accolades not heard there in 75 years. Who was that equally inspiring orator speaking there in the 1930s?

[13] Japanese Imperialism was instrumental, of course, in the Pacific Theater, joining Germany and Italy as the Asian counterpart of the Axis Powers.

days that lie just ahead. *We believe that Democratic Globalism, the current guiding light of our world leaders, will be the ideological means by which this dystopian destiny comes to pass.*

As we come to the end of our study, allow us to pose a number of questions (i.e., equivocations). Can we regroup in time? Can we recover an authentic form of republicanism? Can we wrest control from hidden factions and plutocrats who deride U.S. sovereignty? Can we return to a government which considers our Constitution sacrosanct? Can we be rescued from the fate Democratic Globalism intends for us? Can we long endure the culture of "intolerance" for all but the "tolerant" – aka those who stand for nothing (but fall for anything)?

NO! The opportunity for equivocations is a luxury we no longer can afford. We are flat out of time – the storm has broken full upon us and it will only grow worse. The ascendancy of Antichrist in America is unstoppable – we affirm the Scripture speaks this word to THIS generation – we must stop trying to reform, to fix, to beautify this sow's ear into a silk purse. The system isn't salvageable. We agree that "evil triumphs when good men do nothing" (Edmund Burke) – but we aren't advocating doing nothing. Instead, we must remember the evangelical imperative. We must call this generation, our generation; to repent before it is too late. From our vantage point, we have arrived at the prophetically inevitable; the game (forgive the metaphor) has come down to the final "two minutes" – maybe the final seconds.

We are solemnly called to testify in the street of that Great City. *Babylon the Great* stands condemned – she now unknowingly awaits her judgment. The sooner the Church comes to terms with the fact we're in the final throes of Messianic birth pangs, the better. The Titanic is sinking – stop rearranging the deck chairs! The message couldn't be clearer: NOW HEAR THIS! GET INTO THE LIFEBOATS!

As Christians, we must stop accommodating "Sodom and Egypt" where "our Lord was crucified" – Democratic Globalism inserts itself into every corner of our lives. Despite its pernicious presence, the Church worries over political correctness and acquiesces to Babylon's end-time's fornications. The apostasy of the last days, the "falling away from the faith" surrounds us.

The late intellectual Francis A. Schaeffer in his thought-provoking work on Jeremiah, *Death in the City,* asked, "In what has been called a post-Christian world, what should be our perspective and how should we function as individuals, as institutions, as orthodox Christians, and as those who claim to be Bible-believing?"[14] His answer: "the church in our generation needs reformation, revival, and constructive revolution." But he didn't say revolt against "the government." Frankly, *there isn't time to reform our government, there is only time to awaken the Church to the reality of our situation and sound the refrain of repentance.* Revolution isn't the answer for the government or the Church.

The call is an urgent one: In the words of our Savior and his forerunner "Elijah" – *"Repent for the Kingdom of Heaven is at hand!"* (Matthew 3:2)

True saints in these last days are called to prophesy, to testify, to decry THE FINAL BABYLON'S falsehoods and sins. It is time: don the sackcloth and exhort all within voice shot. We are called to be His messenger: "Believe in the Lord Jesus Christ, the Son of God, Whose coming in glory is imminent and inevitable." For we are but moments from the saintly chorus which will resound throughout all creation:

> *"The kingdoms of this world are become the kingdoms of our Lord, and of his Christ; and he shall reign for ever and ever"*
> *(Revelation 11:15)*

---

[14]Francis A. Schaeffer, *Death in the City*, Downers Grove, Inter-Varsity Press, 1969, p. 209.

# Appendix:
# The Burden of Babylon

Concerning the *Burden of Babylon,* Isaiah writes words of grave warning. And like his vision recorded in Isaiah 17, the "Burden of Damascus", the Burden of Babylon refers to its decimation – perhaps *annihilation* would be the more accurate description.

The Hebrew word translated "burden" literally means "an oracle" uttered by God. Its transliteration from Hebrew into Roman characters would be *nasa*... with the emphasis on the *second* syllable (unlike the acronym NASA, which Americans recognize as the National Aeronautics and Space Administration, with the emphasis placed on the *first* syllable). It can also mean to be "carried, lifted up," or even "swept away." In Isaiah 13, Isaiah "sees" the *nasa* of Babylon. His is a dire vision of desolation. We begin with this preface:

> [1] *The burden of Babylon, which Isaiah the son of Amoz did see.*
>
> [2] *Lift ye up a banner upon the high mountain, exalt the voice unto them, shake the hand, that they may go into the gates of the nobles.*
>
> [3] *I have commanded my sanctified ones; I have also called my mighty ones for mine anger, even them that rejoice in my highness. (Isaiah 13:1-3)*

The context of what transpires at Babylon's destruction unmistakably conveys "when it happens." The timing of the Burden of Babylon is at "world's end", for it indicates that the destruction does not happen until the *Great Tribulation* of the last days; furthermore, apparently it doesn't occur until its conclusion. This irrefutably shows that Isaiah is not speaking of the Neo-Babylonian Empire of Nebuchadnezzar or Belshazzar. His vision, despite being given almost 200 years before Nebuchadnezzar's day, is not for the physical/historical Babylon – but for the Babylon (identified metaphorically) which is spoken of by Jeremiah, Zechariah, and John the Revelator. His vision speaks of THE FINAL BABYLON.

The reference to "my sanctified ones" and "the mighty ones" called forth for purposes of expressing the anger of the Lord are those that also "*rejoice in his highness*" that is, His exalted nature. Revelation 19:1-2 reflects these words, *"And after these things I heard a great voice of much people in heaven, saying, 'Alleluia; Salvation, and glory, and honour, and power, unto the Lord our God: for true and righteous are his judgments: for he hath judged the great whore* [Babylon], *which did corrupt the earth with her fornication, and hath avenged the blood of his servants at her hand.'"* We believe this vast number constitutes the saints who have been translated (the raptured and resurrected – I Corinthians 15:51) and are now come upon the *clouds of heaven* – indeed, their multitude comprises the "clouds of glory" – as they are redeemed, and glisten in their robes of white and in their gloried bodies. Jude in the New Testament quotes from the apocryphal book, Enoch, echoing the same vision: *"And Enoch also, the seventh from Adam, prophesied of these, saying, 'Behold, the Lord cometh with ten thousands of his saints, to execute judgment upon all, and to convince all that are ungodly among them of all their ungodly deeds which they have ungodly committed...'"* (Jude 14, 15) John in Revelation also gives witness to this event at the outset of his vision, *"Behold, he cometh with clouds; and every eye shall see him, and they also which pierced him: and all kindreds of the earth shall wail because of him. Even so, Amen." (Revelation 1:7)*

Returning to Isaiah's writing:

> 4 *The noise of a multitude in the mountains, like as of a great people; a tumultuous noise of the kingdoms of nations gathered together: the* LORD *of hosts mustereth the host of the battle.*
>
> 5 *They come from a far country, from the end of heaven, even the* LORD, *and the weapons of his indignation, to destroy the whole land. (Isaiah 13:4, 5)*

The vision is of Armageddon, when all the nations are gathered together to fight the Lord of Hosts. The noise is in the mountains, the "highlands" of Mount Megiddo (and what we know today as the Golan Heights). The purpose is to destroy Babylon – and this is not just the physical land of Babylon, but the armies of Babylon, which references the armies of the entire Gentile world under the leadership of the Beast. For Babylon refers not just to the "land of the Chaldeans" – the singular nation which has served as the powerbase to the Antichrist during his ascendancy (which we believe is the United States of America) – but to the peoples and their leaders who collectively oppose the Son of God and His Kingdom. This notion references "the kings of the earth" (Psalm 2:2, Revelation 17:2, 18, 18:3, 9, 19:19), the common appellation for those "kings" who stand against Jehovah.

> [6] *Howl ye; for the day of the LORD is at hand; it shall come as a destruction from the Almighty.*
>
> [7] *Therefore shall all hands be faint, and every man's heart shall melt:*
>
> [8] *And they shall be afraid: pangs and sorrows shall take hold of them; they shall be in pain as a woman that travaileth: they shall be amazed one at another; their faces shall be as flames.*
>
> [9] *Behold, the day of the LORD cometh, cruel both with wrath and fierce anger, to lay the land desolate: and he shall destroy the sinners thereof out of it.*

Isaiah's language makes plain what period of history we are dealing with – his meaning is crystal clear: This is the *Day of the Lord.* It is *"cruel with wrath and fierce anger"* – this Day will desolate the land and destroy its sinners. Then Isaiah follows these utterances with a common attribute depicting the most frightening sign of this awesome culminating moment of human history:

> [10] *For the stars of heaven and the constellations thereof shall not give their light: the sun shall be darkened in his going forth, and the moon shall not cause her light to shine.*

This verse incites us to recall Revelation 6:12:

> *"And I beheld when he had opened the sixth seal, and, lo, there was a great earthquake; and the sun became black as sackcloth of hair, and the moon became as blood."*

...and Joel 2:10-11:

> 10 *The earth shall quake before them; the heavens shall tremble: the sun and the moon shall be dark, and the stars shall withdraw their shining:*
>
> 11 *And the Lord shall utter his voice before his army: for his camp is very great: for he is strong that executeth his word: for the day of the Lord is great and very terrible; and who can abide it?*

And then, the climactic verse of Joel, chapter 2: "*The sun shall be turned into darkness, and the moon into blood, before the great and terrible day of the Lord come.*" *(Joel 2:31)* Can there be any doubt that the *Burden of Babylon* speaks of the Last Days?

> 11 *And I will punish the world for their evil, and the wicked for their iniquity; and I will cause the arrogancy of the proud to cease, and will lay low the haughtiness of the terrible.*
>
> 12 *I will make a man more precious than fine gold; even a man than the golden wedge of Ophir.*
>
> 13 *Therefore I will shake the heavens, and the earth shall remove out of her place, in the wrath of the* LORD *of hosts, and in the day of his fierce anger.*

Isaiah continues to describe, with similes and metaphors, the unspeakable fate which has come upon the people of Babylon:

> 14 *And it shall be as the chased roe, and as a sheep that no man taketh up: they shall every man turn to his own people, and flee every one into his own land.*
>
> 15 *Every one that is found shall be thrust through; and every one that is joined unto them shall fall by the sword.*
>
> 16 *Their children also shall be dashed to pieces before their eyes; their houses shall be spoiled, and their wives ravished.*
>
> 17 *Behold, I will stir up the Medes against them, which shall not regard silver; and as for gold, they shall not delight in it.*
>
> 18 *Their bows also shall dash the young men to pieces; and they shall have no pity on the fruit of the womb; their eyes shall not spare children.*

The enemies of Babylon shall have no regard for silver or gold: They are single-minded: they seek death and destruction. There will be no pity. The devastation and carnage shall know no bounds.

Additionally, Isaiah echoes the words of Jeremiah (Jeremiah 50:40): when Babylon is destroyed, it shall be likened to the destruction of Sodom and Gomorrah: "Fire and brimstone" – perhaps the power of the atom – will be unleashed upon the land of the Chaldeans:

> [19]*And Babylon, the glory of kingdoms, the beauty of the Chaldees' excellency, shall be as when God overthrew Sodom and Gomorrah.*

When the Lord judges Babylon, it will be utterly devastated and desolated. Never again will its land be inhabited. It will be more deserted than the deserts of Arabia, than the dry lands where only Shepherds and their flocks can roam.

> [20]*It shall never be inhabited, neither shall it be dwelt in from generation to generation: neither shall the Arabian pitch tent there; neither shall the shepherds make their fold there.*
>
> [21]*But wild beasts of the desert shall lie there; and their houses shall be full of doleful creatures; and owls shall dwell there, and satyrs shall dance there.*
>
> [22]*And the wild beasts of the islands shall cry in their desolate houses, and dragons in their pleasant palaces: and her time is near to come, and her days shall not be prolonged.*

This destruction never happened to Babylon in the days of Isaiah or Jeremiah. However, as Jesus said, "*the scripture cannot be broken.*" (John 10:35) Babylon will be judged. Its judgment will be most terrible.

It is remarkable how many images of the last days attend to Isaiah's description of the *Burden of Babylon*. These words are distressing to hear – but how much harder will they be to endure? The *Day of the Lord*, the wrath of God, is called down upon Babylon for its great sins. THE FINAL BABYLON faces the full force of God's anger.

To consider the possibility that these passages of Scripture are intended for the America as the "powerbase" of Antichrist, defies our imagination. And yet, the evidence is incontrovertible. It is the fate of an empire that has turned on its God, which has forgotten why it was allowed to flourish for so long, and what led to its unequaled blessings.

Can we forestall this ominous fate? Is it possible that we can change our ways, and like Nineveh in ancient Assyria which repented at the preaching of Jonah, altered its fate and deferred God's judgment for yet one more generation?

Or is it now too late?

*******

There is a way to be spared the fate of those who live in the Kingdom of Babylon. If you have never invited Jesus Christ to come into your life and to remake you into the person He wants you to be – now is the time, today is the day. We encourage you to say this prayer, humbly and sincerely, in your heart:

> *"Lord Jesus, forgive me for my sins. Come into my life. Dwell in my heart. Change me by the power of your Holy Spirit that I may live a life that is pleasing to you. Grant me eternal life that I may live in heaven forever."*

If you prayed that prayer and meant what you expressed, you have been transferred from the Kingdom of Darkness, the "empire of Babylon" into the Kingdom of Light. You have been reconciled to God.

However, only the life that is transformed gives evidence that you have truly been saved from sin and from death. You must turn away from those sins that entangle you and keep you from following Jesus Christ in your daily life. This transformation is not achieved by your power, but by the power of the Holy Spirit (the Spirit of Jesus Christ) that has come to live within you as a result of inviting Him into your heart. It is a supernatural life.

Carefully read these words from Romans, chapter 8:

> *Therefore, there is now no condemnation for those who are in Christ Jesus, because through Christ Jesus the law of the Spirit who gives life has set you free from the law of sin and death. For what the law was powerless to do because it was weakened by the flesh, God did by sending his own Son in the likeness of sinful flesh to be a sin offering. And so he condemned sin in the flesh, in order that the righteous requirement of the law might be fully met in us, who do not live according to the flesh but according to the Spirit.*
>
> *Those who live according to the flesh have their minds set on what the flesh desires; but those who live in accordance with the Spirit have their minds set on what the Spirit desires. The mind governed by the flesh is death, but the mind governed by the Spirit is life and peace. The mind governed by the flesh is hostile to God; it does not submit to God's law, nor can it do so. Those who are in the realm of the flesh cannot please God.*
>
> *You, however, are not in the realm of the flesh but are in the realm of the Spirit, if indeed the Spirit of God lives in you. And if anyone does not have the Spirit of Christ, they do not belong to Christ. But if Christ is in you, then even though your body is subject to death because of sin, the Spirit gives life because of righteousness. And if the Spirit of him who raised Jesus from the dead is living in you, he who raised Christ from the dead will also give life to your mortal bodies because of his Spirit who lives in you.*
>
> *Therefore, brothers and sisters, we have an obligation—but it is not to the flesh, to live according to it. For if you live according to the flesh, you will die; but if by the Spirit you put to death the misdeeds of the body, you will live.*
>
> *For those who are led by the Spirit of God are the children of God. The Spirit you received does not make you slaves, so that you live in fear again; rather, the Spirit you received brought about your adoption to sonship. And by him we cry, "Abba, Father." The Spirit himself testifies with our spirit that we are God's children.* (Romans 8:1-16, NIV)

Our prayer is that God will richly bless you as you grow in the knowledge of Him and in His grace! Amen.

# Selected Bibliography


Billington, James Hadley. *Fire in the Minds of Men Origins of the Revolutionary Faith.* London: Temple Smith, 1980.

Brennan, David. *The Israel Omen: The Ancient Warning of Catastrophies Has Begun.* Metairie, LA: Teknon Pub., 2009.

Brown, Dan. *The Lost Symbol: A Novel.* New York: Doubleday, 2009.

Cahn, Jonathan. *The Harbinger.* Lake Mary, FL: FrontLine, 2011.

Church, J. R., Ralph G. Griffin, and G. G. Stearman. *Guardians of the Grail-- and the Men Who Plan to Rule the World!* Oklahoma City, OK: Prophecy Publications, 1989.

Coombes, R. A. *America, the Babylon: America's Destiny Foretold in Biblical Prophecy: An Exegetical Study.* Liberty, MO: REAL Pub., 1998.

Cornwell, John. *Hitler's Pope: The Secret History of Pius XII.* New York, NY: Viking, 1999.

Farrell, Joseph P. *Covert Wars and Breakaway Civilizations [the Secret Space Program, Celestial Psyops and Hidden Conflicts.* Kempton, IL: Adventures Unlimited, 2012.

Flynn, David E. *Cydonia: The Secret Chronicles of Mars.* Bozeman, MT: End Time Thunder, 2002.

Freeman, Kevin D. *Secret Weapon: How Economic Terrorism Brought down the U.S. Stock Market and Why It Can Happen Again.* Washington, D.C.: Regnery Pub., 2012.

Hall, Manly P., and Manly P. Hall. *The Secret Destiny of America.* New York: J.P. Tarcher/Penguin, 2008.

Hancock, Graham, and Robert Bauval. *The Master Game: Unmasking the Secret Rulers of the World.* New York: Disinformation, 2011.

Hapgood, Charles H. *Earth's Shifting Crust; a Key to Some Basic Problems of Earth Science.* [New York]: Pantheon, 1958.

Heron, Patrick. *Return of the Antichrist: And the New World Order.* Greenville, SC: Ambassador International, 2011.

Hislop, Alexander. *The Two Babylons: Or, The Papal Worship Proved to Be the Worship of Nimrod and His Wife.* Neptune, NJ: Loizeaux Bros., 1959.

Hitchcock, Mark. *The Late Great United States: What Bible Prophecy Reveals about America's Last Days*. Colorado Springs, CO: Multnomah, 2009.

Horn, Thomas R., and Cris Putnam. *Petrus Romanus: The Final Pope Is Here*. Crane, MO: Defender, 2012.

Horn, Thomas R. *Apollyon Rising 2012: The Lost Symbol Found and the Final Mystery of the Great Seal Revealed*. Crane, MO: Defender, 2009.

Hunt, Dave. *A Woman Rides the Beast*. Eugene, Or.: Harvest House, 1994.

Hunter, James Davison. *To Change the World: The Irony, Tragedy, and Possibility of Christianity in the Late Modern World*. New York: Oxford UP, 2010.

Hutchings, N. W., and S. Franklin. Logsdon. *The U.S. in Prophecy*. Oklahoma City, OKLA.: Hearthstone Pub., 2000.

Jeffrey, Grant R. *One Nation, under Attack: How Big-government Liberals Are Destroying the America You Love*. Colorado Springs, CO: WaterBrook, 2012.

Johnson, Paul. *"The Almost-chosen People: Why America Is Different"* Rockford, Ill. (934 Main St., 61103): Rockford Institute, 1985.

Johnston, T.C. *Did the Phoenicians Discover America?* 2010 ed. (New York): Nabu, 2010, (1892).

Krieger, Douglas W. *Antichrist-Reflections on the Desolator*. Sacramento: Tribulation Network, 2011. *Www.the-tribulation-network.com*. Krieger, McGriff, 2011. Web. <www.the-tribulation-network.com>.

Krieger, Douglas W. "The Rise or Fall of American Empire by Doug Krieger." *The Rise or Fall of American Empire by Doug Krieger*. The Tribulation Network, June-July 2007. Web. 06 July 2013. <http://www.the-tribulation-network.com/ebooks/rise_or_fall/rise_or_fall_of_american_empire_intro.htm>.

LaHaye, Tim F. *The Rapture*. Eugene, Or.: Harvest House, 2002.

Lambert, Frank. *The Founding Fathers and the Place of Religion in America*. Princeton, NJ: Princeton UP, 2003.

Lindsey, Hal, and Carole C. Carlson. *The Late Great Planet Earth*. Grand Rapids: Zondervan, 1970.

Logsdon, S. Franklin. *Is the U.S.A. in Prophecy?* Grand Rapids: Zondervan Pub. House, 1968.

Lutzer, Erwin W. *Hitler's Cross*. Chicago: Moody, 1995.

Macfarland, Charles S. *The New Church and the New Germany; a Study of Church and State,*. New York: Macmillan, 1934.

Marrs, Jim. *The Rise of the Fourth Reich: The Secret Societies That Threaten to Take over America*. New York: William Morrow, 2008.

McGriff, Dene. "In Search of Mystery Babylon, Dene McGriff, America Is Babylon, American Empire, Apostasy, Deception." *In Search of Mystery Babylon, Dene McGriff, America Is Babylon, American Empire, Apostasy, Deception*. N.p., n.d. Web. 06 July 2013. <http://www.the-tribulation-network.com/denemcgriff/in_search_of_babylon_intro.htm>.

McGriff, Dene. "Recognizing Deception and Apostasy." *Recognizing Apostasy and Deception, Apostasy, Dene McGriff, Tribulation, Antichrist*. The Tribulation Network, n.d. Web. 06 July 2013. <http://www.the-tribulation-network.com/denemcgriff/ Apostasy/recognizing_ deception_and_apostasy.htm>.

McTernan, John. *As America Has Done to Israel*. New Kensington, PA: Whitaker House, 2008.

Morris, Richard B. *Seven Who Shaped Our Destiny; the Founding Fathers as Revolutionaries*. New York: Harper & Row, 1973.

Ovason, David. *The Secret Architecture of Our Nation's Capitol*. New York: Harper Perennial, 2002.

Pentecost, J. Dwight. *Things to Come: A Study in Biblical Eschatology*. Grand Rapids, MI: Academie, 1964.

Perkins, John. *Confessions of an Economic Hitman*. San Francisco: Berret-Koehler, 2004.

Postman, Neil. *Technopoly: The Surrender of Culture to Technology*. New York: Knopf, 1992.

Price, John Richard. *The End of America: The Role of Islam in the End times and Biblical Warnings to Flee America*. Indianapolis, IN: Christian House, 2011.

Putnam, Cris, and Thomas R. Horn. *Exo-Vaticana: Petrus Romanus, Project L.U.C.I.F.E.R. and the Vatican's Astonishing Plan for the Arrival of an Alien Savior*. Crane, MO: Defender, 2013.

Richardson, Joel, and Joel Richardson. *The Islamic Antichrist: The Shocking Truth about the Real Nature of the Beast*. Los Angeles, CA: WND, 2009.

Rosenberg, Joel C. *Epicenter*. Carol Stream, IL: Tyndale House, 2006.

Salus, Bill. *Israelistine*. New York: HighWay, 2008.

Salus, Bill. *Psalm 83: The Missing Prophecy Revealed : How Israel Becomes the next Mideast Super Power*. La Quinta, CA: Prophecy Depot Ministries, 2013.

Skiba, Rob. *Babylon Rising: And the First Shall Be the Last*. [United States]: King's Gate Media, 2011.

Smith, Uriah. *United States in the Light of Prophecy*. [S.l.]: General, 2010.

Viereck, Peter. *Metapolitics: The Roots of the Nazi Mind*. New York: Capricorn, 1961.

Viereck, Peter. *Metapolitics: The Roots of the Nazi Mind*. New York: Capricorn, 1961.

Woodward, Douglas S. *Power Quest Book One- America's Obsession with the Paranormal*. Woodinville: Faith Happens, 2011.

Woodward, Douglas S. *Power Quest Two- The Ascendency of the Antichrist in America*. Woodinville: Faith Happens, 2012.

# About the Authors

**DOUGLAS W. KRIEGER** is Co-Editor of the Tribnet since 2004, having written scores of e-books on Bible Prophecy. He has served as Education Administrator for public schools for 20 years, as well as Public Relations and (formerly) the Executive Director of the National Religious Broadcasters National Prayer Breakfast in Honor of Israel during the 1980s. He holds a BA/Admin. Cred. from CSU-LA/CSUS Additionally, he was a pastor during the *Jesus Movement*. Since 1968, he's been married to Deborah and has three children who love the Lord Jesus. Doug's involvement in Christian Leadership led to several White House briefings during the Reagan Administration with the Religious Roundtable and the American Forum for Jewish-Christian Cooperation.

**DENE MCGRIFF** has 30 years' experience in international business and development with Food for the Hungry and World Relief and several international Fortune 100 companies. The past decade, he has been a Co-Editor and writer for the Tribnet. He has written books on apostasy and deception, the global economy and the role of America in prophecy. He has a unique perspective having worked on all continents and in over 50 countries around the world. He realizes that people around the world are much more likely to agree with the conclusions of this book than the average American Christian.

**S. DOUGLAS WOODWARD** is an author, speaker, and researcher on the topics of alternative history, the occult in America, and biblical eschatology, with 40 years' experience in researching, writing, and teaching on the subject. He has written five books besides the present volume: *Are We Living in the Last Days?* (2009), *Decoding Doomsday* (2010), *Black Sun Blood Moon* (2011), *Power Quest, Book One: America's Obsession with the Paranormal* (2012), and *Power Quest, Book Two: The Ascendancy of Antichrist in America* (2012). Doug has also served as an executive for Microsoft, Oracle, Honeywell Bull, and as a Partner at Ernst & Young. He has served as Elder in the Reformed Church of America and the Presbyterian Church.

Made in the USA
Lexington, KY
22 September 2013